WAR OF WORDS

By the same author

How Can Man Die Better: Sobukwe and Apartheid

Nelson Mandela

BENJAMIN POGRUND

Foreword by Harold Evans

War of Words

Memoir of a South African Journalist

SEVEN STORIES PRESS

New York / Toronto / London / Sydney

Copyright © 2000 by Benjamin Pogrund
Foreword © 2000 by Harold Evans

A Seven Stories Press First Edition

Seven Stories Press
140 Watts Street
New York, NY 10013
http://www.sevenstories.com

In Canada:
Hushion House, 36 Northline Road, Toronto, Ontario M4B 3E2

In the U.K.:
Turnaround Publisher Services Ltd., Unit 3, Olympia Trading Estate,
Coburg Road, Wood Green, London N22 6TZ

In Australia: Tower Books, 9/19 Rodborough Road, Frenchs Forest
NSW 2086

Library of Congress Cataloging-in-Publication Data

Pogrund, Benjamin.
    War of words: memoir of a South African journalist / Benjamin Pogrund.— A
Seven Stories Press 1st ed.
        p.   cm.
        ISBN 1-888363-71-1 (cloth)
        1. Pogrund, Benjamin. 2. Journalists—South Africa—Biography. 3. South
Africa—Politics and government—20th century. I. Title.
PN5476.P64 A3 1998
070'.92—dc21
[B]   97-050423
9 8 7 6 5 4 3 2 1

College professors may order examination copies of Seven Stories Press titles for a
free six-month trial period. To order, visit www.sevenstories.com/textbook, or fax on
school letterhead to (212) 226-1411.

Book design by Cindy LaBreacht.

Printed in the U.S.A.

Dedicated to the journalists
of the *Rand Daily Mail*

Foreword 9
Preface 13

Part I: The Road to Violence

Chapter 1..19
Chapter 2..32
Chapter 3..45
Chapter 4..57
Chapter 5..69
Chapter 6..79
Chapter 7..89
Chapter 8..102
Chapter 9..117
Chapter 10..127

Part II: Into the Prisons

Chapter 11..141
Chapter 12..153

Contents

Chapter 13..171
Chapter 14..184
Chapter 15..210

Part III: The War of Words

Chapter 16..233
Chapter 17..245
Chapter 18..254
Chapter 19..265
Chapter 20..281
Chapter 21..291
Chapter 22..306
Chapter 23..325
Chapter 24..333
Epilogue 345
Sources 363
Index..366

Benjamin Pogrund was the South African affairs correspondent for the London *Sunday Times* when I was its editor. We knew him as a brave, resourceful, thoughtful, and
fair reporter. All those adjectives matter and so does the
noun. South Africa was supposedly a democracy with the
trappings of a free press and an independent judiciary; and
it had its defenders in Britain and elsewhere ready to
pounce on anything that could be dismissed as wrong or
biased. In reality, of course, it was closer to a Communist
police state, certainly for the black population and for anyone, white or black, it considered a threat to state security
which meant, as it meant in the Soviet Union, any critic of
injustice. It enforced apartheid, the law of the land, with
increasing brutality. It brought the full weight of state
power against Pogrund's newspaper, the liberal *Rand Daily*

Foreword

Mail, and a succession of visionary editors when it tried to
report what was going on in the black townships and in the
prisons.

This was Pogrund's seminal contribution. He reported.
In his own time and at night and over weekends he began
to record the accelerating ferment in black politics. No
one, not even the black newspapers, was reporting the
details of life in Soweto and the other townships. He got
to know the leaders and to be trusted by them—Nelson
Mandela and Robert Sobukwe conspicuous among them.
It was to Pogrund that Mandela first publicly espoused
his disenchantment with non-violence.

Pogrund built up a network of contacts. It was risky in
all sorts of ways. Once his contacts misled him with a
story that a man had died from police brutality. Pogrund's
report secured an exhumation. The autopsy showed death
had been from natural causes; he honestly describes it as

his "worst mistake." The severest risk was from the authorities. I lost count of the number of times the security police descended on his home, the panics when he had to try and conceal papers that could give too strong a clue to the identity of a source. He went to prison, just as his baby was being born, because he would not name a politician who had given him documents embarrassing to the Nationalists.

His resourcefulness required bravery and made sense of it. It would have been brave, but pointlessly reckless for a journalist simply to denounce oppression. Pogrund had thought hard about the role of the independent journalist. As a Liberal party member before he joined the *Mail*, he found himself in the middle of a melee in Sophiatown when Liberal Party supporters were attacked by young men from the ANC Youth League. A man built like a tank was about to use a bottle to club someone on the head. Pogrund, as embryo journalist, should theoretically have got out his notebook. Instead, he became Pogrund the citizen, tapping the man on the shoulder and asking, "Can't we sit down and talk about this?" It was the beginning of a long friendship with the astonished bottle-wielder, Steve Segale. Once on the *Mail*, Pogrund had an early crisis of conscience. He got to know ahead of police raids and could have tipped off his contacts; he decided he could not compromise the paper or his own integrity. Then again, he withheld stories of corruption when there was a chance they would endanger his sources.

Pogrund was determined that his news reports would never be propagandist. He had resigned from the Liberal Party straight after starting at the *Mail* because he felt it was wrong for a journalist to have links to any political party. He was intent on reporting dispassionately. He strove to leave out his own judgments when he interviewed people for the news pages or reported events. He took pride in reporting on the Nationalist prime minister and the ANC's president-general with the same absence of favor or hostility. Only in feature articles, under his own name, did he express a viewpoint.

But straight reporting has its own momentum. Simply to report police conduct in a riot accurately, as Pogrund did at Sharpeville and elsewhere, was regarded as revolutionary. Until then, the police report had been taken as definitive.

Pogrund offers us insights into the workings of an embattled newspaper, beset with police spies and with a series of owners and managers of varying moral fibre. He became deputy editor of the paper and has earned international esteem for his prescience as well as his courage. He was, in a real sense, one of the founders of the new South Africa, and typically does not hesitate to describe its disappointments.

This is a valuable, important, and exciting book. It is at once an affidavit in honor of truth, and a moving human testament.

—Harold Evans
December 1999

This is a personal story about a newspaper that should not have died. The story consists largely of my own experiences, recollections, and views during the more than twenty-six years I worked on the *Rand Daily Mail*, from 1958 until it was closed in 1985. My colleagues will have different memories and beliefs, and I hope they will write their own books to add to the record. There are many people and incidents I have not been able to include in this book.

Reflecting on the years of apartheid, with benefit of the knowledge gained from the last terrible years of the Afrikaner Nationalist government until its end in 1994, some of the events seem almost puny in comparison with the murder and destruction inflicted during the last decade of white rule. Yet the events were traumatic when they occurred and they opened the way to what came after. They also created many of the problems

Preface

that the new South Africa is struggling to overcome: damaged people, black rage, a weakened economy, degraded education, a debased press, and a culture of violence.

A favorite phrase used by the *Rand Daily Mail* in the apartheid era was that South Africa was on a "slippery slope." It became increasingly more relevant than any of us could have believed as the Nationalists extended their power and undermined and demolished opposition. This book covers the period of the slippery slope.

In telling the *Rand Daily Mail*'s story, I hope that it constitutes a warning primer about would-be authoritarian rulers. There is no easy way to resist them. The *Mail* did try. Sometimes it was heroic and sometimes it wasn't, sometimes it was visionary and other times shortsighted. But ultimately, it served South Africa well.

A note is needed about how I describe the people in *War of Words*. The need for clarity still requires references to color groups, and especially when speaking of the South Africa in which every aspect of existence was dominated by racial ideology. In describing different ethnic groups I have mainly followed the *Rand Daily Mail*'s style: *Asian, black, colored, white*, with *black* sometimes also used as a generic term for people who are not white.

Not everyone will agree with this approach, but it has the benefit of being similar to current official usage in the new South Africa. The government's census carried out in October 1996 asked people to describe themselves under these headings: African/black, colored, Indian/Asian, white.

Most of this book was written in a house overlooking Frenchman Bay near Bar Harbor, Maine, during the winter of 1995-96. My wife, Anne, and I were there at the invitation of Bernice Silk. I first met Bernice's husband, Leonard, in 1976 when he was a member of the editorial board of the *New York Times*, and the friendship was renewed many years later. He was the newspaper's economics columnist and spent summers at the family house in Maine writing articles and books, which were both knowledgeable and suffused with his humanity and humor. Leonard and Bernice had an emotional bond with South Africa: their son, Andy, spent time there and wrote a fine book about squatters before his early death. Leonard died in February 1995.

I am indebted to Bernice for her warm and unstinting hospitality and her constant encouragement. I am glad that my writing this book in Leonard's study gave her pleasure. The months in Maine provided a bonus in enabling Anne and me to enjoy the loveliness of that part of the United States.

For the actual writing I had the benefit of a computer from our friends, Holly and Bob Doyle in Cambridge, Massachusetts, plus their generous help with all computer problems. They welcomed us as extended family whenever we visited Boston.

Many others helped in the preparation of this book. I thank the several score of former *Rand Daily Mail* and South African Associated Newspapers (Saan) colleagues and others who gave me information: except for a tiny number whose anonymity has to be preserved, their names are listed at the end under Sources. I am also grateful to friends who were supportive and helpful in the process of producing recollections—

whether happy, or tinged with regrets or pain—about a quarter century of my life, and in checking information. Especially notable among my friends were Perdita Huston, Carol Marks and Paul Stopforth, Tina and Jay Kirsch, Tom Karis, Randolph Vigne, Hazel and George Palmer, Josie and Morrie Simon, Riva Krut, Michael Polonsky, Arthur Chaskalson, Raymond Louw, and the late Laurence Gandar, who in his quiet way kept reminding me that this was a book that must be written.

I am indebted to Michele Pickover, of the Cullinan Library at the University of the Witwatersrand, Johannesburg, for putting me on the track of my apartheid-era security dossier.

Anne shared many of the original experiences and shared, too, in remembering and trying to understand them; the warmth of her presence runs through these pages.

Thanking my publisher, Dan Simon, is more than a ritual: he was the first person to read the draft manuscript and his continuing approval and eagerness spurred me on to a greater extent than he can imagine. And my thanks to others at Seven Stories Press, some of whom I have met via e-mail—the people whose labor and enthusiasm have ensured publication: Kera Bolonik, who edited the text, and Daia Gerson, who was copy editor; Nicole Dewey and Greg Ruggiero, who planned and put into effect the promotional campaign; Jon Gilbert, who handled production, and designers Cindy LaBreacht and Annette Flaster.

As always, final responsibility for what follows is entirely mine.

Part I

The Road to Violence

The telephone on my desk in the *Rand Daily Mail* newsroom rang. I picked it up and heard the deep, warm voice of Nelson Mandela. It was midmorning on Monday, May 29, 1961, and the moment I recognized the voice, I began to stammer an apology.

"I am sorry, Nelson, that we reported so wrongly. I feel terrible about it."

He replied, "It's all right, Benjie-boy, I know it wasn't your fault."

That was a response of startling generosity. Only two hours earlier the *Rand Daily Mail* had dealt him a heavy blow, undermining his months of dangerous organizing work against the South African government. Thirteen months before, in the aftermath of unrest after police opened fire on an unarmed crowd of black people at Sharpeville, killing sixty-eight, the African National Congress (ANC) had been banned. Mandela, its leader

Chapter 1

in the Transvaal province, had forsaken his family and his attorney's practice and gone underground.

Mandela became the mastermind of a nationwide strike call, urging black workers to stay away from work for three days starting on Monday, May 29th. That was the week when whites—and especially the ruling Afrikaners—were to celebrate Republic Day.

The entire police force hunted him. But, sheltered by supporters, he traveled around the country from his base in Johannesburg to plan, exhort, and organize. He became known as the "Black Pimpernel."

I was a young reporter on the *Rand Daily Mail* and my specialized field was black politics. I had gotten to know Mandela and other leaders of the ANC since becoming a journalist on the *Mail* in 1958. During Mandela's months of underground activity I had been meeting him secretly and, in part through my reporting, the *Mail* had published more information than any other newspaper about the coming strike.

The first day of the strike marked the climax of Mandela's months of work. South Africa waited to see what would happen: how many black workers would heed the call to stay home? Without the masses of blacks filling the low-grade jobs, would factories and offices be paralyzed? If blacks proved their political clout, where would the next challenge to white authority emerge?

The *Mail* rushed out a special edition, sold in the city and in the black townships twelve and a half miles (20 km) away. "Most Go To Work: All Quiet" read the headline, and "Police Patrol Townships Before Dawn—Officials Say Stay-Home Unsuccessful."

The strike had failed, according to the report, which drew on quotes from the manager of Johannesburg's Non-European Affairs Department, claiming that blacks were coming to work as usual. The police echoed this.

In fact the headline and the report were fatally flawed, the result of rushed and sloppy journalism. Though the strike was not the total success Mandela had hoped for, it certainly wasn't the failure that the *Mail* reported.

The effect of the *Mail's* special edition was significant. At this point, the *Mail* was the country's foremost newspaper; its breadth of reporting and liberal stance had earned it respect among many blacks as well as liberals in other racial communities. Its report of the strike's failure would influence countless numbers of black people who were wondering what to do: If so many people were refusing to obey Mandela's call, they would reason, then whatever minority stayed at home would have to face wrathful action, starting with instant dismissal from jobs. Yet here was Mandela on the phone exonerating me, holding me blameless for what my newspaper had done to the strike, and to him.

We were in contact again that night. He phoned shortly before 8:30 P.M., and again an hour later. Reports were coming in of shootings and deaths in the black areas, and his mood was quieter than it had been earlier.

For publication the next day he said, "We are not disheartened," even while he admitted that "the people did not respond to the stay-at-home to the extent to which we expected them to do." He told me that it had been yet another attempt by blacks to mount nonviolent action, but the response of the government was to display intransigence backed up by the military might of its police force, the same as always. He was clearly talking about a shift to violent struggle. And that fateful step, long debated behind the scenes, was indeed taken by the ANC within weeks of our conversation.

The inglorious contribution made by the *Rand Daily Mail* in putting the boot into the strike testified, if nothing else, to the acceptance that the newspaper enjoyed among many blacks. That was a recent phenomenon. It had come about rapidly, within the previous four years. The change in the newspaper, and in the public perception of it, had begun in October 1957, when Laurence Owen Vine Gandar became editor.

There would have been little reason at that stage to believe that anything revolutionary was about to start. Gandar gave every appearance of fitting comfortably into the world of the *Rand Daily Mail*, a newspaper that, as he later said to me, "tended to reflect the outlook of the typical, middle-to-upper-income, English-speaking, urban group, very Rand Clubbish and Chamber of Mineish." The Rand Club, in the center of Johannesburg, was the city's all-male, all-white WASP club. A short walk away sat the headquarters building of the Chamber of Mines, the organization of gold and coal mine owners and one of the dominant players in South Africa's economy.

The *Rand Daily Mail* had come into being in 1902 when Johannesburg was a mere sixteen years old. The city was there because of gold. A geological quirk, some 270 million years earlier, had created a saucerlike depression, a huge inland shallow lake. Torrential rains and rivers washed debris containing particles of gold and other minerals from the surrounding high mountains into the lake. Over millions of years thin layers of gold accumulated, separated by thick strata of rock. With the gigantic shifting of the earth's crust, rock tilted and twisted, leaving seams of gold running from near the surface to thousands of yards underground.

By historical fate the area was within the boundaries of the Transvaal republic established by Boers (the name derived from the Dutch word for "farmer") of Dutch and French Huguenot ancestry who trekked north during the first half of the nineteenth century to escape British colonial rule. In February 1886, according to legend, a prospector tripped over an outcrop of rock exposed by erosion and dislodged a piece of ore. He panned it and found what proved to be the fabulous Main Reef. Prospectors and adventurers poured in. Overnight a tent town sprang up. Later that year Johannesburg was on the map, taking its name from burg, the Dutch word for "city," and, perhaps, from Field-Cornet Johannes Petrus Meyer, an official of the republic. In time the gold mining industry was to stretch over a three-hundred-mile (500 km) arc, radiating east, west, and south of Johannesburg and producing up to fifteen hundred pounds (700,000 kg) of gold a year.

Within a year of its founding, Johannesburg's population was 10,000. It grew to 100,000 in the next ten years. Horse-drawn trams came by 1889, followed by electricity the next year, as well as the growth of fashionable suburbs on the town's northern edge for the new rich elite. But the wealth beyond dreams also brought trouble: the ruling Boers were horrified by the burgeoning mining camp, with what they saw as its greedy, sinful ways. They sought to fend off the demands of the "Uitlanders" (foreigners) for political representation because of the taxes they were paying. Britain, covetous of the gold, precipitated conflict, and war broke out in 1899.

On May 31, 1900, British troops occupied Johannesburg and also took the Transvaal's capital, Pretoria, thirty-four miles (55 km) away. The war, it seemed, was over. But the Boers refused to accept defeat and continued to wage guerrilla warfare. Eventually Britain had to bring in some 250,000 troops from its far-flung empire to crush 25,000 citizen soldiers, and even then it succeeded only by resorting to a scorched-earth policy, burning down farmhouses and destroying crops to starve the insurgents into submission. The old men, women, and children evicted from their homes were herded into "concentration camps." It was apparently intended as a humanitarian gesture, but it backfired as disease struck the camps and thousands died.

The war and the savagery of the suppression embittered the Boers, with dire effects that were to endure through most of the 20th century. The Boers became known as the Afrikaners and their original language, brought from Holland, developed into Afrikaans. English- and Afrikaans-speaking whites were to become obsessed with their struggle for political and economic power. But at the time, with the war ended, Britain and some Boer leaders made their peace; for the moment, reconciliation between whites became the order of the day. The people of color, who formed the majority, were excluded from power and were increasingly debarred from any right of equal access to South Africa's wealth.

One of the indirect casualties of the war was a Johannesburg newspaper, the *Standard and Diggers News*, which had been subsidized by the Boer government. The newspaper collapsed, leaving behind, among other things, a stock of Linotype machines and presses, and its worried owner, Emmanuel Mendelssohn, a substantial person in the property market. In Heath's Hotel one day in June 1902 he bewailed his loss. What was he to do with the machinery? Harry Freeman Cohen, a man with a thousand mining and speculative interests, offered, "I'll buy the lot, if the price is cheap." It was—the printing press was obsolete—and in a few minutes Freeman Cohen was the owner. The deal was celebrated with a magnum of champagne.

According to the version carried in company publications in later years, that same evening a young man with a mustache and an extravagantly long cigarette holder strolled into the hotel. "There's a likely-looking chap for you! Who's he?" asked Freeman Cohen. "That's Edgar Wallace," Mendelssohn told him. "Kitchener [the general who headed the British forces] can't stand him. He scooped everybody with his news of the peace negotiations [with the Boers] for the *London Daily Mail*."

"That's Wallace, is it? Well, I'll start a daily paper here and make him the editor," said Freeman Cohen. And, as the tale runs, Wallace had hardly finished another cigarette before, at the age of twenty-seven, he was editor of the still-to-be-published newspaper.

It's a pity to spoil a good story, but the reality seems to have been less fanciful, even in its most minute details: Not until ten years later did Wallace take to using the extravagantly long cigarette holder, which became his hallmark. The publishers of a Wallace biography, issued in London in 1939, noted that few people knew the real story of his life. According to Wallace's biographer, Margaret Lane, when Freeman Cohen bought the printing plant, he already knew Wallace and had discussed the newspaper plan with him, including the offer of editorship at a salary of princely proportions: £2,000 a year compared with the £336 he was earning from the London newspaper.

Wallace was, by then, a journalist with a considerable reputation as a result of being first with the news of the peace agreement between Britain and the Boers. The talks between the two sides had been held in a camp surrounded by a barbed-wire fence near the town of Vereeniging. Journalists were not allowed inside and were subject to strict military censorship. Wallace surprised his colleagues with the scoop because he had supposedly never gone near the place, spending his days sitting in a train that chugged to and from the Vaal River. When he wasn't doing that, he was using Freeman Cohen's office in Johannesburg to send cables to London to buy and sell shares.

This was all a cover. Wallace had previously been a medical orderly in the British army stationed in the Cape. The Vaal River train passed the peace-talks camp, where an old crony served as a guard. Whenever the train went by, the guard strolled to the fence and used a handkerchief to blow his nose. A red handkerchief meant "nothing doing," blue was "making progress," and white was "treaty definitely to be signed." Using a simple, prearranged code, the information was hidden in Wallace's stock exchange cables that went to Freeman Cohen's brother in London for transferral to the *Daily Mail*.

Wallace's disclosure of the peace agreement was published a sensational twenty-four hours before the British government announced the news in the House of Commons. An enraged General Kitchener punished Wallace for breaking the censorship rules by having him barred from working as a war correspondent and denying him the Anglo-Boer War medal. This did not lessen the sweetness of Wallace's triumph, however. On a visit to London, the *Daily Mail* honored him with a banquet at the Savoy Hotel.

Returning to Johannesburg, Wallace launched the *Rand Daily Mail*. The first issue appeared on Monday, September 22, 1902. Even by mining-town standards, the newspaper's working conditions were unpleasant. The office "was in the top floors of a ramshackle and depressing brick warren behind the corner of Rissik and Commissioner streets" in the center of town, wrote Lane.

Originally built to house sample rooms for commercial travelers, the building was hidden from the street by a row of shops, and separated from their back wall by a narrow alley in which garbage was thrown, and nearby restaurant workers cut chickens' throats. There was no staircase. Instead, the upper floors "were reached by broad wooden ladders; draughts, noise and smells pierced the comfortless building from top to bottom. A goods hoist clattered gustily from floor to floor in that part of the office set aside for the sub-editors, and the screech of chickens, held to bleed over the garbage bins in the alley, punctually heralded the approach of lunch and dinner."

Wallace's office was a closetlike room partitioned off in a corner, large enough only for a battered desk, a chair, and an old bookcase. The only telephone hung on the outside of the partition and was answered by whoever happened to be near it. But Wallace reveled in the dignity and prominence of being editor, lived well, and entertained lavishly.

His prosperity was quickly apparent. According to Lane, "His figure began to fill out, and his mustache grew bolder. He indulged his taste for large pale-colored hats with rolling brims, and strolled to the office in high-buttoned suits of a sporting and opulent character. The gold-headed cane, the solid watch-chain festooned across his waistcoat, the ring on his little finger, the immaculate yellow gloves carried importantly in the left hand, bespoke him a man of consequence in Johannesburg."

As was newspaper practice then, the first and last of the closely printed eight pages were devoted to advertisements. Notices of sales of oxen, land, and bicycles appeared alongside advertisements for "The People's Tailors—Suits to Measure at 90s" and Non-Intoxicating Lager (NIL) beer. There were also advertisements for companies and products that remain household names in today's South Africa: Castle beer; H. W. Markham, Gentlemen's Outfitter; and Mutual Life Assurance, which today is the Old Mutual.

Personal links with Britain were all-important: hence the *Mail* published a news report that the train bringing the "English Mails" from Cape Town was eleven hours late. In the aftermath of the Boer war, British-imposed martial law was still in force, and the newspaper carried the names of those who had been given permits to travel to and from the Johannesburg area from the coast and other towns. The political attitude was made abundantly clear with a sharp editorial rebuke for "a manifestly injudicious manifesto" issued by former Boer generals in which they begged the world for help because Britain was not doing enough to repair the ravages of the war.

"The [Boer] Republics," the generals wrote, "were ready to sacrifice everything for independence but now the struggle is over and our people are completely ruined."

There were problems finding space for all that was happening in the burgeoning town. Within its first week the newspaper told readers, "Owing to a rush of telegrams just before going to Press our report of the prize-giving at the Johannesburg Public School for Boys and a mass of other interesting material has been crowded out of this issue."

Among the items that pushed out the prize-giving was the fact that "some little excitement was caused yesterday morning about 8:00 o'clock by a small outbreak of fire which, but for the prompt action of the Jeppestown Fire Brigade, would in a short time have assumed serious proportions."

"Money, Brains, Energy, are employed without stint in making the *Rand Daily Mail*," the paper boasted. Wallace had grand plans. "We'll race the paper by special train to Pretoria," he told his staff. "We'll have a fleet of motor vans. We'll have correspondents in every capital of the world. Johannesburg is a great city and it is going to have a great newspaper."

The fantasy of a fleet of vans went unfulfilled, but the special train—the 699 Down—became a reality, albeit an expensive one, costing more than it earned.

Wallace was, fifty years later, described by an official company publication as having carried out his editorship with "a lavish and brilliant Bohemianism." Too lavish, however. The reaching for foreign news lasted only as long as it took for the bills to come in—at ten shillings and threepence a word for cables from Tokyo, and six shillings and twopence a word from Buenos Aires. Those were huge amounts. Lunch in a Johannesburg cafe could be had for one shilling and sixpence. After less than ten months Freeman Cohen had to clear his bank account and borrow money to settle the debts, using the newspaper as security. The 699 Down ran no longer.

Wallace wrote "Finis" on his desk blotter and sailed back to England to become a world-famed writer of crime novels, churning out close to 150 in twenty-seven years and spawning many movies such as *Sanders of the River*. Some eighty years later his daughter in Britain was still in contact with the *Rand Daily Mail*, sending out copies of the Edgar Wallace Society newsletter. The desk Wallace was believed to have used as an editor was given a polish and kept in the boardroom, on display to visitors.

One of Wallace's innovations was a Christmas Comfort Fund—soliciting money from readers to provide food parcels for the poor of the city and its surrounding areas. The fund's image of sympathy toward the underdog soon came to be associated with the *Mail*. As with so much in the South Africa of then and later, the image was not a true likeness: the comforts provided by the Christmas Fund were for whites only, a situation that was to persist for many years.

Wallace's immediate successor was George Adamson, born in Scotland and described in later company publications as a "sound and steady figure." But Freeman Cohen died in 1904, and the *Mail* was put up for sale. The "Nationals," a group that supported the cause of the postwar Boers, put in its offer. The sale, however, was stymied by Abe Bailey, a mining magnate who was later to be knighted by Britain. He shared the newspaper's declared support for Lord Milner, the British governor set on the primacy of English and imperial British rule. Bailey put his money into the paper, but took an indirect role in the operation during the next thirty years, ensuring only that it remained in approved hands.

The *Mail's* early years, and those of its afternoon rival, the *Star*, set patterns that continued into the modern era. Both newspapers were owned by gold mining interests: the British-owned Central Mining Investment Company, known as Corner House, kept a tight rein on the *Star*. On the other hand, Bailey and the others who came after him seemed to have been more haphazard, and the *Mail* developed a volatile and maverick character. Corner House thoroughly disapproved. By 1914 its London headquarters was saying that the way in which the *Mail* and its sister paper, the *Sunday Times* (started in 1906), were conducted was "detrimental both to the mining industry and to the general population."

With Bailey as the dominant shareholder, it followed that the newspaper supported the views of the gold mining houses. That was evident as early as 1905 under the shrewd editorship of Ralph Ward Jackson, a former British cavalry officer in the Eleventh Hussars.

Many gold mines had closed during the Anglo-Boer War, and altogether 100,000 black laborers were dismissed. As mining got under way again, there was a severe shortage of labor. Mine owners, through their Chamber of Mines and with the approval of Lord Milner, imported laborers from China. Within months 50,000 had arrived, setting off howls of protest from local whites. The *Mail* backed the arguments of the mine owners and government that the Chinese were vital for the industry to survive; it also suggested that they were there temporarily and would return home when their contracts ended.

At the same time the newspaper's fundamental tenet was to support a "white labor policy," which would ensure full and privileged employment of whites. That could hardly draw kudos from the Chamber of Mines, which, intent on reducing costs, made sporadic attempts to use poorly paid blacks to take over some of the work of highly paid whites.

The contradictions were already evident in 1905 when Sir Lionel Phillips, chairman of some of the biggest mines, sued the *Mail* for libel because of its reports of terrible conditions in gold mines, and charges that miners were "dying like flies from phthisis" (the lung disease caused by dust underground).

Over the years the *Mail* earned a reputation as a friend of white workers, and especially of white miners. Giving support to white workers would be viewed today as naked racism—except that "racism," then and for many years after, carried an entirely different meaning: it was used in an all-white context, and referred to relations between South Africans of British stock and Afrikaners. Bailey and the *Mail* denied being racists, by which they meant that they believed in the two white groups cooperating for the sake of the country.

Prejudice against people of color was different. In today's terms the newspaper's attitudes were indeed racist. At the time, they were within the mainstream of South Africa's white-controlled society, which believed implicitly in white rule, then and forever. In the period immediately preceding the creation in 1910 of the Union of South Africa, which brought together the Cape, Natal, Transvaal, and Orange Free State, the *Mail* did not merely take it as an article of faith that there was no question of voting rights for blacks, but even vehemently opposed— unsuccessfully, it turned out—the white liberals in the Cape who wanted mixed-race coloreds to retain their voting rights. Only for the unimaginably dim and distant future was there some acceptance of what might lie ahead, for as the editor wrote, "We feel strongly that the principle of discrimination between black and white is an absolutely essential principle of any successful policy for the peaceful governing of South Africa. Perhaps generations hence such a principle may be abandoned. But to abandon it today must inevitably lead to serious complications in the near future."

In 1912, George Kingswell, acting for the company that owned the *Mail*, struck a blow for segregation at a congress of the Newspaper Press Union (NPU), the organization of newspaper owners. Until then the NPU had included among its members a black editor, Tengo Jabavu, of *Imvo Zabantsundu* (African Opinion). Kingswell proposed that "no colored or native newspaper proprietor should be admitted as a member of the Newspaper Press Union." The motion was carried and the point was rammed home with the added requirement that members had to be "European" (the word for whites, used until the 1960s and even later). Not until sixty-three years later, in 1975, did the NPU drop its color bar.

The *Rand Daily Mail* echoed Bailey's harsh views, this time on the subject of Asians, a large number of whom had been brought in from India from the second half of the nineteenth century onwards, primarily to work in the sugarcane fields on the east coast. A speech he made in parliament in 1922 was reported: "Mr. Bailey said there could be no denying that the presence of Asiatics had a deteriorating effect on the white race. The Asiatics were the white ants of South Africa, destroying the foundations of our institutions and the roots of the livelihood of the white race." The next day, under the headline "Asiatic Menace," the *Mail* said the government should heed the numbers of unemployed whites and "should check the Indianizing of the country and give its own sons a decent chance against the lower standard competition of Asians."

That was during the brief three-year editorship of L. E. Neame. After him, in 1924, came the New Zealander Lewis Rose McLeod, who came to Johannesburg via the *Daily Mail* in London, and steered the paper for the next seventeen years with the same rigid color and class attitudes as his predecessors.

The simple fact for the editors—and this did not apply only to the *Rand Daily Mail* but to all the mainstream newspapers in the country—was that blacks featured in the news only in so far as they were responsible for division among whites. They were the "Native problem"—sometimes with a capital N, sometimes not—and political differences among whites occurred in large part around differing views of how to deal with it.

Blacks did not exist as ordinary people. The speeches of black political leaders were reported only in isolated cases. Reporting black activities was confined to occasional statements by white liberals, sometimes issuing from the South African Institute of Race Relations. Newspapers catered to readers who were, overwhelmingly, whites. The advertising they carried was directed exclusively at white consumers, and the government's activities that were reported were at all levels in white hands.

There had been, however, one occasion when blacks were treated as flesh-and-blood newsmakers. In 1936 the United Party government, led by General J. B. M. Hertzog—a Boer leader in the Anglo-Boer War— was in the final stages of altering the constitution to radically reduce the voting rights of blacks, and limit their "reserves" to about 16 percent of the country. He sought the views of black leaders until the day that he achieved his needed two-thirds majority among white members of parliament (MPs). Literally from one day to the next, blacks disappeared from the news.

Throughout the 1930s, under McLeod, the *Mail* served as a pillar of the Chamber of Mines, and supported the United Party government, lining up with the rest of the English-language press but opposed by the smaller number of Afrikaans newspapers. The *Mail's* support swiftly turned to criticism if the government did anything that might adversely affect the mining industry, such as increasing taxes.

McLeod's last few years were dominated by the events in Europe, separated by a fortnight's passage by sea or several days by air. The political divide among South Africa's whites deepened as many Afrikaners looked with admiration at the rising German colossus, both because of the appeal of the ideas of National Socialism and because of Germany's challenge to Britain. When Britain and France declared war on Germany on September 3, 1939, South Africa's parliament was fortuitously going into a special session. The deputy prime minister, General Jan Christiaan Smuts, also a former Boer general, seized the occasion to propose that South Africa enter the war against Germany. Prime Minister Hertzog opposed him, but lost by eighty votes to sixty-seven, and war was declared on September 6th. Most English-speaking whites backed Smuts, as did many Afrikaners. But large numbers of Afrikaners backed Hertzog. With opinion so divided, Smuts as the new Prime Minister did not dare order conscription; as it was, he had to put down rebellion and cope with agitation and subversion by two Afrikaans extreme right-wing organizations, the Greyshirts and the Ossewa Brandwag (Sentinels of the Ox-Wagon).

Both English and Afrikaner South Africans volunteered for service on the side of the Allies and wore an orange flash on their shoulders to show that they had agreed to fight outside the country's borders. This they did in East Africa, Abyssinia (now Ethiopia), North Africa, and Italy. Blacks were also recruited, but as truck drivers, stretcher bearers, and laborers who were allowed to carry only spears or clubs. The black response to recruiting drives was unenthusiastic, although at first some had reasonably, if naïvely, hoped that they might benefit from the war for democracy.

The *Mail* gave unstinting support, in its reporting and comments, to the war. The belief in the fight against the Nazi menace was total. So, too, was its opposition to those Afrikaners who were now in the Nationalist party (later renamed the National Party) led by Dr. D. F. Malan, a former minister of the Dutch Reformed Church, and former editor of the *Burger*, the Afrikaans newspaper in Cape Town, the party's official organ.

Smuts had won an election during the war years and, in 1948, called a general election. To widespread surprise and shock, he narrowly lost to Malan and the newfangled cry of "apartheid"—Afrikaans for racial separateness. During electioneering, Malan also promised there would be white bread. This was a potent promise to a public tired of being restricted to brown bread because South Africa relied on wheat imports. These had been affected by the war, and afterward were neglected by Smuts's government, as was much else in the country, through complacency and incompetence.

To the *Mail* and to English-speakers, the unthinkable had happened. The Nazi supporters—the *Sunday Times* had set the fashion of calling them Malanazis—were in office. Just as bad, they were Afrikaners, intent on regaining through political means the power that Britain had taken from them in the war nearly half a century earlier.

Thousands gathered on Burg Street in Cape Town to watch the results of the May 26, 1948 general election flashing on a screen outside the offices of the *Cape Times*, the local English-language morning newspaper. Through the second night, in between singing "The Londonderry Air" and other popular ballads, the sense of shock in the crowd was palpable as results from the rural constituencies came in and the Nationalists headed for a small majority in parliament. Prime Minister Smuts was defeated even in his own Standerton constituency.

I was in the crowd, aged fifteen, a junior in high school, and an intense admirer of Smuts. I considered him an extraordinary man of learning who had studied at Cambridge University in England, written about his holistic view of life, fought as an Afrikaner general during the Anglo-Boer War and then made peace with his British enemies. He had gone on to hold the army rank

Chapter 2

of field marshal in Britain and served in British imperial cabinets during the half century's two world wars, and was one of the founders of the United Nations. As a teenager who was conscious of being a Jew, I felt grateful to him for leading the Union into the Second World War and helping to destroy Nazism.

Later, my starry-eyed view of Smuts would change as I came to know more about the contradictory roles he adopted—a statesman of vision and humanity on the world stage, while at home a politician who pandered to white racial (antiblack) attitudes. Later still, Harry O'Connor, long one of South Africa's foremost political journalists, used to regale me with stories about Smuts's contrived folksy ways. When Smuts went to speak at a hall in rural villages and towns, he did not walk up the stairs to the platform. Rather, he made a point of climbing on from the front and, as he did, would flip up his jacket to show his backside—and the neat patch on his trousers; a murmur would go through the hall, "Ouma [Granny, as Smuts's wife was known to all] sewed it on."

On another occasion, O'Connor remembered, Smuts was in London for his first visit since losing the election the previous year. The great and the good of the world's press came to interview him in his hotel suite. Smuts, who was due to go on to Buckingham Palace, came in from his bedroom dressed in formal morning suit—and wearing slippers. The journalists were duly impressed by this evidence of small-town homeliness, and hung on his every word.

Even while a teenage admirer of Smuts, I had already begun to grow skeptical of his United Party because of its narrow devotion to maintaining the interests of whites. I was coming to believe that the future of South Africa rested with its majority—blacks, mixed-race coloreds, and Asians—who comprised more than 80 percent of the population.

I had had no meaningful contact across the color line except a very personal one: Lizzie Adonis was a colored woman who had been with my family since I was a few months old. She brought me up and worked for us until I was twenty. I could do no wrong in her eyes; when as a boy I misbehaved and my father was threatening me with a spanking, Lizzie would passionately spring to my defense and put herself between my father and me.

My parents had come from Lithuania in the 1920s. My mother's two brothers had arrived earlier, settled in, and then sent for my father, who later brought out my mother. My parents owned a busy grocery store in the suburb of Observatory, down the street from our home, and I worked there, mainly on Saturday mornings, serving behind the counter and making up customer orders. Later my parents switched to a more sedate drapery store. Every one of their friends was Jewish, and many hailed from the same area in Lithuania. The only semisocial contact they had with non-Jews were customers who occasionally came to our house. The signature feature of our home was our wonderful library. My father was a storekeeper out of necessity and a scholar by inclination. He spent much of the day in the drapery store at a table reading and studying languages—he knew about eight—with my mother as the driving force in the business. I became a voracious reader at an early age, working my way through my father's library and moving on to the public library down the street. I could always use my pocket money to buy any book I wanted, certain to get a refund from my father.

The Zionist Hall near the city center was the Jewish community's social hub where, as a child, I went with my parents to innumerable weddings and *bar mitzvot*. All followed the identical pattern: food was served in abundance to the several hundred guests seated at long tables covered with white cloths, and lengthy speeches were made; then with a lot of clattering the waiters removed the tables, and the band struck up for dancing.

Many in the community followed Orthodox Judaism, which in the South African context meant a more relaxed and tolerant observance than the word orthodox usually means these days. Traveling by car and working on the Sabbath were widely accepted as necessary. But it did mean a kosher home, with only ritually slaughtered meat and separate crockery and cutlery for meat and milk foods. When I was five, I spent the afternoon at an Afrikaans friend's home, and when I returned home, my mother wanted to know whether I had eaten anything. I told her I'd had a plate of soup, which earned me the biggest beating of my life. The next time I ate *treyf*, nonkosher, was when I was sixteen, on holiday at the farm of cousins near Oudtshoorn, the small town famous for ostriches. I discovered that steak actually had flavor, compared with the salt-cleansed fiber I had known until then, and my eating habits changed from then on.

The rabbi of our local synagogue was a *landsleit*—he came from the same region as many of his congregants. One of the rabbi's duties was to carry out ritual slaughtering of chickens: sent by my mother, I would carry a live one to him and watch while he slit its throat and it hopped around on the ground until it died. Then I would carry it home to be plucked over a small fire in the backyard. The rabbi was also the teacher in *cheder*, the Hebrew school at the synagogue where I went each afternoon for several years, culminating in studies for bar mitzvah when I turned thirteen.

Before apartheid began, in May 1948, Cape Town's suburbs were already largely segregated. Three hundred years before, it was the way of life initiated by the Dutch settlers who settled at the Cape in 1652—except that there was no shortage of sexual relations for the men, producing the mixed-race colored people. Segregation and discrimination were carried forward and enacted into law by the British, who, at the start of the nineteenth century, took over the Cape to control what was then the primary sea route between Europe and the important colonies of India and the Far East. But the segregation was not total, at least in regard to coloreds: in our adjoining suburbs of Salt River and Wood-stock, working-class whites and coloreds lived side by side, and there were also pockets of coloreds, in modest houses, in middle-class suburbs such as Newlands.

It was different for blacks. Few lived in Cape Town at that time. Elsewhere in the country, where blacks predominated, as in the Transvaal and Natal, the discrimination against them was severe and entrenched. But in Cape Town, because the black population was smaller, the rules and habits of segregation were mostly absent. Buses in Cape Town were not segregated, unlike most of the country. The local suburban trains were also not segregated, even though they were run by the state-owned South African Railways, whose intercity and suburban services in the Johannesburg area were segregated. Cape Town's City Hall, the venue for classical concerts, was also not segregated. But beaches, whether by law or by custom I don't know, were racially divided.

Had May 1948 not altered the course of events, it is conceivable that Cape Town could have muddled along, with segregation slowly breaking down and the city's traditionally more relaxed attitude spreading throughout the rest of the country. That, at least, was the belief of many Capetonians, which I shared. We saw ourselves as gentler, more civilized people living in the shadow of Table Mountain amid scenery of surpassing beauty; all this in contrast with the hardness, in geography and outlook, of the Transvalers, who came on holiday each summer.

Of course we were presented with practical problems when apartheid was enforced. What to do about the auditorium in the City Hall, where a roped-off area near the back of the hall delineated the places that people of color could sit: Did you share the space? Not go to concerts any longer? On the segregated suburban trains all the first-class carriages with their comfortable seats had boards saying, "Whites only." But one first-class carriage was left unmarked and was open to everyone. Was this the carriage to use as a gesture of solidarity—even though it was often already overcrowded with coloreds and blacks whose comfort you were lessening by crowding in?

As a boy my contacts with people of other colors were infrequent. One was on my daily walk to and from *cheder*. En route I passed a fruit and vegetable shop owned by people known as Cape Malays, Muslims whose forebears had come from the East Indies during the seventeenth century. Under apartheid the owner was later dispossessed of his shop. His son, a boy much my own age, was Dullah Omar, who would later become South Africa's minister of justice in Mandela's postapartheid government.

As I grew up, there was little politics at home. My father seemed to be a United Party supporter. I was immersed in Jewish affairs as a member of *Habonim* (Hebrew for "builders"), a Jewish youth movement akin to the Boy Scouts, but with a strong Zionist and socialist bent. Our uniform shirt was blue, in solidarity with the workers of the world, and we regularly sang the "Internationale." With Israel just coming into existence in May 1948, my ambition was to go there to live as an intellectual peasant on a kibbutz, working in the fields by day and at night listening to Beethoven on scratchy seventy-eight records. I spent school holidays on *hachsharah* (preparation), doing exactly that on a farm in the Transvaal, happily accepting that the toughening process included sleeping on stony ground in midwinter and taking cold-water showers in the open at the end of the working day in the fields. But my mother opposed my desire to move to Israel, insisting that I first acquire "a career." I enrolled at the University of Cape Town (UCT) and there for the first time I became directly involved in South African affairs.

The university occupies a site on the slope of Devil's Peak. It is set against the changing colors of the mountain, and from the campus the view over the Cape Flats, the stretch of flat, sandy land that links the city with the north, is breathtaking. UCT prided itself on being an "open" university, which meant that, together with the University of the Witwatersrand (Wits) in Johannesburg, it admitted "nonwhite" students; that is, coloreds, blacks, and Asians. Alone among universities in the country, UCT and Wits practiced academic nonsegregation: students who were not white were admitted on merit, even though the numbers were not high at that time.

The few who were medical students suffered discrimination, however: at Wits, white pathologists on staff carried out autopsies at the government hospital where students trained, dissecting white cadavers with only white students present. Then the white bodies were covered up or removed and the pathologists began autopsies on black cadavers, at which point the black students waiting outside were admitted for the lesson.

Socially, black, colored and Asian students were excluded from sports and dances at both UCT and Wits. At Cape Town the social segregation was quaintly known as a "gentlemen's agreement." At Wits it was a matter of some contention, with calls by white students for the ending of all racial barriers. In some years the annual intervarsity rugby match against

Pretoria University was suspended because of the refusal of the Afrikaans university to play against a Wits team if there was a student of color on it.

At Wits, blacks had their separate residence, but there was no such provision at UCT. It took me a long time to come to understand the hardship in time, energy, and money that this imposed on black students, forcing them to live in rudimentary conditions far away in the then small black townships.

I made my first friends across the color line. They were chiefly coloreds and those I knew mostly belonged to the Non-European Unity Movement (NEUM, known nowadays as the New Unity Movement). It dated from the 1930s, and membership was strong among colored intellectuals, especially teachers. Its policy was rooted in the concept of noncollaboration with the oppressor, which was fine except that members who were teachers were employed by the white government, and they went on with their jobs.

My growing political interest and liberal outlook led to my being drawn into the National Union of South African Students (Nusas). I was a protégé of Patricia Arnett, who had just become president, the first woman to hold the office. She schooled me in a lifelong lesson: respect for facts. My motto, which I came across in my studies, was a quotation from Charles Booth, the nineteenth century English pioneer of social research who carried out a monumental study of life and labor in London:

> In intensity of feeling, and not in statistics, lies the power to move the world. But by statistics must this power be guided if it would move the world aright.

My first elected position was as the Nusas director of research at UCT. We launched a range of research projects into social and medical problems in the Cape Town area, with scores of students taking part and preparing reports. During my term of office, I was elected national director of research because the previous director, a Communist, became ill.

Soon after, it was time for the next annual Nusas conference, held that year at Pietermaritzburg in Natal. As national director I was required to approve all the research papers to be presented to the conference. I rejected a paper submitted by a Wits student, Harold Wolpe, on the grounds that it was not research but a Marxist polemic. (In years to come Wolpe managed a daring escape from police detention and went on to become a distinguished Marxist scholar in Britain.) Suddenly I found myself a target of left-wing fury.

One of my friends, a medical student named David Cooper, was ordered by the Left to stand against me. He came to tell me about it late at night with tears rolling down his cheeks. It was all the more painful because I had close links with the Left, both because so many of my friends were among them and because of my socialist background in *Habonim*. The new Afrikaner Nationalist government was giving expression to its fear of the *rooi gevaar* ("the red danger")—which went with its fear of the *swart gevaar* ("the black danger," meaning the majority of South Africans)—and was setting about enacting legislation to proscribe the Communist Party. However, around that time I was reading Arthur Koestler's testimonies of a disillusioned Communist, *Darkness at Noon* and in *The God That Failed*. Both powerfully pointed to the discrepancies between the beauty of theory and the ugliness of reality. Whatever lingering beliefs in Communism I might have held were forever ended by those books and my Nusas experience. I came to view Communism as inimical to South Africa as apartheid was; both failed because they did not care about the individual and cared nothing about the damage they inflicted putting their ideology into effect.

We won the vote and I was reelected. It was a triumph for the liberals in Nusas, and a turning point too. The liberals, centered on Cape Town, were vying for control with the left wing at Wits. A running cause of dispute, which exemplified the differences between the two camps, was Nusas's membership in the International Union of Students (IUS). The IUS, headquartered in Prague and run by the Communist nations, was a propaganda weapon in the Cold War. Nusas was the only Western body that still held its membership, and many of us believed that we were being used as pawns in the world struggle for influence and that our name was supporting policies that did nothing but savage the West. The Left was determined to keep Nusas in the IUS, but the liberals were equally intent on getting out. With the liberals now in the ascendancy, Nusas was finally able to quit. (At the time a number of student leaders in the Communist countries had not been heard from. There was also a Yiddish poet, Yitzik Pfeffer, who somehow became a rallying point for us. "Where is Yitzik Pfeffer?" we chanted at our fellow-traveler colleagues, often more in jest than in earnest. The terrible truth about what had befallen Pfeffer and student leaders began to emerge only with Nikita Khrushchev's revelations to the Twentieth Communist Party

Congress in Moscow in 1956: they had been killed, victims of Stalin's paranoid suspicions.)

Whenever possible I went to Saturday night meetings held by the NEUM at its New Era Fellowship. One night they had a speaker about Nusas. He made so many inaccurate statements that I stood up repeatedly, demanding that he speak truthfully. My aggression finally set off an eruption, with the audience yelling at me. One of them let loose with what was considered the worst insult a NEUM person could utter: "Liberal, liberal, liberal!" The chairman stopped the meeting and ordered him to apologize for using such unseemly language.

My links across the color lines were developing all the time. Through Nusas I assisted in running a community center for coloreds in the Athlone suburb, a paternalistic exercise, although I did not understand this at the time. On campus I became an effective vote-getter and applied this after persuading Jairus Mutambikwa, a social science student from Rhodesia and one of the small number of blacks on the campus, to stand for election to the Students' Representative Council. Aided and abetted by a sassy first-year student, Monica Menell, whose father was head of Anglovaal gold mining, we made history when he won at the polls. He was the first black student elected to the council, and it drew cross comments from government people in parliament. They would probably have been even nastier had they known that the irrepressible Monica, when asked by would-be voters about the candidate's unusual name, would gaily say that it was Italian.

It was through student politics that I had my first contacts with journalists. I had no interest in working on the UCT student newspaper, nor did I aspire to be the campus representative for local newspapers. But the Afrikaner Nationalists were moving against the universities, to deny UCT and Wits in particular the right to admit whom they pleased. However imperfect the treatment of Asian, black, and colored students, the essential point was that the universities decided their own admissions policy, as they did their policy on hiring staff and their curriculum. Academic freedom was at stake. Huge efforts went into fighting for it, not only at the two "open" universities but at the other English-language universities in Grahamstown, Durban, and Pietermaritzburg, which were even more restrictive in admitting students and actually applied their own apartheid to the extent that some had lily-white student enrollment. The efforts staved off government action for years; only in 1959 was legislation to destroy academic freedom finally enacted under the title of the Extension of University Education Act. This wording was as inaccurate as it was cynical. What the act did was to exclude students who were not white from virtually all the existing universities. They could attend only with permission from the government. Asians had to apply to the Department of Indian Affairs, coloreds to the Department of Colored Affairs, and blacks to the Department of Native Affairs (whose name underwent changes over the years), and each in turn dealt with the Department of National Education, which handled the "white" universities. The "extension" of the act's title was in the creation of new segregated and inferior universities for different tribal and ethnic groups.

The fight against university apartheid, while it lasted, was intense. As the Nusas executive representative at UCT, and later as secretary of the Students' Representative Council, I was involved with the protests and began to meet journalists like George Clay and Dave Marais of the *Cape Times* at press conferences. Marais became a newspaper cartoonist and was adept at lampooning the madder aspects of apartheid: when beach segregation was enforced, with signs posted on beaches declaring "Whites Only," Marais drew a suntanned little boy pulling down his bathing costume to show his white backside to a policeman.

Between classes I worked in an attorney's office in the city. As part of my job I often had to go to the Deeds Office, the land registry that happened to be across the street from the entrance to parliament. I would grab a file and announce that I was off to the Deeds Office, and rush over to supervise the picket line of several hundred students holding posters opposing university apartheid, which I had organized, with grim-faced Nationalist MPs walking past. Or I would walk a block to the city center to check the afternoon picket line strung along Adderley Street. Picketing protest was still possible, and many students were willing to take part. A couple of years later the Nationalists barred demonstrations in the precincts of parliament and later, step by step, extended this until little picketing was possible anywhere.

By its very nature student politics had to do with national politics. We looked at newspapers from universities in the United States or Canada where student conflict revolved around how much parking space should be provided for cars. In UCT elections the dominant issue was a candidate's stand on university apartheid and, year by year, the elected majority opposed the government's plans. Even engineering students, known for their conservatism and right-wing views, had to declare themselves.

The fate of universities was but one battlefield. Immediately after their victory in 1948, the Afrikaner Nationalists set about putting their ideology into practice. They had won the election with a majority of parliamentary seats, but actually polled fewer votes than the combined United Party and tiny Labor Party. (The latter was a political oddity. Its then few MPs were fine liberals, but the party's heyday had been in the 1920s when it fought for the interests of white workers and had several members in the cabinet.) A system of loading votes, legitimately instituted at Union in 1910 to compensate the *platteland* (countryside) for sparse populations and long distances, favored rural constituencies by up to 30 percent over urban seats. The Nationalists were strongest in the *platteland*, among farmers and in *dorpe* (villages).

The first aim of the Nationalists after so unexpectedly winning office was to ensure that they could not easily be unseated, and all the better from their point of view if this accorded with ideology. A great drive was launched against the colored vote. Although coloreds had only a restricted right to the franchise, there were enough of them to influence a number of constituencies. The Nationalists set out to do what had been done to blacks in 1936—create "Colored Representatives," a handful of white MPs elected by coloreds on a separate voters' roll. The struggle went on for years until the Nationalists succeeded, by hook and by crook. There were stirring scenes in Cape Town with a march by thousands up Adderley Street. No one had ever thought to see Sam Kahn, the solitary Communist MP, arm in arm with George Golding, who until then, had been as toadying a colored leader as anyone could be.

Kahn was a magnificent parliamentarian, a strong voice ringing out in the debating chamber. He was evicted by the Suppression of Communism Act in 1950. Many years later I ended up alongside Kahn on a public platform in London: he had grown old and, tactlessly, in addressing the Jewish audience, assailed Israel, Zionism, and most things Jewish. The audience grew angrier by the moment, yelling at him to sit down and shut up. My reaction was Voltairean. I rose to say that as a schoolboy I had gone to the South African parliament to listen to Kahn's impassioned denunciations of apartheid, how they had stirred me, and how I could still remember the heavy shouts of "*Jood*" (Jew) and "Go to Israel" from the Nationalist benches. Sam Kahn had paid his dues and deserved better than what the audience was giving him. It silenced them.

The Suppression of Communism Act of 1950 was the granddaddy law, with the main purpose of banning the Communist Party, which had, in any event, a short while before met and voted itself out of existence. The act also included provisions for depriving the personal liberties of anyone "deemed" to be a Communist. This became the basic Nationalist club for dealing with opponents, with the law extended and broadened year by year and loopholes closed. Within less than a decade the law would be used to muzzle many with strong anti-Communist views, including liberals such as David Craighead, a prominent Catholic, and Patrick Duncan, editor of the fortnightly newspaper *Contact*.

But a new yeast was at work. Blacks were getting themselves organized and were trying to fight back. Muriel Horrell, for many years editor of the annual survey of the South African Institute of Race Relations, described the process as "action, reaction and counter-action." The government did something, people reacted with outrage, and the government snuffed out the protest, arming itself with ever-spiraling power at each stage. The developing black militancy confirmed my belief that it was black politics that counted for the future.

The Liberal Party was a natural postuniversity home, indeed the only home for me given the alternative. The also newly formed Congress of Democrats (COD) was objectionable to me both because it was a cover for the extreme Left and because it was for whites only. This was one of the contradictory aspects of the Congress Alliance with separate organizations for blacks—the ANC—and each of the other two major ethnic groups. The phrase was multiracialism. The Liberal Party, on the other hand, was predicated on the primacy of the individual; it was nonracial, anti-apartheid, and anti-Communist. Margaret Ballinger, a "Native Representative" in parliament under the law passed in 1936, was the president. She was a large and formidable woman, very sure of herself and her role after her years of opposition to racial discrimination. Her husband, William, was a "Native" senator under the same law and lived in her shadow. But the Ballingers, as I was soon to discover after joining the party's Cape Provincial Committee, belonged to a fading era when whites spoke for blacks. Far more in tune with developments was Alan Paton, author of the classic South African novel *Cry, the Beloved Country*, who was an executive member of the party from its start in 1953 and became its leader two years later.

The drawback to the party, for me, was that it believed in a "qualified franchise," that everyone should meet educational and/or property qualifications in order to have the right to vote. It was a convenient policy for whites and was thought to be appealing to white voters because virtually every white man or woman would automatically qualify by virtue of historical education and privilege; in other color groups, there would have to be a transition period. But I rejected the qualified franchise as insultingly patronizing to blacks. Nor did it achieve what it was supposed to since in fact the party made little headway among whites. It had a core of supporters and the numbers barely grew. Two of the Cape Provincial Committee's members stood out for their opposition to the qualified franchise: James "Jimmy" Gibson, handsome, charming, and an impecunious barrister. He had been a prisoner-of-war in Germany during the Second World War and then in the foreign ministry until the advent of the Nationalists. Peter Hjul was editor of a fisheries magazine and possessed the twin gifts of boundless energy and enduring optimism. I became the junior partner of the team and through them made friends with local black leaders and went to meetings in the black townships. We were viewed with deep suspicion by others on the provincial committee. Our efforts to work across the color line at the grassroots level unnerved them. They saw us at best as irresponsible radicals, and at worst as Communists.

Gibson ran for a parliamentary Native Representative seat, opposing a candidate farther to the Left, Len Lee-Warden. Our campaign seemed to be going reasonably well. Then, shortly before the polling day, Lee-Warden was banned: it meant that although he remained a candidate and his name was on the ballot paper, he could no longer campaign because he was not allowed to attend meetings or issue statements. Whatever chance Gibson might have had evaporated overnight. He became "the government's man," whereas Lee-Warden was "the people's choice." We thought that the banning was done deliberately to put Lee-Warden's election beyond doubt. The government wanted someone from the extreme Left to be elected so that they could say, "You see, they always elect these Communists and Leftists. We must get rid of these Native Representatives." Which is what they eventually did.

We had some political fun when Hjul and I presented ourselves at a conference of the South African Colored Peoples Organization, part of the Congress Alliance, and enrolled as members. They were too embarrassed to turn us away on the grounds of color. The conference was poorly organized, and we succeeded in getting Hjul elected to the national executive. But he was never invited to a meeting, and when he took it up, he was bluntly told the organization was not for him.

A couple of years later, when the ANC was still legal, it faced a similar situation: a white supporter, Ronald Segal, the flamboyant editor of *Africa South* magazine, spoke from the platform and applied for membership at a public meeting in Johannesburg. He dramatically threw a £1 banknote, enough for eight years' worth of subscriptions, onto the table in front of the conference chairman, Oliver Tambo, then the national deputy president-general. Another white man, Baruch Hirson, a lecturer at Wits, and later jailed for involvement in sabotage, also demanded the right to membership. Although the crowd wildly applauded these assertions of nonracialism, Tambo would have none of it. I asked for his comments, and Tambo sent me this terse note:

> I do not consider that Segal and Hirson intended to do more than demonstrate their wholehearted and unreserved support of the program and policy of the ANC. Applications for membership of the ANC are not made from conference platforms and European members of the liberatory movement know this very well.

What the ANC was really afraid of, and what Tambo could not admit, was, justifiably, that if it opened its membership to non-black people, it could be handing a potent weapon to black nationalists who were already claiming that the organization was under heavy influence from people of other colors. It would take many years, and proscription and exile, for the ANC and its linked bodies eventually to make nonracial membership a fact.

G. **Rayner Ellis,** British-born, had succeeded McLeod as editor of the *Rand Daily Mail* in 1941—another in the line of orthodox editors, at least in his views. "He was very pompous but terribly shy; he always had his head down and never looked you in the eye," recalls Colin Legum, a reporter at the time who later became a renowned writer with the *Observer* in London. Rayner Ellis went for lunch to the Rand Club but, unlike McLeod, who had been one of the boys, he usually ate alone. Yet he was a highly capable editor with a feel for good writing as well as the author of well-written editorials.

When Sylvester Stein joined the *Mail* as a junior reporter in 1948, after war service and completing an engineering degree, he was older than the other juniors, but like them was paid a paltry £15 a month. Stein remembers Rayner Ellis's light-gray striped suits and

Chapter 3

extreme shyness: "The eccentric thing about him was that he would not acknowledge his staff. He would rush up to the first floor and go straight to his office. If he saw anybody in the corridors he wouldn't say good morning. If he saw a member of the staff in the street then he would stop and stare at a shop window."

World news at this time was normally carried on page one, called the cable page, and local news was in the middle of the paper opposite the leader page. Although news about blacks was ignored, Stein was sent to report on a concert given by a celebrated white pianist, Elsie Hall. The concert was performed in the black suburb of Sophiatown and the headline zeroed in on the novelty of the event, explaining why it was being published: "Elsie Hall Plays To Natives."

"In South Africa in the 1930s and 1940s blacks were not humans. You just didn't think of them like that," Stein recalls. "I did have feelings and relationships with blacks and that's why I was surprised that the *Mail* did not want stories about them. I would come with a jolly little piece but they didn't want it."

It was a known policy that photographs including black subjects were not published, with the notable exception of photos depicting riots.

After the Afrikaner Nationalists began to enforce apartheid, violent disturbances in black areas in and around Johannesburg early in 1950 created considerable unease among whites. The *Mail*'s view, limited and paternalistic, was conveyed in an editorial on February 16th:

> The fact is that the Natives, already irritated by laws which they consider unjust, have been driven to far more active resentment by the increasingly stringent restrictions which are now being placed on them. This is not a question of political representation or anything of that sort, but of constant interference with people's daily life.

It went on:

> Either the government must be turned out and replaced by one that will treat the Natives more considerately; or, before very long, the whole of the Union will have to be placed on a civil war footing.

A few days earlier the newspaper had, unusually, given publicity to black views as expressed in evidence to a commission of inquiry investigating the riots. It reported the testimony of Absalom Gxogyia, who had previously held a minor post as a member of the Native Advisory Board in a small location, Munsieville. Presumably his views accorded with what the *Mail* believed was typical of blacks, which was why he was given such prominence for saying, "Natives are queer people to handle, I admit, but at least we are always ready to listen to those in authority." He continued to say that the stage had finally been reached, however, "when Natives will just not tolerate oppression and take instructions as in the past, but will question the right of anyone giving instructions."

Apart from the *Mail*'s blindness about blacks, it was a newspaper that strove for excellence. That was its ethos, and in the postwar period it had exceptional talent on its staff: Claud Cook, the labor correspondent who enjoyed such authority that trade unionists came to consult him—white unionists, that is, because, again in the spirit of the times, he wrote only about white workers. Hugh Carruthers, a former fighter pilot, was the top air correspondent. George Oliver was a court reporter, and Isaac Goodman a Supreme Court reporter. The paper also benefited from the flow of journalists from Britain who were part of the postwar emigration to South Africa. They brought British standards of journalism with them, with the downside that they did not know Afrikaans or any other indigenous languages and had limited understanding of South African politics. For many of them, "home" was across the sea, and they overloaded the pages of the *Mail* with photographs of the British royal family.

Britain remained the focus of attention and provided the context for local events. "We were only the colonies," Stein says. Thus, when in January 1950 the head of South Africa's defense force suddenly resigned, the headline "General Beyers Resigns As Defense Chief" was followed by the subhead "Move Causes Surprise In London; No Official Comment On Successor."

The newspaper was bitterly opposed to the new Afrikaner Nationalist rulers, and Rayner Ellis criticized their authoritarian policies in full measure in editorials. He had a deep anger because of their support for Nazism during the war. He did not attack them as Afrikaners, but there was anti-Afrikanerism in the air. Raymond Louw, who was English-speaking but had an Afrikaans name, recalls trying to get a job on the paper for two years and was finally told by the night editor, "Bully" Joffe, "You can forget it. You've got the wrong surname." (Later, when the *Mail* took on half a dozen juniors, Louw was hired. Twenty years later he was editor.) The *Mail*'s antagonism toward Afrikaner Nationalists was fully reciprocated. They called the paper the "Rand Daily Liar" or the "Jingo" or "Big Jingo" (*jingo* meant "a blustering British patriot").

Sylvester Stein was appointed to the parliamentary press gallery in 1951 and later became the political correspondent covering the lobby. He had virtually zero relations with the government. Members of the cabinet did not speak to him, nor did the Nationalist MPs. At best he had a bit of contact with Afrikaans journalists who might occasionally even pass on a tip. That was the situation of English-language newspapers in general. They relied for background and inside stories on reading the Afrikaans press, information from the opposition United Party, or pure invention. The only Afrikaners who regularly spoke to Stein were those in the United Party. The *Mail* attacked the Nationalists vigorously, and tension grew between Rayner Ellis and the board. He was judged too liberal and too anti-Nationalist, thus imperiling the newspaper. In his twelfth year in the editor's chair he was away for long periods. Illness was blamed. In 1953 he was fired and an assistant editor, A. P. Cartwright, was appointed to succeed him.

An era of "floppiness," in Stein's phrase, set in because Cartwright, while an excellent leader writer, shrank from confrontation. The newspaper became less aggressive, which was exactly what the board of directors wanted. A British journalist, Alex Botting, was imported as managing editor to bolster the paper. Not only was he ignorant about South Africa but he did even more damage in inflicting the rough and tough values of Fleet Street tabloid journalism, in which entertainment ruled over news. The *Mail* went into sharp decline.

I was well aware of it because, starting in 1957, I became a daily reader. That year I moved to Johannesburg to work for African Explosives and Chemical Industries (AE&CI), the world's biggest manufacturer of dynamite, owned jointly by Imperial Chemical Industries (ICI) in Britain and the local De Beers diamond mining company. With three degrees, in psychology and social science, I was hired as an executive trainee, handling personnel matters in the headquarters office. That meant I dealt only with the several thousand staff members around the country who were white. The many thousands of black workers were handled separately. My bosses were kind, but it was a miserable year. With the thick book containing the company's personnel rules lying on my desk, I could project what size office and carpet I was likely to have in ten years, twenty years, etc. The predictability of my future stretching ahead gave me nightmares.

Inside the Liberal Party I found that the Transvaal Provincial Committee, to which I was co-opted, was way ahead of the Cape in wanting to be rid of the qualified franchise policy. I became active in the Sophiatown branch. Sophiatown, on the city's western edge, was noteworthy because blacks enjoyed freehold tenure—they could possess full title to land, one of the only two areas in Johannesburg where they had inherited that right. Across the street was the more traditional Western Native Township—tiny, rundown houses surrounded by a metal fence. Both were anathema to the Nationalists because they were in the midst of "white" suburbs, with coloreds and Asians also living nearby, and when I arrived in Johannesburg, the process of evicting the people was under way.

Sophiatown was crime-ridden, and gangs proliferated, with names like Berliners, Americans, Gestapo, and Vultures. Some devoted themselves to stealing from whites, but most preyed on their neighbors. It was certainly true, as the Nationalists claimed, that much of the land was owned by landlords, most of whom were not black, and that they charged exorbitant rents to tenants crammed into badly maintained houses and crude backyard shanties. But it was home to the people there, many wanted to stay there, and the place had zing.

I met Can Temba, who was then among the surging black writing talents. He surfaced through the monthly *Drum* magazine and its sister weekly newspaper, *Golden City Post*. Both were started early in the 1950s, by a son of the *Rand Daily Mail*'s Sir Abe Bailey. The *Mail*'s Sylvester Stein later became editor of *Drum*. Temba was an exuberant writer of features and short stories, a heavy drinker, and a strong talker. We spent long nights sitting in a smoke-filled room in Sophiatown—a large refrigerator dominated the room—drinking brandy and arguing over how best to overcome the ills of the country. The experiences made my days at AE&CI seem ridiculous to me, and probably hastened their end.

In Sophiatown there were also noisy fights involving the Liberal Party because our chief supporter was a black landlord who did not always get on well with the ANC. I was sitting on the platform at one of our meetings when a melee erupted in the hall as young men from the ANC Youth League attacked our members. A man built like a tank, with a heavy neck sunk into his body, was leading the charge. I ran into the hall, and as he was about to use a bottle to club a man, I tapped him on the shoulder and asked, as he turned around, "Can't we sit down and talk about this?" Clearly astonished by my innocence, he put down the bottle and nodded. It was the start of a long friendship. He was Steve Segale, and as I discovered, he had a checkered history that included imprisonment for robbery. But he was in the process of reforming himself and later became head of the ANC Youth League in the Transvaal.

My fiancée, Astrid, studying Zulu at Wits, told me about her marvelous teacher, Robert Mangaliso Sobukwe. I was also hearing his name in political circles as one of the leaders of the African Nationalists, a dissident group inside the ANC. One day when I went to fetch Astrid, she introduced me. Sobukwe and I started meeting in his office to talk about events. We could not go and have tea or a drink together because there was nowhere to go: cafés and bars did not allow it. Sobukwe soon started visiting us in our apartment, and as he was black, this opened us to the risk of being evicted for creating a "nuisance" under our lease. I also used to visit him at home in Mofolo, which was a new area deep inside the fast–growing sprawl of houses for blacks. The Johannesburg municipality ran a competition for a suitable name and came up with Soweto. Although only a geographical description—southwestern townships—it had an African sound. It was also better than saying "location," which was the usual usage for black townships and which I thought conveyed the idea that although something was there, it had no real existence or future.

These were exciting days in the ANC because the African Nationalists were pushing their criticisms harder and harder. Essentially these came down to two points: first, they believed that the ANC had reneged on the Program of Action it had adopted in 1949, which called for noncollaboration. That program had led to the Defiance Campaign of 1952 in which thousands of people of all colors had deliberately broken apartheid laws and been imprisoned. The campaign came to an end when the government enacted a law that escalated the possible, and probable, imprisonment to five years—plus a bonus of lashes for a repeat offense. Second, the African Nationalists said that the ANC was under the influence of Communists, and especially white and Asian Communists, and that this had taken hold since the banning of the Communist Party in 1950 because party activists had been driven to channel their energy and efforts into other organizations. To add to the ANC's woes, the Transvaal province was in an uproar because of poor leadership and mismanagement, with many of its leaders among the 156 people facing charges of high treason. This mass Treason Trial, as it became known, began in 1956 and would continue for five years before the last of the accused were freed. Not a single person was convicted of anything.

Professor A. H. Murray, who taught philosophy at UCT, was known as the prosecution's chief witness and its guide on Communism. I had attended his political philosophy classes and like many other students had expected evidence of his Afrikaner Nationalist outlook in slanted presentations that would reveal his favoring totalitarianism of one form or another. But his lectures in class gave no clue to his outlook: they were brilliantly lucid and evenhanded.

Murray didn't do so well in the trial, however. While under cross-examination, various texts were read to him and he was asked to identify which were clearly and blatantly Marxist in origin. This he did, until it was pointed out that he was the author of a text that he had so identified.

The basis of the prosecution case was that the Freedom Charter, adopted by the ANC and its allies in 1955, was a Communist document and underpinned efforts to overthrow the government. An expert witness, an American scholar, was imported to testify to this effect. I met him at a party before the trial and asked whether the Charter was indeed a Communist document. "It is not," he declared heatedly, "and that is the evidence I am going to give." Murray was standing next to us and I looked at him and said incredulously, "That's your expert witness?" He smiled and shrugged.

I never did understand how the trial kept going. Either the prosecutors were so dim and caught up in their crude anti-Communism that they did not perceive the weakness of their case, or perhaps the government was satisfied merely to damage the ANC by pinning down its leaders for so long with the trial itself.

Meeting Sobukwe and spending hours of debate with blacks awoke me to the significance of African Nationalism. I saw it as the next step on the road to black self-empowerment. I urged the Liberal Party's Transvaal Committee to make contact with Sobukwe and his followers. But there was a widely held view that the African Nationalists were antiwhite and that the party should therefore give them a wide berth. The view was understandable: Sobukwe was nonracial to the core of his being, viewing all people alike and treating all people with equal courtesy, regardless of color or class. But with him were people like Potlako Leballo, who espoused a heavy dose of antiwhite feelings whenever he got on a public stage, electrifying the crowd. Inevitably, too, as African Nationalists sought to fight their own battles, they rejected the helping hand of white liberals. The dividing line between that and an outright hostile antiwhite racism was not always clear. Sobukwe and I had countless discussions in which he argued that black nationalism was a necessary weapon to be used to forge unity and that it would not lead to racism. I would argue that I understood its potency as a weapon, but if it succeeded, then the leadership would not simply be able to press a button and return the weapon to its box. We never reconciled these differing standpoints through the years of what grew into a close friendship. The issue continues to dog South Africa. Black nationalism hovers in the wings, and a deep uncertainty remains among some black South Africans about how best to deal with whites.

Political work aside, life on the job at AE&CI allowed time to read the morning paper each day. I was accustomed to the *Cape Times*, a good newspaper. I also knew about the *Evening Post* in Port Elizabeth whose editor, John Sutherland, was rated the most liberal in the country. In contrast, the *Rand Daily Mail* carried little news and was insubstantial, poorly written, and badly presented. The newspaper's reactions to the Nationalists, like other English-language newspapers that I saw, seemed to derive more from outrage that Afrikaners were in power than from any principled opposition to the racial laws the Afrikaners were inflicting on South Africa. The United Party, which received largely uncritical backing, was responding to the Afrikaner Nationalists by aping them, offering a watered-down version of apartheid. It never worked, and for four decades there was a nearly unbroken line of increasing support among whites for the Nationalists. They preferred unadulterated racism above any ersatz version.

After a few months I noticed that the *Rand Daily Mail* had begun to change. It had a new editor, Laurence Gandar, and under his stewardship had already switched from using the word Native to using the word African. The *Mail* was the second mainstream paper to do so, after the *Evening Post*. Using the word preferred by black political leaders reflected a new mindset. Most excitingly of all, in mid February of 1958, the *Rand Daily Mail* published a set of three articles assessing the state of the country ahead of the April general election. They were signed "Owen Vine," which I later learned were Gandar's middle names. The articles were the start of the "Political Viewpoint" column, written whenever the spirit moved him. The insights and quality of writing had a freshness and clarity unknown in South Africa.

The first article went right to the heart of the country's situation:

> Perhaps the most remarkable feature of election activity so far is its similarity to the electioneering of 1953. How little anything has altered in five years. For the rest of Africa and the world at large, this has been a period of turbulent and bewildering change. Everyone accepts that we are living in a different age from that of 1953—an age of nuclear science and space conquest, new concepts of warfare and power, new nations and alliances of nations, new emancipatory movements affecting millions of people. Fresh currents of thought are blowing through the world, stirring the minds of men everywhere. Yet here in the Union the calcification of political attitudes persists. We are confronted with an election that seems largely a repeat performance of the one five years ago.

Gandar went on to argue that below the surface, however, there was "a ferment of feelings and ideas" and he saw hope of change.

In a follow-up column the next week, Owen Vine/Gandar argued,

Apartheid is meaningless because it cannot, on the highest admission, bring separation to the economic sphere. Apartheid is unrealistic because it is geared to a timetable that will be surely and completely overtaken by events. Apartheid is a sham because there is no evidence of any willingness to face the sacrifices it involves. Apartheid is unworkable because it is set to run counter to the massed forces of world opinion and the tides of contemporary human progress.

That was the nub of the argument to which Gandar and the *Mail* were to return over the years, relentlessly rubbing it in and exposing the weaknesses of Afrikaner Nationalist policy.

I decided to move into journalism because my interest in politics and world events far outstripped my interest in anything else. I made the *Rand Daily Mail* the newspaper I hoped to write for. Apart from becoming an admiring reader of these political columns, in more practical terms I chose the *Mail* because I had a slight contact—the friend of a friend—in Hank Margolies, an American cigar-chomping journalist who worked at the *Golden City Post*. He knew the *Mail*'s news editor and agreed to introduce me. We met outside the *Rand Daily Mail* offices on Main Street, went upstairs, and not only did he introduce me to Harry O'Connor, a short, burly man with white hair, but he delivered an embarrassingly flattering spiel about me. O'Connor asked me to return for an interview, and when we left, I thanked Margolies.

"But how could you say all those things about me?" I asked. "You hardly know me."

He replied, "If I had said this guy needs a job, Harry wouldn't have bothered to look at you. They have guys all the time coming in off the street wanting jobs. But I got him to look at you and now it's up to you."

I had an interview with an assistant editor, Ivor Benson. He was cold and brisk. I had been warned in advance to be careful. Although Gandar was liberal, the paper was divided and Benson did not like liberals.

He asked me, "Are you interested in politics?" I crossed my fingers and responded, "No, no, not at all."

He gave me a hard look and said, "There were three liberals on this newspaper. I have got rid of one and two are left."

Benson then hired me as a junior reporter. O'Connor's initial greeting to me when I joined the fifteen or so reporters in the newsroom was frosty. He was a journalist from the old school where it was believed that the only training was to come up through the ranks. At that time few journalists in South Africa had been to university, although this was beginning to change. Those who did have university degrees seemed to be clustered in senior editorial posts. There were few in reporters' ranks. Here I was with three degrees, and he was not pleased that I was actually joining his staff. I would have to prove my worthiness.

"I've no time to train you," he told me. "I'm dropping you in the deep end. Sink or swim." (When I was arranging for the printing of my first visiting cards, O'Connor asked how I was going to describe myself. "Reporter," I said. O'Connor beamed. "That's a great word. Never mind all these people who say they are journalists. You're a reporter and be proud of it.")

In the absence of any formal training, the "deep end" meant writing reports from press releases, covering whatever might arise on Sunday duty, and reporting at the law courts in Johannesburg for several months under the tutelage of a senior reporter, Lou Meyers. I learned the trade wandering around the long corridors and going into courts for a few minutes to sniff out stories. Making contact with lawyers was part of the game, especially those with offices at the bottom end of Commissioner Street near the courts, specializing in defending small-time criminals and handling divorces. They could always be relied upon for a tip-off about a case that could provide an offbeat story and publicity for them. The best and cleverest among them was Jimmy Kantor, who was one of the sights around Johannesburg with his Cadillac convertible. He would come into the pressroom at the courts to tell us when he had an interesting case coming up. In court he had a talent for putting questions to witnesses that would yield newsy angles for us. And he would even on occasion pause during the questioning and turn to those reporters sitting at the side of the court and whisper, "Anything else you want me to ask?"

Kantor wasn't the slightest bit interested in politics. But his brother-in-law, Harold Wolpe, who worked with him, was caught in a government crackdown, detained, and then escaped. The authorities, led by Dr. Percy Yutar—of whom more to come—harassed Kantor mercilessly, in revenge for having been Wolpe's brother-in-law. Kantor was detained without trial and then prosecuted. The judge discharged him at the end of the prosecution case, saying there was no evidence for him to meet.

Kantor was never the same man after his ordeal, and after emigrating, suffered an early death.

Lou Meyers, my tutor at the law courts, was from Rhodesia and had countless stories about his previous life there. He told me that he had gotten out one jump ahead of the police, who wanted him for fraud. I thought these were tall tales. Reporting courts was not onerous, and we conceived a get-rich scheme: we started a secondhand car business. We scraped together a small amount of capital and began to buy and sell cars. We agreed to run a clean business: no putting string in the oil sump or cardboard in the differential to conceal a car's serious defects as the sharp end of the market was wont to do. Not only did we have to buy and sell cars, but we also had to get them repaired and road-tested at the municipality's car center. Everyone at the *Mail* knew what we were doing, and we were nicknamed "Straight Lou" and "Honest Ben." O'Connor sent a cub reporter to us, even more junior than me, for training at the courts. At the end of his first day we returned to the office and went to see O'Connor.

"This fellow's no good," we said. "He hasn't a driver's license and we can't use him to take cars for road-testing." O'Connor's face went blood-red, then he burst out laughing and assigned another cub to us who could drive.

I began to worry about Meyers when, without consulting me, he rented an expensive salesroom in the center of the city. Early one morning there was a knock on the door of my apartment: it was a bailiff with a sheaf of summonses to pay for cars bought in my name. Unknown to me, Meyers had sold the cars without paying off the money owed on them. The debt was in my name, and so was the fraud that had been committed. I could not take any action against Meyers because that would have exposed me to criminal prosecution. It was a lot of money for me and I had to borrow it in a hurry. My father-in-law, Arnold Schonfrucht, thought the whole affair very funny and wanted to let me have the money as a gift. I insisted it had to be a loan, and eventually paid back every cent. He thought it the best business lesson I could possibly have. It was some time before I could say I felt the same. But I never again got embroiled in any business ventures. Meyers drifted off into the unknown. I realized that he must have told the truth about being on the run from the Rhodesian police.

Johannesburg's magistrates' courts, like all courts, had their quota of sad and bizarre human stories, and I learned to write my own purple prose to liven up the *Mail*'s news pages, such as, "While his wife solicited on a

Johannesburg street corner, the husband followed—pushing a pram with their two babies." (The husband drew twelve months' suspended imprisonment for living on the proceeds of prostitution.)

Another was, "A man who feared being kicked to death dived under a car and slashed his wrist in a frantic suicide attempt."

A case that ran over several months and rated regular space in the newspaper because of its gruesome nature was the preliminary trial of Matthew Shadrack and sixty-six members of his Msomi gang. They faced ninety charges of murder, robbery, arson, and extortion of the people of Alexandra township. A black bus inspector, for instance, testified that when two gang members boarded his bus, one of them was "enthusiastic about having me shot" and kept telling the other one who carried a gun, "Shoot him, shoot him." Two policemen riding guard on the bus were armed only with sticks and "were shivering and could not do anything."

The accused were a fearsome bunch, crowded into long rows in the front of the court with only a few policemen in attendance. Some, like Shadrack, were well dressed in smart suits, others wore overalls, and most had tattered clothes. Just about every man had a scar on his head and/or face. In reporting the case I sat within touching distance. They ignored me.

Even as the case wound its way through the courts, a terrible retribution overtook the gang members. They were housed in the Fort, the turn-of-the-century prison used for people on trial and short-term prisoners. Blacks were held in large cells, with more than one hundred men sleeping on rubber or sisal mats on the concrete floor. Some of the Msomis were locked up with another gang, the Spoilers. As ruthless as were the Msomis, the Spoilers were even tougher. The cell door was opened one morning to reveal that four Msomis had been battered and kicked to death during the night. It turned out that while the murders were being committed, everyone else in the cell had been made to sing and clap hands and then wipe the blood from the floor.

When **Laurence Gandar** took over as editor of the *Rand Daily Mail* on October 1, 1957, he had no clear objectives in mind, only a generalized aim to make the *Mail* a better and more relevant newspaper. As he later told me, he felt that the paper was in the same dreary rut as all the other English-language newspapers making ritual, predictable attacks on the government and stereotyped responses to issues of the day. It lacked insights and penetrating analysis and needed higher editorial quality. Without any specific formula, Gandar set out with a rather woolly intention to play it by ear.

He had an important letter in his pocket: a written promise of complete editorial independence. He insisted on getting this because he had heard that his predecessor had suffered from managerial interference.

Gandar had been recruited from the public relations department at Anglo American Corporation. The general

Chapter 4

manager of South African Associated Newspapers (Saan), Henri Kuiper, had been scouting for an editor, and the Argus Company strongly recommended Gandar, who had begun his career on their Sunday newspaper in Durban, Natal, and rose to an assistant editor and political columnist in the group. He had spent a year in London on a Kemsley journalist's scholarship. Born and raised in Durban, the very center of English-speaking conservatism, Gandar enlisted in the army in 1940. Starting in the ranks he fought in North Africa and Italy and ended with the rank of captain as a brigade intelligence officer in the Sixth South African Armored Division.

When he joined the *Mail*, he was not in any way viewed as a courageous visionary. Nor was that expected of him. His job was to perform a rescue operation. Journalists on the newspaper respected his professional competence, though he was perceived more as an ivory-tower writer than a news-driven journalist.

There was also some skepticism about him because he was coming out of the Anglo American Corporation, the power behind the English-language press. But even Harry Oppenheimer, the Anglo chairman, apparently did not expect too much. On the one occasion that I had dinner with Oppenheimer and mentioned a campaign that Gandar was about to launch, he made a slighting comment to the effect, "Oh, is Laurie going to show some courage?" The campaign was launched and was as strong as I had said it would be. A few days later I was at lunch in a restaurant, and Oppenheimer was at another table. On his way out he stopped to say, with a warm smile, that he was glad to see that he had been wrong about Gandar.

As editor, Gandar had the arduous task of cleaning house. He hired Ivor Benson, whom he had known in Durban on the former *Daily Tribune*, to handle the brutal task of firing while also seeking new talent. Gandar thought Benson was an interesting person with penetrating views and was not aware of his extremism. The editorial staff saw it differently, and there was open talk that Benson was trying to white-ant Gandar.

Benson revealed his true face while Gandar was away. He wrote an editorial favorable to Sir Oswald Moseley, who had been interned during the war as leader of the British Union of Fascists, and who was on a visit to South Africa. The editorial described Moseley as "a man with exciting political associations" and as standing for "the strong Right wing in political thought." Kuiper suspended Benson amid uproar with Jim Bailey, a member of the board of directors, pounding the table and threatening a shareholders' meeting unless Benson was thrown out immediately. That is exactly what Gandar hurried back to do. There was an added twist: the *Mail*'s reporters had searched high and low for Moseley, but could not find him. It turned out he had been staying with his friend, Ivor Benson, who had concealed this from his reporters.

Benson was still on staff for several months after I joined the *Mail*. I resigned from the Liberal Party immediately upon starting my job, not because of Benson's warning to me about politics but because I felt it was wrong for a journalist to have formal links with a political party. I was intent on reporting dispassionately, and that did not go with personal membership of a political party.

The usual word is *objectivity*, and while it's a worthy aim, how valid is it in reporting the views and deeds of people? To what extent can any reporter leave behind his or her emotional baggage and prejudices? Right from the start I preferred the word *dispassionate*, striving to leave out my own judgments when I interviewed people or reported events. The approach served me reasonably well over the years. I took pride in reporting on the Nationalist prime minister and the ANC's president-general with the same absence of favor or hostility. That was for news reports. I believed feature articles under my own name were of a different order, allowing me greater personal latitude to express a viewpoint.

Personal links with liberals continued, however. A pattern swiftly developed whereby my friends were my newspaper contacts and many of my contacts became my friends. Apart from making for a largely seamless life between personal and professional worlds, it was the road to forging mutual trust. Freed of the party connection, I could now also take my interests further. Little of the accelerating ferment in black politics was being reported, save for the occasional brief item in the mainstream press. In my own time, at night and over weekends, I attended and reported meetings and got to know leaders. Benson must soon have woken up to my interest in politics. But I got away with it, probably because I was producing stories that no one else had, and in any event they were from across the color line and did not rate as politics in the usual white way.

Once I was a full-time journalist, I also began to write for *Contact*, the fortnightly newspaper owned and edited by Patrick Duncan in Cape Town. He had been a judicial officer in the British Colonial Service in Basutoland—in 1966 it became the independent Kingdom of Lesotho—before joining the Liberals in Cape Town. His father had been the first South African–born governor-general, the British king's representative. Duncan published everything that I sent him. I wrote under the pseudonym "*Umhlabeni*," a Zulu translation of my name coined by Sobukwe, meaning "on or over the ground."

One of my early reports for *Contact* late in 1958 assessed the state of the ANC. It referred to a conference that I had missed but that had entered folklore: strong-arm men had beaten the heads of dissidents. It was popularly called "the conference where blood flowed."

I did a lot of painstaking research, wrote the story, and took it for comment to Oliver Tambo, who was in charge of the Transvaal. Tambo was a partner with Nelson Mandela in a law firm, and their offices were on the first floor of Chancellor House, a small building across the street from the magistrates' courts. Tambo read my typed pages, and when he got to the part about the violence at the conference, he looked up and said in a surprised voice, "This did not happen. What is this?" I was taken aback and wondered whether I had totally misunderstood. I argued, setting out all that I had unearthed, point by point. After a few minutes Tambo dropped his innocent front. As I was to see on other occasions, he had a reserved, deceptive air about him that concealed a nimble mind and talent for political maneuvering. These characteristics were to stand him in good stead during the thirty years he later spent in exile and keeping the ANC alive and strong.

Tambo's office was like no attorney's I had ever seen. A basic lesson I had learned while doing legal articles in Cape Town was that it was vital to keep track of clients' files; order was essential. In Tambo's office there were half a dozen piles of brown file covers standing three feet high on the floor near his desk. He and Mandela ran their practice amid huge difficulties. By government decree Mandela had been under intermittent banning orders since 1952. He was prohibited from attending meetings, which meant he could not be with more than one person at a time, and could not leave Johannesburg without permission. He was also an accused in the ongoing Treason Trial, which took him to Pretoria most days. Despite this, eluding the police's watchful eye, he was active behind the scenes in ANC committees. Tambo, on the other hand, had a high public profile from supervising the Transvaal and serving as national deputy president-general. Somehow they still managed to run their legal practice, and the waiting room was always full of silent, care-worn people.

Being a reporter at the magistrates' courts at that particular time had unexpected and far-reaching consequences for me because of the government's actions in forcing black women to carry the hated *dompas* (Afrikaans for "stupid pass"). Black men from the age of sixteen were compelled to carry this identification document and were subject to instant arrest if they could not produce the "pass" on demand, and if it did not show that they were allowed to be where they were, and had paid taxes. Every aspect of a black person's life was at stake: permission where to live and work, whether husbands and wives could live together, where children could live, the fate of grandparents. The language was officialese at its tortuous worst. And all of it was backed by criminal sanctions and the full weight of the law, giving employment to armies of petty officials, policemen, prosecutors, magistrates, and prison warders.

The pass laws were enforced with ever–greater ferocity after being tightened and extended in 1952 through the misleadingly titled Natives (Abolition of Passes and Coordination of Documents) Act. They were a maze of bureaucracy that was corrupt through and through. With enough money, a pass could be bought from a clerk, or a needed official permission stamped in it, or a policeman making an arrest could be bought off. It was nonracial in the unfortunate sense that black clerks battened on their fellows as much as whites did.

At the *Mail* we were fully aware of the corruption, but could not expose it apart from the few details which seeped out during occasional court cases. To expose it, we would have had to report what had happened to someone, or alternatively lay a trap for a crooked official. Whichever black person took part in the exposé would face certain retribution and be damned for life, and we would be powerless to offer protection.

In the late 1950s the government was moving to extend the pass laws to women. There was stiff resistance with protests throughout the country: in 1956, twenty thousand women had marched on the Union Buildings in Pretoria, and the next year seven thousand women had marched to Johannesburg's City Hall. Not only was there deep resentment at the mere idea of degrading women by forcing them to carry the *dompas*, but instances of inevitable abuse were already surfacing.

Margaret Ballinger told parliament of a case of a woman returning to Nyanga township in Cape Town after a day's work who had been stopped by a policeman demanding to see her permit. She had left it at home, for safekeeping, and offered to retrieve it within minutes. He arrested her and took her to a police cell. She remained there, without food or water, even though she managed to send a message to a friend who brought her permit to the police station. The next day she paid an admission of guilt, amounting to more than a third of her monthly wages.

Teams of officials began to issue passes to women on October 16, 1958, in Johannesburg. Thousands queued up for the document, but large numbers illegally demonstrated in opposition. Some eighteen hundred women were arrested, nine hundred of whom were freed on bail. The other nine hundred refused to accept being released on bail. Hundreds gathered in sympathy outside the front entrance of the magistrates' courts on West Street. I had a front-row view standing on the steps behind the line of uniformed policemen, facing the noisy but peaceful, predominantly female crowd. I heard the officer in charge order his men, "Take three steps forward and push them back." The policemen took one step, a second step, and then tore into the crowd, using batons and lengths of wood. I ran with the police as they hit the women, some of whom had babies on their backs, carried inside blankets in traditional style. The policemen were laughing and shouting to each other, "By the end of today this will be Blood Street."

It was my first sight of a police attack, and I felt sickened. I was horrified by the lack of discipline among the police. They had gone wild like dogs. I saw a policeman deliberately throw a tear-gas glass bomb at a television crew across the street.

When the police attack on the crowd was over, the courts went on grinding away at the cases involving hundreds of women who had been arrested elsewhere. The basement in the Johannesburg courthouse, which housed cells, was turned into a giant impromptu courtroom. Press and public were excluded, but Mandela, who played a leading role in arranging for the defense of the women, told me what was happening. I managed to get in to see the chief magistrate, and demanded that the press be admitted. He backed off and the court was opened. Nearly six hundred accused women sat patiently on twenty-six rows of benches. Quite a few of them had their babies with them. The trials there and in other courts in the building were spun out over the next six weeks. The charges usually involved congregating in a public place or holding an illegal procession, and alternatively failing to disperse after being ordered to do so. Police witnesses described how women were singing and proclaiming that they wanted to be arrested. Magistrates reacted predictably: most imposed imprisonment for six weeks with the option of a fine. One magistrate said he was imposing both, as a punishment and a deterrent to others; another, in paternalistic vein, told the women they should realize that if other people urged them to protest, "you will have to bear all the consequences while the others sit and watch."

I wrote the story of the police attack as I had witnessed it. Gandar called me to his office. He was sitting at his desk, with my report in front of him. Next to it was the report written by the crime reporter, Harold Sacks, who had also been at the scene. "These two reports are very different," Gandar said. "Tell me what you saw." I went over the details and, after a few questions, Gandar said, "We'll use your report. Take Mr.

Sacks's report and extract whatever you think is necessary to give the police point of view and add it to your report." I did that, and the story, in a style uncharacteristic of me, appeared on page one under a crime reporter byline: "Teargas bombs were hurled at a mob of 1,000 screaming Africans… but those who suffered most were European office workers, television photographers and a traffic inspector. As the bombs were thrown, police charged the crowd."

Late that night Sacks came into the office, as he often did to collect the first edition. I could hear his bellows of fury from down the passage as he read his altered report. After a lot of shouting he went off into the night.

From then on, the crime reporter no longer wrote the definitive version of any political episode involving the police. In the past the crime reporter had often merely transcribed police statements. Now the police would no longer so easily determine how conflicts with the public were reported. No longer was the reporting routinely, "The police said last night that they had been forced to open fire on a mob of rioting Natives…" Sacks would contribute to the overall picture. Increasingly, as I came to cover the black political scene, what he wrote was meshed in with what I saw and reported so that the practice of joint reports from different perspectives and angles became normal for the paper. And, as was increasingly to happen in the press, what the *Rand Daily Mail* did, other English-language newspapers followed. The change marked a major turning point in South African journalism.

After Sacks's initial outburst of rage, he accepted the situation and worked with me. In a period of frequent Security Police raids on anti-apartheid activists, Sacks—a hugely overweight man and a heavy drinker—would lurch into my office in the afternoon and say, "Stick around tonight. There's going to be a *klopjag* (police raid)." I would remain at my desk and every hour or so as the night wore on Sacks would come in and tell me to stay on, as it was still going to happen. He knew that a raid was planned but did not know the targets. I spent the night drawing up the names and phone numbers of likely people around the country who might get raided. It was invidious to be in possession of advance information like that, especially as the names of friends appeared on the list. Those were long nights at the office as I sat and wrestled with my conscience. I dared not contact them. I felt bound by confidentiality, and any leak would have compromised the paper.

At around six A.M. Sacks would finally come to announce, "Okay, it's begun, you can get to work." I would start phoning to check who had been raided, whether anyone had been arrested, or what documents had been seized. Quite often I phoned while a raid was still in progress, with either the victim or a policeman answering the call.

Sacks had started working in the late 1930s, and was far and away the foremost crime reporter. But he had personal problems and tried to commit suicide. On his second attempt he succeeded, using a hose attached to the exhaust pipe of his office car.

Protests against passes continued. In January 1959 I covered a meeting in Johannesburg's Gandhi Hall, a block away from Anglo American Corporation's imposing headquarters. Called by the Federation of South African Women, linked to the ANC, nine hundred women condemned the passes and voted to make June 26th "a mighty day of protest." Members of the Security Branch were inside the hall throughout the day, according to my report in the *Mail*. When the organizers asked them to leave, they produced a warrant entitling them to remain. They took notes of all the speeches. The protests, however, did not halt the government.

A group that did stand firm, and whose resolve even grew with the passage of the years, was the Black Sash. The movement began in 1955 when white women banded together in protest against the government's actions to deprive coloreds of their remaining nonracial voting rights. The women wore black sashes to mourn the death of the constitution adopted by the Union forty-five years earlier, and took to staging silent vigils at places where cabinet ministers and MPs were expected. The government derided them, but the vigils went on and on and clearly got under the skin of the Nationalist politicians.

At first, I was dismissive about the Sash: any defense of the color-ridden Union constitution was misplaced, I thought. But as the Sash developed I became a fervent admirer. The Sash women broke new ground by offering free advice and aid to blacks caught in the pass system. They set up Advice Offices, staffed mostly by volunteers, first in Cape Town in 1958 and then in Johannesburg, Pretoria, and other towns. The Sash asked me to edit a booklet explaining the pass laws. I pored over it for months but had little success in translating the complex and heavy-handed rules into plain language.

The Sash women made their way through the pass laws by getting to know the system. As their expertise and experience grew, they often understood the ins and outs of the laws and regulations far better than the officials with whom they dealt, and that made their hand all the stronger. For years I sent every visitor from abroad with whom I came into contact to the Sash Advice Office in Johannesburg. "Go and sit there for a couple of hours and just watch and listen," I urged them. "You will be looking into the soul of this country."

The Sash women's contribution to making possible the new South Africa is beyond estimation. Not only did they rescue countless numbers from the pass laws but they helped to keep alive rudimentary but crucial ideas about decency and justice, and stiffen opposition to the Nationalists. A natural partnership developed between the Sash and the *Mail*. Jean Sinclair, the Sash president for many years, was a guide through the byways of the pass laws, and when she retired in 1975, her equally tenacious daughter, Sheena Duncan, took over as president and as a friend of the *Mail*.

Occasionally I put my ear to the ground by going to the Bantu Commissioners' Courts in Johannesburg, where pass offenders were prosecuted. The ritual was always the same: I made sure that I walked into a courtroom just after the morning tea break. There was no seat for defense lawyers because they appeared so rarely, nor was there a designated area for the press. I would sit down, and after a few minutes either the magistrate or the prosecutor would beckon an orderly, whisper to him, and the orderly would approach me.

"Who are you?"

"*Rand Daily Mail.*"

He would tiptoe back and whisper the information. For the next two hours I would sit and listen to court cases: the prosecutor questioned the accused in what could be said to be a normal way and the magistrate jailed them or sometimes acquitted them. Whenever any case looked as though it might be a little more complicated, the prosecutor either immediately withdrew the charge or asked for a remand to a later date.

When the lunch break came and the magistrate left, I would ask the court clerk for the magistrate's record for that morning. Invariably he would refuse to give it to me and I would point out that this was a public document and I was entitled to it. Now and again I had to threaten an immediate application to the Supreme Court.

When I had the record in my hand, I compared the number of cases I attended with the number during the two hours before the tea break: the difference was always staggering. In my absence it was a sausage-machine process, with an average of one and a half to two minutes per case and with the vast majority of people jailed or fined. In contrast, while I was in the courtroom, the number of cases dropped to a crawl, and acquittals soared. At one stage the Sash tried to get Johannesburg lawyers to take part in a roster system to assist pass offenders, and wrote to about one hundred firms in Johannesburg. Only a tiny number bothered to reply, and even most of these found it impossible to be available on the occasional Saturday morning.

My knowledge of the pass laws came nowhere near that of the Sash women, but as black workers in the *Mail* building saw what I was writing, they came for advice, and gradually my desk became a minisocial welfare agency. I used the *Mail*'s name in approaching officials. There was a world of difference between dealing with Johannesburg's Non-European Affairs Department and dealing with the central government's bureaucracy. The city's officials were watched by the central government and, conscious of this, they wanted as little trouble and exposure as possible. So I could phone an official, and after he had said that there was nothing he could do about a case, I would respond, "You know, this is an upsetting story. But I don't really want to write about it. I'd far rather have this fellow fixed up." And there would be a short silence, and then, "Send him over to my office and I'll arrange his papers." But that was my bluff (these were often stories that I could not have gotten into the paper). It did not work with government officials, whose jurisdiction overlapped or went beyond the city. Time and again I was curtly rejected when I asked for compassion for someone in trouble. "The law is the law" was the stock answer.

A man I employed as a gardener one day a week at my home asked me for help with his pass. He did not have the right to work or live in Johannesburg and thus faced instant arrest wherever he went. He had a driver's license and this should have enabled him to get a more secure and better-paying job than itinerant gardening. I checked with the Johannesburg Labor Bureau, through which all legal hiring of blacks had to be done. There was a surplus of drivers in the city, so they refused to register my man. But a friendly official told me that Kempton Park, a town adjoining Johannesburg, was currently below its quota of drivers.

I phoned the Kempton Park Labor Bureau and confirmed they could place my gardener in a job, and with this they would give him legal registration. I sent him to the bureau, but he returned with a message: before he could be registered he had to be resident in the town. I sent him to the Kempton Park department that dealt with accommodation for black workers. He returned with the message that accommodation was available—in a men's hostel, which would be awful, but it would be a roof over his head and legal. However, they would not give him accommodation until he was registered to work. I went back to the Labor Bureau, but they insisted they would only register him if he had accommodation. I went back and forth between the two offices, getting nowhere. It went on for several weeks. One day I lost my temper and started yelling at the official in charge of the hostels: "This is crazy. How do I break through this cycle where we are going round and round?" Somehow this time it worked, and instead of the usual uncaring arrogance, the official opened the hostel door. With that done, employment as a driver was secured. It was only achieved—and for one man—because I was the big white boss able to throw some weight around.

The magistrates' courts were also the place of ongoing trials arising from the abortive nationwide strike called by the ANC in April 1958. Protestors were demanding better pay and were opposing the pass laws. Months later, in August through November, groups of people were still being hauled up in courts to be charged with having "advised, encouraged, incited, commanded, aided or procured" blacks to stay away from their jobs.

Opposition to the government was at a low ebb, accentuated by the drift among whites toward apartheid. In April the general election saw the Afrikaner Nationalists return to office with a bigger majority, and in September the National Party chose Dr. Hendrik Frensch Verwoerd—already known as the arch-apostle of racial "separate development"—as its new leader and new prime minister. The ANC wasn't able to fight back much because the Transvaal province was so divided, and the arguments took up so much time. To resolve matters, a conference was called for the first weekend in November at the Orlando Communal Hall in Soweto. The African Nationalists were determined to have a make-or-break confrontation. There was much talk on all sides about the probability of violence. On the first day about a dozen journalists were there, both white and black. By the time the conference adjourned well after midnight, I was the only white journalist remaining, together with one or two black journalists. I had to flee when Tambo sent me a message that he had heard I was going to be attacked. I did not have a car, and there were no phones. Two security policemen took me into their car parked across the street, gave me cigarettes and chocolates, and when the meeting adjourned, gave me a lift home—and all without asking a word about the meeting. I surmised they probably had their informers inside.

The next morning a few journalists attended, but since nothing was happening, most left. Finally the story broke: the Africanists had been barred from the hall. I had been puzzled by Tambo's conciliatory behavior, giving the dissidents every possible opportunity for long rambling speeches. In the light of day it was all clear: he had been sizing up the strength of the opposition and had arranged to have his own strong-arm men in greater numbers than the other side. The dissidents were kept out of the hall by having their credentials as delegates rejected. They went off, later forming a new organization, the Pan-Africanist Congress (PAC), with Robert Sobukwe as president.

My story led the *Rand Daily Mail* the next morning: "After tense and angry scenes that threatened at any moment to break out into open violence, a section of the African National Congress, known as 'the Africanists', yesterday broke away from the parent body to start what they called 'a political battle against white domination.'" Benson, still at the *Mail* at the time, had supervised the placing of the story and used a subsidiary inaccurate headline: "Powerful Splinter Group Proclaims 'Anti-White' Policy." I was dogged by that headline for years to come, as the Africanists held me responsible for tarring them with the racism brush—although, ironically, in their ranks were some men nakedly hostile to me simply because I was white. When the PAC was formed, there was a marked difference between attending one of its conferences and going to an ANC event. Ordinary ANC members, whether or not they knew who I was, always accepted me without demur. In contrast I was often conscious of animosity when I went into a PAC conference. Often I was the only white person present, and always made a point of sitting near an exit, whether a door or window. Once, fearing attack, I made a rapid exit through a window so high that I would not have considered doing it normally.

My working pattern settled into arriving at conferences and meetings earlier and staying later than anyone else. The cost to me included countless cigarettes smoked, many missed meals, bad food when I could get it, and innumerable hours spent in utter boredom, in overcrowded halls listening to interminable speeches or in the hot sun outside. But time and again I was one of the few journalists, and always the only one from the mainstream press, who was still around when there was a real story to write.

Editors were faceless, nameless beings as far as their readers were concerned, as were most reporters in an era of few bylines and with names of writers appearing only on the feature pages. It took time for word to get around that the Owen Vine who was writing the challenging "Political Viewpoint" columns was Laurence Gandar. Both opposition and government circles began to watch the *Rand Daily Mail*. The daily editorials were blowing the cobwebs out of the white political scene.

Meanwhile the news reporting was coming alive. At the heart of it were the senior appointments made by Gandar. For the first time in the *Mail*'s fifty-plus years of existence, it had a South African-born editor and its key news operations were also run by South Africans.

First among the appointments was Harry O'Connor as news editor: his sharp news sense gave the paper direction, and Gandar left him to get on with it, making suggestions

Chapter 5

about the stories he thought should be covered. The night news editor was Raymond Louw, who, after overcoming the handicap of his name and getting on to the paper, had spent six years in Britain gaining experience on small newspapers. A knowledgeable financial writer, Harold Fridjohn, gave weight and quality to the financial pages at a time when business journalism was just getting started. Two assistant editors added their own luster: A. B. "Barno" Hughes, who had read Classics at Oxford and wrote the twice-weekly "Just In Passing" humor column—clever, gentle, and beautifully written to an exact word-count. The other notable assistant editor was Lewis Sowden, who served as both the book review editor and the drama critic and had written an important play about black-white relations. In 1961 Sowden got into trouble while visiting New

York: he was at the United Nations listening to Eric Louw, the minister of foreign affairs, give a speech to the General Assembly, and he lost his cool. He shouted from the public gallery that Louw was telling half-truths. The sentiment was worthy, but it wasn't the way a journalist, let alone an assistant editor of a major newspaper, should behave. Gandar suspended him, and the *Mail* publicly criticized his emotional outburst. Sowden returned home and apologized, and was subsequently reinstated. More than three months later the government withdrew Sowden's passport, and the *Mail* reacted in an editorial by condemning this as "an act of petty vindictiveness."

The new era on the *Mail* opened up life for me. I wanted to delve into an ignored area of South African existence exactly when, for the first time, an editor had arrived who accepted the validity and relevance of that reporting. Gandar's personal interest in the reporting I did led to a personal relationship between us, and I often went into his office to tell him about developments in the black political world.

Gandar, medium height and slender, was a quietly spoken, shy man and many, including *Mail* staff, mistook that for coldness. But in case anyone could not guess from his writing and his dedication to justice, his friends knew him as a warm and concerned man with a dry wit. His happy and long marriage to Isobel Ballance, a schoolteacher who was also from Durban, was a secure anchor in his life.

Even before emerging from the magistrates' courts, I was being assigned to cover news attuned to my interests and special knowledge such as the dying kicks of the decade-old struggle against university apartheid. In late 1958 I wrote that a debate planned at Wits on the government's intentions had to be canceled because white Afrikaans student leaders refused to address a racially mixed audience. And in early 1959 my article about a protest outside Wits began: "Security Branch detectives and uniformed police attended an hour-long poster protest staged yesterday afternoon… There were no incidents." It would not be long before the police *not* being in attendance would be newsworthy. Shortly after, I reported that a planned all-day multiracial tennis tournament had been halted at lunchtime because, as a Wits spokesman said, "non-whites" were not allowed to use sports facilities. One tennis court, he said stiffly, was set aside for them.

As the *Mail*'s news columns opened up, I was allowed to ease into full-time reporting on black politics, and from this into reporting on every possible aspect of everyday black existence. This was new territory. No one, not even the *Bantu World*, the newspaper for blacks owned by the Argus Company, the *Golden City Post*, or the left-wing *New Age*, tried a consistent approach to reporting the minutiae of life in Soweto and other townships. That was my aim, and I began to pour out the words.

I would spend the day collecting information, going to the townships or making phone calls, then late in the afternoon I would sort out my notes and start writing: six reports of varying length was normal, though it could go to ten or more.

The articles were not meant to be antiapartheid. That would have been totally unacceptable to the newspaper, and offensive to my own sense of journalism. Rather they were an attempt to report what had not hitherto been reported. The term *advocacy journalism* was unknown at that time in South Africa; ignorant reporting and sins of omission existed in abundance, but reporting in an ideological context was in the domain of Afrikaner Nationalist and left-wing newspapers, plus the government-controlled radio. In any case Gandar's aims for upgrading the *Mail* required all our news reporting to be as accurate and free of bias as possible.

The range of issues I reported in the second half of 1959 included:

"The only home for unmarried African mothers in the Union is to close because the government will not allow a white person to supervise it or a white managing body to administer its affairs." (July)

"Eighty-two families are still living in the streets of Sophiatown because their houses have been demolished by the Bantu Resettlement Board." (September)

"Indians find happiness in Lenasia—Most want to stay in 'Group Area'" (September)

"Tribal colleges will be on trial to vindicate or damn." (December)

The casualty rate of my reports was high—if nothing else the *Mail*'s news balance would have become lopsided if all were published—and many were discarded or cut to the bone. But through the weight of what I was producing, allied with my internal lobbying, the infusion of such material into the newspaper became significant.

In banging up against the copy editors (called subeditors in South Africa and England) day after day, I knew that I was encountering resistance, not merely to the volume of what I was writing but to the subject matter. All the copy editors were whites, many had the prejudices of most of the country's whites, and they just didn't like all these reports about blacks coming at them. Even though Gandar had filled the executive positions, including those in charge of the editing process, there was resistance to change internally.

The whole character and direction of the *Rand Daily Mail* was changing, and it was charting a new course for the country's press; as with large ships that need a lot of open sea to come to a halt, newspapers need time to school their people in a different culture. Gandar put in long hours, returning after dinner most nights to check the first edition's page proofs. But the *Mail* was large and sprawling, and he was not the hands-on editor—a shirtsleeves editor—who could shape it totally.

He was also facing opposition outside the newspaper. In early 1959, not much more than eighteen months after his appointment, Gandar encountered his first problems with the board of directors. The United Party had a new leader, Sir de Villiers Graaff. He resented Gandar's sharp criticisms and complained to him repeatedly. When the criticisms grew even stronger, de Villiers Graaff took his complaints to his close friend Clive Corder, chairman of Syfrets and a member of the Saan board. This was heavyweight stuff because Syfrets, an old-money investment firm in Cape Town, represented a majority of shareholders on the board. Corder was a staunch United Party supporter, as were other members of the board. But Gandar had two strong allies in the Saan management: the managing director, Henri Kuiper, and Leycester Walton, the general manager, who came from an Eastern Cape newspaper-owning family and had himself been a journalist. They tipped off Gandar that some members of the board were becoming restive about his attacks on the United Party. But they, along with the chairman of the board, G.R "Bob" Edmunds, believed in what he was saying, and backed him, fending off the criticisms.

On one side of the United Party were those who supported de Villiers Graaff's belief that the road back to government was by offering white voters a lesser version of apartheid. United Party policy was "white leadership with justice" in an integrated South Africa. On the other side was a small group who shared Gandar's outlook in aiming for a multiracial society. They were embarrassed by the United Party's pusillanimity. Their unhappiness was extensively reported in the press, though they were clearly a small minority. If they broke away or were expelled, they risked political oblivion. What dramatically changed the situation for them and for South Africa was that Gandar argued on their behalf.

The *Mail* was out in the open, the only newspaper that supported the criticisms voiced by the progressives in the United Party. One night while I was in Gandar's office, he took a phone call from someone about the *Mail*'s policy. I heard Gandar say, "I suppose one of these days I had better go and see the chairman and tell him what I am doing. He must think I've gone out of my mind." I was astonished that the newspaper had made such a significant policy switch without the editor consulting his chairman and board. Years later Gandar told me that he had agonized about this. He felt he should inform Edmunds, if only as a courtesy and especially because of his unwavering support. But he decided that if he went to see the chairman, he would in all likelihood be putting him into a situation where he would be formally giving him an opportunity to veto the *Mail*'s changed direction. It was best to stay away.

At the United Party's annual congress in August 1959, twelve out of the party's fifty-three members of parliament resigned and formed the Progressive Party. The "Progs" were lively and enthusiastic, and gingered up opposition to the Nationalists. The Syfrets people were certainly unhappy about Gandar's actions, but Kuiper and Walton once more believed he had done the right thing in encouraging the emergence of new ideas in opposition and again won the day for him.

I was not enthusiastic about the Progs or the paper's support for them. I viewed them as a considerably watered-down version of the Liberals and not much of an improvement on the United Party, especially because they initially restricted membership to whites. There were, however, some exceptional MPs among them, especially the incomparable Helen Suzman, who represented the Houghton, Johannesburg, constituency. Since I lived there, I always felt it was worthwhile to cast a vote in parliamentary elections. I would not have bothered to vote for most of the other Progs of that time and would certainly not have voted for the United Party.

The *Mail* was part of the South African Morning Group, an association of English-language morning newspapers that gradually became more formal, with nearly all coming under the Saan umbrella. All watched the *Mail*, some with horrified interest. Victor Norton, editor of the *Cape Times*, was friendly, as was John Sutherland of the *Evening Post*. But word reached Gandar that Mac Pollock of the morning *Eastern Province Herald* in Port Elizabeth was complaining, "Who the hell does Gandar think he is, preaching to everybody about what they should think and how they should behave?" John Robinson, editor of the *Natal Mercury* was outright hostile. And when I drove to Durban for the annual ANC congress that year (which turned out, because of events three months later, to be the ANC's last congress in the country for the next thirty years), I was going to telex my reports to the *Mail* through the *Mercury*. This was standard practice inside the Morning Group. Before leaving Johannesburg, I sent the *Mercury* news desk a courtesy telex that I was visiting their area for the ANC congress and would come in to file my reports. I stopped for the night in Pietermaritzburg, fifty-six miles (90 km) short of Durban, and found an urgent message from the *Mail's* news desk waiting for me: Don't go near the *Mercury*. They won't let you use their telex. They want to have nothing to do with reporting the ANC Congress.

The congress was the usual ANC meeting as I had come to know them. Each session began several hours late. Resolutions that had been written in advance were passed without much disagreement coming from the floor. Delegates were drawn from all classes, but most were poorly dressed people. They had come from all over the country, traveling long distances through the night in crowded hired buses. Some delegates never arrived because the police blocked them en route. Above all, you could sense from the gathering a shared humanity, and with it, an enthusiastic belief in the ANC's ability to bring relief from the misery of life under apartheid. The hall near the city center where the meeting was held was meant to hold 600 or 700 people, but more than twice as many were crammed in. When all 1,500 sang loudly and danced energetically, as they did frequently, the midsummer temperature and humidity in the hall soared.

After the congress I drove up the north coast to visit Chief Albert Luthuli, the ANC president. Eight years earlier the government had forced him to decide between legal status as a chief or membership in the ANC. He chose the ANC and had released this statement announcing his decision:

Who will deny that 30 years of my life have been spent knocking in vain, patiently, moderately and modestly at a closed and barred door? What have been the fruits of moderation? The past 30 years have seen the greatest number of laws restricting our rights and progress until today we have reached a stage where we have almost no rights at all.

Although Luthuli was no longer a chief, many people continued to use the title out of respect. He could not be at the congress because he was banned and confined to the small area of the Umvoti Mission Reserve at Groutville, where he lived. As a white person I had to get a permit from the local Bantu affairs commissioner to enter the area. The typed document ordered:

> Under no circumstances must the holder hereof interfere in the domestic or other affairs of the Natives. In his dealings with the Natives the holder hereof must behave in a dignified manner and refrain from criticism of the administration of the Government or any of its officials. Under no circumstances must the holder hereof publish or cause to be published in any newspaper or periodical any article of a political nature or a criticism of the Government or its officials which may stem from the interview.

It was a wacky document even for those times, and I ignored its restrictions on what I could write. Subsequently Luthuli would be denied the right to receive visitors at home, but I was able to sneak in because I knew I could drive along a back road, park, and walk through the sugarcane fields to his house.

I was the first visitor he had had since the congress in Durban. I sat in his living room and told him about the meeting—how impressed I had been because I thought there was a new mood of militancy and determination. I mentioned the membership figures I had been given during the congress by the Transvaal secretary, James Hadebe. It reflected a claimed total paid membership of something over twenty-five thousand. "That is interesting," said Luthuli enthusiastically, "I must write that down." I found myself standing next to the president-general of the ANC as he sat at a desk and I dictated his organization's membership figures around the country. I was upset for him that ANC leaders had not yet come to report to him.

That the ANC enjoyed widespread popular support was clear to anyone who had any dealings with it. Just going to the movement's Transvaal offices in the basement of a building two blocks from the magistrates' courts was an eye-opener. For this was a time when the government was forcing blacks in rural areas to accept a system of local "Bantu Authorities," which were the building blocks to create Verwoerd's separate development. The forms of pressure on recalcitrant tribes ranged from withdrawal of schools to the deposing and banishment of local leaders and hereditary chiefs. On my visits to the ANC office I would find groups of people there, their clothes reflecting their poverty, who had come to report their plight and were waiting for guidance and help. The power of the state was so overwhelming that not much could be done for these people except a very occasional legal intervention and, in my case, a story in the paper. Some stories were published, such as a group's complaint about being beaten by the police. This piece holds a special place in my memory because the ANC office phoned me at home on the Jewish New Year and after thinking through the competing ethical demands I went to interview the group of country people. It was the first time in my life that I worked on that holy day.

The ANC was a ramshackle body, its heart bigger than what it could achieve. Money was always in short supply, making it difficult to hire full-time organizers, authorize travel, or even print publicity material. Albertina Sisulu, wife of Walter Sisulu, who was the ANC's full-time secretary-general at the end of the fifties, recalls that she was supporting the family by working as a nurse. One day she gave her husband a list of groceries and money. He came home at the end of the day without the groceries, and confessed that he had used the money to pay the ANC's office rent. The phone bill was seldom paid and it was widely believed that the Security Police kept the Post Office from cutting it off because they were tapping it. Eventually the phone bill must have reached such proportions that the Post Office rebelled and the phone service was suspended. The unthinkable had happened, and so great was the consternation at the ANC that Hadebe had to put together some money. Only part of the amount owed was paid, but either Post Office honor was saved or the Security Police prevailed and the phone link was restored. In antiapartheid circles the telephone account became a litmus test to find out if your phone was being tapped: if you didn't pay and were not cut off, then you were being watched. I always paid but found that I enjoyed special treatment in the speed with which I could get my phone at home repaired—a big plus in life because of the fault-ridden telephone system.

Part of the ANC's broad appeal was the lack of tribalism—divisions caused by adherence to one or other of the dozen different black tribes, whether the Xhosa, Zulu, or whatever. This was a continuing strength, but it also put the ANC entirely beyond the pale as far as the government was concerned. There was no possibility of the Afrikaner Nationalists entering into discussions with the ANC because their own policy was heading in entirely the opposite direction, toward fragmentation and tribalism. To protect white power, they set out to destroy national unity among blacks.

But while the ANC seemed free of tribal tensions, cultural differences did play their part. Hence the story told me by Joe Matthews, prominent in the ANC: Walter Sisulu had traveled from Johannesburg to Durban on the overnight train for an organizing mission. As secretary-general he was met at the station by a welcoming committee of local ANC leaders, and this being Natal, they were Zulus. They politely asked to carry his suitcase, but Sisulu, traveling light, merely held up a brown paper bag in which he had a change of underwear and a toothbrush. From that point on, said Matthews, he might as well have climbed on the next train and returned to Johannesburg because to Zulus, a gentleman always traveled with a suitcase; it didn't matter if the suitcase was empty. As Sisulu had shown that he was no gentleman, they felt it was not worth talking to him. Years later Sisulu told me it had grown even worse because he stayed at the home of a Natal leader and when the time came to go to bed that night, his host asked where his pajamas were. Sisulu lamely said that he had been late for the train and did not have time to pack them.

An area of notable success for the ANC at that time was in farm labor. A Johannesburg lawyer, Joel Carlson, was brave and enterprising in exposing a system of farm-labor exploitation. Black men arrested for pass–law offenses, petty crimes, and "vagrancy" were offered the option of working out their two- to six-month sentences on white-owned farms in lieu of prison. "Offered" was a loose term, and what emerged was that men were bundled off to the farms without knowing what they had contracted to do. Even if they were aware, once on the farms, they could face savage mistreatment with rudimentary living conditions, poor food, and wholesale assaults, sometimes even leading to death at the hands of farmers and their "boss boys," the black supervisors. For the authorities the system reduced overcrowding in prisons, and farmers were guaranteed a constant flow of cheap labor: pass-law arrests were at 500,000 a year. Carlson exposed abuses through urgent applications he brought before the courts and dramatic rescues of men from farms in the Transvaal. The disclosures were heavily reported in the press. I went out on several visits to farms with members of the Black Sash, who also exposed the legalized outrage. During my own investigations I visited a farm, passing myself off as a traveling salesman, which was just as well because the farmer told me in bloodcurdling terms what he would do to any reporter who dared come on his property.

The ANC weighed in with a call to boycott potatoes, a major crop of the region. It was effective propaganda, appealing to emotions by speaking about the blood of laborers on potatoes. The farm-labor system was suspended. However, as I reported, this left intact the whole vicious circle of "arrest, prison, release, arrest," to which blacks in the city who lacked jobs or permission to be there were subject.

One man I wrote about was named Jeremiah, aged sixty-five, who lived in Alexandra township. He had arrived there eighteen years before from the Transkei.

> Until a year ago Jeremiah was employed as a watchman. He lost his job because he was too old. Now, from the official point of view, he must return to his home in the Transkei. But although he has visited his old home sporadically, his roots are in Alexandra. And even if he wished to return to the Transkei, he has no money to pay for his train-fare. His alternatives: to remain here and to become part of the vicious circle. Or else he can accept work in a rural area in the hope of saving money. But at his age what work can he do? It is a problem for which officials see no solution at present.

Unfortunately the solution was to continue the arrests, and in due course, as I was to learn, farm labor was again flourishing.

Nineteen-sixty put the *Mail's* reporters to the test. The year opened with a disaster in mid January at Coalbrook, a coal mine thirteen and a half miles (22 km) from Vereeniging. When we arrived within a few hours of the event, rescue teams were already underground and other rescue teams were rushing in from gold and coal mines up to two hundred miles away.

Using a carhood as a desk, I wrote as much as we had been able to learn, then went to the nearby clubhouse for whites. We had to beg for use of a manual call box linked to the mine's tiny exchange, which was overwhelmed by emergency calls. Standing on the veranda, shouting over a poor line within yards of a cluster of sobbing women and children, I felt terrible as I dictated our first wrap-up story:

> At least 250 men—and perhaps 500—are trapped 600 feet underground... They were trapped by a

Chapter 6

> heavy fall of rock. At 2:00 this morning—nearly seven hours after the fall—the fate of the trapped men was still unknown.

With colleagues joining in, the story went on,

> Relatives knelt on the ground within the shadow of the pithead and prayed. A minister led them. He moved among the weeping women and children, talking to them. Mothers, fathers, wives, daughters stared at the pithead.

In fact 435 men were entombed in the worst mining disaster in South African history. Speculation at the mine was that the collapse had happened because too much coal had been cut from the underground pillars left during mining to support the roof. An inquiry later exonerated the mine management. The *Mail* began to pour out special editions that morning and every day for nearly a fortnight as rescue efforts continued. Two drills were trucked in and erected, and hour after hour, as they bored their way down, we stood around ceaselessly discussing the diminishing chance of finding anyone alive.

Eleven days after the cave-in I was among the group of miners, officials, and reporters waiting silently in the early-morning sunshine when, at 6:45 A.M., a drill broke through into the underground workings. A microphone was lowered: only the sound of running water was heard.

Every possible reporter and photographer was thrown into round-the-clock reporting of the story at the mine. The teamwork and coordination were unmatchable. The new abilities the *Mail* had been developing were tested to the nth degree, and the paper passed with flying colors. The tough approach to reporting and the techniques for making it work put together by O'Connor and Louw became the standard for coverage for years afterward. If the story was big, the *Mail* went after it, marshaling every possible resource, going for saturation coverage of every nook and cranny, and outstripping everyone else.

I saw what I was often to marvel at over the years: the willingness of badly paid reporters to throw themselves into the story and not stop until it was safely back with the news desk. At Coalbrook the mine management soon turned truculent and uncooperative, and attempted to keep reporters off the mine property. *Mail* reporters responded by eluding the guards by lying on their stomachs and crawling through the surrounding cornfields made muddy by heavy rain.

Only six of the entombed miners were whites, and we had access to their families, their personal information, and to the whites working in the rescue attempt. But the compounds housing several thousand black workers were out of bounds, and we could not gain information about how they were taking the news of the loss of their friends.

At Coalbrook the rescue teams had whites heading teams of blacks. As they prepared to go underground on their hugely perilous missions, I would see the whites joshing with the blacks in what seemed to be the usual South African master-servant relationship. But amid the rough talk I also watched the leader almost unobtrusively but carefully check the equipment of each man.

Color did not matter when they got into the dark and unknown below. Everyone depended on one another. I witnessed the same thing when I covered other mining accidents later. But there was no equality under the law. Skilled jobs were reserved for white miners. In particular, only whites could hold "blasting certificates," which gave the right to set off explosives underground and ensured high pay for white miners. It was, however, common practice for white miners to order blacks to do the job while they sat at their ease. Any suggestion that this should be made legal drew instant strike threats from white miners, who argued that it was too dangerous to allow blacks to set off the charges.

A few days after the end of the Coalbrook rescue attempt, I covered British prime minister Harold Macmillan's visit to South Africa. Addressing parliament in Cape Town, Macmillan gripped the country and the world with his declaration: "A wind of change is blowing through Africa." Although elegantly phrased, his speech, which caught the feeling of the black rush to independence in the continent, was a blunt challenge to the course on which the South African government was set. I listened to him on the radio, as well as the following speech by Verwoerd, who spoke politely to his guest though his voice was shaking as he struggled to control the fury of his reaction.

Verwoerd had taken the original apartheid doctrine and translated it into racial "separate development," which pretended to promise blacks "separate freedom" in their own tribal areas. But in practice it merely put a gloss on continued control by whites. Verwoerd was so fixated on his own rectitude and his racial ideology that he was probably genuinely unable to understand world abhorrence of his policies. He and his fellow Nationalists, for example, felt there was nothing wrong with what they were doing at that time to the one thousand Asians in Rustenburg, north of Johannesburg. The Asian community had been in the town for seventy years, and many were traders or storeowners. They lent money to the white farmers in times of drought and were repaid in the good years. Now they were being evicted en masse from their businesses and homes under the Group Areas Act, first introduced in 1950 and steadily and remorselessly implemented since. They had to start their lives again on undeveloped land two and a half miles (4 km) outside the town. I went to see leaders of the community.

"This means economic ruin for us," they said. The Rustenburg story was being repeated throughout the Transvaal. Each village and town was the same. Publish one story and it told the whole story, as did the coldness of Rustenburg's white deputy mayor's response. He told me, "The Group Areas Act must be carried out—it is the law of the country."

Even while the shock of Coalbrook was still reverberating, the government was pressing down on blacks: the pass laws were ferociously applied and worker protests over poverty pay were stifled. On Monday, March 14th, I reported on an ANC Women's League conference in Lady Selborne township, Pretoria, where fifteen hundred women had gathered in a hall to protest against passes. Black Security policemen brought their own chairs and sat in front of the platform. The women ordered the detectives to take off their hats out of respect and to go to the back of the hall. The detectives sheepishly obeyed, but their white Security masters promptly ordered them to return to the front. It soon turned nasty, and armed white policemen came into the hall. The Women's League leaders urged their people to remain calm. The black detectives remained at the front, taking notes of the speeches.

Alongside the ANC Women's League conference article was another report by me. The three paragraphs began, "Circulars are being distributed to Africans throughout the Union urging them to save money and food in preparation for a campaign aimed at the abolition of the pass laws. The date of the campaign being organized by the Pan-Africanist Congress will be announced on Friday."

Those words proved to be a curtain-raiser on events that would shake the country to its foundations. Sobukwe did announce the date of the planned pass-law protests, and the campaign opened on Monday, March 21st. By the end of that day the police had killed sixty-eight people at Sharpeville, and a new chapter had begun for South Africa.

At five-thirty that morning I began my "dawn patrol" inside Soweto, my usual drill in times of protest and unrest. I went to Sobukwe's tiny house in Mofolo to say goodbye to him before he set off to walk close to three miles (4.5 km) to the Orlando police station, where he and other PAC leaders offered themselves for arrest. Sobukwe had called on blacks to break the law by leaving their passes at home and turn themselves in to the nearest police station. The idea was to swamp the prisons and bring the pass laws to a standstill. He said he would not ask anyone to do what he was himself not willing to do. But only some two hundred men joined him from throughout the vast sprawling townships. The police were confused and did not know what to do with them, so they told them to wait outside the station fence.

I was with Sobukwe and his supporters in midmorning when Harold Sacks arrived with the news that in other townships thirty-five miles

(50km) away thousands of black demonstrators had gathered to demand that they be arrested, and the police had opened fire, killing two men in the first deaths of the day.

Jan Hoek, a *Mail* photographer, and I drove to Bophelong, an hour away, and watched Harvard propeller planes, used by the air force for training, flying not much higher than the telephone poles in an effort to frighten people. Once the crowd realized the planes were only going to make a noise, they stood and shook their fists.

Hoek and I followed the police in their armored Saracens to the township of Sharpeville a few miles away. The police ordered us to stay out, but we drove in. The crowd of thousands gathered around the police station was peaceful, and once they found I was from the *Mail*, people were eager to tell me their grievances—how they suffered under the pass laws and their struggle to pay rent and buy food.

I decided to drive around the side of the crowd, and suddenly there was the sound of a fusillade of gunshots. Instinctively I swung the car to the left toward the shooting. People were running toward us, shouting, "Watch out, watch out, they'll shoot you." Then there was silence and we saw the ground strewn with bodies. I was inching the car along when one man came running toward us, screaming, "Who are you? What do you want?" and in slow motion I watched him pick up a stone to fling at us. In an instant a mob was let loose, and amid the noise of shouting and stones striking the metal of the car, shattering the glass, and sticks beating on the car, I pushed down on the accelerator, ramming us clear. Shaken and frightened, we took off over open land, bumping along until we reached a road and drove back to Johannesburg, passing truckloads of soldiers heading for the scene. The car was badly damaged, and my ear was cut from flying glass.

As the world later learned, the police shot 705 bullets at the crowd. Medical evidence revealed that more than 70 percent of the sixty-eight killed and 186 injured were shot from the back; at the most only 15 percent of wounds could be identified as inflicted from the front. Three policemen were reported slightly injured by stones.

The name Sharpeville leaped onto the world's news agenda. A generation grew up identifying Sharpeville with apartheid repression. At home the massacre triggered an outpouring of rage. As the PAC pushed ahead and the ANC called for protests and the burning of passes, unrest and violence spread. The government declared a State of Emergency and proscribed the ANC and PAC. The detention without trial of more than 1,900 political people of all colors was a travesty. The police unearthed the names of every possible suspect, seizing people who had been out of politics for years. Arrests like these were blamed on "Spengler's List," the accumulated names that, it was said in left-wing circles, had been collected and stored by Colonel Att Spengler, head of the Security Branch in Johannesburg.

Many of my friends were detained. I was so immersed in dealing with radical politics that I thought I might be among them. I kept few notes about stories I was working on and used codes to disguise sources if I had to record them. Whatever possibly compromising paper I had with me at night I put in a bag tied with string, ready to hang out the window of our first-floor apartment if the police should come knocking. It probably wouldn't have been much protection, but in fact nothing happened. Those seized included my closest friend, Ernest Wentzel, a lawyer.

Many political leaders and activists were able to evade the police during the State of Emergency and went into hiding or escaped over the borders. The most notable was Oliver Tambo, who led the ANC in exile and was only able to return home again more than three decades later, when victory was in sight.

Swaziland, which was a five-hour drive from Johannesburg and had an unguarded border, was one of the havens for those on the run, and I went there in search of them. As I drove down the main street—the only tarred street—of the capital, Mbabane, I saw several people I knew on the sidewalk. By the time I braked and swung into a parking space, they had disappeared. It took several days of negotiating through intermediaries before any of the refugees would see me.

The refugees in Swaziland and Basutoland were in difficulty because the only way to get to Europe, short of driving through South Africa, was to fly over. Basutoland was entirely landlocked, and Swaziland was bordered to the east by Mozambique, where the Pide—the Portuguese secret police—were in cahoots with South African security. With Britain's assistance most refugees were eventually able to get out.

There was a particular newspaper search for the Anglican bishop of Johannesburg, the Right Reverend Ambrose Reeves. The previous year he had set up a united front through the Bishop's Committee of Thirteen Anti–Apartheid Organizations. The police came for him when the Emergency arrests began, but the bishop had fled.

My *Mail* colleague Oscar Tamsen traced Reeves to Mbabane, to the home of an Anglican priest. Tamsen knocked on the door. The priest came to the door and denied that Reeves was there.

"Of course I have heard of the bishop," he said. "But I do not know him and have never met him."

At that moment there was the sound of a toilet flushing and Reeves stepped from a bathroom into the hallway. With great courtesy Tamsen asked the priest, "Can I introduce you to Bishop Reeves?"

Reeves fled from sight. Subsequently he, too, reached Britain safely, and flew back to Johannesburg a few months later. The police detained him at the airport, refused to let him see his lawyer—Wentzel—and deported him as a British subject. Reeves had followed bad advice in leaving South Africa in the first place. Many of his loyal flock felt that their spiritual leader had deserted them in time of need. Those of his white parishioners who had objected to his taking on a political role, and there were many of them, were pleased that the troublesome priest had destroyed himself.

From this point on, the surrounding countries became a regular route for people without passports. But care was necessary in reporting someone fleeing the country. The *Star*'s early edition once carried a front-page report giving names of Johannesburg barristers who had escaped to Lesotho. It was a startling list until, shortly after the newspaper went onto the streets, it was discovered that these were barristers who had enrolled their names so that they could practice in the Lesotho courts. It must have cost the *Star* a fortune in damages.

Steve Segale, my ANC friend from Sophiatown times, was also caught up in the State of Emergency. When it began, he was in prison for a nonpolitical offense. His sentence expired a few weeks later, and Segale queued up with a crowd of other prisoners waiting to be released. A Security policeman came into the prison yard, and as Segale ducked away, he heard him tell the warder in charge, "You have Segale here. Don't release him. We are detaining him under the Emergency laws."

Segale went to a friendly warder and pleaded, "Please, man, let me out. I've been waiting long enough." The warder obligingly took Segale to the gate and he was off. The police spent several months hunting for him until they finally found him walking in the street. Segale told me that he was taken to Security headquarters in Johannesburg, and as he was brought into a room, a Security policeman, Carel Dirker, who was tall and heavily built, punched him to the floor. Segale, no slouch in a fight, picked himself up and promptly knocked him down. Dirker, swearing angrily, started going for Segale. But Att Spengler was watching the incident, stepped forward, and ordered, "Leave him alone. You asked for it."

Spengler behaved in like manner during a raid on the home of Vic and Marcelle Goldberg, white and left-wing. In an age when old-fashioned courtesies still held sway, Marcelle told a Security detective to take off his hat in her home. He rudely refused, and Spengler ordered him to do it.

Spengler belonged to a dying breed, one of those Afrikaners who had entered the police force during the Depression years of the 1930s and who viewed himself as a professional policeman. He told me that he had served General Smuts, he was serving Dr. Verwoerd, and he would serve Chief Luthuli just as faithfully if the ANC ever came to power.

The difference between him and others was made clear to me on a Sunday morning at a planned protest meeting at "Freedom Square," a corner plot of wasteland in the suburb of Newclare. The meeting had been banned overnight by magisterial decree. I went to check it out, but the only people there were a few truckloads of armed policemen. I saw Spengler standing with someone whom I recognized as the national head of the Security Police, General "Sampie" Prinsloo. I walked across and Spengler introduced me to Prinsloo, who, without even a nod or a look in my direction, asked, "What are you doing here?"

"I'm just hanging around to see if anything happens," I replied.

"Nothing is going to happen," he said, looking at his watch, "I'm giving you three minutes to get out of here before I arrest you."

I was taken aback and looked at Spengler. He was embarrassed but did not say anything.

I drove to the nearest pay phone and reported to A. B. Hughes, the editor of the day. I asked his permission to go back in and get arrested, but he refused. The police were in control and could do what they wanted, he said.

Spengler was involved in the police shooting at Sharpeville. According to some witnesses he was in the process of arresting someone in the crowd when one of the uniformed policemen behind him panicked and fired the first shot.

Another policeman in the same mold as Spengler was a Major Bill Murray. I covered many street demonstrations and meetings where Murray was in charge of the police, and I could see and hear how he kept tight hold of his men. If he said, "Take three paces forward," that's what they did, no less and no more.

Policemen like Murray and Spengler were thin on the ground to start with and were declining in number as Nationalist ideology bit deeper and whites came into line to defend the ramparts of privilege.

Time and again the Nationalists protected their police from all charges of wrongdoing, and brutality became accepted as the standard means of operation. That attitude seeped through to all levels of behavior, whether in political action against the government's opponents or in everyday police work.

The Murder and Robbery Squad in Johannesburg for many years had a commendably high rate of success in cracking cases. A bitter price was paid for this, however, as it had a reputation for stopping at nothing, starting with the basic technique of forcing suspects to hold, with arms extended, a water-filled car innertube and beating them if their arms sagged. Occasionally details like this emerged in court cases. I had my own example of police attitudes when my car was stolen and I phoned the Flying Squad. Two constables arrived at my home and I offered them a drink while they took down the details. They were friendly and helpful and wanted to cheer me up about my car.

"Don't worry," one said, "we've sent out a message on the radio and when our men find your car, they'll shoot the thieves dead."

On Saturday, April 9th, the day after the government banned the ANC and PAC, Verwoerd came to Johannesburg to open the annual Rand Show of agriculture and industry. The tension in the country was palpable: the killings by the police, the bannings, the ongoing mass arrests. Widespread belief that something had to break was focused on the prime minister's attendance at the Rand Show in its grounds neighboring the University of the Witwatersrand. There was a feeling that anything might happen. Many foreign journalists were present, drawn by the turmoil and Verwoerd's presence.

Verwoerd delivered his speech and sat down. Most of the journalists promptly fled—listening to Verwoerd's avuncular, talking-down-to-you style was always a trial—and sought refreshment in the bar. A few minutes later a wealthy trout farmer, David Pratt, shot Verwoerd. A local journalist, Desmond Bagley, who had stayed behind, witnessed the shooting. He ran to the bar with the news—but unfortunately he had a stutter, which became worsened by his excitement. He fought to get out the words: "Ver-Ver-Ver-Ver-Ver-wo-wo-wo-erd's been shot" as journalists crowded around him.

As the moment of understanding came, they stampeded back to the stadium. Meanwhile a BBC photographer had had two television cameras mounted on tripods during Verwoerd's speech. The film in one had run out. He was lifting a camera off the tripod when he heard a crack, and instinctively held up the camera to point it at Verwoerd and pressed the start button, not knowing which camera it was. It proved to be the loaded camera, and the remarkable film shown around the world opened with Verwoerd staring ahead as though nothing was amiss. A split second later blood spurted from a small hole in his face caused by a .22 caliber bullet, and he slumped to the side.

David Pratt was, in due course, declared mentally unfit to stand trial, was jailed, and committed suicide the following year. Verwoerd survived for the time being.

The State of Emergency gave the Nationalists all the power their hearts desired. They could do, and did do, much as they pleased, and that included the control of information.

An earlier Nationalist prime minister, General J.B.M. Hertzog, had been on the verge of legislating to curb the press, but was halted by the Second World War and the loss of his job to General Smuts. Hertzog, it seemed, was prompted to act because of complaints by Nazi diplomats that South African newspapers were being unkind to their country. "Hertzog warned editors that he would pass a law for the control of the press unless they desisted from attacking Hitler and Mussolini," a Labor MP, Alex Hepple, noted in a booklet about censorship.

Over the years the English-language press was a particular target for the Nationalists: they repeatedly flayed it as unpatriotic, disloyal, given to telling outright lies,

Chapter 7

and controlled by foreign-owned gold mining companies. The fact that so much of the ownership resided in Britain for so long, that the presence and influence of British-born editors and journalists was so strong for even longer, and that so much of the news revolved around London, fueled their cause.

The Nationalists were not alone in their criticisms. On the English side of the fence there were anxieties about the monopolistic control of the press. Dr. Bernard Friedman, at the liberal end of the political spectrum and a United Party MP when the party was still in office early in 1948, put a motion before parliament calling for the appointment of a select committee to investigate "whether the financial and technical control of the press in South Africa is such as to prevent a completely free expression of editorial opinion and presentation of news." It was rejected.

A year later, with the Nationalists in government, a call by one of their MPs for an inquiry into the press drew a readier response. An official commission was appointed in January 1951, and set to work compiling dossiers on local and foreign journalists, demanding that journalists fill in lengthy questionnaires, and summoning them for questioning behind closed doors and without legal representation.

Dr. Albert Hertzog, the son of General Hertzog, declaimed against "important English-language newspapers, which are today controlled by the mine magnates... the time is overdue, not only for a thorough investigation into this matter, but for drastic action." Hertzog became minister of posts, where he fought to keep the world at bay by refusing to allow television, which eventually entered South African living rooms as late as 1976.

In August 1954 J. G. Strijdom, a firebrand Afrikaner leader nicknamed the "Lion of the North," accused the English-language press of writing material "the effect of which must be that the Natives are incited against the laws of the land." Three years later Strijdom was prime minister and described the English-language press as South Africa's greatest enemy.

In February 1958 Eric Louw, the minister of foreign affairs, who was given to brandishing sheaves of press clippings as he attacked journalists, set off a particular storm when he told parliament that "stringers" were sending abroad distorted and false reports and were "selling the interests of South Africa for thirty pieces of silver." He went on to say that foreign correspondents had descended on the country "like a swarm of vultures." The South African Society of Journalists—a trade union body confined to the English-language press because Afrikaans newspapers would not allow staff to join it—predictably and understandably challenged Louw to name the "stringers" outside the protection of parliamentary privilege so that they could sue him for libel. The Foreign Correspondents Association said they did not know whom he was describing.

A week later Louw returned to the attack, as aggressively as before. He said he particularly had in mind the "itinerant press correspondents who, during the past year, have flocked to South Africa with instructions from papers and agencies to send unfavorable and, if possible, sensational reports." His attacks never stopped.

The commission of inquiry into the press toiled and toiled. Responsibility for it was shunted from one government department to the other amid repeated promises that it would soon report. It went on for fourteen years, so long that it became somewhat of a national joke, but only up to a point, because its existence cast a dark shadow over the press. The threat of what might result prompted caution in English-language journalists. Eventually, in February 1962, the commission handed in its first report of 700 pages plus 1,566 pages of appendices. Its second report in 1964 ran to 1,400 pages with 3,000 pages of appendices. Among the welter of confused words were proposals for sundry restrictions on the press. But the Nationalists did not have to bother to take these up because by then they were well on the way to doing what they had always wanted to do: the noose already encircling the neck of the press was being tightened.

The chilling effect of the press commission went in tandem with another commission of inquiry into "Undesirable Publications." This commission's report in 1957 dealt not only with pornography but also with fundamental press freedoms, and recommended prepublication political censorship. The government put this into a bill and brought it before parliament but backed off because of the combined protests of the Afrikaans and English press. The law eventually enacted toughened censorship but excluded newspapers. The price was that the press, through the Newspaper Press Union, agreed to set up its own disciplinary system.

In 1962 the NPU announced a Free Press Code and Board of Reference. Saan was among a minority of newspaper owners who expressed dissatisfaction with the code, but agreed to go along with it. Having led the way, Saan expected its editors to follow, but there were ruffled feelings when Gandar said he would wait before expressing his position. He went on to express his doubts, arguing in an editorial on March 14, 1962, that, whatever the denials, the press code was the result of political pressure and what might otherwise have been an innocuous code—an elaborate exercise in the obvious—had a sting in the tail.

The particular clause he objected to was this one: "While the press retains its traditional right of criticism, comment should take cognizance of the complex racial problems of South Africa, the general good and safety of the country and its people."

No one could be sure exactly what this sweeping statement meant or even how it might be used. It became another reason to look over one's shoulder, especially as in the years to come the Nationalists continued to push for a tightening of the code.

Until 1948 the press in South Africa enjoyed considerable freedom in terms of the law. The great struggle for press freedom had been waged 120 years earlier against the Cape's autocratic British governor, Lord Charles Somerset. The principle of the right to publish was maintained, disturbed only in times of war or insurrection. Defamation had to be avoided because the law, based on British law, was tight, and a defense had to be founded on truth and public interest. If publication could not be shown to have been in the public interest, then the greater the truth, the greater the libel.

Section 83 of the Criminal Procedure Act provided for imprisonment for up to eight days at a time, to be repeated without end if necessary, for anyone who withheld information demanded by the police. The only known case involved a *Rand Daily Mail* journalist. George Heard, the political correspondent, was jailed in the late 1930s over a leak of details about the budget. Various laws on the statute book had the potential to prevent publication of information, but they did not seem to have caused much difficulty because they covered black activities, which were then of minimal interest to most of the press. So, until 1948, the picture was of a press with enviable freedom but which did little to apply that freedom in covering the totality of South Africa.

Then the inroads began. One Nationalist law after the other assaulted individual freedom and, in doing so, eroded the freedom of the press. New laws and extensions of old laws meant that by 1960, at least twelve statutes were in place that in one way or another denied or inhibited press freedoms.

Then came the State of Emergency, decreed in terms of a law bullocked through seven years earlier, specifying that it was a crime to publish any "subversive" information. *Subversive* could mean anything that questioned or criticized the government. Backed by a heavy fine and/or five years' imprisonment, it ensured that much information did not see the light of day. Under the State of Emergency, the identities of the 1,900 political detainees held without trial could not be published.

At the *Mail* and other newspapers, we worked to get hold of names and to rush them into print, and many were published before the prohibiting law came into effect. But there was no avoiding the threat in Emergency laws. Newspapers could be closed down (and two were, *New Age* and the NEUM's weekly *Torch*), and the police could search without warrant and detain whom they wanted for as long as they wanted.

The five months of the Emergency honed the *Mail* into a fighting instrument. The two and a half years of Gandar's editorship were bearing fruit. His editorial analyses had cogency and strength. He had transformed the *Mail* into a magnet that was attracting talented reporters; the newsgathering had a bite and aggression new to South African journalism.

The *Mail* was also usually a good-looking newspaper, with innovative and daring layouts that set the standard for the country's press. But the newspaper's mercurial character was well in place, and perhaps, too, because the *Mail* and its journalists were pushing so much at the edges, there wasn't always consistency. When it was good, in content and appearance, it was unrivaled; when it was bad, it was awful.

While quality was soaring, the downside was that the traditional white readership was dropping away. The *Mail* was simply too far ahead of their outlook in its opinions. They felt alienated. It reached the stage, I thought, where some whites bought the paper almost as a means of getting going in the morning: they read it, exploded with rage, and with adrenaline pumping through their veins were ready for the day's work.

The circulation department pointed out a curious phenomenon: when the *Transvaler*, the Johannesburg morning National Party organ, ran an important political story, the *Mail's* sales jumped. It seemed that Afrikaans readers did not trust their own paper and wanted to hear from the *Mail*, or sought an additional, alternative view. Many Afrikaners read English newspapers, although few English-speaking read Afrikaans papers.

As with much in South Africa, where traditions are quickly established, the country soon settled into the State of Emergency. For most people life went on pretty much as usual, especially as most of the press attention was increasingly given to the referendum called by the government for October—in which only whites could vote—about whether South Africa should become a republic and end its constitutional ties with Britain. After a couple of months the *Mail* took to displaying an occasional reference on page one along the lines of: "The State of Emergency has now lasted 95 days." It didn't seem to do much to arouse people, but we thought it important to remind our readers.

After the initial burst of anger among blacks about the killings at Sharpeville and the vast response to the ANC's day of protest, feelings subsided. Three weeks later the ANC and PAC sought to bring the country to a halt by urging blacks to strike for a week in protest against passes. It was almost a total failure.

"The level of political consciousness has now ebbed," I wrote. "The emotional impact of the events of late-March and early-April has dissolved under the daily pressures of having to exist. A man who lives under the breadline cannot for long ignore the hand-to-mouth demands which he has to face for himself, his wife and his children."

Within the limits of Emergency laws, the *Mail* published occasional reports about what was happening to detainees, putting together scraps of information gleaned from families and detainees as they were released. Once having arrested people without trial, the authorities seemed hard pressed to know what to do with them.

In mid June I reported that the male white detainees in Pretoria were "well treated and are living under good conditions... The major causes of distress among them are boredom and the continued separation from their families. This is intensified because they do not know when they will be released."

A few days later I recorded the desultory pace of dealing with the detainees: "The questioning of the white men detainees who are in a Pretoria prison has started again after a break of about four weeks. During the first round of questioning, the men being questioned were separated from the others and were kept in a separate section of the jail. Several of these men have since been released."

The treatment of black detainees was very different because not only were political activists past and present seized but so were some eighteen thousand people described as "vagrants" under the pass laws. The definition—anyone with "no fixed place of residence, means of subsistence and a regular occupation, or who cannot give a satisfactory account of himself"—allowed the police to cast a wide net.

The Defense and Aid Fund came into existence to give help, but with so many in need it could dole out only small amounts. The fund, in due course, became the main way of paying for the legal defense of antigovernment activists and supporting their families. After eventually being proscribed—it had proven too successful in maintaining the bodies and keeping up the spirits of activists—it continued its work from London. But in 1960 the needs were basic: "A bag of mealie meal (corn) was all that an African mother had in her house last night to feed herself and her two children," ran one of my reports. "But even the mealie meal could not be cooked because there was no money to buy coal for the fire." The woman's husband was a detainee and his already poverty-level weekly wage of £7 had stopped immediately when he was arrested. The mother was getting £2 a month from the Defense and Aid Fund, said the report, setting out the details of what she was spending and how her debts were growing. It also contained a reaction that I often found: "I do not want to ask the fund for money too often, because I know they have to help many, many people," she said.

The Emergency ended in August, but the banning of the ANC and the PAC remained intact. Their absence from the public stage suited the government, which at this point did not have to deal with national movements representing blacks but could push ahead with tribal divide-and-rule. It also fitted in with Prime Minister Verwoerd's refusal to consult with blacks. Get rid of the organizations demanding democracy and the issue falls away, was the government's attitude.

But while this was all convenient from the Afrikaner Nationalist standpoint, blacks were seeking a way forward. This was done through locking onto an appropriate focus for protest, which was May 31, 1961, when white South Africans were going to put into effect the majority decision they had taken in the previous year's referendum: to become a republic.

For Afrikaners it was the achievement of their dream—breaking away from the British Crown and restoring the Boer republics that had been vanquished by Britain sixty years earlier. The All-in African National Action Council came into being to organize the protest. From the start the ANC was behind it, but non-ANC people took part and broadened its image. A plenitude of money, whose origin was unknown, seemed to be available for the Action Council's work.

More than one thousand people went to a two-day conference in Pietermaritzburg in March and, as expected, went along with the prepared resolutions that condemned the new republic constitution as "fraudulent," calling for a three-day strike at the end of May. As strikes by black workers were prohibited by law, it was a criminal offense to urge anyone to go on strike or even to report that a strike was planned; in attempting to circumvent this, a strike was referred to as a "stay-at-home." The hall was jam-packed: to get from the back to the front meant literally climbing over bodies. Again I was struck by the ready acceptance of me, a stranger to most people and for much of the time the only white person inside the hall. The Security Police were thickly clustered outside.

The conference had a surprise speaker: Nelson Mandela. At that stage, although the Mandela name was well known, he had been out of the direct public gaze for several years and was a relative stranger to many in the hall. He had been under on-off banning orders during the previous eight years and his latest five-year banning, and its prohibition on attending meetings, had expired only a few days before the conference, coinciding with his acquittal in the five-year-long Treason Trial. While Mandela is not a scintillating speaker, he impresses people with his sincerity and the quality of his thinking. On this occasion, he spoke in solemn terms and did little to arouse the emotions of the audience after the initial excited response to his unexpected and dramatic appearance on the platform. Mandela finished speaking, left quickly before the police could do anything about him, and the conference continued.

A few days later the government, worried about the Action Council's plans, resorted to repeated large-scale raids and arrests. They sought Mandela, but he had gone underground.

For the next month the police did everything they could to find him, but never succeeded. I saw him regularly, usually at the small home—at 74 Avenue Road, Fordsburg, in Johannesburg—of Adelaide and Paul Joseph, who were in the Transvaal Indian Congress.

Paul had at one time also been an accused in the Treason Trial, and with that sort of political background they took great risks in giving shelter to Mandela. The only other journalist I ever encountered there was Charles Bloomberg of the Johannesburg *Sunday Times*, and he and I never spoke about it when we met elsewhere.

At other times I would drive at night to a street corner in the suburb and pick up Mandela. We would go to a secluded street nearby, and sit and talk in my car. This was a period fraught with danger, and he would speak in serious tones as he assessed the state of his organization around the country. He would be disguised in a pair of worker's overalls. The clothes did not do much to hide his tall, imposing figure, but he was never caught.

If Mandela wanted to see me, a note was handed in at the *Mail*. I did not know at the time how it was done, but later learned that Adelaide drove her eleven-year-old niece, Letchmee Iyer, and dropped her off a block away from the *Mail*. Letchmee would go to the reception desk, hand in a note for me, and leave. If I wanted to see Mandela, I went to the Josephs' home, taking care not to be followed, and left a note for him if he wasn't there. The personal contacts were dangerous for everyone, and we arranged that whenever needed I would be phoned at the *Mail* at five P.M. and a voice would read a statement to me from Mandela and/or the Action Council. I was not supposed to know whose voice it was; that was the procedure we followed. I was always at my phone at that time and a voice at the other end of the line would read a statement. I kept Gandar fully informed of what I was doing.

Later a member of the cabinet spoke rousingly in parliament of Mandela being a fugitive from the police, "but every morning on the stroke of the clock he communicates with his people via the *Rand Daily Mail*," which he added, was one of "the most traitorous institutions we have ever had in this country." There wasn't anything we could do in response except to hope that the minister of justice would not act on the words of the outraged cabinet member.

Eventually I was summoned to Gandar's office. Spengler was there and wanted to know how I was getting these statements from the Action Council. From a telephone caller, I told him. Was it Mandela who was phoning me? No, I was sure it was not Mandela. Did the caller have a "Bantu" accent? No, I wasn't sure, it might be a South African black accent, but it could be a foreign accent.

After going around the tree like this for a while, Spengler turned to Gandar and warned him that he could face prosecution because he was publishing details about a strike that was illegal. Gandar went completely cold and firmly told him that we had a responsibility to the public and that, even though he was aware of the laws making "incitement" an offense, he intended to continue publishing essential information so that people would not be caught unawares about whatever might happen on May 29th.

Spengler was clearly unhappy about our noncompliance. He left, which was a relief since he had neglected to ask me one very basic question: did I write reports derived from anonymous telephone calls? Had he thought to ask that, I would have been hard pressed to think up a credible answer.

In the predawn hours of Monday, May 29th, I stayed in the office, monitoring the reports coming in from the townships and around the country. Until then I had always gone into the townships in times of unrest, usually in the company of a photographer. I was painfully aware that if violence erupted, the *Mail* would be no one's friend. One of the *Mail* photographers carried a revolver and I secretly derived comfort from this when he was my partner, even though I knew that it would be of no practical protection when surrounded by a mob. The police did not want us around and could not be expected to help should we land in trouble. So I reacted with relief to being told to work from my desk because of my overall knowledge.

While I was trying to assess what was going on the paper was rushing ahead toward producing a special edition, to go on the streets as soon after eight A.M. as possible.

Information and statements were flooding in, and amid the rush a splash report was cobbled together that relied on statements issued by the city's Non-European Affairs Department and the police chiefs. These, predictably, said that the strike was a flop. It wasn't, and our report was inaccurate.

The *Rand Daily Mail*'s standing was so high that our negative front page undoubtedly helped to dissuade many people from taking part in the strike. Word of the *Mail*'s report must have spread rapidly among people scared about what to do that day. Even before the *Mail*'s report appeared, the popular response did not match Mandela's hopes; however, the turnout was significant, involving almost 50 percent of people in Johannesburg's townships, although far fewer in other cities.

The stay-at-home had been intended as mass, nonviolent action by people who had no vote, and no other means to register their anger. Yet the government had thrown its vast resources into destroying the strike call. In advance of the event the government hounded the leaders, mobilized troops, and sent them through townships. It carried out mass arrests, and in concert with employers, gave black workers dire warnings that if they failed to go to work, they faced retribution through immediate dismissal and, twisting the knife for some, threatened the official punishment of "endorsement out"—eviction from the cities into rural starvation.

The pressure on workers was a prime reason why the strike call had not enjoyed wider support, I wrote in the next day's *Mail*. An increasingly common attitude was "What can we do against the government?"

That is why Mandela was in a quieter mood when he phoned that night, still underground, hunted by the police, but as relaxed and friendly as ever. I asked how he was, and in the note I later put through to Gandar, I reported him as saying, "I am not feeling as I would otherwise, but we must remember a number of things. The government had to mobilize the entire military and police forces to deal with the situation, and this alone is a measure of our strength." He went on: "The people did not respond to the stay-at-home to the extent to which we expected them to do. We are not disheartened. This is not the end of the matter. We have learned our lesson. Next time we will not be caught napping. It raises a very serious matter—whether we can continue talking peace and nonviolence in the face of the way the government responds to such a policy, if they deal with what is patently a nonviolent protest by show of force."

He was sending out orders for the strike to continue for the planned three days, he said, and on the "same basis"—in other words, nonviolence was to be maintained. My questioning him on this issue clearly caused him to think further, because he phoned again an hour later. He said he had terminated our earlier conversation because he had had to flee from the public phone booth. I thought it more likely that he wanted to clarify the nonviolence point, and indeed he gave me a more considered comment, which was an historical watershed as his first public espousal of violent struggle: "The events of today and the reactions of the authorities closes a chapter insofar as our methods of political action are concerned. I don't think, speaking for myself, that I can continue speaking peace and nonviolence in the light of the methods adopted by the government to suppress our peaceful protest. The setback will not in any way deter us. The grievances against which the people are protesting still remain, and we will continue struggling to remove these grievances. I want to stress that it is futile to continue talking peace in the light of the show of force and intimidation put out by the government."

The strike fizzled out—Mandela called it off on the second day—but within a month he sat down with other leaders of the ANC, the Congress Alliance, and the Communist Party and argued that violent opposition could not be avoided. They created Umkhonto weSizwe (Spear of the Nation), to undertake military action. Mandela was appointed commander.

Mandela slipped out of the country at the start of 1962 and went traveling in Africa and Britain to drum up support for Umkhonto and to undergo military training. He returned to South Africa eight months later and was arrested soon after while traveling near the town of Howick in Natal. There is no certainty about who tipped off the police as to where to find him. He was jailed for having left the country illegally—which proved but a prelude to the life imprisonment, which came two years later.

Luthuli was present at the meetings in which they agreed on violence, but judging from what transpired in subsequent months, this intensely honest man seemed to have blanked it out of his mind. In October the Nobel committee in Oslo announced that he was the recipient of the Peace Prize. In a profile I wrote of him, I concluded that his tragedy was that the government "still refuses to accord him any recognition; and many of his followers, who do not have his idealism and his Christian devotion, are increasingly turning away from him as they see that he cannot bring material help to his people."

When this was published on October 30th, I had no idea that the switch to violence had already been agreed. Nor did I know it when I went to visit Luthuli—although banned for the past nearly three years, he could still be quoted at that stage—and asked him to answer the question: How could blacks, restricted and harried by the laws of the country, still legally express opposition to government policy?

Luthuli's uncompromising reply was published on November 14th:

Africans dare not forsake the oath of nonviolence. To do so would lead to disaster both for themselves and for South Africa... [W]e shall still continue to exert pressure through nonviolent means. It will continue to be the legitimate kind of pressure used all over the world.

In his acceptance speech at the award ceremony in December—the government, although seething with rage, deferred to world opinion and allowed him to attend—Luthuli echoed the same theme. Through all the years of cruel treatment suffered by blacks, he said, "our people, with few exceptions, have remained nonviolent" and they would continue along their "chosen path of disciplined resistance."

Shortly after lunch on December 15th, Ernie Wentzel phoned me at the *Mail*, his voice choked with laughter. "Come uptown right away," he said. "I've just seen something very funny." I met him on the corner of Eloff and Market streets, in the heart of the city, and he told me that he had been walking there when a small car came along with black smoke pouring out from inside. It stopped and he recognized Ben Turok, the secretary of the Congress of Democrats (COD).

A small crowd gathered, and two traffic officers approached Turok. He told them that firecrackers had exploded inside the car. Wentzel saw Turok kick something out of the car, roll up the window, and zoom away, his face pressed up against the windscreen in the smoke-filled car. Wentzel and I looked around, and in the middle of Market Street, in the leftover tracks of the trams that Johannesburg once had, we found small pieces of a clear plastic.

We surmised that Turok had been carrying a smoke bomb that had gone wrong. Back at the office I wrote a three-sentence story about this amusing incident, without naming Turok. That night, out of sheer devilment, an Afrikaner colleague phoned Turok at home and, deepening his accent, asked him, "Mr. Turok, where were you between one and two P.M. today?"

Turok was only too clearly a worried man and demanded to know who was phoning him. We taped the conversation and played it several times, hooting with laughter. We thought we were having some harmless fun.

Reality came the next day, on December 16th, when Umkhonto weSizwe's first bombs went off around the country. We realized that we were into something far bigger and more serious than we had bargained for. The car incident took on fresh meaning: Turok, we now surmised, must have been carrying acid that, when mixed with other chemicals, would make an explosive. The acid must have been in a plastic jar, and lying on the back floor on a hot summer's day probably heated up, letting off the thick smoke that Wentzel had seen. Turok must have kicked the jar out of the car, hence the pieces of plastic in the street.

We hurriedly erased the tape and waited apprehensively in case the police had been bugging the phones and descended on us. To our relief nothing happened, and the incident disappeared amid the consternation of the country waking up to the fact that the ANC had turned to violent protest.

Turok and I dealt with each other regularly because he was part of my beat, but we did not like each other. In due course he set off a real bomb—timed to go off at night inside a divorce court for blacks—was caught, and was jailed for three years. When he was released, friends urged me to see him. I did, and either prison had improved him or I had changed, for I found that I liked him. He went into exile, returned to South Africa in another era, and became an MP for the ANC.

"Heresy? Did you say you've been charged with heresy?"

I was sitting with Albert Geyser at his home in Pretoria. He was professor of New Testament Theology at the university there and my mind was trying to catch up with what I had just heard. Heresy was medieval, evoking the image of people burned at the stake. But now, in October 1961, Geyser was telling me that he had just been served the charge sheet by the Nederduitsch Hervormde Kerk, one of the three Afrikaans churches.

Religion was in turmoil: the Afrikaans churches were under challenge by the world religious community and South Africa's English-language churches because of their support for apartheid. I was covering the struggles: religion, like everything else in South Africa, was intertwined with politics and even more so because "the Almighty" was used by all shades of opinion to justify their policies.

Chapter 8

The Afrikaans churches, all sternly Calvinist, were closely aligned with the National Party. Their ministers— the *dominee* or *predikant*—were respected leaders in parishes up and down the country. They were crucial in keeping Afrikaners together and forging their political purpose.

During the Anglo-Boer War in 1901, before becoming the *Mail*'s first editor, Edgar Wallace evoked the tone of their sermons in a dispatch to the *Daily Mail* in London:

> The predikant prayed with fervor—with head uplifted, with hands clasping and unclasping in agony of spirit. In his prayers he did not refer by name to the Boer Republics; he simply asked for Divine intervention for the Lord's chosen. He did not speak of England; he said Philistines and

Amalekites. He did not refer directly to Sir Alfred Milner nor to Mr. Chamberlain [the British leaders], but with all the passion he could command he called for vengeance on the false counselors who had initiated the persecution of the people of the land.

Already in the 1950s the Afrikaans churches were being challenged by the World Council of Churches to justify their belief that apartheid could be defended on biblical grounds. The Nederduitsch Hervormde Kerk believed it did. Article 3 of its Church Law had always barred blacks, coloreds, and Asians from membership. The church appointed a two-man commission to prepare its case, but one commissioner, the promising young theologian and dominee, Albert Geyser, reported to a meeting of ministers that apartheid was contrary to the Bible, and pandemonium broke out. In 1960, Geyser took a leading part in writing *Delayed Action*, a book in which eleven theologians from the Afrikaans churches condemned race discrimination and called for a new outlook in racial attitudes. The book was a milestone, and the *Mail* had broken the story because I had been given an advance copy.

At the end of 1960 the World Council of Churches held a Consultation in Johannesburg to bridge the widening gap between the churches within Africa over color policy. The Consultation denounced apartheid, leading to the end of the Afrikaans churches' links with the World Council.

Alan Paton was an Anglican lay representative at the Consultation. I wanted a statement from him as leader of the Liberal Party about a current incident of government abuse of power and went to see him at the meeting, held at Wits. "Let's go to my room and write it," he said. I was an admirer of Paton's books, and this was an exciting chance to watch him at work. I stood next to him as he wrote out a short statement of protest, saying the words aloud as he went along. It seemed simple, almost trite, and I was disappointed. I went to my office to type it out, and suddenly realized the strength of what Paton had given me. I marveled at his ability to use everyday language to bring alive hoary old subjects such as liberty and the freedom of the individual. Thereafter, I often contacted Paton for statements and always had the same experience.

Geyser showed me the charge sheet, which ran to thirteen pages and was written in a mixture of Afrikaans, English, Latin, Hebrew, and Greek. The complaint had been lodged by three of his theology students, who had been put up to using their notes of Geyser's comments in classes as well as his answers to their staged questions. One of the charges derived from his interpretation of the Greek word *agape* ("love"), a common concept in religion. He was accused of committing heresy because he had argued that agape crossed racial lines. He was also charged with failing to obey a church order prohibiting criticism of its laws and decisions by telling his class that apartheid had no biblical basis, and with conveying an invitation to his students to meet Roman Catholic seminary students for a friendly discussion.

To protect Geyser, I could not reveal that I had actually seen the charge sheet. I wrote up the bare bones of the heresy accusations and that evening phoned the moderator of the church, the Reverend A.J.G. Oosthuizen, to put the seal on the story. He denied any knowledge of the charges. "Is it conceivable that heresy charges could be brought against a minister of your church without you, as moderator, knowing about it?" I asked incredulously. He assured me it could not happen. If I had not seen the charge sheet only hours before, I might have believed him, so calm and definite was he. Oosthuizen proved to be the first in a line of priests who destroyed my innocent faith in the purity of men of the cloth.

Geyser was duly hauled before a church court to face the penalties of defrocking and expulsion. Oosthuizen was the chairman. Everyone who took part was sworn to secrecy, but the court leaked like a sieve, and we published near-daily reports about the proceedings. The court found Geyser guilty and defrocked him, but he appealed to the secular courts, which overturned the church's finding. He quit the church and went to teach theology at Wits.

Geyser was not a worldly man, but he demonstrated awesome intellectual courage and emotional strength in reexamining the religious ideology in which his family was steeped. His family had come to South Africa from Holland in 1752. His great-grandfather and grandfather were among the nineteenth-century founding members of the Nederduitsch Hervormde Kerk, and his entire family was closely involved with Afrikaner nationalism. As a *dominee* and university professor, he was among the elite in Afrikanerdom, and yet he walked away from it after concluding that apartheid was non-Christian. He and his family paid a heavy price because they were driven out of the world they inhabited, restricted as it was, and were ostracized and despised, with only a few friends and a tiny handful of colleagues standing by them.

Though there was a small contingent of Afrikaans ministers who followed their conscience, ranking among South Africa's bravest of the brave, changes in the Afrikaans churches did not come about for another twenty years, and only when apartheid rule was going into decline.

South Africa's English churches were generally opposed to apartheid, though the extent of their opposition varied. However well-intentioned their leaders and pronouncements were, none of it seemed to have much effect on the mass of white adherents who, year by year, gave greater support to Nationalist apartheid. The more church leaders opposed apartheid, the more they were rejected by their white congregants— chief contributors to church funds—while also drawing government ire. The government felt that priests should stay out of politics. Because so many of South Africa's high-profile archbishops and bishops from the Anglican Church came from Britain, they were viewed as outsiders.

In trying to capture some of the spirit of the times, I did seven question-and-answer interviews in 1963 with religious leaders, most notably with Denis Hurley, the Roman Catholic archbishop of Durban, who was especially outspoken in criticizing South African lip service to Christianity. The *Mail* published the series as a booklet, *The Church and the Race Problem*, with an additional interview by the *Mail*'s political correspondent with Dr. F. E. O'Brien Geldenhuys of the largest Afrikaans church, the Nederduitse Gereformeerde Kerk (Dutch Reformed Church), which had its "mother church" for whites and three separate "daughter churches" for blacks, coloreds, and Asians. Asked whether "nonwhite" members ever attended "white" services, Geldenhuys replied, "Yes, at funerals, for example, the trusted servants of the deceased often attend the service in the European church."

The next year, I went to Zambia (then Northern Rhodesia) to cover a Consultation at the Mindolo Ecumenical Foundation held by the World Council of Churches and South Africans to discuss the responsibilities of Christians in dealing with racial problems. The meeting was held behind closed doors, so I sat outside in the sun, the only journalist there, and friends came and told me about the discussions. The church people in attendance were haunted by the memory of Dietrich Bonhoeffer, the German pastor who opposed Hitler and was murdered only weeks before the Nazi capitulation in May 1945. Bonhoeffer posited a question that clearly alluded to Hitler: If a pastor saw a madman driving down the road and killing people, did he do enough to discharge his responsibility by warning people to get out of the way, or must he try to grab hold of the driver and get rid of him by force? Leading on from this, the question at the Consultation arose: If blacks were denied the vote in South Africa and could not effect change, and if they were denied recourse to nonviolent protest and could not effect change, what alternative was open to them but violence?

The Mindolo Consultation did not reach a definitive conclusion. Instead it left violence to the individual Christian's conscience. The individual was warned that he or she must be fully aware of the implications and the danger of his or her actions. This was a significant, if cautious, shift in Christian thinking because until then nonviolence had been a creed. However, there was no unanimity and some delegates, including South Africans, dissociated themselves from any suggestion that industrial disruption, international intervention or internal violence were permissible in order to secure social justice.

As white rule in South Africa grew more repressive, there was greater need to debate the philosophical, religious and practical pros and cons of violence. But this could not be done because it was a forbidden area with reporting and discussion severely limited by law. The enforced silence did not, however, halt the steady increase in violent opposition.

A decade earlier Father Trevor Huddleston of the Anglican Church had been the epitome of a priest who meddled to good purpose by standing up to the government in defense of his black flock in Sophiatown. His book, *Naught for Your Comfort*, was an early wake-up call about apartheid, and I was one of those profoundly influenced by it. And even when he was no longer in South Africa—his church was embarrassed about him and pulled him out—he became a leading force in the anti-apartheid movement in Britain. Ambrose Reeves was brave and visionary while in Johannesburg as the Anglican bishop in uniting opposition against the pass laws and poverty wages, but destroyed himself by fleeing in 1960. And during the late 1960s and early 1970s the city's Anglican dean, the British-born the Very Reverend Gonville Aubrey ffrench-Beytagh used money sent to him by supporters in Britain to help political prisoners and their families. I was among those who dispensed his aid for Robert Sobukwe on Robben Island. The dean did so much for so many people that the government raided his home and planted illegal Communist Party and ANC leaflets in a cupboard. He was found guilty and sentenced to the five years' minimum jailing of the Terrorism Act but was acquitted on appeal and deported to Britain.

I was unwittingly caught up as a result of my financial connection with the dean. Hunting for evidence against him, the police raided the homes of several people around the country. They came to my apartment at 6:30 A.M. with a search warrant. I had been on night duty at the *Mail* and had returned home only a few hours earlier. I stumbled into my study where my research papers were kept, and on top of the six-foot-high pile lay notes from my interview with Johannesburg lawyer and former ANC Youth League leader Godfrey Pitje. He was banned and I immediately realized he could face prosecution for giving me a statement for publication. I panicked at the prospect of landing him in serious trouble, and hid the papers before handing over all the other documents.

Security policemen poured in. For eight hours nine of them methodically searched the apartment. Knowing what had been done to the dean, I was more concerned about what the police might plant on me than what they might remove. I fought to have a lawyer present to check what they were seizing.

My wife, Anne, and I had been married for only a few months and she was not yet accustomed to dealing with Security policemen. Whereas I wanted polite formality toward them, she was outraged at their intrusion and made her feelings known loudly and clearly. As the raid continued, we moved the Pitje papers ahead of the police. Anne finally dropped them over the balcony into the flower bed below. I went onto the balcony and gestured to a cluster of journalists, sent to report the raid, to remove the papers. Robert Botha, formerly a photographer with the *Rand Daily Mail* and then with the *Sunday Express*, did so, returned to his office, and told his colleagues about it. Unfortunately a police informer apparently overheard him. There was a swift police raid and the papers were seized.

Bell, Dewar and Hall, the *Mail*'s lawyers, made representations that I should not be charged because I was using the papers to prepare the outline for a doctoral application at Wits. The Security Police replied that they were determined to prosecute me because Anne had "insulted" them during the raid. Among the papers they had seized were three issues of the South African left-wing *Guardian* newspaper, which had been banned twenty-five years before. This drew a charge under the Suppression of Communism Act. They also accused me of stealing my Pitje papers from them; this "theft" charge was an attempt to smear me because they and I both knew the papers had never been in their possession. During the trial a Security policeman testified that they had seized the papers in the apartment. I could not give evidence about this because

I would have had to implicate Anne. When the tea break came, I walked up to a clump of policemen outside the court and angrily told the witness, "You lied under oath to get me convicted." He drew himself up and responded, "We will stop at nothing to get you."

There was a postscript to the court case. To "prove" that the Pitje papers had been in their possession, the police initialed each page, as they had done with all the papers they seized. Robert Botha was a witness for the prosecution, but was asked by my lawyer, Wentzel, if the papers looked the same as those he had picked up in the flower bed. He replied that the initials in the top right-hand corner were not there when he saw the papers originally. Despite Botha's evidence on this vital point, I was found guilty on both counts. The prosecutor spoke darkly about the need for imprisonment because I had "again deliberately defied the authority of the State," but a Wits lecturer, Nome Pines, testified about my academic status and I got away with a suspended sentence of six months. We went on appeal, and the theft conviction was quashed on the technical grounds that the search warrant did not cover the Pitje papers.

The Suppression of Communism Act conviction remained, however, and I took it to the Appeal Court. After the hearing by five judges, Wentzel felt we had a reasonable chance, as at least two of the judges seemed to favor us, but the conviction was confirmed, 5–0. Wentzel told me the judgment made no logical sense. The only explanation he could offer was that the judges were not willing to breach the laws against possession of banned material. So there I was: a "statutory Communist," despite my vehement anti-Communism.

When I first visited Israel, in 1976, I went to Yad Vashem, the Holocaust memorial museum in Jerusalem. A few paces inside the entrance was a glass case containing a court register from Germany of the 1930s: the two open pages listed the names of German Jews and non-Jews who had had sexual relations and been found guilty of "Rassenschande," racial disgrace. It was an exact analogy with the hounding and prosecution at home under the Immorality Act of whites and blacks who went to bed together. How could any Jew from South Africa looking at that court register not be stirred to vehement rejection of racist apartheid?

It wasn't as straightforward as that. For many years, hardly a single Jew in South Africa openly supported the Afrikaner Nationalists—not surprising in light of their pro-Nazi record. There was the story of the

Nationalists in their early years in power holding a public meeting in the Zionist Hall in Cape Town and putting a token Jewish man on the platform. The largely Jewish audience was restless at the sight of him, and someone shouted, "When you were circumcised, the wrong piece was thrown away!"

Gradually a few Jews publicly allied themselves with the Nationalists, but the number was never large. There was talk of big businessmen donating money to the Nationalists by way of "insurance." Of course individual Jews, like other whites, did shift to voting for the government be it out of fear, or belief. But more significantly, many influential Jews consistently gave effective help to the Nationalists. This arose from the twin-track existence of the 120,000 Jews of the time (immigration has reduced the number to 60,000–70,000). On the one hand, Jews were strongly represented out of all proportion to their numbers in commerce and industry, and were thus often in the front line in the exploitation of black workers. At the least, their compliance and cooperation with the system helped to prop up Nationalist rule. Some, like the Frame empire—in its day said to be the world's biggest manufacturer of blankets—had an unsavory name during the 1970s for its atrocious pay and work conditions. But Jews were also strongly represented, again out of proportion to their numbers, in the professions of law and medicine, and in liberal and left-wing political organizations, and played an exceptional role as leaders in attacks on apartheid and in defending and helping victims.

The prominent Jewish presence in political opposition drew out the anti-Semitism lurking beneath the Afrikaner surface. Helen Suzman was taunted in parliament as a Jew, and Afrikaans newspaper cartoonists took their cue from Nazi times and drew caricatures of her with a large hooked nose and heavily bejeweled fingers. For unknown reasons, the Security Police seemed to believe that Ernie Wentzel was Jewish and, on the occasions that they arrested him, began interrogation by cursing him in lurid anti-Semitic terms. From what I could see, the more that Jews moved to the left, the less they adhered to their Jewishness, but that did not deter the Nationalists from hating Joe Slovo, the Communist leader then in exile, not only as the devil incarnate, but as a Jewish devil.

The Jewish community was supposed to be represented by the South African Board of Jewish Deputies, which protested that it could not get involved in "politics." Every now and again I had contact with the board when I was invited to a meeting of leaders to hear their anxieties about the future of the community should black majority rule eventually prevail. Each time I urged them to start making friends across the color line. A year or so later, I would again be asked to come to a meeting. It happened about three times. Only towards the end of the 1980s did the community start to make genuine attempts to mend fences. They were held back over the years by the fear of anti-Semitic action. I thought this was exaggerated because the Nationalists could not afford to put their prejudices into action: they dared not divide the white group.

Zionist pride was strong, and the community raised a lot of money each year for local Jewish and Israeli causes. The Nationalists used the foreign exchange regulations to keep the Jewish community in line by controlling how much money could be sent to Israel each year. This went even further because pressure from the community helped to ensure that Israel regularly abstained on anti-apartheid votes at the United Nations. The community was also hypersensitive about the way that Israel was portrayed: a legitimate headline in the *Mail* read "Israel dithers" (it was to do with some issue at the U.N.) but was enough to draw a complaint to the editor from local Jewish leaders. They were not assuaged when told that a "nice Jewish boy" (me) had written it.

The community might have offered more resistance had it been given more of an ethical lead by its rabbis. A few did speak out, and some grew so much at odds with their congregants that they quit, or if they were immigrants, were pushed out of the country by the government. But most played it safe and kept silent. I had a traumatic personal experience of this. I was a member of the Oxford Orthodox synagogue in Johannesburg and its American-born Rabbi Norman Bernhard was both my religious counsellor and a treasured friend. Suddenly, with no word of explanation, he stopped seeing me. Some months later, in a chance encounter, he told me what had happened: the government had withdrawn the permit entitling him to work in South Africa and the congregation's leaders had rushed to Pretoria to ask about it. They were told it was because of his sermons against apartheid and his friendship with me. Bernhard's permit was reinstated. I never saw him again but in recent years he has constantly spoken of his fight against apartheid.

The Orthodox Chief Rabbi Bernard Casper, an import from Britain, presided at the Great Synagogue in Johannesburg until the late-1980s. I listened to scores of his sermons and never once did I hear him refer to the South African racial situation. Never once did I hear him say a word about racism, critical or otherwise, or express distress or sympathy about the lot of black people. Very occasionally, in sermonizing about the meaning of a biblical or rabbinical text, he would seem to be inching towards dealing with the realities outside the synagogue, and then would say, "But I must not speak about politics," and move away. He finally changed.

In August 1985, banks in the United States refused to roll over loans for South Africa. The crisis that followed set in train events that some years later brought the Nationalists to understand that their rule was doomed. A few weeks after the banks' action, for the first time I heard Casper speak about South Africa in a sermon. He urged his congregants who had friends or business contacts in the United States to tell them to do all they could to end sanctions—because, he explained, of the suffering it was causing among the country's poor deprived black people.

Desmond Tutu is the most well known of all South African religious leaders. He did more than any single churchman to take the lead in bringing apartheid to an end. And when it did collapse he walked away from the political scene, although he continued to raise his moral voice in the new South Africa by criticizing some ANC cabinet ministers for "hopping aboard the gravy train" and by saying it was "monstrous" that South African weapons were used in the tribal slaughter in Rwanda.

Tutu's rise to prominence had begun in earnest in 1978, when he was appointed general secretary of the South African Council of Churches. We were friends and met once in a while over lunch at a restaurant to share ideas. He always bowed his head and said grace, and if I sometimes forgot my manners and picked up a bread roll before he had done so, there would be a swift reproving flash of his eyes.

John Rees was Tutu's immediate predecessor as general secretary of the South African Council of Churches and the most committed Christian layperson I have ever known. I first brushed up against Rees in the late 1950s when I was a young reporter and he was a "location superintendent" of the city's Non-European Affairs Department in charge of Mofolo in Soweto. He was unlike the other superintendents I was meeting. Each of them controlled the lives of many thousands of black people, and they were arrogant and unfeeling in exercising their power. Rees was discernibly different. He was also English-speaking, which made him even more unusual in that setting. He and I did not initially take to each other. Rees did not like an eager young reporter prying around his bureaucratic patch and stirring things up, and I found him prickly and uncooperative. Our ways parted until years later I noticed that a John Rees had become general secretary of the Council of

Churches. It couldn't be the same man, I thought; location superintendents were incapable of making such a leap in life. Finally we met, and I discovered he was in fact the same John Rees. As our friendship developed, I came to realize that it was his devout Methodism and his drive to apply it to his everyday life that had taken him into his work in Soweto.

Eventually Rees and I shared a personal trust through a project that we jointly conceived and developed and which, had it come off, might have made a substantial contribution to peaceful change. As we got to know each other we found that we were each desperately concerned about the hopelessness so prevalent in South Africa in the 1970s and the lack of contact between people of opposing viewpoints. We believed that an entirely fresh approach was needed and that instead of trying to apply known solutions, we should reverse the process and start with South Africa as it was and seek to develop unique ways to meet its needs. We proposed a structure of twenty-five think-tanks, each of which would consist of five people—a rough microcosm of the country's people—who would spend time together on specific topics with an infusion of a small number of experts brought in from abroad. There were no boundaries and the whole point of the project was that we did not know where it would lead. Non-violence was the only principle.

We called it the "Search for Alternatives," and raised seed money from the Carnegie Corporation of New York and the Johnson Foundation in the U.S. We opened an office in a building across the street from the *Rand Daily Mail.* Rees worked fulltime on the project. At an early stage, we took the decision that hostility and suspicion were so rife that we had to avoid publicity like the plague; many people would only be willing to meet across the color and political lines if they were reasonably sure that it would remain secret. We achieved this by going to the editors of major newspapers to tell them what we were doing and inviting them to participate on a basis of confidentiality. We thought it best also to tell the government what we were doing on the premise that they would in any event learn about it and we wanted to show that we had nothing to hide. I went to see a cabinet minister, Piet Koornhof. Rees and I also met Johan Coetzee, who was then head of the Security Police, and we had a surreal discussion because we knew that we were being watched (we had evidence of surreptitious searches of our office), and yet we all had to pretend (including Coetzee) that this was the first time that he had heard what we were doing. He wished us well and said he would not interfere with us as long as we did not contravene any laws.

Rees did the main contact work around the country and reported enthusiasm for the project. Those who were initially skeptical quickly changed their minds when he indicated who was already on board. We set about commissioning position papers as the basis for discussions, on the constitution, law, education and social welfare. Over months, we built up a list of over one hundred people willing to participate. We believed it was the broadest spectrum of South Africans that had ever agreed to come together. The only people who stayed out were extreme right-wing Afrikaners. Otherwise every color and economic interest group was represented, even the tough and radical young men in the townships. The notable exception whom we decided to leave out at that stage were the exiled movements; we thought we would first establish trust and contact inside the country before taking the next step. That proved a fatal error, although given the circumstances of the time it was probably unavoidable.

The Search was going well but we were still negotiating the financing from abroad, from the United States and West Germany, when the *Citizen*, the right-wing government newspaper in Johannesburg, ran a smear story saying that the Search was a C.I.A. project. Rees and I realized that someone behind the scenes had given us the thumbs-down and this was the method being used to destroy us. A project as fragile as the Search for Alternatives could not survive this sort of mudslinging. The *Citizen* report was untrue, but it achieved what it was intended to do. We started losing our Afrikaner support. We pushed ahead, but a German foundation with which we were negotiating, and one that seemed on the brink of putting in several hundred thousand rand, said no because the anti-apartheid movement abroad criticized the Search as white and liberal.

We spent five years pursuing the project until we finally gave up. The Search was ahead of its time. But perhaps some of the contacts we made and the bridges we created helped to pave the way for the talks which began behind the scenes only a few years later and which culminated in the coming of democracy.

June 1976 was the turning point for South Africa. Although no one could realize it then, it was the beginning of the end for white rule. As school-children took to the streets in protests, at least six hundred by official claim, and certainly many more, were killed by the police, others were maimed, and thousands were detained. The Council of Churches launched the Asingeni Fund, and Rees took the lead in raising millions of rand from abroad to ease the suffering and to ensure aid and legal representation for families of people shot or arrested. That angered the government, yet there was even more to it than met the eye because Rees used his discretionary powers to channel money to people who were defying apartheid laws. Those payments were not entered in the books. They couldn't be because they would have imperiled both the recipients and Rees, as for example the money he gave to black-consciousness leader Steve Biko to enable him to move around the country to continue his political work even though he was banned. Rees told me he accepted the fact that one day he might be called to account for the money he had secretly disbursed and would not feel able to disclose the details. He was prepared to accept the consequences, whatever they might be.

That is exactly what happened in 1983. Rees was charged with fraud, alternatively theft, concerning aid moneys. It began when Eugene Roelofse, the Council of Churches' ombudsman who dealt with consumer affairs in general, complained about poor bookkeeping on the part of the Council. This led to a police investigation and the prosecution, unsuccessfully, of a bookkeeper. While the Council moved to set up its own commission of inquiry, the government seized its chance to get into the Council's affairs and appointed a judicial commission of inquiry, which went on to hear evidence about the Council's support for the banned and exiled ANC. The unfolding investigations created some tension at the *Mail* because of the attention that Roelofse was drawing. I did not think that we should dig too deeply into the Council of Churches, because I felt Roelofse was a loose cannon. The crime reporter Mervyn Rees (not related to John Rees) disagreed, and thought we had a duty to pursue the story, and did so.

The issue illustrated a dilemma in which we found ourselves from time to time: to what extent should we attack our few friends, the reduced and embattled elements in the antiapartheid camp? At first sight it seemed that we should never hold back, that it was our duty to investigate and report without fear or favor. In practice, however, total purity of purpose was not always possible.

The dilemma presented itself, at its crudest level, in a reporter coming across a banned person at a social party: the law was being broken and there was some public interest to be served in showing that the banning law was being contravened. But it was unthinkable to publish such a story. To do so would have been to act as a police informer. Indeed one of the nagging anxieties of our reporters who dealt with the political scene was to avoid being forced into court to testify against people who broke their banning orders. The Johannesburg flatland suburb of Hillbrow was another example: although reserved for whites in terms of the Group Areas Act, by the early 1980s, large numbers of coloreds and Asians were living there illegally because they could not find housing in their assigned segregated suburbs. Though it was widely known, and made for an interesting story because it exposed the government's difficulties in enforcing its racial ideology, we could not touch it because we did not want to precipitate official action.

In regard to the Council of Churches, I was worried about Roelofse. I was not protecting John Rees from the bookkeeping mess, which in fact had occurred after he ended his tenure as general secretary. But knowing that John Rees had disbursed Asingeni relief funds in ways that he could not account for was the issue on my mind, and I thought that Roelofse was blindly serving up Rees and the Council of Churches to the government, in the process doing grave damage to apartheid victims who needed aid. The government, of course, was happy about the propaganda value of embarrassing the Council of Churches and prosecuting a high-profile person involved in bringing in cash from abroad. Tutu was one of the witnesses called by the prosecution, and testified in court about a loan that Rees had advanced to him to buy a house. Inexplicably the Council was obstructive when Rees sought access to information for his own defense, his lawyer told me.

During Rees's trial I went to the Supreme Court several times as a way of demonstrating support for him. I happened to meet the presiding judge, Richard Goldstone, at an evening wine festival organized by the *Rand Daily Mail*. I knew him from his student days at Wits. As we stood aside from the crowd, he said he had seen me in court and guessed that I was a friend of Rees, and went on: "I know that he is innocent, I am sure of it, but on the evidence before me I shall have no option but to convict him. He is in the witness box and tomorrow is the critical day. If he provides the evidence I need, then I will acquit him, otherwise I must find him guilty."

It was an agonized admission, all the more intense because it was said in a quiet voice amid the cheerful hubbub of the crowd of wine lovers. I wondered whether I should go to see Rees that night and tell him how vital the next day would be, but decided against it. I felt I had to treat Goldstone's disclosure as a personal confidentiality and, knowing Rees, I had no doubt that he had drawn a line in his mind and conscience about what information he was prepared to yield and he would not go beyond it.

Rees did not provide the evidence the judge needed, and was found guilty and sentenced to a heavy fine. After the trauma of his trial Rees poured his energy into a job as director of a home for the mentally retarded. By law it was only for whites, so he raised the funds to build a home for blacks in Soweto. He ran a soup kitchen for the aged, and was heavily engaged in devising schemes for black empowerment in business and in planning mass housing. But early in 1994 he was diagnosed with leukemia, and no amount of treatment was able to save him. In mid September, as death approached, he wrote to several of those who had been involved in his criminal prosecution. A copy of his letter to Judge Goldstone was sent to me. By then, Goldstone had distinguished himself by investigating and exposing government-inspired murders in South Africa and was also chief prosecutor of Bosnian war crimes at the International Court of Justice in The Hague.

By the time this letter reaches you, I will be dead and buried and have wanted to write to you for a long time, firstly because I am a great admirer of the work that you have achieved for South Africa... I have lived a very full life and done everything that I have ever wanted to do for my fellow human beings. Interestingly enough just out of curiosity I tried to calculate how much money I had raised for projects and other ventures and it is well over R50 million, much of that was achieved since the case.

Turning to the case for a moment, it must have been a puzzling matter for you, a seeming fool who has lived in the same house for thirty-three years, had no aspiration other than that to bring up a family in a deeply Christian manner and suddenly be accused of pinching R256,000 out of the millions that he handled. I am grateful you never sent me to jail—it was a possibility.

Just in case you ever had any lingering doubt, I would like you to know that I never touched one lousy penny of the money I was accused of pinching and the secret of how and to whom I managed to get the money will go to the grave with me. Suffice it to say that the majority of people that I helped hold very high office today and are known to you and me personally.

John Rees died a month later, at the age of fifty-seven.

The scope of my beat, covering black existence, grew apace, spreading from the Johannesburg area to the rural "reserves" for blacks, plus the three territories then under British colonial rule that adjoined South Africa. Dictated by my need to cast a wider net and to multiply my sources of information, I developed a network of sources among blacks who were either already journalists but having problems getting jobs or who aspired to become journalists, paying them the *Mail's* money for tip-offs to stories. We paid only paltry amounts, but it was a start. Gandar agreed to give me my own byline, and starting in 1960 I wrote under the proud new title of African affairs reporter.

Reporting the territories, which were in the early stages of nationalism and striving for independence, was logistically complicated: they were in opposite directions, west, east, and south of Johannesburg. To get to the bor-

Chapter 9

ders, it was a four-to six-hour drive along roads that were only partly tarred. Inside Bechuanaland the corrugations in the 310-mile (500 km) south-north dirt road were smoothed now and again by tying together a clump of thorn trees and having a tractor haul them along, raising a huge trail of choking dust. You either coasted along behind it at walking pace for up to thirty miles (50 km), baking in the sun, or did a dangerous pass through the dust, praying that another car wasn't coming toward you in the near-zero visibility.

The hotel (for whites only) in Lobatse, the main but tiny town in the south, served excellent food, with beef from local herds. Its rooms, however, were infested with bugs brought in from the interior. I made a point of charging extravagant amounts to my expense account for antibug creams and fumigants, daring the *Mail*'s accountants to question me, but they never did.

The legislative council of Bechuanaland met in the then-capital, Mafeking—because of a quirk of history, it was a short distance inside South Africa—and I covered its early sessions. Sitting on a front bench was Dr. S. M. Molema, a local medical doctor. A decade earlier he had been treasurer-general of the ANC, and we spent many hours talking about that era. Sharing the bench with him was a white farmer from Bechuanaland, Hendrik van Gass. It was a unique sight: whites and blacks simply did not sit next to each other like that, let alone be so obviously friendly, not in South Africa or Bechuanaland.

When a session ended, I caught the two of them as they were leaving the chamber, and Molema introduced me to van Gass. I told them how amazed I was to see the two of them together. Van Gass said he was an Afrikaner and a Nationalist from South Africa, but had come to Bechuanaland and had done well. He owned a large farm and this was a different country from across the border, and color did not matter, and everyone had to work together to make it prosper.

Molema stood by, smiling benignly. When he left, I went on talking to van Gass, telling him again how strange and moving it was to come from South Africa and see him and Molema so friendly with each other. Van Gass looked around to make sure that no one was within earshot and whispered to me, "*Ja, maar 'n kaffer bly 'n kaffer.*" ("Yes, but a kaffir remains a kaffir."). Kaffir was a term of rank abuse for blacks. I felt like throwing up.

The second British-ruled territory I covered was Basutoland, which became the independent Kingdom of Lesotho in 1966. At an early stage I was granted an interview with Moshoeshoe, the Paramount Chief, a title used by the British (and in South Africa, too) for the chief of chiefs. As I was being ushered into the interview, a colonial official told me that I could address him as "Motlotlehi," which, I understood, was a title coined by officialdom to denote respect. Regardless of its exact meaning, it fell short of "Your Majesty." Britain had a queen, and Basutoland was under her reign, so "Your Highness" and "Your Majesty" were reserved for her. Under no circumstances, the official said, was I to address him with those titles. But I did, because I knew that the Basotho viewed Moshoeshoe as their king, and anyway I was feeling mischievous that day. Every time I peppered my questions with

"Your Highness" or "Your Majesty," I could see the official getting red in the face.

Moshoeshoe set out to be a constitutional monarch but was overwhelmed by the political struggles that followed. His country's poverty makes it reliant on South Africa. The nation held its first independence elections in 1966, and Chief Leabua Jonathan won. He enjoyed support from South Africa; it was never certain exactly what the support was, but at the least a lot of money was given to him for organizing purposes. In return, Leabua curbed the activities of South African liberation movements inside Lesotho. His leading opponent, Ntsu Mokhehle, was a firebrand African nationalist with personal and ideological links to the PAC across the border, formed when he was a student in the 1940s at Fort Hare University College. He was viewed as being antichurch, which did not help him in a country where the Catholic Church exerted strong influence.

In time the Lesotho political scene turned topsy-turvy. Leabua became more and more outspoken against apartheid, for reasons that I never fully understood. It eventually led to his downfall: most of Lesotho's income came from the labor it exported to South Africa, with about one third of wage-earning men working in the gold mines of the Free State, not much more than an hour or two's drive from the capital, Maseru. Whenever South Africa wanted to squeeze Leabua, it would slow down immigration procedures at the border crossings. The queue of Basotho miners wanting to get home for a holiday break or returning to their jobs would rapidly build up; crossing from one country to the other could take days. Leabua, fearful of the miners' anger, would soon come to heel.

Finally the South Africans overdid it: they pushed once too often and too hard, and Leabua was overthrown by his country's tiny military. Mokhehle, meanwhile, had been driven into hiding by Leabua and eventually fled the country. But based in Botswana and Zambia, he could not travel over South Africa to return home. It seems that he did a deal with South Africa and was not only allowed safe passage but was enabled to set up and run the Lesotho Liberation Army. A messy military dictatorship followed Leabua's fall until free elections finally put Mokhehle in the prime minister's office in 1993.

Revelations that emerged in 1996 about South African Security Police undercover activities included details about Mokhehle's links. It was said that his insurgents had been trained at the police undercover headquarters, Vlakplaas, notorious as the headquarters of South Africa's assassins, and that he had also been there. Mokhehle described the reports as "blatant lies."

King Moshoeshoe was an ill-starred monarch. After years of marginalization, the military exiled him to Britain in 1990. He became a prime mover in the Institute for Democracy in Africa, which, as the name indicated, promoted democratic government in the continent. He brought together a small group for a weekend's discussion at an hotel outside London; I was among them and had great pleasure in sitting down next to him at breakfast and saying, "Good morning, Your Majesty." Moshoeshoe was allowed to return to his throne early in 1995 but died in January 1996 when his chauffeur-driven car went off a mountain road.

After being banned, the PAC set up shop in Basutoland. Like the ANC, it, too, turned to violence but went along a different, murderous road through Poqo ("our own" or "pure" in Xhosa, and pronounced *Pawcaw*), an offshoot group that had grown among blacks in the Transkei and in Cape Town townships out of the frustration of the antipass campaign. Poqo had no discernible political philosophy but aimed at overthrowing white rule by killing whites. The PAC's leaders were either in jail or in exile and the organization was rudderless. Its president, Robert Sobukwe, was in prison, first serving a three-year sentence for incitement arising out of the antipass protests, which had resulted in the Sharpeville killings; then, through a special law rushed through parliament soon before his sentence ended and renewed each year, he was kept without trial in virtual solitary confinement in Robben Island Prison for six more years.

The island, a half-hour boat ride from Cape Town harbor, had been used over four centuries successively as a prison, a leper hospital, and an army base. In 1960, with the surge in black resistance, it became the site of a maximum-security prison, holding up to 1,400 men: blacks, coloreds, and Asians, chiefly sentenced political prisoners, with white guards. Nelson Mandela spent eighteen years in a tiny cell there. The island upheld its reputation that no one without a boat could escape alive from the rough shore and freezing water. It was closed in 1991 and later became a popular tourist site, with former political prisoners working as guides. Meanwhile Potlako Leballo, a fiery member of the PAC national executive, was released from prison in August 1962, went to Maseru and took over as acting president. A few months later Poqo began to attack whites: five were killed in the bloodiest episode at a road camp in the Transkei.

In Johannesburg, early in 1963, I began to get information from one of my contacts that Poqo was active locally. My informant belonged to two Poqo cells, and several times a week came to me with details of the meetings he was attending. After a while he told me that mass action was planned for the weekend of April 7–8. Poqo members were going to go through the streets of Johannesburg to kill whites and invite blacks in general to join in. They were going to attack police stations and seize arms. Domestic servants were to poison their employers' food. It sounded way out. I doubted that many people would follow Poqo's lead in chopping up whites in the streets. I thought that most people would do the sensible thing and run as fast as they could in the opposite direction.

But the information was so consistent, detailed, and cumulative that I felt it had to be treated with the utmost seriousness. I was giving Gandar regular reports, and we were both in a considerable quandary as to what to do. It was information that we had a duty as a newspaper to publish, but if we did so, the police would demand to know our source, which I would not be willing to divulge. I would face jail, and would be isolated from the public because no one would have sympathy for a journalist concealing information about a plot as murderous as this. On the other hand, how could we keep silent? If the Poqo plan worked, the lives of heaven knows how many people would be on our consciences.

We agonized over these issues. I had sleepless nights grappling with a moral issue: keeping my own wife and child at home while giving no warning to others. Who else among family and friends should I warn?

I finally came up with the idea to go and confront Leballo with the details in my possession and then reveal the plot in the *Mail* in the context of his reaction. Leballo was certain to be desperate to maintain secrecy, so I planned to stay overnight in a hotel near the Basutoland border, drive to Leballo's office in the morning, and have a driver sitting in the car with the engine running ready to get me out of the territory. Gandar approved the scheme, but the night before I was to go, he phoned me at home to say that it was too dangerous and he wanted to think more about what to do. We still had ten days until the launch date.

Leballo helped to precipitate events. Always a big mouth, late in March he issued an announcement that an uprising was imminent. It also turned out that the Special Branch in Basutoland was getting its own information about Leballo's intentions and was alarmed because the small number of whites in the territory were also among the targets of the planned action. With the approval of the British government in London, the Special Branch passed word to South Africa's Security Police that Leballo was sending two couriers across the border. The couriers, two young women, were carrying letters to be put into the mail, giving Poqo cells their final go-ahead instructions. The women were arrested, and the addresses on the letters led the police to the cells. At least 3,246 Poqo members were rapidly seized throughout South Africa, put on trial on a range of charges, starting with murder, and were sentenced to jail.

The moment that Leballo spoke publicly, I rushed to Basutoland, but he had fled into the mountains. My contacts in the Basutoland government dropped heavy hints to me that they were not searching too hard for him. The British did not want to cooperate with the South Africans, but had Leballo been caught, they would have faced demands to hand him over for trial. When the dust died down, Leballo was allowed to escape from the country and he went to Tanzania. He made an utter mess of the PAC, murdering rivals and engaging in wholesale corruption by misusing money donated for the freedom struggle. He was expelled in 1979, and died in London two years later.

Swaziland was free of tribal rivalry because it was home only to the Swazi people. They gave absolute allegiance to King Sobhuza, known as the Ingwenyama, the Lion. He was reputed to have more than seventy wives, and hundreds of children. The wind of change was touching this small, beautiful country and the local white settlers were resistant to it. Early stirrings were represented by the Swaziland Progressive Party, which pushed for nonracism to be built into the constitution being prepared for future independence. Its president, J. J. Nquku, was anything but a radical, but that did not spare him the attentions of the South African Security Police when he flew to Britain or Ghana, which he had to do via Johannesburg's Jan Smuts Airport. Even though he was in transit, police and customs officials went through his luggage and his pockets each time. "They were courteous about it," I recorded him as saying after one of these searches.

A far tougher political movement sprang up, led by Dumisa Dhlamini, who was connected to the royal house. Dhlamini was the royal family name, but almost one third of Swazis carried it. Dumisa was young, charismatic, and totally in command. Unusual for a political leader, he was also right on with his information. He phoned me in Johannesburg one day to tell me to come to Mbabane, the capital, because a general strike was going to start the next day. The idea of a strike by the tranquil Swazis was almost bizarre, but knowing Dumisa, I went there the next day.

As my driver went into the main street of Mbabane, I was startled to find the place deserted. The township was atop a hill, and I could see a large cluster of people. Up we went and, being cautious, I told the driver to turn the car around to point downhill. I walked toward the crowd, asking for Dumisa, and began to get the feeling that something was wrong. No one answered or looked me in the face. I saw Macdonald Maseko, a friend and former ANC leader in South Africa. "Hello, Mac, where's Dumisa?" I asked. I got really worried when he nervously responded, "You must go away, it's not good for you to be here."

I started walking back to my car, slowly, despite mounting apprehension. I was surrounded by a growing crowd, whose voices were getting louder. I reached the car and climbed in, with people pushing me. The driver looked as scared as I probably did, and we raced away down the hill.

Three days later I met Dumisa when he came to town for a court case.

"Where have you been?" he wanted to know. "Why aren't you reporting our meetings?"

I told him in lurid language what I thought of his followers and how I had escaped from them. He laughed and said he had heard about it and it was all a misunderstanding.

I agreed to go back, on the condition that I have an escort in my car. So we set off, together with the *Mail*'s Jill Chisholm and a photographer who had come in to help report events. There was again a large crowd on the hill. I was made to stand on a table in the middle while Dumisa made a speech, chiding them for having given me such a fright. Everyone laughed. They were no longer the potential lynch mob they had been.

A few days into the strike the authorities called on London for help and a small detachment of British soldiers was flown in. The news that they were coming scared the Swazis. This was unlike anything they had ever experienced. Literally overnight the township was evacuated as thousands trekked over the mountain ridge to the king's home. By dawn they were seeking royal protection. They waited until the afternoon before Sobhuza addressed them.

Sitting on a chair, in Swazi sarong-type tribal dress, he spoke in a quiet voice, initially sympathetic but ultimately upbraiding them for participating in a nontraditional action such as a strike. There had to be progress but the nation must not be destroyed, was his message. I was filled with admiration for the brilliance of his speech. He had the crowd in the palm of his hand, and moved them where he wanted them to go.

The soldiers were to fly into Matsapa Airport, and I went there with a television photographer, Ernie Christie. He was working for an American network, and went on to achieve award-winning distinction for his footage in the Vietnam War. During protest meetings on the steps of the Johannesburg City Hall, when they were still allowed, he would heft his heavy camera (as TV cameras were then) and bring it crashing down on the arms of policemen foolish enough to block his filming. He regarded the dents on his camera as badges of honor in defense of press freedom. He also had a quick temper, and I saw policemen wilt under the lash of his tongue.

After years of working abroad, Christie returned home to Johannesburg. Early one morning he took off in a hired light plane and, with seeming deliberateness, flew into an apartment building, killing himself and several residents. Exactly why Christie committed suicide in this gruesome way or if that building was his particular target was never known.

At this time, however, he and I were together at Matsapa Airport, with only one other person in sight: a white colonial police officer. He officiously ordered us to stand behind a waist-high fence and took up station on the other side with his back to us. It was the wrong way to treat Christie. He leaned over the fence, held his camera two inches (5 cm) from the officer's face and pressed the button. As the camera whirred, he said softly, "I'm going to show people in America what a British fascist looks like." I watched the blood slowly rising in the officer's neck, but he did not say a word.

Once the troops arrived, and Sobhuza instructed his people to return to their jobs, the battle was waged between the modernists led by Dumisa Dhlamini and the tribal traditionalists. The whites backed the traditionalists and opposed the breaking down of racial barriers. I was writing about the attacks on those barriers, and on the growth of African nationalism. As the *Rand Daily Mail* usually arrived at lunchtime each day—by the daily bus, the link with the railhead that was some distance across the border inside South Africa—my reports were well known. They led to verbal skirmishes in the hotel bar at night, and I had a particular run-in with a magistrate who told me, "If you come up before me, I'll send you away for a long time."

A notable exception to the white community's resistance to non-racism was Vincent Rozwadowski—full name, Wincenty Maria Jordan-Rozwadowski—who owned a dairy farm outside Mbabane. Polish-born, he had been an officer in the Horse Artillery, an aristocratic territorial army unit, when his country was overrun by the Nazis. He escaped and made his way to France and joined the Free Polish Army. When it, in turn, was defeated, he was captured, but escaped while en route to a prisoner-of-war camp.

Rozwadowski was able to pass himself off as a Frenchman, became part of the underground, and rose to a high position in intelligence, sending copious reports to London about German troop dispositions in advance of the Normandy landings. After the Allies invaded Europe, he went behind the German lines, posing as a laborer and retreating with them, sending back intelligence reports. He told me he was dismissive about the French Maquis, which he believed had been riddled by informers. His own organization, he said, had consisted of tightly organized small cells. It was accepted that anyone seized by the Gestapo would crack under torture. No one was expected to resist it. The only instruction was to hold out for twelve hours if possible so as to allow time for word of the arrest to get around and for other members of the cell to go into hiding.

I spent evenings at Rozwadowski's fireside listening to these stories of daring and courage—they had a good deal of relevance then, and later, to events in South Africa in the struggle between the Security Police and underground movements. High honors were heaped on Rozwadowski: Poland conferred the Virtute Militari, the Polish VC; France gave him the Croix de Guerre and he was appointed to the Legion of Honor; and Britain gave him an MBE.

He had to show a different sort of courage in Swaziland because he had to live with being treated as an outcast by other whites. When he walked through the town, people crossed the street to avoid him. For some time one of his few friends was the Government Secretary, Athol Long, who was number two to the resident commissioner. Long's liberal views were known, so the whites did not like him either. But because of his rank and the social status that went with it—extremely important in a restricted colonial milieu—they could not ignore him. Rozwadowski's day finally came: after a few years, as the king began to move toward nonracism, he suddenly found whites going out of their way to greet him on the street and invite him to parties.

My first call on arriving in Mbabane was usually to Long, who would give me a full briefing on all that was happening and what might happen, all of it on a clearly understood off-the-record basis. Then I would tell him which stories I wanted to write and we would argue back and forth. Finally he would agree to three or four, and send me to the government press officer to get the details for publication. This could be an embarrassing meeting because, quite often, the first that the press officer knew that something was happening was when I came and asked for the story and he had to pretend that he knew all about it. Long was the only government official I was ever so close to. I never felt that my integrity as a journalist was compromised.

I had another source whom, several times, provided information that was so hot it could not be used then because I could not, if pressed, disclose where it came from.

In one episode a light plane took off from Matsapa Airport and headed over South Africa. Within minutes a South African Air Force jet was in the air and forced the light plane to land at a South African airport. The story was given a giant headline in the *Sunday Times* in Johannesburg. It was intended to convey that the ever-vigilant air force ensured that no one could fly over South Africa from the territories without permission. In fact, I was told it was a wholly put-up job on behalf of the South African authorities wanting to scare political exiles from traveling across South Africa by air.

A second episode concerned Frans Erasmus, who was successively South Africa's minister of defense and then justice. He had been found in the veld in Swaziland having sex with a local black woman. A few days later the minister's private secretary arrived in Mbabane to convey Erasmus's apologies for what had occurred and to explain that he suffered from "amnesia." This was at a time when the Afrikaner Nationalists forbade sex across the color line, and to be caught even attempting it was a criminal offense.

The Erasmus story was dynamite. Prosecutions under the Immorality Act were frequent—they ran to several thousand a year with about one thousand convictions—and even the private secretary of a Prime Minister had been charged and found guilty. But to name a senior member of the cabinet would have unleashed serious anger, and I could not do it without a reportable source.

The slide into South Africa's dark years began in March 1960 with the shooting at Sharpeville and the State of Emergency that followed. The Nationalists tasted the power of detention without trial, and liked it; equally so, the suppression of black voices through the bannings of the ANC and PAC.

Among whites, opposition was fading through a combination of persuasion and coercion. The Liberal Party had only tiny support, and the COD even less. The colored and Asian communities were ineffectively organized. On the parliamentary stage the opposition to the Nationalists came from the Progressives, the eleven MPs who had broken from the United Party late in 1958. With another general election set for October 1961 the *Rand Daily Mail* argued hard for the Progs. Gandar's comment column insistently spoke for them. The week before the election he ran daily editorials on page one.

Chapter 10

But the results proved disheartening. The Progs were wiped out with one exception: in the largely wealthy Houghton constituency in Johannesburg, Helen Suzman retained her seat by a narrow margin against a former mayor of the city. "Waves Of Cheering Greet Prog Victory—Tearful Mrs. Suzman Mobbed," was the *Mail*'s headline among the otherwise bleak news of that morning.

Helen Suzman was a superb parliamentarian, hardworking, dogged, meticulous about her facts, a speaker who held her audience and whose sharp, witty tongue squashed hecklers and cheered supporters, and all of it done while retaining her femininity. Above all, she was willing to fight for anyone who was a victim of injustice. She didn't care about political views or affiliation. If someone needed help, she gave it, through public speeches or by importuning and pursuing cabinet ministers and their officials. For thirteen years she was the lone representative of the Progressives in parliament. She spoke for the helpless and helped to keep alive the notion of the multiracial democracy South Africa could become.

Her platform inside parliament, however, was small. Other MPs could listen to or ignore her speeches as they wished, and although the speeches were circulated to newspapers and radio by the South African Press Association (Sapa), all else being equal the effect would have been minimal. But she reached hundreds of thousands of South Africans, and the world outside, through the *Rand Daily Mail*. Gandar was a close personal friend, and so were succeeding editors. She worked closely with the *Mail*'s political correspondents and anyone from the paper who contacted her.

In reporting on the townships, I was already working with her, asking her to put questions to cabinet ministers to get information that I could not otherwise obtain. Every letter I wrote to her came back with an answer. We published her speeches day after day, not out of any sense of duty but simply because she was speaking our kind of language, saying what we also believed.

She was always good value if comment was needed about an event; it wasn't a cheap "rent-a-quote" but someone in harmony with us whose keen eye could see the nub of a situation and sum it up wisely. Many editorials were written that picked up on something she had said. Slowly, as the strength of her criticisms of apartheid came to be acknowledged and her stature grew, other English-language newspapers came around to supporting her. Eventually she also earned the respect of many in the government itself.

Backing Helen Suzman was part of the goal that Gandar had come to set for the *Mail*, as he later described it to me: "Apart from wanting to make the *Mail* a better all-round paper in the straightforward professional sense I wanted it to become a beacon of light, an instrument of change, an engine of reform. Those were the darkest days of apartheid, of Verwoerd's brand of granite apartheid, and [minister of justice] John Vorster's lock-'em-up, shoot-'em-down war against opponents of the government." Gandar wasn't so naïve as to think we could change the thinking of the white supremacists who backed the Nationalists or even the white-leadership-with-justice supporters of the United Party. Indeed he was prepared to concede that the *Mail* may even have angered such people to the point of increasing their stubbornness. But, at the time, he thought it "was absolutely essential to help keep up the spirits of the small embattled forces of liberal-minded people who might otherwise have been crushed, to demonstrate to blacks that there was at least one sizable white institution that understood and was prepared to fight for the removal of their grievances, and to show the outside world that there were still some upholders of Western norms and values alive and kicking in South Africa."

At the English-language universities, after the fight against the imposition of apartheid had been lost, the years saw a gradual diminution in support for liberal opposition. Every now and again there would be a flare-up of student protests, but the time between them lengthened. It became more difficult and hazardous to demonstrate against the government. Protest marches through the city ceased because they were no longer allowed. Reporting one of them, I dashed into a small shop on the route to buy cigarettes. Standing alongside me at the counter was a man who ordered a dozen eggs. He was one of the hooligans pelting the marchers with tomatoes and eggs. I kept an eye open for him during the rest of the march but was at least glad that he was using fresh eggs. Passports could be and were denied to students who fell foul of the government. There was also the great deterrent of parental pressure, especially from parents who were in business or industry and had to have permits from the government to import goods, or approval to export money for payment or investment. The arguments around the dinner table were often, "What are you trying to do to us? You are going to lose me my business. Stop going to these meetings against the government."

Academic staff, with a few notable exceptions, retreated to their ivory tower. Little research or writing about the racial situation or the effects of apartheid was done, and rarely could students look to their professors for inspiration. I always thought that the academic boycott, which began in Britain early in the 1960s and spread wider, had a decisive effect in this regard. Boycotted by the academic world, the universities and South Africa were deprived of the infusions of fresh thinking and courage the country so badly needed. The *Mail* was also affected by the boycott. There were fewer local academics wanting to write for us, and fewer on whose ideas we could draw. The sterility and laziness extended even to the sphere of book reviewing. When, after 1972, I was in charge of the *Mail*'s book reviews, it was difficult to find academics—except for a handful—willing to put themselves out to make their knowledge available to the wider community.

Apart from marches and vigils, a thousand and more people would gather at lunchtime on weekdays on the steps of the Johannesburg City Hall to hear protest speeches. When thugs molested them, the police moved in to break up the meeting. The flower beds in front of the hall suffered from the scuffling and fighting, and some city councilors said this was outrageous and no meetings should be allowed there. For once, wiser heads prevailed in favor of the right to demonstrate whatever the cost in flowers.

Eventually, of course, starting in 1962, the government prohibited the meetings entirely. At least the flowers bloomed. The usual Sash vigils of a line of women also fell under what was forbidden: they had to stand at least fifteen feet apart from each other so as not to constitute a "gathering." One of the bravest actions of all was carried out by Jill Wentzel (Ernie Wentzel's wife) and Esther Levitan in 1979 after the police had killed Steve Biko, the black-consciousness leader. The two of them went to a National Party meeting in Pretoria and took a long, lonely walk up the aisle of the hall carrying a wreath, which they put in front of the astonished cabinet minister and party leaders on the platform. The audience was slow to understand what had been done but when they did it was only remnants of old-fashioned courtesy that saved the women from the mauling that men would have gotten in their place. As it was, a crowd, screaming obscenities, gathered around them and pushed and shoved them out of the hall.

With authoritarianism creeping through the country, I encountered a new level of difficulty in dealing with an apartheid showplace, Baragwanath Hospital. Located on the main road running past Soweto, it had been built during the Second World War for British troops based in South Africa. It retained its appearance of a sprawling army barracks as it grew into the country's biggest hospital for blacks (in the 1990s it was said to be the world's biggest hospital). For many years most of its doctors were white and so were the head nurses. It provided a high level of medical care and foreign visitors were taken to see it as a prime example of what the white man was doing for blacks. This was one of the standard bits of white belief and propaganda: the line was that whites paid most of the taxes therefore the services that the government provided for blacks were funded by white generosity. The fallacy of the argument, of course, was that blacks paid so little in taxes because they were poorly paid, whereas the taxes paid by whites derived from exploitation of blacks.

Baragwanath was treated as above reproach. But I had friends among the doctors there and their description of conditions was different from the official version. They were telling me this informally, over dinner tables, and I could not use the information. The day came that one of them, Archie Stein, a surgeon, came to see me to say that he had reached his breaking point and wanted to get the true story into the open. He said he had to operate for so many hours nonstop that he believed he was killing patients out of exhaustion.

Using other sources, too, I put together a harrowing report. A *Mail* photographer went in and surreptitiously took photographs showing gross overcrowding with scenes of patients lying under beds and in passages. I went to see the hospital superintendent, put the pictures in front of him along with my report—the sources were concealed—and asked for comments. He looked at the pictures, read my report, and asked, "Who gave you this information? I want to know. I will not have them in my hospital." That was all the comment I could get: not a word about the conditions, only a punitive attitude toward those who had blown the whistle.

On the other hand, I learned a useful lesson about worming out information from official sources. For weeks I tried to get the statistics of black unemployment in Johannesburg from the Non-European Affairs Department but was given the runaround. Then the figure appeared in the *Star* and I asked the reporter how he had managed this. "It was easy," he said, "I phoned the department and said I understood more than 30,000 blacks were unemployed and the official responded, 'That's a lie. There are only 16,812.'"

By the early 1960s the *Rand Daily Mail* was established as the leading newspaper in South Africa. One result was the added strength of the reporting staff. The *Mail* seemed to attract both the best and the weirdest. Terence Clarkson was a veteran reporter, gray-haired for as long as I knew him, and wore the same suit every day, a bluish-purplish pepper-and-salt cloth. Every few years, when it had grown too shiny, he went to a tailor and had the identical suit made up. He seemed to specialize in writing about jackals being spotted in Johannesburg suburban gardens. In the newsroom he used a desk until its drawers were crammed full with old notebooks, scraps of paper, and leftovers of sandwiches. When not another piece of paper could fit in, Clarkson picked up his current note-book and pen and found another vacant desk. He told me he had been on the staffs of newspapers around the country in his many decades in journalism, and had never once cleaned out a desk drawer.

Wessel de Kock had studied for the Dutch Reformed Church ministry at Stellenbosch University before he became a journalist. He was Afrikaans and seemed to be a Nationalist sympathizer. He would come into my office in the mornings, lean over me, his face red as he banged on the desk, "I hated every word of Gandar's editorial this morning." And then he would add, "But I admired the way he wrote it and, man, I love this newspaper. It's a real newspaper."

Two other Afrikaners fared less well. J. J. Oosthuizen was a member of the Liberal Party, and it was later rumored that he was also a secret member of the Communist Party. He committed suicide. Ferdie Noffke had a more checkered career on the *Mail*. He was sent to report tribal trouble in Sekukuniland, a long way away in the Northern Transvaal. He wrote a graphic account of an outbreak of rioting during which a rock shattered the windshield of his *Mail* car. The report carried weight because people there had been resisting the government, and this seemed to be evidence of renewed violence. It then emerged that the windshield had been smashed during a drunken spree: Noffke had flung a brandy bottle at it. He was fired and joined the *Vaderland*, the afternoon Nationalist newspaper, but did not last long there. His method was to write a blood-and-guts story that the ANC was planning a major campaign, and then a few days later another equally blood-and-guts story that the ANC had called off its campaign out of fear because the police had learned about it. Both stories achieved front-page prominence and both were his inventions. The *Vaderland* woke up to what Noffke was doing and fired him. He, too, committed suicide.

Chris Vermaak was crime reporter for a time and then joined an Afrikaans newspaper. In the mid 1960s he wrote a book, *The Red Trap*, which purported to tell the story of Communism and violence in South Africa. He had been a solid reporter, but the book was a wretched piece of work, filled with factual errors. It also contained a statement of breathtaking absurdity, but which probably reflected the beliefs of most whites. He wrote, "Much has and is still being said in South Africa about 'oppressed' peoples and 'peace.' It is not my intention to write an essay on why nonwhites in South Africa cannot be called 'oppressed' people. This is a fact which is plain for everyone to see."

In a time of ever-increasing police activity, the *Mail* was caught between young radicals on the editorial staff and the police spies planted on the editorial staff to watch them. Paul Trewhela, who was among the radicals, was one of the brightest prospects among the younger reporters. While working for the Argus Company he was active in the COD and was arrested twice, and convicted and cautioned for handing out leaflets protesting against the government's latest abuse of personal freedom. He was warned that he would be fired if he continued political activity. A month later he was arrested again for putting up a poster, which showed the bottom of a boot with a swastika on it. He was fired. He applied to the *Rand Daily Mail* and Gandar, knowing what had happened, took him on as a general reporter. "I did anything that came up," Trewhela remembers. "You had opportunities that could not have existed anywhere else in the world. As a cub reporter, with only half a training course behind me, I could be sent anywhere to do anything. I did a wide range of stories, as a court reporter covering criminal and political cases, or going out when explosions went off, or covering the murder of a woman by her lover." He continued as a member of the COD and also joined the underground Communist Party. Shortly after doing so he quit the *Mail* and went to work for a magazine. "I was rather pleased to be leaving the *Mail*," he says. "It wasn't possible to be active in the underground without knowing that you were almost certain to be arrested or have to flee the country," and he realized that this could be a major embarrassment to the *Mail* and preferred not to be on the paper when it happened. Trewhela was indeed arrested for his Communist work and jailed for two years. A witness against him was Gerard Ludi, a police spy who had been his colleague on the *Mail*. There had been suspicions about Ludi, so Gandar confronted him with what was being said. Ludi flatly denied it, and Gandar felt he could do nothing further. Not long after, however, the police blew Ludi's cover and he was revealed as a Security Police agent who had successfully penetrated the Communist Party. He testified for the State against Trewhela and others in several trials. His book, *Operation Q-018*, did not reflect well on the competence of the Communist Party or the intelligence of Security Police agents.

After Harry O'Connor was promoted to assistant editor, M. A. "Johnny" Johnson became news editor. His style was that of a galley master, whipping the slaves to greater effort. He was also a superb newspaperman, driving for hard news. I did more work with Johnson as news editor than at any other time of my life, simply because I feared his wrath. During one altercation he grabbed me by the tie, spoke his menacing words, and then released me with the snarling comment, "Now you can go and complain to the union that your news editor assaulted you." It was easier to achieve the impossible and deliver the story he wanted than to have to face his anger.

Raymond Louw, who succeeded Johnson as news editor, brought system to the *Mail*'s news-gathering operation. A man of extraordinary energy, he was totally absorbed in the hunt for news. As with every specialist reporter, each day saw a clump of newspaper clippings landing on my desk, sent by Louw, often with notes to ask what I was doing about this or that. Otherwise he left me to develop the African Affairs beat pretty much as I wanted—provided that I kept producing enough reports that he considered newsworthy.

The kind of investigative reporting that focused on a particular issue was still in its infancy. We knew there was a good deal of hunger among blacks, but it received only sporadic attention. The full extent of the situation had never been exposed. The creation of the non-profit-making Nutrition Corporation, known as Kupugani, triggered our interest. The Kupugani people were in contact with Gandar, and what they were saying was so devastating that he decided to launch a campaign under the heading, "Starvation—A National Scandal." It kicked off with two days of front-page reports by Keith Abendroth of the *Mail*'s Pretoria bureau, after visiting the remote northeastern Transvaal.

At the best of times people in the tribal lands there lived at poverty level. After two years of drought he reported, "For many African families their meal now is a handful of maize porridge bought with cents scraped together and accompanied by sprigs of cooked blackjack grass once every two days." As the campaign picked up momentum, I weighed in with information provided by Kupugani officials: "Mass starvation has driven Africans in parts of the Eastern Transvaal back to Stone Age conditions. They are living on wild fruit picked from bushes."

Digging deeper, I found screeds of little-used details tucked away in government statistics and in the annual reports of medical officers of health in cities and towns. When placed together, they portrayed malnutrition on a scale that few had understood. It was especially seen in children with kwashiorkor, the protein-deficiency disease. Doctors at Baragwanath Hospital helped me find information, and the chief pediatrician, Dr. Sam Wayburne, took me on a tour of his kwashiorkor wards, where babies were kept two to a cot.

A baby suffering from kwashiorkor can look plump and healthy at first sight, but the plumpness is merely water, and once treatment starts, the fatality rate soars as dehydration sets in and a baby is literally reduced to skin and bones.

I sat up through the night writing one of the articles, searching for an introductory sentence that would convey the pain I had seen at Baragwanath. Five hours later, surrounded by discarded paper and hundreds of attempts, I came up with what I have always considered my best opening statement. It ran to four words: "The children suffer most." And it went on: "Underfed, wrongly fed, their bodies offer no resistance when illness comes." Alongside was a photograph of an emaciated baby.

As our other reports examined the effects of widespread malnutrition on the economy and the roots of the scourge, a tidal wave of emotion swept through readers, and money poured in for the starving and for Kupugani. We ran daily lists of the names of the contributors. One of the many stories we recorded was of the businessman who phoned to ask the cost of 1,000 pounds (450 kg) of concentrated soup powder. Advised that it was 175 rand, he said that he would send that amount. "It is not from me," he explained. "It's my children of fourteen and twelve who have asked me to do something."

The *Mail* also came in for savage criticism. Our reporting of starvation in the Northern Transvaal was "unfavorable and distorted" and "entirely without foundation," said the minister of Bantu Administration, Daan de Wet Nel. A government MP went further and called me a "liar." While the politicians damned us, with the usual charge that we were unpatriotic and writing for overseas consumption, from behind the scenes I was receiving verbal messages from several highly placed government officials. "Keep going," they told me. "We need to have this in the open so that we can do something about it."

The Nationalist press did not hold that view. The *Transvaler* took to referring sneeringly to the *Mail* as "*die hongersnood koerant,*" (the malnutrition newspaper). It claimed that our photographs of kwashiorkor babies were fakes. It sent a reporter to Baragwanath and he arrogantly told Dr. Wayburne that his instruction was to walk in my footsteps and disprove everything we had published. Wayburne invited him to tour the kwashiorkor wards. After going through the first ward the reporter looked ill and declined to visit the others, Wayburne told me afterwards. But that did not stop the *Transvaler*'s attacks.

At the end of the first week I wrote a memo outlining the points I thought should go into the front-page editorial that Gandar was planning. It was a job I did from time to time on important issues, and this time, as always, I was filled with admiration and envy for the way in which he took my pedestrian words and wove them into an editorial of facts, passion, and power. From my university days—though still a lodestar to me—I offered him Charles Booth's words: "In intensity of feeling, and not in statistics lies the power to move the world." To my delight, Gandar put the words at the head of his page-one editorial, which urged "prevention, prevention, prevention." However, alongside the report—as a reminder, if any be needed, of what the *Mail* was up against—was a story that reported Justice Minister Vorster's searing attack on liberalism and his call: "Let us purge ourselves of this danger."

The first flush of the campaign over, I went to Zululand with Kupugani's national organizer, Neil Alcock, a farmer who was also a visionary about people and land. I incessantly asked questions about the use and abuse of the land. We spent a week moving from one mission station to the next to check on the state of the corn harvest, local health conditions, and what Kupugani should be doing. For me every hour was eye opening: the rudimentary level at which rural blacks were living; the harmful effects on family and land of the long absences of the men as migrant workers in the cities and the mines; the ignorance among many peasants about how to care for babies, resorting to milk powder in place of mother's milk; and their failure to use wild-growing spinach as a valuable food.

I also learned from doctors and nurses in the mission hospitals what a medical emergency meant: if a woman in a distant *kraal*, a collection of huts inside a fence, experienced difficulties during labor, they said, she was put on a sled, which was dragged across country to the nearest track while someone set off with a message for the hospital to send an ambulance to an agreed meeting place. By the time the woman and the ambulance met up, which could be three or more days later, it was likely that the baby was dead. By the time the ambulance reached the hospital, the mother could be dead. I also learned that no one had any real idea about the size of the black population: few births were registered and few deaths. The five-yearly census was at best a rough guess about numbers.

Because Alcock and I were traveling so much, we could not help but arrive on a Sunday morning at a mission station in the mountains. It was run by a Christian church based in the American South and the missionaries welcomed us. We sat down with them in an office to discuss the district's food needs and what Kupugani should ship in. I was a heavy

smoker, and without giving it a second thought, pulled out my cigarettes. I offered the pack around, but no one took one, so I lit up. I
looked for an ashtray but there wasn't one, so I used the pack's cello-
phane covering. After only a few minutes Alcock and I found the meeting had ended. They were ushering us out and said that they did not
want any food aid from Kupugani. They gave no explanation. All I could
think was that I had mortally offended them by lighting a cigarette on a
Sunday, which thus put Kupugani and me beyond the pale. How many
children died in the mountains that year for lack of food?

Throughout the early 1960s the Nationalists were systematically
enforcing separate development, forcing tribal communities to accept
what they were ordered to accept. After covering a four-day visit to the
Transkei and Ciskei with de Wet Nel, I wrote, "There were gifts in plen-
ty from tribal leaders for the Minister of Bantu Development and
Administration... But all this could not hide the fact that tribesmen are
skeptical of the government's promises of self-government and intend
forcing the pace. It was by no means a triumphal tour for the minister.
Most of the crowds were not very big, and applause for his words was
thin." I also lightheartedly listed the gifts the minister had been given,
from beads to spears, and wrote about the number of times his dour face
appeared in the department's propaganda magazine. The minister was
not amused by my reports and barred me from entering tribal lands. He
was able to do this because whites needed permission to enter these
areas. Gandar reacted by sending a stiff message that the *Mail* would
continue to assign me and would not substitute any other reporters. His
decision was open to argument because he was depriving readers of
information. On the other hand, he rightly refused to allow the officials
to decide who should represent the *Mail*—and in any event he knew that
they only invited us if they thought their propaganda would get into the
paper.

The new policy of separate development was intended to make old-
style racial apartheid more palatable to blacks and the increasingly hostile world outside. South Africa was to be partitioned. That could have
been a way of resolving the racial problems except that it was a colossal
and cynical con: whites, about 16 percent of the population, were keeping about 84 percent of the land; blacks, who formed about 70 percent of
the population, were to have 16 percent. The colored and Asian minority groups were in an uneasy no-man's land. Even further, in applying
divide and rule, the land for blacks was split into some ten "Bantustans,"

each a mini-state for a different tribal group. Not all were unified territories—Zulus, for example, were handed twelve separated parcels of
land, a "nonsense state," as a tribal leader put it.

The white govenment said that blacks could practice their own separate freedoms in their own separate Bantustans—with the corollary that
they were stripped of citizenship in "white" South Africa, and if they
were in the country then it was only to work in lowly jobs, and only for
as long as they were needed, as "guest workers." That was supposed to
mean that South Africa could no longer be accused of racial discrimination because there were no blacks to be discriminated against. Only
some of the Bantustans opted for "independence," and were recognized
by South Africa and no one else. They were poverty-stricken and corruption was rampant. No mercy was shown in creating the Bantustans:
several million black people were compulsorily shunted around, backed
by the pass laws to control the number of blacks allowed to enter
"white" South Africa.

Part II

Into the Prisons

The Prisons Act of 1959 was a highly detailed piece of legislation that provided for the administration of jails. But Sections 44 (e) and (f) dealt specifically with dissemination of information about prisons and prisoners.

Section 44 (e) said that it was an offense to sketch or photograph any prison, prisoner, or burial of a prisoner without the written permission of the commissioner of prisons.

Section 44 (f) said that it was an offense to publish any "false information" about prisons or prisoners, "knowing the same to be false or without taking reasonable steps to verify such information." The onus of proving that "reasonable steps" had been taken rested on the accused and a conviction could mean up to a year's imprisonment and/or a fine.

These sections were appended to the Prisons Act at the last moment because an issue of *Drum* magazine had

Chapter 11

contained photographs of black prisoners in the Fort prison in Johannesburg doing the *tausa* dance. The *tausa* was a widespread practice of ordering blacks returning from court appearances or outside work to strip naked and jump up and down with arms and legs spread out, while warders kneeled on the ground and looked for forbidden material, such as knives or dagga (marijuana).

Drum had been enterprising in taking its photographs from atop a high building that overlooked a courtyard in the Fort. The intention was to show the undignified nature of the *tausa*. The minister of justice, C. R. Swart, had a different view: "People should not be allowed to photograph such scenes not so much for the sake of the prisoners but for the sake of the staff." He also complained about reports covering the last moments of prisoners sentenced to death and the publication of photographs of people with the noose around their necks as they were about to be executed. "That should not be allowed. That man is serving his sentence; he is paying the highest penalty one can pay, with his life, and then certain newspapers publish these stories just for the sake of sensation and to build up their circulation." He said he did not want to restrict the freedom of the press, but he did want to curb their license to publish untrue, sensational reports about the experiences of prisoners. The "decent press," by which he probably meant newspapers that supported the government, had complained to him that they could not see their way clear to publishing reports of this kind, "but they lose circulation, and the sensational papers make money out of the troubles of other people by publishing fictitious stories."

Swart was already notorious for his harsh outlook. As minister of justice since the Nationalists first came to office in 1948, he had pushed the repressive Suppression of Communism Act through parliament and had had much to do with the creeping erosion of individual liberties since then. He had brandished a *sjambok* (leather whip) in parliament when he introduced a law to impose lashes on criminal offenders. He stood firmly by the police, tolerating whatever they did, thus opening the way to the police abuses that would continue for so many years. And already by then the freedom-versus-license line was the standard Nationalist excuse for assailing the press. Sections 44 (e) and (f) were simply part of the Nationalists' growing dislike of criticism and their antagonism toward the English-language press. That indeed is how the English newspapers viewed the proposed law, and we attacked it.

Less than two months after the Prisons Act became law, information was passed to the *Rand Daily Mail* about an outbreak of typhoid at the Fort. The source was unimpeachable—Lewis Sowden at the *Mail* had a friend who worked as a doctor at the Fort. On May 9th we reported that sixteen black prisoners had been taken to hospital and four of them had died since April 24th. Contacted by the *Mail*, the jail's superintendent said there had been "an unusual number" of cases of gastroenteritis, and added, "I know of no cases of typhoid in the Fort, or of any deaths from typhoid there."

That afternoon the *Star* quoted the assistant director of prisons, Colonel J. C. Steyn, as saying that officials had the cases of "stomach sickness" under control at the Fort. With Sowden getting daily reports from his medical friend, however, the *Mail* knew exactly how incorrect these official statements were, and on May 11th we insisted that there was indeed typhoid at the Fort. So specific was the information that we were able to reveal that the first two prisoners had been taken to hospital on April 10th, both had died, and that the typhoid diagnosis had already been confirmed by tests on April 18th. On May 12th the *Mail* reported that the number had risen to twenty-seven cases in hospital, fifty suspected cases at the Fort and five deaths.

Later that day the minister of justice confirmed, in a statement to parliament for the first time, that there was in fact a typhoid outbreak at the Fort, and he described the steps being taken to seal off the prison.

In addition to the outright lies of denial, the *Mail*'s early reports were severely attacked by Nationalist newspapers, which were blindly taking their cue from government officials. Yet the gravity of the outbreak could hardly have been overstated: the Fort (which has since been closed) stood at the edge of the densely populated Hillbrow flatland suburb and had two major hospitals immediately across the street. Medical opinion was that a single fly could spread the disease. Doctors blamed the outbreak on medical incompetence allied with the Fort's sanitation system, which dated to the turn of the century, and the use of buckets as toilets in cells.

By the end of the week there were nearly two hundred confirmed or suspected typhoid cases in Johannesburg and nearby towns, all traceable to the Fort. By then, after the initial admission of the existence of the disease, an official shutdown on news was enforced and little more was heard about it.

Although Gandar had begun by publishing information about the typhoid outbreak in defiance of official denials, he was saved from any prosecution under Section 44 (f) because the authorities could not conceal the facts for long. Indeed it was behind-the-scenes pressure and threats of action by alarmed city councilors in Johannesburg that finally forced the government to inform the public and adopt remedial measures. There was a subsequent internal prisons-department inquiry into the negligence of the doctor in charge at the Fort, but it was held in secret and its deliberations and findings were never revealed.

Sixteen months later the *Mail* immersed itself again in prison-condition investigations. I wrote articles about white political detainees during the State of Emergency, but they were not submitted to the Department of Prisons. Our lawyers advised us that since the reports were essentially noncritical of conditions, because whites were being looked after fairly reasonably, we need not fear prosecution. This proved correct.

However, it was a different story on the black side. Prisons were overcrowded. There were more than 1,800 political activists of all colors, plus 18,000 blacks arrested as "vagrants." I began to receive information that bad things were happening inside Modderbee Prison in Benoni, recently converted from a gold-mine labor compound.

At that time there wasn't a single black reporter on the *Mail*, and I could not do the investigation on my own. I arranged to work with Obed Musi of the *Golden City Post*. Musi spoke so rapidly that it was always a struggle to understand him, but he was a superb and fearless reporter. We spent many days outside Modderbee. He lounged around on the road leading from the prison waiting to buttonhole released prisoners. I skulked among a grove of bluegum trees nearby, waiting to work with Musi in interviewing ex-prisoners as he got hold of them. We gave them absolute assurances that their identities would not be revealed and we kept as few notes as possible. Over weeks we interviewed scores of released prisoners, and meticulously built up a picture of people crammed into cells, sleeping on concrete bunks or on the floor and with too few blankets and clothing to ward off the midwinter cold. The stronger men seized what was available from the weaker ones. Food was in short supply and the daily diet lacked milk, fruit, and vegetables. Prisoners showered in the open and had no towels. The men were coming down with pneumonia: eighteen had died.

This time we were advised by our lawyers that the material was explosive, and publication could not be risked without prior submission to the Department of Prisons. I phoned the acting commissioner, General J. C. Steyn, the same official who had denied the typhoid reports the previous year, and read our report to him. He commented on each point. Musi and I wrote our own stories. With simultaneous publication in the *Mail* and *Golden City Post*, we published all of it, even those details that Steyn had specifically denied. He confirmed the eighteen pneumonia deaths. But as it turned out, he either knew even less than I thought he did, or he lied again, for soon afterwards the news leaked out, and was confirmed, that there had in fact been forty-two deaths.

There was one legal casualty: Dennis Kiley, the *Post* news editor, used the material in an article for a London newspaper. His report went a bit farther than ours had, and he was prosecuted and found guilty under the

Prisons Act for allegedly publishing false information about prisons. An important precedent was established, one that hung over all foreign correspondents and stringers from then on: Kiley had cabled his report to London, and the act of handing the cable to a post office counter clerk in South Africa was held to be publication, added to which a policeman had been able to read his report because the London newspaper was distributed in South Africa. If a cable couldn't be sent, would a letter be safer? Some years later Patrick Laurence of the *Star*, who later became one of the leading reporters on the *Rand Daily Mail*, mailed a report to the *Observer* in London in which he quoted Robert Sobukwe, who was banned after Sharpeville. The police intercepted the letter, pretended that it had gone through the normal post and been sent back to them in South Africa by a sympathizer, and were able to prosecute Laurence for publishing the statements of a banned person. He, too, was found guilty.

My concern about finding out what was happening to arrested people led me, in 1960, to perpetrate the worst mistake of my career. At that time I frequently dealt with members of the Nyasaland ANC, people working in South Africa and hailing from what was to become the independent state of Malawi. I liked and respected them. The leaders came to tell me that they were convinced that one of their members had been beaten so severely while in prison that he died. They had visited him in hospital as he was dying, and although he could not speak, he had conveyed this to them. I questioned them at length and believed them. I then persuaded Gandar, the newsdesk, and our lawyers, that the allegation was reasonably founded. We instructed a lawyer to obtain an exhumation order—it was a considerable effort to get this from a court and was very seldom done—and the body was dug up a couple of weeks after death and taken to the Johannesburg Mortuary.

We hired the foremost pathologist to be present at the autopsy to keep check on the government pathologist. The pathologists set to work, and I paced up and down outside, puffing away at cigarettes. After an hour the private pathologist emerged, gave me a disgusted look, and said, "There isn't a mark on his body. It's a toss-up as to whether he died because his lungs or heart or kidneys packed up. He was rotten internally." I felt crushed and so embarrassed that I could not face dealing with the story again. I also did not dare ask how much money it had cost us. But the *Star* heard about the exhumation, and carried a report about it; that led to Gandar sending me a brief note, polite but filled with implied reproof, asking why I had failed to report our own story in the *Mail*.

There was never another word from him about my blunder. Nor did I reproach my informants; I believed they had made a genuine mistake.

My interest in prisons was taken farther and became more personal when I ran into Robin Scott-Smith, an old Liberal Party friend, on a Saturday morning in July 1961. He was laughing about an article in the *Mail* that morning about the minister of justice, Frans Erasmus, who had told parliament the previous day that the police had uncovered and foiled a dastardly plot to disrupt the celebration of Republic Day. Erasmus and the police had fallen for nothing more than a political prank, according to Scott-Smith. He offered to bring me the document, but I had to promise not to reveal that he had given it to me. The next evening he brought it to my home. In pseudomilitary style the three-page typed text—headed "Operation Damp Squib," signed "Thundercracker"—gave instructions to "disrupt and make a farce" of celebrations. "Leaders" in every town were to have groups of "Rockets" and "Crackers" working for them. They were to phone and reduce the orders for soft drinks, food, and portable toilets. Attached to the document was a note: "This is the political joke of the year. Ex-army officers drew it up as a students' rag joke. This is the minister's 'plot.'"

I thought it was quite witty and wrote the story. The night staff agreed and gave it strong play on page one. The day after publication I was at home with a migraine headache when the newsdesk phoned: "A police officer has been waiting here for two hours. He wants to speak to you about a story you wrote." I groaned and drove to the office and met Major Hendrik van den Bergh of the Criminal Investigation Department (CID). He asked for the source of the Damp Squib report, and I declined to give it. He was very pleasant: "You must decide whether you are going to give me the name," he said, "otherwise I must make arrangements for you in jail tonight. It's going to be cold and I want to arrange extra blankets for you." By late afternoon I was standing in front of a magistrate in a specially convened court, flanked by the *Mail*'s attorney, Kelsey Stuart. We had been instructed to come to the courthouse, but endured some comic opera because the guards on the main door initially refused to let us in as it was after hours.

The magistrate, C.J.M. Durr, briskly dismissed Stuart's argument that I was bound by my promise of confidentiality, and consigned me to prison for an initial eight days, ordering that I then be brought before him again if need be for further imprisonment. In theory the eight-day jailing could be repeated without end. This was "Section 83" in operation, a clause in the Criminal Law Amendment Act, one of the omnibus changes to laws enacted now and again. Van den Bergh drove me to the Fort, took me to the registration desk, shook my hand, and wished me well. He could not have been nicer. As I was put into a cell and the heavy metal door clanged shut, I peered through the peep-hole in the door, looking at my narrow world of a passageway, and stood back laughing aloud. Going to jail had been hanging over me for a long time. I had written any number of articles and dealt with any amount of dangerous information that I thought could bring the police down on me. I had often been worried that writing one story or another might land me in jail, and here I was, unexpectedly, in jail for a story written as a joke, without having given a moment's thought to the possible repercussions.

The prison authorities were nervous about having me thrust upon them. Although Section 83 hovered over reporters' lives, it had seldom been used until then. The only cases I knew of were George Heard's jailing in the late 1930s, and the year before me, Patrick Duncan's three-week imprisonment for an editorial in *Contact*. He refused to divulge the source of his information about the reemerged South African Communist Party. He told the magistrate he was prepared to stay in prison for twenty years if necessary.

I was given the best possible treatment by being put in the prison's "hospital section." My cell was nine-by-nine feet, with a bed, and a wood floor instead of the usual cement floor. A bucket in a corner served as a toilet, and a small table and chair were brought in as a special concession. As van den Bergh had warned me, the cell was bitterly cold, but he had not, from what I could see, arranged for extra blankets. The blankets on the bed were filthy, the sheets stained, and only once did I lift the bottom sheet: one look at the mattress and its encrusted dirt and I decided to close my eyes. But I knew what I was doing in fulfilling my promise to Scott-Smith, and slept soundly.

My wife came to visit me the next day. She was eight months' pregnant with our first child, and I was angry that we were pinned behind high wire fences separated by three feet of space. I protested, and a contact visit was allowed. My wife, familiar with my penchant for reading thrillers in times of stress, delivered a half dozen to the prison. The next morning the commandant came around for inspection, grimacing. "Someone sent you the most terrible books with pictures of gallows and naked women on the covers," he told me. "I can't let you have books like that, an educated man like you." I sighed but kept silent. I didn't want to lower his estimation of me.

Jill Wentzel sent me a large jigsaw puzzle. After struggling to put it together on the small table while wearing fur-lined gloves, I developed a permanent hatred for puzzles. Raymond Louw visited and handed me two cartons of cigarettes: one brand was my regular one, Westminster 85, and the other was a toasted brand I didn't like. I tried to give the toasted ones back to him, but he kept pushing them at me. Suddenly I realized what these were for, and indeed they did come in very useful: cigarettes were the currency of prison and a pack handed to a warder or a prisoner achieved wonders.

I learned some of the ways of prison. Because I carried a blue card, classifying me as awaiting-trial and not as a sentenced prisoner, I wore my own clothes and food could be sent in. Louw came up tops with excellent dinners delivered from a nearby hotel. The food came in a wooden box, with all of the cutlery removed, presumably to prevent me from committing suicide, so I always had to ask a "trustee" to lend me his spoon (all serving prisoners carried a spoon for eating).

It was all easy apart from the physical discomfort and the nagging worry that I did not have the slightest idea how long it might continue. It lasted six days, as it turned out. I was released because the *Mail* lodged an appeal. It was rushed forward and was heard three weeks later in the Supreme Court in Pretoria. The two judges needed only a short time to reject my plea of journalistic ethics. This was the first time that Section 83 had been clarified. The implications were grave for me and all journalists: we had no right to protect our sources of information. I sneaked a suitcase packed with clothes out of the apartment in case I had to return to prison that day. However, at the end of the court hearing the police said they weren't ready to return me to prison yet.

The afternoon my appeal was dismissed my wife went into a long labor. The next morning, a Saturday, I walked out of the hospital for a break. As I was returning, a car came up the street, its horn blaring. A Security policeman rolled down the window and said, "I've been sent to take you back to jail." I don't know what sort of look of fury came over my face when I told him, "I'm not going anywhere until my baby is born," but it was enough for him to shrink back in his seat. "It's okay, man, I'm also a human being. Promise me that you won't leave here and I'll see what I can do," he said. He left and I rushed into the hospital, timing contractions in between phoning Stuart and Louw. An hour later the police phoned to say that I could stay out over the weekend. Jennifer

Solange was born that evening. That Monday the *Mail* published her photograph, aged fifteen hours.

I returned to court, this time armed with a statement I had prepared:

> I have a pride in my profession. I believe in my work and I try to do it as honestly and responsibly as possible. During the course of each day I meet a great many people. Some are simple people, others hold important positions in the community. Many of these people honor me with their confidences. I cannot betray one of them without betraying all of them. Yet this is what the State is asking me to do… The prosecutor said that the code of the law transcends the code of ethics of journalism. But I wish to submit that, for the State to function, every citizen must have a moral standard. The State is meaningless if citizens do not live according to moral values. I want to submit that the State is asking me to be immoral.

Durr served as the magistrate again. He listened stonily and then sent me back to jail. This time the treatment accorded me was different. No longer was I cosseted, but was peremptorily ordered downstairs into the cells of the magistrates' courts to wait to be transported to the Fort. My fellow inmates were there for petty crimes, such as buying liquor for blacks, which was illegal, thefts, and assaults of various kinds. We were loaded into a truck with wire-mesh sides; we could be seen as we trundled through the city. I was embarrassed and ashamed. Me, a gentleman, exposed to the public gaze in the company of the flotsam of Johannesburg! As panic swept over me, I fought back by reminding myself why I was there. Later, reflecting on my initial reaction, I remembered reading how the Chinese had broken captured American GIs during the Korean War: uniforms were removed and this denial of a soldier's dignity was the first deliberate step in a softening-up process. The same basic principle applied to my experiences. The idea of standing up to an official insult was also engraved in South African prison life, where "stand on your dig," keep your dignity, was a common motto.

Arrival at the Fort provided yet another experience. A truckload of black prisoners was being unloaded at the main gate. We whites had to wait as they ran into the prison. A white warder was in charge, and I stood looking at his pleasant, smiling face, when suddenly his face contorted as he stepped forward to lash a black prisoner who had stumbled.

His face resumed its pleasant and smiling expression. The transformation was both rapid and bizarre.

During the day, Scott-Smith sent a message to Stuart permitting me to identify him. I was hauled back to court and named him. That was still not the end of the affair, though. A few days later, together with Stuart, I was ordered to Colonel Att Spengler's office at Security Police headquarters. We found some angry policemen who had gone looking for Scott-Smith and discovered that he had left the country. They accused me of having stalled in identifying him to give him the chance to get away, and threatened to lock me up again, but then dropped it. Scott-Smith later settled in Swaziland and did not return to South Africa for another thirty years, until apartheid rule was ending.

During my time in prison assorted doggerels went up on notice boards in the Saan building:

There was a young man named Ben
Who spent eight days in the pen,
He refused of course
To disclose his source
And so he went back again.
Ad infinitum.

And:

Uncle Att has much improved
Since he had Ben removed
Now he sits and smiles all day
Because the riot consultant has been put away.

Jokes aside, Damp Squib hardly justified all the brouhaha. It seemed to me that I had made the minister look like a fool, he had kicked the next fellow down the line, and the kicks had progressed until they finally got to me. The situation may, however, have been more serious than I realized. A Cape Town lawyer, Tom Walters, was accused of authoring the Damp Squib document and was charged with incitement. He was acquitted, but, as I was later to understand, although he wrote the document in jest, there were others—members of the recently formed underground group, the African Resistance Movement (ARM)—who had wanted to put it into effect.

Writing under the name of Candide, a political columnist in a Durban Nationalist newspaper, the *Nataller*, derided the reasons I had given for not identifying my source of information. I had used high principles to conceal "the most unprincipled behavior," wrote "Candide," who turned out to be Ivor Benson, the *Mail*'s sacked assistant editor who had hired me.

I sued for defamation. The *Nataller* published an apology and paid me enough money to buy a new car. A few years later Benson popped up again, as a media adviser to the white minority government in Rhodesia. Later still he reappeared to give evidence to a commission on the press in South Africa. He said that both Argus and Saan were controlled by the powers behind the "international capitalist-Communist conspiracy." Even the most fervent Nationalists probably would have had trouble swallowing that one, or so one hoped.

The real eye-opener of the jail experience for me was the unstinting support I received from the *Mail*. Not the slightest pressure to cave in was applied. Gandar and Louw visited me in jail, arranged whatever could be arranged, and went to see my wife to give her encouragement. Kuiper, the Saan managing director, was also supportive and backed the defamation action against the *Nataller*, agreeing that I would not bear any costs if I lost, and let me keep the cash settlement. He accepted that whatever had happened had resulted from my work for the newspaper and I was therefore entitled to support.

Our legal advisor, Kelsey Stuart—a partner at Bell, Dewar and Hall, the firm that had done the *Mail*'s work from the start of the century— became my friend. As the government piled up one law after the other and the hazards multiplied, Stuart became the country's foremost expert on media law. His knowledge was unsurpassed and he had a quick mind, able to grab hold of the essentials of a story. He served all the Saan group newspapers in Johannesburg and persuaded the board to stop paying expensive insurance premiums against the risk of being sued and instead pay his firm a retainer and fees.

Stuart made it possible for the *Mail* to publish as freely as it did because he went beyond the usual legal role of advising us what we could not publish; instead he was willing to explore how much could be published. He was unflappable. A story would break at 1:30 A.M., on deadline, and we would call him. He'd wake up, listen to a lengthy, perhaps complicated report, and immediately give advice. It eventually got to the stage that, when a hot story landed, within fifteen minutes other newspapers in the Morning Group phoned to ask for Stuart's assessment and how we were going to handle it.

The advice he and his colleagues gave us was only that; whether or not to publish was an editorial decision. But it would have been a foolish editor who did not follow his counsel, and I do not know of any time that his advice was not followed. Stuart was not infallible, though, and some of his assessments went wrong, particularly when his recommendations had to take into account both the law and the malevolence of many Nationalist politicians, judges, and magistrates toward the *Mail*. But he was not arrogant about his knowledge: if he felt it necessary, he sought the advice of senior barristers. He wrote a book, *The Newspaperman's Guide to the Law*, that proved so useful that its scope broadened in later editions and it became the standard work for journalists and lawyers.

Although Section 44 (f) did not totally prohibit the publication of information about prisons, everyone believed that it did. A great silence descended over the country's prisons. The most probable explanation for the self-deception is that it came about as a result of the wave of new restrictions on personal liberties that was the government's response to the growing resistance movements.

Underground activity was flourishing: Umkhonto weSizwe, the ANC, PAC, Poqo, the Communist Party, the African Resistance Movement, the Yu Chi Chan Club, plus others in tribal areas. Detention without trial—initially for 90 days at a time, later stepped up to 180 days, and then indefinitely—became an integral part of existence.

The public was provided with less and less information, and a climate of fear ensured that people did not want to know too much. Newspapers consciously or unconsciously accepted that it was safer not to dig too

Chapter 12

deeply into sensitive issues. Prisons, in any event, were considered a low priority when there was so much else to delve into, and with less risk.

The curbing power of 44 (f) was believed to be even greater after June 1965, when its scope was extended from "publishes" to "publishes or causes to be published," lengthening the chain of those who could be held responsible for publication. At the same time, the Section 44 (e) prohibition on taking photographs was tightened to close a loophole the press had been using, especially in regard to political cases. Thus, for example, when Nelson Mandela was on trial for sabotage in 1964, although newspapers were prohibited from photographing him, pictures of him taken prior to his arrest were published. The new 44 (e) prevented publication, without permission, of any photographs and sketches of anyone in custody, or anyone who had escaped from custody, or anyone who had been executed or died in prison. The minister of justice, John Vorster, offered seemingly reasonable reasons for concealing the images of arrested political leaders and activists. He claimed that it was in the interests of families and arrested people that their photographs not be published. The principle of protection also applied after a person had been convicted, he said, and in addition, unlimited publication of photographs was disadvantageous for the prevention of crime.

Even though little appeared in print about prisons, I was receiving bits and pieces of information from men who had been jailed for pass offenses. I also knew many of the people who were arrested for political activities, and word circulated about their experiences. But they were usually political detainees kept in solitary confinement away from other prisoners. Ernie Wentzel was detained for a month and returned to tell the story of being kept in isolation in a suburban police station. The cell door was opened to let in a priest, and a surprised Wentzel told him, "I don't think I am allowed to have visitors." The priest said that he was glad to have the chance of coming to offer comfort and prayer. "I'm a political detainee," explained Wentzel, at which the priest went pale and hurriedly backed out of the cell, calling as he went, "God bless you, my son, God bless you."

Another detainee and close friend was Norma Kitson. Around the time my first marriage broke up in 1964, she was separated from her husband, David. But when he was detained, she stood by him. I learned, at close hand, what it was like to worry each day about the unknown: to examine clothing returned from the police station for signs of blood in case of torture, to smuggle in cheering messages by inserting a thin roll of paper into a tube of toothpaste, or sewing it into a shirt collar. In due course David was found guilty of membership of the High Command of Umkhonto weSizwe and was jailed for twenty years at Pretoria Local. He managed to sneak in a tiny radio, hidden in his groin.

While Norma was campaigning against detention without trial, I went to Zambia for a fortnight. On the way back she phoned me in Salisbury (now Harare) to say the Security Police had hauled her in that day and questioned her about our relationship. She thought they were going to detain me when I came back. Two days later I returned to Johannesburg. She had been detained that afternoon. They did not torture her physically, but the Security Police used other techniques. An interroga-

tor invited her to sit down, she later told me, offered her tea and a cigarette, and chatted amiably until he suddenly asked, still in a pleasant
voice, "Have you heard about your daughter? What's her name? Mandy,
isn't it?" Out of touch with the world while in jail, Norma reacted with
fear: "What's wrong with her?" "Don't you know? She's got cancer."
And then the interrogator switched tactics and started screaming at her
that she was a Communist who didn't care for her children. He marched
out, leaving her distraught. They kept Norma in jail for four weeks, and
although her courage held, the experience took its toll on her. After her
release she had to go into a private sanatorium for a few days, and her
inner distress was evident in the nightmares she suffered for many
months to come.

Nonviolent interrogation could be successful. A detained leader
cracked when tape recordings were played of him in his mistress's apartment. A woman started off defiantly, but crumbled and told all she knew
when a tape was played of her with a lesbian lover in her own bedroom.
A directional microphone was used to eavesdrop on a discussion
between two members of an underground movement who thought they
were safe because they were in the countryside.

But force rapidly became the norm. People were either beaten
straight out or ordered to stand on a brick. The brick treatment was
used a great deal. People stood hour after hour under the threat of punishment. Weariness led to disorientation and an overwhelming desire
for rest. That is when people confessed and signed statements. The stories about interrogation got around, but could not be published because
nothing could be proven. Only occasionally did details emerge into the
open, when defense lawyers presented the testimony of the accused in
court. It was seldom done, because lawyers knew that most judges were
hostile. If the accused said that he or she had been tortured, the prosecution could put three police colonels or a general into the witness box
to swear that the fingered policeman couldn't have done it because he
was lying on a sunny beach five hundred miles away at the time. Faced
by a choice between an accused charged with terrorism or subversion
and a bevy of senior police officers, it was hard to imagine a judge finding for the accused. Once the judge rejected the accused's claim, the way
was open for the prosecutor to say that the accused had been found to
have lied about torture, clearly for political reasons so as to besmirch
South Africa. What other lies was he telling to worm himself out of the
serious charges against him?

Early in 1965 Gandar decided it was time for the *Mail* to set up an investigative unit, and asked me to head it. The unit was to be modeled, in a very modest way, on the *Sunday Times* of London, which under the editorship of Harold Evans, was probably the finest newspaper in the world. I had become its Southern African correspondent, so I was reading and admiring it every week.

I was then reporting the *Mail*'s labor beat, which chiefly dealt with the Trade Union Council of South Africa (Tucsa). It was a body of considerable size and importance and its leaders were well-intentioned in opposing apartheid. But they were grappling with a dilemma: on the one hand, they had the demands of their overwhelmingly white members, who wanted to preserve their status and high pay; on the other hand, the leaders knew whites had to link with black workers to avoid being undermined. Tucsa never resolved the dilemma. A while later it excluded black unions from membership, and never recovered from this retreat from reality.

The labor situation in the mid sixties was undergoing transformation because the government's attempt to protect white workers by decree—restricting specific jobs only for whites through "job reservation"—was collapsing since there simply were not enough white workers to do the jobs.

Employers were pressing for the entry of blacks into more skilled work and were being resisted, not only by the government but also by the white trade unions, which feared for their members. For example I reported that the attempt to reserve housepainting for whites had to be diluted by decreeing that at least the final coat had to be applied by a trained white worker. But since modern PVA paints needed one, perhaps two coats, it was a nearly mad-hatter decree. In the construction industry blacks were not allowed to drive trucks above a certain size, but in the engineering industry they were.

The Garment Workers Union in Johannesburg had its own unique and complex identity. Among its ranks were many white Afrikaner women who had come from the farms into the garment industry during the Depression of the 1930s, and in the waiting room of its offices in the city were three photographs reflecting the contradictory strands of its history. One was of Paul Kruger, the president of the Transvaal Boer republic defeated by Britain at the start of the century. Facing him was Bill Andrews, the first chairman of the Communist Party of South Africa in 1922. The final portrait was of Solly Sachs, Jewish and a onetime Communist who had organized the women and won their eternal loyalty.

To get the investigative unit going, I drew up a memo for Gandar outlining possible topics. Prisons were at the top of the list. I proposed a couple of articles. Apart from my prison reports, Gandar was getting information from other reporters and people in public life with whom he was in contact, and he believed that it was time for an investigation. Coincidentally the *Mail* was invited on a press visit to a new model prison at Kroonstad, a couple of hours south of Johannesburg by car.

I went to Kroonstad, which seemed impressive, and in an article carried on page one the following day I reported that it was the "pride" of the Prisons Department, "setting the lead for a new outlook towards criminals, with the stress on rehabilitation and reformation." The typical image of prison warders was contradicted by the head of the women's section, an attractive twenty-three-year-old university graduate. The white prisoners—468 men and 28 women—were the main focus of the visit, but I was also shown the living quarters of the nearly 2,000 black prisoners.

One large cell was home to eighty black political prisoners. It was clean and airy, with the bareness broken only by sisal mats and blankets neatly rolled up at the side. There were no lockers because, I was told, black prisoners only had one set of clothes. I stood in that large, desolate room and wondered which friends of mine were housed there. I asked to meet the politicals but was turned down. The closest I got was seeing a line of men walking past a doorway, in the distance. I could not recognize anyone, but ten years later I met Thami Mhlambiso in New York, where he was working for the United Nations. Mhlambiso had been in jail for his ANC activities, and was one of the prisoners who walked past the doorway. They had recognized me then, he said, despite the distance, and were excited to see me there.

Kroonstad was interesting because of the new buildings and the officials' fine words in speaking of their "unflagging belief in the inherent good of a man, even when he has been convicted of a serious crime against the community." But it did not accord with what I was hearing about other prisons and, as I later learned, there was a great gap between uttering well-sounding phrases from psychology and criminology books and understanding and applying them. Nor did Kroonstad fit with a letter that reached Gandar at that time, smuggled out of Zonderwater jail by white prisoners. It began, "We are appealing you most humbly to come to our assistance." It conveyed twenty-six complaints, including allegations of large scale corruption and theft by warders, toleration by warders of sodomy among prisoners, the watering of milk, jam, and the tobacco ration, and the withholding of legal documents. Gandar and I agreed the letter had the ring of truth about it.

How to meet the requirements of Section 44 (f)? The vital point, clearly, was to take "reasonable steps" to ensure accuracy in reporting on prisons. But what were "reasonable steps"? I already possessed a lot of background information about prison conditions. What else should I do? I consulted Stuart, who agreed that I would be safely within the law if I interviewed a cross-section of prisoners and built up a portrait of conditions, much as Obed Musi and I had done four years earlier at Modderbee. He said that as an additional safeguard he would question my informants and require them to testify under oath to the accuracy of their statements.

Gandar gave the go-ahead to start work. I made appointments to see Johannesburg lawyers with large criminal practices for the purpose of gaining access to their clients. Several months would be needed to interview a sufficient number of ex-prisoners, and relatives and friends of political prisoners.

Fate intervened. Norma and I went to Durban, 375 miles (600 km) away, on holiday, and while there, she visited Harold "Jock" Strachan and asked me to fetch her. Strachan had been released from jail a few weeks earlier after serving three years. I wasn't eager to meet him and did not know much about him except that he was a leftist who had been involved in teaching people to make bombs. We met and I liked him. His face was thin and bearded, his nose crooked, giving him a pixie look. After an evening of conversation I was totally sold on him. His memory was remarkable. I had no doubt that he was truthful, and he was not only highly articulate but invested his recollections with human detail and humor. There was also a sense of balance in what he said, both damning and praising prisons. I spent hours with him, recording him on tape.

Thirty-nine-year-old Strachan had joined the South African Air Force immediately after completing high school during the Second World War. He qualified as a pilot with the rank of lieutenant. At the end of the war he studied art in Britain and Germany before returning to South Africa to teach and paint. He was among the first to get involved in underground activity when a lot of it was amateurish. He laughed as he told me that because he had been in the air force, he was presumed to know about making bombs. He had served his full jail term because, as a political prisoner, he was denied the one-third remission for good behavior given as a matter of course to murderers, robbers, and rapists. As his sentence approached its end, he was charged for a second time, but was ultimately acquitted of having recruited people for Umkhonto weSizwe and training them for sabotage.

When I met Strachan, he was living on borrowed time. A few days earlier the Security Police had visited him and asked the questions that often preceded banning and house-arrest orders: they wanted to know about his family and servants, his daily movements, his health, and whether there was a bathroom in the house. Once the banning decree was served, he would not be allowed to prepare any material for publication, nor would the press be able to quote him in any way without the permission of the minister of justice. I thought the statement I had recorded was so comprehensive that it would be a useful base from which to prepare a questionnaire for other ex-prisoners.

I returned to Johannesburg, had the tapes transcribed—they ran to thirty-five thousand words—and gave copies to Gandar and Stuart. Stuart was skeptical. "If what he says is true, then our jails are nothing less than concentration camps," he said. One of the improbabilities he picked out was Strachan's statement that the blankets he had been given at the Port Elizabeth North End Prison were stained, partly due to masturbating by prisoners. That apart, as a measure of Strachan's good faith, said Stuart, I should have him sign the transcript as a sworn statement and explain to him the dangers of making statements about prison conditions. I drove to Durban, gave Strachan the transcript, and offered my explanations. Strachan attested to the truth of the transcript in the presence of his lawyer.

During my return drive to Johannesburg, I mulled over Strachan's vivid account. There were his own experiences as a political prisoner, but he had also witnessed the degradation suffered by prisoners in general, both white and black. I did not believe that he was out to manipulate the *Mail*. I had asked him if I should concentrate on political prisoners or examine prisoners as a whole, and was impressed by his immediate response: "You must deal with all prisoners. You are dealing with human beings and you must try to help all of them." An idea sprang into my mind: why not publish Strachan immediately as a first-person story? I rushed to see Gandar the next morning, and he shared my enthusiasm. It was now a race against the imminent banning order: within less than a week I poured out twelve thousand words that captured the facts and sought both to evoke the feeling of Strachan's statement and render a portrait of the man. I had never written so fluently.

I sent a message to Strachan and he came to Johannesburg. Stuart spent several hours questioning him, and one of the first issues he raised was about the stained blankets in Port Elizabeth. Strachan described in some detail the different masturbatory methods he had witnessed, and Stuart declared himself convinced—as he finally was of the entire twelve thousand words.

Strachan and I worked a few more hours that night to incorporate changes as required by Stuart, and the text was finalized. Strachan flew back to Durban, narrowly escaping identification by a Security policeman at the airport. As far as we were concerned, we had met the requirement for "reasonable steps" to ensure accuracy. We also decided not to ask the Department of Prisons for comment ahead of publication. To do so would alert the Security Police and precipitate an immediate banning order for Strachan. In any event, the commissioner of prisons was General Steyn, who had misled us twice before.

I still had one question for Stuart. I had spent many hours with Strachan, written the series, checked and rechecked details with Strachan and against my own knowledge of prison conditions. But I still did not believe that it was possible to ensure 100 percent accuracy when reporting a man's life over a period of three years. I estimated that I was working to an accuracy level of 98 percent. Was this sufficient for the Prisons Act? If the government wanted to bring charges, could it select bits and pieces from here and there or would my text have to be taken as a whole? Stuart was emphatic: any prosecution could not pluck out sentences, but would have to keep them in the context as they appeared in the report.

The three-part series, which began on a Wednesday morning in June 1965, provoked widespread astonishment. Most people assumed that the *Mail* had contravened the Prisons Act through the mere act of publishing details about prisoners. "What happens behind the high walls of South African jails?" read the page-one teaser. Inside, the article, "By Harold Strachan as told to Benjamin Pogrund," reported such details as:

We had a flush toilet in the cell, which is quite unusual as far as prisons I have been in. But an interesting thing about this toilet was that you didn't only defecate in it, but you also washed in it; you brushed your teeth in it.

They had sufficient bathroom facilities. They had a very spick and span shower room with hot water and everything laid on, but we weren't allowed to use this because it had been beautifully polished

In Cape Town, in 1957, with, from the left: Peter Hjul (standing), Joan Hjul, Athol Fugard, and Jimmy Gibson.

Press conference given by World Council of Churches after Cottesloe Consultation, Johannesburg, December 14, 1960. From the top right: Fred van Wyk (with cigarette) of South African Institute of Race Relations, Dr. W.A. Visser t'Hooft, WCC general secretary (next to him, with cupped hands). I am on the left.

Reporting on the Bechuanaland Police Camel Corps
at Tshabong in the Kalahari Desert, August 26, 1963.

On the left are two police detectives serving a search warrant on me (second from the right) and Laurence Gandar (at right) at the *Rand Daily Mail*, June 1965.

As night editor, during a police raid on the *Rand Daily Mail* led by Lieutenant Barend Celliers (right).

With Laurence Gandar (right) emerging from the Supreme Court in Johannesburg at the end of the Prisons Trial in 1969, surrounded by well wishers.

Johnny Scholes, ranked as the toughest prisoner of South Africa, in 1969.

At the University of Witwatersand, Johannesburg, after Laurence Gandar received an honorary Ph.D. on December 14, 1974. From left: Raymond Louw (the editor of the *Mail* at the time), Isobel Gandar, me, Laurence Gandar, Mark Gandar (his son), Jean Louw, and Anne.

A "re-education camp" for dissidents, criminals, and prostitutes in Marxist Mozambique in 1980. The sign reads, "In Unango, reconstructed men grow."

The Pan Africanist Congress leader, Robert Sobukwe in 1977 in Kimberley, to which he was banished for six years before his death.

While Deputy Editor (I'm on the left in my office) in May 1982, I dealt with the police (the two on the right) about the *Rand Daily Mail* report on Seychelles mercenaries (note the newspaper headline on my desk). *Mail* reporter Eugene Hugo is sitting second from the left.

President Samora Machel of Mozambique emphasizes a thought during an interview at his presidential palace in Maputo, April 1984. The interview appeared in the last issue of the *Rand Daily Mail*. Machel gave me the interview as a tribute to the paper.

Squatters on the Cape Flats, Cape Town, in the early 1980s, who were continually harassed by the police.

Anne with my close friend and advisor, Ernest Wentzel, in Johannesburg, 1984.

Dr. Mamphela Ramphele while under government banishment in the rural slum of Lenyenye in the early 1980s.

Anne with Mandela's daughter, Zinzi (left), and Winnie (right) in Brandfort.

With Nelson Mandela (and my son, Gideon, far left) at Witwatersrand University to mark the presentation of my Robert Sobukwe papers to the university's library, and the reissue of my biography, *How Can Man Die Better: Sobukwe & Apartheid*. (Natalie Scrooby)

With Rabbi Michael Rosen (left) and Archbishop Desmond Tutu at Yakar's Center for Social Concern, Jerusalem, February 1999. (Debbie Bernstein)

—floor, taps and so forth—and mats were laid on the floor to keep it nice and tidy, and prisoners were seldom allowed to go in there. It was kept clean for inspection.

I saw constant assaults on African prisoners. There was a particular prisoner—a longtimer whose name was China. He was reputed to be half Chinese and half Xhosa, and a terrible brute.

He looked like a gorilla. He stood around in a reception office in one of the passages and he beat up prisoners. The white warders did not say to him "Slaan hom" (Hit him), but they said, "Vat hom raak." (Get hold of him).

This apparently was to make it kosher so that no one could ever say that they had told him to assault prisoners. When told to "vat hom raak," China would beat up men unmercifully.

Even the duster that I used for cleaning my cell I put around my neck. Everything you could get hold of you put on. And you just sit and freeze...

We did nothing all day. You just sit. You are not allowed to lie down. No. That is an offense. You just sit. I used to wake up at half past five in the morning when the gong rang and just sit and hope and wait and shiver and pray for half past four in the afternoon when you were allowed to go to bed [on two felt mats on the concrete floor, and with four thin blankets].

At Pretoria Central Prison, the condemned prisoners are in a special section on their own, but right in amongst other prisoners. This is one of the most terrible parts of being in that jail... Executions were held about every ten days. Days beforehand, the condemned start singing, and being Africans most of them, they can't help singing harmoniously. But as the time wears on the singing gets more and more ragged.

The last two days and nights they just sing right through. 'Nearer my God to Thee' and stuff like that. I never want to hear any such hymns again.

Then you would hear the condemned walking to the gallows cells singing hymns. You would hear the door shut. Later, you would faintly hear the sound of the trapdoors opening. I would feel a tremble run through the part of the building where I was as the trapdoor fell.

I ended the second article with the teaser "Tomorrow, I want to talk about assaults." That was the last straw for the government. Later that day a posse of policemen arrived at the *Rand Daily Mail*, bearing search warrants to seize my notes and transcripts. I had destroyed or hidden anything that might have helped the police, but they were not bothered about this. Their mission was to halt publication of the third and final article.

I did not have the text, I explained, as I had given it to the printing department. I suggested I fetch it, and they agreed. I handed it to them and they left with broad smiles. What they did not know was that the previous afternoon the chief copy editor, Rex Gibson, had told me that production was slack, and if I had the third article ready, he could have it edited and set in type a day ahead of time. When the police let me loose, I ran to the production department, checked that the article had indeed been typeset, and frantically told the foremen to hide it. Foremen and linotype operators grabbed the trays of lead type and ran to hide them in the bowels of the building.

Word leaked out, perhaps through a police spy in the office, that we were still able to publish. That evening Gandar received an extraordinary phone call at his home from Brigadier Louis Steyn, commandant of the police in the Johannesburg area (and no relation to General Steyn). Steyn said he was a supporter of the opposition United Party, that he had great difficulties in his job because of his political views, and as a personal favor to him, he wanted Gandar to stop the publication of the final article. The reports, Steyn said, were causing him great concern because of the potential harm to South Africa's image abroad. He asked Gandar as a personal favor to him to hold back the final article for a few days so that they could discuss it "like gentlemen."

Gandar pressed him to learn about the rationale behind his request. Steyn indicated that he was speaking on behalf of a person or persons in high authority, but would reveal nothing more. Gandar was taken aback by the call. He did not even know Steyn. He phoned senior members of the *Mail's* staff, and all agreed we should not accede to this strange request. We anticipated further action, but the night was quiet and the third article duly appeared with the opening statement:

I did not see any serious assaults at Pretoria Central. The worst assaults I have seen were on non-European prisoners at Pretoria Local Prison. For example, I remember walking back to our section from the exercise yard, conducted by a head warder. There were two doors on either side of the passage through which we were walking and through these two doors across the passage Africans were carrying heavy bags of food on their shoulders, bent forward.

We had to walk past and as a political I was never allowed to come into contact with any non-European prisoners.

Instead of asking the men to keep away, the head warder kicked one of them in the belly. The man sort of staggered back holding on to the bag on his back.

This is typical—this happened often. I saw it from my cell window. Orders were often accompanied by a blow. We saw Africans being driven into their section—we peeked through our windows—they were driven in like animals by *poyisas* (black warders) with sticks and with leather straps.

They used the long double strap of their truncheons or keys as a whip. Each man as he came past running would get a blow with the whip... we could see these men being driven across the yard for showering or other purposes by these *poyisas* with these straps.

We could see these men also being hit with fists and open hands. We could see them coming in a column two-abreast, that is, "two-two" as they put it in prison, and being thrashed as they rushed into the prison.

We could hear the same men rushing up the stairs and then into the section above us with the same cries as we had heard in the yard and we could hear the blows following.

This was general. But the worst assaults I saw anywhere in jail were those on Africans at the hospital and sometimes non-European patients in the hospital at Pretoria Local. For most of my time there the hospital yard was straight under my window.

Non-European prisoners who had to see the doctors were brought out at about 6:15 in the morning, and it could be freezing cold in Pretoria. They stood naked: sixty, seventy, eighty of them at a time. Huddled up like birds trying to keep warm. Like poultry. Stark naked. They had to stand with frost thick on the ground, barefoot, clutching each other to try to keep warm. Shivering.

And they would stand there until the doctor came at nine o'clock, sometimes later. Now and then one of the *poyisas* would allow them to pick up a garment to drape over their shoulders. Otherwise they just stood naked until the doctor came.

I have seen prisoners get a blow as they were inoculated, from a *poyisa* or from one of the prisoners who worked in the hospital. Sometimes this happened in the presence of a doctor.

Later that day Strachan returned to Durban with his wife and two young children from a fishing holiday. He and I had arranged for him to leave town while publication was under way. The *Mail* paid the modest cost, but made no other payment. Outside his house was a car filled with unshaven, disheveled, and irritable Security policemen, who promptly served banning and house-arrest orders on him. They had been waiting there since the previous evening. Now we understood the attempts to delay the third article: if the banning orders had been served on Strachan, we would not have been able to publish. We never learned whether Brigadier Steyn was party to the deception, but thought it likely that he was simply used. Within hours of Strachan's banning, Security policemen visited Gandar to warn him that nothing Strachan said or wrote, past or future, could be published. Next day the *Mail* told readers, "As a result, the three issues containing Mr. Strachan's story have now become 'collector's items'. His story… may now not be sold or disseminated in any way. However, there is no onus on any person who has copies of the three issues to dispose of them."

The *Mail's* policy, then and after, was never to seek permission from the minister of justice to publish statements of banned people. This was done on the principle that the minister would only authorize publication when it suited the government's political ends. We could see the policy in practice because, every now and again, Sapa circulated a report quoting a banned statement with the added advisory note to editors that the minister had approved it. In fact Sapa only distributed statements if it had official permission; otherwise it would have been breaking the law. The statements were of the sort that the government wanted to see publicized because it believed they reflected badly on the author or speaker. On this occasion, however, we broke our own rule: I persuaded Gandar to let me write to Vorster for permission to continue distributing copies of the *Mail* containing the Strachan articles. It was a tongue-in-cheek letter with no prospect of success, and sure enough Vorster curtly said no.

Gandar called for a commission of inquiry in a front-page editorial the day after the series ended. It was not an altogether satisfactory way to go forward, as the Nationalists had already shown the extent to which they would pack a commission with yes-men to whitewash an issue. But it was the best we could do.

The prison reports caused profound public shock. Helen Suzman told Vorster that he shouldn't ignore the complaints "or adopt his usual stubborn defense of his police or prison authorities. Even if the prison regulations are adhered to, South Africa is years behind the times and jail conditions are medieval." The United Party also spoke out strongly, although its spokesman hedged his bets by saying, "I cannot think of anything more wicked than the conditions described. And if these allegations are false, I cannot think of any more wicked lies. Either way, the government must take very strong action and a judicial inquiry is called for."

No minister or official responded. But the government's view was conveyed via the *Transvaler*. According to them, our reports were an "abominable smear campaign"; they were viewed in a very serious light, a top-level inquiry was under way, and "further action can result soon." The Nationalist Sunday newspaper, *Dagbreek*, also weighed in. A judicial inquiry was rejected at the highest government level, it said. The politicians calling for it were trying to embarrass the government and put it in a bad light. As for Strachan, he was a former political prisoner whom the government had banned. What was of concern was that the articles could have "serious consequences" because they would be publicized overseas.

Indeed they were. The *Mail* and Gandar were already well known abroad, and the police raid and the clumsy attempts to block publication drew international interest. I added to that with my report to the *Sunday Times* in London. I had intended a straightforward summary of Strachan's accusations, but instead wrote, "I am not allowed to cable any details of the shock exposure of South African jail conditions published this week in the *Rand Daily Mail* and which I compiled for the paper. The former prisoner, Harold Strachan… was placed under house arrest and he therefore cannot be quoted even in the most general way. Although the banning has not yet been published in the *Government Gazette* I dare not risk prosecution and jailing by cabling his story."

The journalist who spotted the potential in that was Derek Ingram, deputy editor of the *Daily Mail* in London. The *Daily Mail* led with the story under the headline "The Shock Report That No Journalist Dare

Cable—Inside South Africa's Jails." Over the next two days the paper published lengthy extracts from the Strachan reports.

The floodgates opened. We were inundated with cables, phone calls, and letters from newspapers and magazines in the United States, Europe, and Africa asking for publication rights. This put us in a quandary, as the *Mail* would contravene Strachan's banning by permitting anyone to reproduce it. On Stuart's advice we sent tactful replies to papers as widely dispersed as the *Guardian* in Britain, *Trouw* in the Netherlands, and the *Nation* in Kenya: we cannot distribute the articles, but there is no copyright. In other words, please publish.

As publication spread through the *New York Times Magazine* and *Africa Today* in the United States, Nationalist fury boiled over. We had not remotely taken overseas reaction into account before publication, but now that it was happening, we sought to take advantage of it. The Nationalists believed otherwise. To them our sole purpose in publishing the Strachan articles was to gain international attention. At the best of times they were hung up about articles sent out into the world, and never understood that it was their own actions that were the cause. They always blamed hostile journalists, who were usually also viewed as agents or dupes of Moscow.

Helen Suzman once summed it up perfectly in parliament when a cabinet minister, goaded by her perpetual questions about abuses of civil rights, yelled at her, "You put these questions just to embarrass South Africa overseas." To which she replied, "It is not my questions that embarrass South Africa—it is your answers."

The Nationalist afternoon newspaper, the *Vaderland*, said that Gandar must surely have realized the reports would be used for a "smear campaign" abroad and that the public required an answer to this before going into the merits of what the *Mail* had published. The *Burger*, in Cape Town, also an official party organ, referred to an interview by Gandar with an overseas newspaper in which he'd said that the banning of Strachan was an attempt to suppress the truth; it also referred to my *Sunday Times* article. These were a "black reflection" on South Africa, and a heavy responsibility rested on us to prove the truth of our statements, said the *Burger*. In other words, how dare we say that banning was oppressive. *Dagbreek* published a wild and muddled article that sought to establish a link between Gandar, the prison reports, the multiracial National Union of South African Students, various people convicted of sabotage, Dr. Martin Luther King, and threats by "Freedom

Marchers" in the United States to fall upon South Africa. Finally, after three weeks, Vorster made his first statement, but in the threatening way that was his style, telling a party newspaper that it was all a smear campaign and promising action against "certain people."

Despite these attacks, there was a heady atmosphere at the *Mail* based on the belief that we had presented an unanswerable case about prison abuses and that the government would therefore be pressed to take urgent remedial action. Among the many letters published, one reader defended prison officials, "who cannot strike back because of their status as public servants." Gandar attached a cocky footnote that the officials we had named could sue us for damages if they felt they had been wrongfully accused of misdemeanors, but "so far we have heard nothing from them."

In a front-page editorial Gandar pressed forward with our case:

In any normal society allegations so serious as those set out in the articles would have made some response from official quarters mandatory. Either the allegations would have been denied or, if there were some doubt about the true state of affairs, an inquiry would have been instituted, as a number of responsible citizens have already demanded.

Nothing of the sort has happened. The minister of justice, Mr. Vorster, has maintained a stony silence even though he is not usually slow in coming to the defense of his department when it is under criticism. The director of prisons has been equally tight-lipped.

And referring to Nationalist newspapers that had gone on record stating there was no need for a commission of inquiry because Vorster could be trusted to ensure that all was well, the editorial ended, "We do not share this trust in Mr. Vorster. We want something done about prison conditions and we are going to see that it gets done. We have opened up a chink in the curtain of secrecy surrounding our prisons. We are now going ahead to bust it wide open."

In that spirit, I continued seeking out former prisoners, taping lengthy interviews, and taking the men to Stuart and other lawyers in his firm to have the statements checked and sworn to if possible. I used a 112-point questionnaire I had put together, and planned at least two additional articles, one on white prisoners and one on the far worse conditions of black prisoners.

Then I heard about a head warder named Johannes Theron at Cinderella Prison, Boksburg, who was willing to speak out. I went to see him at his small house on prison property. He seemed like manna from heaven: a warder of warrant-officer rank who was willing and eager to lift the lid on the maltreatment of blacks in his prison. Theron was a tall man, strongly built, and excitable. The words poured out of him as he told me there were terrible things he wanted to expose. He had already been interviewed by Brian Kennedy, a reporter with the *Sunday Times* of Johannesburg (the *Mail* was in greater competition with the *Sunday Times* than with any other newspaper), and indeed, it broke the story. It went deep into the sins of the Department of Prisons, starting with the bold headline "Head Warder Condemns Conditions—Speaks of Brutality, Victimization and Bribery." Stuart was also legal adviser to the *Sunday Times*, and he had taken a sworn statement from Theron and approved publication of his story:

"I have seen electric shock treatment being given to prisoners—as a punishment and in order to make them talk. Once a prisoner has had the treatment he is prepared to sign anything," said Theron.

And, saying he had made a statement earlier that year to the Department of Prisons giving details of assaults, he went on:

"The conditions in Cinderella Prison are among the worst I have seen in seventeen years' service... During the past two years I have fought a running battle of protest against the victimization of both prisoners and staff. I have seen brutality absolutely contrary to prison regulations. Warders who have spoken out against these appalling conditions have been victimized."

Theron amplified the details in his conversations with me, and also introduced me to Gysbert Johan van Schalkwyk, a young warder who said he was leaving the prisons service at the end of the month and who confirmed the gist of Theron's statements. I saw another warder at Cinderella, Nooientjies van Rensburg, and he, too, confirmed Theron's account. But there was tension in the van Rensburg house because his wife opposed him getting involved. Van Rensburg said that if Theron landed in trouble, he would testify for him. Theron also offered me the chance to interview a black Mozambican, Filisberto Taimo, who had suffered electric shock treatment and was being released from prison in a few days.

Theron acted as the go-between, and I had someone meet Taimo when he came out of jail. To round off the picture, I had separately met another former prisoner, Isaac Setshedi, who also told me about assaults and torture at Cinderella.

The four men complemented one another. Their stories stood as a package. Stuart interviewed each of them, and cleared all their reports. But we were too hasty in trying to beat the *Sunday Times* and drive the government into appointing a judicial inquiry. Taimo's statement, the last of the package, was cleared by Stuart at 9:30 P.M. for the next morning's paper. Only at 1:00 A.M., when I got home and looked through the first edition, did I spot that a previous jail sentence of Setshedi's read as six years instead of six months.

A quick phone call to the office and the error was chiseled out of the lead plates on the printing machines for the following editions. Was there also a more serious error? Vorster was quick to claim that van Schalkwyk had not resigned but had been fired. We were dismayed about this but thought it insignificant when set against the weight of accusations leveled at Cinderella.

Gandar wrote another editorial: "Well, Mr. Vorster, are there now some anxious doubts in your mind?" Referring to the Cinderella revelations, "What does Mr. Vorster say to all this? In contrast to his reticence over the now famous Strachan disclosures... Mr. Vorster was quick off the mark yesterday in an unworthy attempt to discredit one of our informants, claiming that he had been dismissed from the prison service for bad conduct. Significantly, Mr. Vorster sidestepped the warder's allegations about electric shocks, merely saying that these would be investigated in the usual way. But he then prejudged the matter by adding that he was not prepared to allow the good name of his officials to be besmirched by unfounded lies." Repeating the need for a judicial inquiry, Gandar ended provocatively: "Get cracking, Mr. Vorster. Evasion is impossible now." For good measure, alongside the editorial were statements by the leaders of the United and Progressive parties backing a judicial inquiry.

That was the day our innocence ended. The Cinderella reports pushed the government into action. Van Schalkwyk was arrested as he came off duty, en route to a meeting with the *Sunday Times*'s Kennedy. Also arrested just after his last shift in the prisons was another young warder, Gideon Prins. He, too, was to meet Kennedy, who instead saw him being driven away in a police van. The next day Theron was suspended from duty and ordered to remain home. As the police ransacked his house, Theron grabbed his National Party membership card and publications and threw them at the policemen. "Here, you take these also. I don't want them anymore," he told them.

The same day, the *Mail* was raided for the second time, with the police seizing all documents about Cinderella. Gandar reached me at home to tell me that the police wanted another document, which I had. I phoned the *Mail* news desk to say I would drive to the office immediately. Fifteen minutes after I arrived, the police returned—the first indication, with many more to come, that we were being watched.

Raid number three came within a few days, with search warrants demanding the tape recording of my original interview with Strachan. I phoned Stuart and he advised me that, as Strachan was banned, I would commit an offense if I handed over the tape; I would be disseminating his views. I conveyed this to the three waiting detectives and they grew somewhat choleric. They assured me that they had no intention of prosecuting me on that score.

"I know you gentlemen and I am sure I can accept your word," I replied. "But what of your superior officers? For all I know this could be a trap to get me to break Strachan's banning order."

The argument grew more heated until Gandar realized that nothing was to be gained and brought it to a close. The tape, as it turned out, was in Stuart's office and the detectives went off to obtain a fresh search warrant. I rushed a messenger to Stuart's office and had the tape brought to the *Mail*. We knew we could not keep up this game of tag, so I phoned the police and they returned to seize the tape from me, and insisted on using my tape recorder to confirm that the tape I was giving them was the right one. They had decided that I was not to be trusted.

The first police moves went together with a fierce war of words in the public arena in 1965. On one side were the *Rand Daily Mail*, several other English-language newspapers, and the anti-Nationalist opposition inside and outside parliament. Their demand for a judicial commission of inquiry gathered strength. The *Sunday Chronicle*, a serious Sunday newspaper that unfortunately had only a short life span, said that nothing less than a commission would "clear away the stench that is building up over our jails." The *Golden City Post* carried interviews with black leaders backing a commission. The Anglican archbishop of Cape Town and the bishop of Johannesburg also backed it. Black Sash members held a poster demonstration calling for a commission, and were abused by passing motorists shouting, "Go back to Russia."

On the other side were government leaders, principally Vorster, his Nationalist newspapers and the government-

Chapter 13

controlled South African Broadcasting Corporation (SABC). In interviews with his party newspapers Vorster put to good effect his practiced art of speaking in ominous terms. The prison accusations would be tested in the courts as soon as possible "without regard to persons." Gandar cracked back at him in the *Mail* the next morning, "Even if court proceedings are instituted—and we doubt that they will be—these will necessarily be confined to particular individuals and particular circumstances." Vorster replied within hours, "The editor of the *Rand Daily Mail* can set his mind at rest and watch the dock. Perhaps he will be surprised who will land there."

To add to government belief in some kind of a conspiracy, Vorster and his colleagues were convinced that we had deliberately timed our disclosures for a United

Nations conference on prisons in Stockholm. General Steyn was there, and was subjected to a failed attempt to evict him from the meeting. To Vorster the "liberals"—that is, us—were looking for a platform to bring the government and South Africa into disrepute. A few days later, without referring to the prisons issue, he spoke about the forces of Communism, which were waging a campaign directed toward trying to halt a Nationalist victory in the general election due the next year. The climax was imminent, he said darkly. In another speech to a party congress he said that people sometimes spoke lightly about prisoners and prisons—people who had never been inside a jail and did not know what prison meant. As delegates applauded loudly, he continued, "There are some people who have not been there and want to know, and perhaps they will have the chance."

That might sound like nothing more than a politician's histrionics. But in the tense atmosphere of the time, with attacks and threats raining down on us, it was sinister and frightening, especially because once Vorster had set out the line of attack, the SABC was quick to follow. Already guilty of selective presentation of news, its regular "Current Affairs" commentaries now zeroed in on us. One evening "Current Affairs" accused the *Mail* of not being interested in social criticism but of providing propaganda material for South Africa's enemies. The following evening, while the *Mail* was not directly mentioned, the announcer read out a circular allegedly seized from the South African Communist Party saying that the Communists had the duty to publicize abroad reports of horror and other conditions so as to maintain external pressure on South Africa.

The two broadcasts taken together were intensely alarming. Gandar and I had no doubt that we were being set up for a Communist smear.

To be the target of a Nationalist onslaught was a scary experience. It was ferocious and sustained, with vitriolic words, snide suggestions of impropriety, and threats pouring out from newspapers and the SABC. The Nationalist media establishment picked up their line from what their leaders said in public or presumably told them privately. Gandar had been subjected to it before for his editorial attacks on apartheid. Three years earlier he had won a defamation action against the *Transvaler*. This was my first real personal experience, and I was astonished at the capacity for distortion and smear. The previous attacks on me had been small stuff compared with what was unleashed.

It reached such a level that Gandar devoted a think piece to the "political hate campaign" being waged against the *Mail*. "Hardened as I am to the rough and tumble of South African politics, I cannot recall a campaign of such savagery, especially as funneled through the Broeder-bond-controlled South African Broadcasting Corporation," he wrote. "All of this is an extraordinary commentary on the state of affairs in South Africa today. For almost anywhere else—and this is certainly true of the Western world of which we claim to be part—our series of articles on jails would have been treated as a straightforward newspaper enterprise, a standard exposé of a social wrong." Yet, he said, Vorster seemed determined "to treat this as a political vendetta and the Nationalist press has taken up this line with vigor." The *Star* shared Gandar's concern, and spoke about "the curious and sinister campaign" against newspapers that had sprung from the prison reports. "The disclosures were… seized upon not as a case for inquiry and reform but as evidence of a campaign to besmirch South Africa's name abroad," it said. "All kinds of insinuations, some of them wildly far-fetched, were built into this indictment in the government-controlled press and radio."

As the attacks mounted, ex-warder van Schalkwyk was brought before a magistrate on a charge of perjury. He was given bail, but apparently could not raise the money, so we sent a reporter to pay the bail. He returned without van Schalkwyk and reported that the clerk of the court had "stalled" him for two hours and then said bail had already been paid and van Schalkwyk had been released. We did our best to find him, but he was kept hidden. Though we did not know it at the time, the failure to find van Schalkwyk would have catastrophic consequences.

The next time he was seen in public was in a crowded courtroom less than two weeks later. He pleaded guilty to charges of making false statements about the ill treatment of prisoners at Cinderella. He did not have a lawyer.

A deputy attorney general of the Transvaal, Dr. Percy Yutar, served as prosecutor. He was well known for his role as the chief prosecutor in the Rivonia Trial of Nelson Mandela and other leaders of Umkhonto weSizwe the year before. The trial was named for the suburb outside Johannesburg where the police found Umkhonto's secret headquarters. Yutar was a zealous agent for the government, and the Security Police thought the world of him. I knew this because they told me so. There was little doubt that Yutar created a courtroom climate in which only the international protests at the time deterred the judge from imposing the death penalty on Mandela, sentencing him to life imprisonment instead.

With van Schalkwyk in the dock, Yutar played the propaganda game from the start. He had copies of his opening statement available for the press, which was unusual for a South African court. He went straight in: van Schalkwyk had made his statement to the *Mail* under oath, he said, "knowing it to be false, and false in every material respect." Of the eighteen paragraphs in the statement seventeen were false. Van Schalkwyk had made the statement for financial gain and Theron and I had added a "good deal" to it.

Nineteen prosecution witnesses followed, each denying van Schalkwyk's claims, and all went unchallenged because there was no defense lawyer. Van Schalkwyk asked witnesses only three questions. The general refrain was that the electric-shock machine alleged by van Schalkwyk to have been used to torture prisoners was for the treatment of the prisoners' sore muscles.

I was horrified. I knew that van Schalkwyk had spoken to me freely, and I was absolutely certain that he had told the truth about the abuse of prisoners. I remembered talking to him in the Theron house. Theron had offered a few suggestions, which I politely turned away. Mrs. Theron was also present, however, and at one point, as van Schalkwyk was describing how warders had applied electrodes to prisoners' genitalia, she cried out in horror, "You don't really mean that." Van Schalkwyk had turned to her and replied, "That's nothing. I could tell you about a lot of other things, too."

In the courtroom I heard day being turned into night by an unscrupulous alliance between the prosecutor and the police. Van Schalkwyk's not having a lawyer was deeply troubling. With Stuart's approval I tried to speak to him, but the police and Yutar foiled me. Stuart said there was nothing we could do, as we were not a party to the proceedings. I rushed a letter to Yutar offering myself as a witness, but was ignored. Van Schalkwyk went into the witness box and said that he had had a car accident and had hoped to get compensated for the information he gave me. Asked by Yutar whether the Cinderella reports were "infamous lies," he replied, "Yes." Newspapers throughout South Africa shouted the story: "Van Schalkwyk Admits He Told 'Infamous Lies'" and "Ex-Warder Says: Story on Jails Untrue."

At the *Mail* we were all stunned with disbelief. I could hardly look anyone in the eye. I felt I had done something wrong but did not know what it was. It was beyond my comprehension how the newspaper could be flayed in open court without having the chance to reply. I could not understand how the truth could have been so distorted and destroyed. I urged that we publish a front-page statement the next morning and wrote a draft: "If the court finds that van Schalkwyk is a liar, then readers will ask themselves: at what point did he start lying?" It also noted that Yutar had not called witnesses who had offered themselves, including *Rand Daily Mail* photographer Geoff Bridgett, to whom van Schalkwyk had complained outside the courtroom that he had landed in all this trouble and not been offered compensation by the *Mail*. We discussed it at length, but decided not to publish anything for fear of falling foul of the *sub judice* rule. Finally, Gandar wrote a letter overnight to Yutar stating that the *Mail* had made no financial promise to van Schalkwyk, and he drew attention to Bridgett's availability as a witness.

If the first day of the trial had been a catastrophe, the second day was a nightmare. It opened with Yutar telling the court that because van Schalkwyk was not represented, and because "he has neither the intelligence nor the ability to plead on his own behalf, I deem it my duty to plead for him." Poor van Schalkwyk. He would have been better off without Yutar pleading for him. Yutar ignored the Bridgett evidence, and instead used Gandar's letter to drag me into the case. He said that he accepted that the *Mail* had not paid or offered any money but that I had been "the nigger in the woodpile," determined to get a story that would hit the headlines in South Africa and abroad. Probably the most aggravating circumstance, he went on, was that "the image of this country here and abroad has been damaged almost irreparably." In van Schalkwyk's eighteen-paragraph statement, about the only correct things were his name and that of the attorney who signed the statement. "Not only did he sell his birthright for a mess of pottage but he also sold his land for a mess of pottage—and even that he has not received," said Yutar. The magistrate sentenced van Schalkwyk to the maximum three years' imprisonment.

Months later I learned what had happened behind the scenes: Van Schalkwyk was out on bail after lodging an appeal, and I met him. He was a bit embarrassed talking to me. I asked why he had gone back on his statement to me. He said that he had been very frightened when he was arrested. A plain-clothes detective gave him a choice: he could either stick to his *Mail* statement, and get a three-year jail sentence, or he could give the police another statement denying what he had said and get a much lighter sentence, if not an acquittal. "What else could I do?" he asked. He said he had refused to speak to me during the trial on the instructions of police.

I felt some sympathy for him. Apart from the false inducements offered to him by the police, he was under severe social pressure. After his statement appeared in the *Mail*, he was treated as an outcast by many of his own people, especially since his father was also in the prisons service. He was an Afrikaner and lived inside the tight prison world. His fiancée broke off their engagement. It wasn't only that he was weak; even a strong person would have struggled to keep his feet on the ground.

The van Schalkwyk verdict had instantaneous effects. It was as if the white public heaved a deep sigh of relief. They could now dismiss all those terrible stories about the jails, which had caused such an unwelcome sense of responsibility. The *Mail* received abusive telephone calls and letters. Strict security was enforced at the Saan building: strangers visiting the building were screened and the garage entrances were guarded.

A lot of the threatening phone calls were directed at me. I was still listed in the telephone book under my previous address, and my ex-wife received a stream of phone calls threatening to throw bombs into her apartment and demanding to know where I was. For several weeks I did not stay in my apartment. I only went there to fetch clothing, always accompanied by a "guard," one of the two young *Mail* reporters who happened to be karate experts. I took care whenever I crossed a street.

On the afternoon of the van Schalkwyk judgment Gandar was subjected to police raid number four. The search warrant listed all photographs and negatives of the five people whom we had already published, and went even farther, demanding all documents "relating to conditions in prisons and the experiences of prisoners in jails throughout the Republic of South Africa." Gandar handed over the photographs, but on Stuart's advice demanded a copy of the search warrant before he would yield anything else. Strangely, the detectives would not do this. They left and said they would return later with a copy of the warrant. They did not return, and the next morning Gandar and Saan sought an urgent interdict in the Supreme Court, arguing that it was abuse of court process and harassment. The judge ruled that the police could keep what they had seized but that the rest of the warrant was too broad. The government took the case to the Appeal Court. It was heard months later, but we won that one.

The breathing space afforded by this court case could not have come at a better time because the problem of keeping documents away from the police had become acute. I had accumulated dozens of transcribed interviews with ex-prisoners, and their photographs. My informants would have been in great danger if the police learned their identities. I had an additional worry: I was researching a book on the history of Communism in South Africa and had a mass of documents and banned political books in my apartment. The consequences of a police raid on my home could be serious (later my fears were to be proven correct). My research papers were too bulky to cart around. I had difficulty searching for new hiding places for the prison papers that had some degree of easy access. I always told at least one other person where the papers were currently hidden. During one raid, while the police were questioning me in my office, a batch of papers was rushed out of the building through a back entrance. Several times there were false alarms and papers were unnecessarily moved. As it happened, the Gandars lived next door to the Yutars, and Isobel Gandar offered to hide the papers in their garden. It was one of the few jokes among us during that grim time.

Yutar was the hero of the hour. The night of the van Schalkwyk conviction he told a meeting of law students at Pretoria University that this was "just the start" of rebuttals. "I wonder what all those who have been shouting for a commission of inquiry into prison conditions, here and abroad, are going to say now that the very first case in the matter has shown matters to be blatantly untrue," he said. "And I wonder whether the editor of the *Rand Daily Mail* will be so eager to appear on television now." Government prosecutors did not talk like this in public, and the fact that Yutar did demonstrated his closeness to the Security Police. The *Burger* in Cape Town fueled the fire by saying that "lies of an unbalanced, unintelligent and unsuccessful warder were seized upon as evidence of unbelievable abuses in South Africa's prison institutions, and were spread around the world as part of an antiSouth African campaign which did our country terrible and wicked harm."

The Transvaal congress of the National Party was being held that week, and the "liberalist press" (a Nationalist derogatory term for liberals) came under attack for disturbing relations between whites and blacks and "poisoning" world opinion against South Africa. While such language was typical of these congresses, it was particularly distinctive because the minister of information, Frank Waring—a lightweight but valuable to the Nationalists because of his crossover from the United Party, and one of the first in the English-speaking community to give public backing to the Afrikaner government—gave delegates a soothing message: he promised that the government was considering taking action against some journalists who were "abusing the freedom of the press... Basically this government intends to retain the freedom of the responsible press—I say the responsible press—but it does not consider the freedom of the press the freedom to publish dangerous and distorted criticism." That was threatening enough, but his further words were even more chilling. He spoke about "agitating journalists" who published damaging material about South Africa "for money or because they wanted to harm their country." This was considered "treason."

Soon after, a detective went to Gandar's home to seize his passport. I was returning from Cape Town that evening, after trying to track down a warder who was willing to speak out. Gandar sent a telegram to the plane to warn me, but the message did not get through. While on the flight, I was chatting with a beautiful actress who was about to star in a play. As we walked into the terminal building together, I saw a knot of journalists and thought to myself, "How nice for Sophie. The press have come to interview her." When a couple of detectives stepped forward, I realized it was me they had come to see. As with Gandar, they seized my passport too. We joined the long list of South Africans stripped by ministerial decree of the right to travel out of the country. I did not get the passport back for more than five years.

As if that wasn't enough, Dirk Richard, editor of *Dagbreek*, wrote, "I have never encountered among National Party congress participants so much displeasure and scorn towards a publication as there was [for the *Mail*], never such agreement that the paper and its editor should encounter some trouble. The series of articles on the jails was, as far as the delegates were concerned, the final proof that South Africa has a growth in its midst which should be cut out." He gave yet another ominous indication of what was lying ahead. Was the *Mail's* editor, he asked, the only guilty party in promoting a smear campaign against South Africa by publishing the prison reports? Weren't the owners and directors of Saan also a party to this, since they had done nothing to alter the "direction" of the *Mail*? In case anyone hadn't fully understood the message, he then listed the names of the *Mail's* directors. To underline it still further, a news report in the same issue of the newspaper said all involved in the prisons series would be charged in court. "This includes journalists and editors," and "the public may be astonished at the other men of standing in the business world who will be called to account in court."

We never learned if this was merely a scare tactic, but given the hysteria of the time, and the degree of *Mail*-bashing, I thought it was for real. There was another possible threat: all the warders we had named in the beating or torturing of prisoners were going to sue for defamation in a series of almost never-ending court cases. The threats were especially troublesome because of the pressure they put on members of the board. The businessmen on the board would have considered it unthinkable to be hauled into court, and we were concerned what they might do to escape the danger. But they did not back off.

The *Mail* fought back. Gandar, still reeling from the shock of the van Schalkwyk verdict, reread the lengthy report of the trial published the previous day in the *Star*. To his surprise he noticed that Van Schalkwyk's confession to the police was anything but the outright denial of his *Mail* statement as described by Yutar. Gandar showed it to me. I was equally taken aback. It was clear that, even in the police confession, van Schalkwyk had adhered to the bulk of his accusations against Cinderella Prison. The combination of the hysteria surrounding the first day's court proceedings, the speed at which the trial had been conducted, the vehemence with which Yutar had condemned van Schalkwyk's statement in the *Mail*, and the lack of a defense lawyer had masked the truth. The *Mail* reporter who covered the trial had not spotted it. I had been in court for part of the time, but my mind had become fixated on Yutar's opening address and even I failed to see it.

"The Case With The Question Marks" read the headline over Gandar's two-column editorial on page one the next morning. "On the surface of it, it appears to have been an open-and-shut case," he wrote. "The accused pleaded guilty and there was never any doubt as to what the outcome would be. His original statement in the *Rand Daily Mail* on jail conditions and electric shock treatment of prisoners has been branded as a pack of lies, discredit has been cast on our reporter who interviewed van Schalkwyk, the *Rand Daily Mail* has been held up in an extraordinarily bad light and Mr. Vorster has seemingly emerged triumphant from a new round of his public fight with this newspaper.

"There is more to this case, however, than meets the eye," Gandar went on to write. First, Vorster had said that court cases, and not a judicial inquiry, would test the *Mail's* accusations. But "the State produced a string of witnesses, most of them employees of the State, who gave evidence in accordance with the State's view of the case. There was no cross-examination of these witnesses and no argument on the issues raised. The court was presented, in fact, with a series of *ex parte* statements that were, at no stage, challenged or subjected to closer scrutiny. The State put its case and that was it. There was no counter-case for the court to consider. It was a walkover for the prosecution. So much for the broad contention that prison conditions are exposed to judicial examination in cases of this kind." Second, despite Yutar's claims about van Schalkwyk's confession to the police, it "scarcely adds up to a wholesale rebuttal of his original statement to the *Rand Daily Mail*."

Third, Yutar had said that van Schalkwyk made his statement to the *Mail* out of spite and for financial gain:

> And what did the prosecutor base this assertion on? Hearsay evidence from the accused's girlfriend's mother who was conspicuously vague both about the amount involved and when it was supposed to be paid. Van Schalkwyk himself had said in his confession that "nothing was said about remuneration" when he made his original statement; he had merely understood from Theron that the press would "see him right." Had Dr. Yutar wished to establish the point he could have called the editor of the *Rand Daily Mail* and questioned him under oath but he preferred to rely on slighter, indirect evidence. And even when the editor wrote him an urgent letter yesterday pointing out that at no stage was any money offered or paid to van Schalkwyk, Dr. Yutar continued to maintain that van Schalkwyk sold his birthright and his country for a mess of pottage. This seems odd, to say the least, seeing that Dr. Yutar accepted our statement that no money had been offered or paid.
>
> The more discerning members of the public at any rate will be left with the uneasy feeling that something less than full justice was done to a matter of grave public importance and intense public interest.

A few discerning newspapers shared our opinion. The *Cape Times* published the editorial in full, and the *Star* latched on to the issues at stake:

> It is because this trial was much more than the trial of a not very important young warder that it was unsatisfactory in the wider context in which it occurred. For there is no doubt that in this and other cases which the public has been assured will take place it is the newspapers that gave publicity to the prisons "scandals" that are really on trial, yet court procedure did not permit them to be

represented in the van Schalkwyk case and may exclude them from the others. The result was that there was no cross-examination of witnesses on what actually happened in prison or between the accused and the newspaper, and the prosecutor's attack on the journalist concerned was allowed to go unchallenged.

We were cheered, too, by the fact that overseas opinion was not fooled. The *New York Times* summed up the widespread attitude: "Typically, the government is trying to persecute and prosecute those responsible for the disclosures instead of ordering a judicial inquiry to determine actual prison conditions." Others seemed unsure. As a result of the first prison reports *Life* magazine was preparing a feature on Gandar and the *Mail*. A photographer had spent days taking hundreds of pictures of him at home and at the office. The feature was now dropped.

The best response came from the *Sunday Times* in Johannesburg. A quiet word was passed to its editor, Joel Mervis, about the disparities between van Schalkwyk according to Yutar, and van Schalkwyk according to his original statement. Mervis, who had been a lawyer before turning to journalism, seized the issue with gusto, and personally wrote the damning report under the banner headline "How Prosecutor Misled The Court." The documents in the case "prove beyond doubt" that Yutar's statement in court about van Schalkwyk "is inaccurate and misleading," Mervis wrote, and point by point compared the two versions of van Schalkwyk's statement that the *Rand Daily Mail* published and his confession to the police, for example:

> Affidavit to *Mail*, paragraph 6: 'I have seen this shock treatment being done many times. I've seen at least 15 to 25 convicts getting this shock treatment. Chief Warder van der Merwe was present sometimes, not always.'
> Confession to police: 'Paragraph 6 is the truth. I did see it.'
> Affidavit to *Mail*, paragraph 7: 'All the warders at Cinderella Prison know that it happens. But they are too scared to talk about it.'
> Confession to police: 'Paragraph 7 is also the truth.'

There had never been so devastating a denunciation of a public official. Nor was the *Sunday Times* alone, because the *Post* had spotted the same discrepancies. But the only discernible effect was to confirm existing prejudices and beliefs. Those who thought ill of the *Mail* brushed the facts aside and did not change their minds, while our supporters were given a factual basis for doing so and stood with the *Mail* even more firmly. Yutar later sued the *Sunday Times* for defamation and won, which was a commentary about the subservient courts at the time.

There were risks in being too supportive of us. Dr. Geoffrey Dean was a specialist physician in Port Elizabeth with an international reputation for his research on porphyria. He wrote a letter to the *South African Medical Journal*, the sober magazine of the medical profession, on August 14th:

> You will remember that I wrote to you two years ago when I found that, over a ten-year period, a number of the deaths among white men between the ages of 15 and 60 occurring each year at the Provincial Hospital, Port Elizabeth, followed assaults in our local jails and police stations, and that I felt sure, from logic, that this only represented a small proportion of the total assaults that were taking place. Assaults on non-whites possibly exceed assaults on whites. I suggested to you at the time that you might consider writing an editorial pointing out the moral duty of Government Medical Officers, for instance district surgeons, to use their power and influence as doctors to prevent assaults and cruelty in our prisons and police stations by seeing that, when they occurred, suitable action was taken against those concerned.
>
> The articles in the *Rand Daily Mail* by Strachan and the repeated accounts in our newspapers, both English and Afrikaans, United Party and Nationalist, of assaults by the police and warders must, I am sure, have convinced you that assaults and deliberate cruelty are really taking place.
>
> I spent a year in Germany at Frankfurt University from 1937 to 1938 and, at that time, decent men and women were aware of the atrocities that were being perpetrated against the Jews and no one, including the medical profession, had the courage to speak up about it. I can't help feeling that we as a profession in South Africa are becoming guilty of a similar sin of omission and that, unless we do something about it now, the world of the future will always remember it against us.

It was a remarkable letter for so conservative a publication as the *Medical Journal*, and reflected the extent of public concern provoked by the Strachan series. The sequel was sad. Two days after publication Dean was visited by Lieutenant Barend Celliers, the detective investigating several of the prison cases. Celliers said he had flown from Johannesburg in the private plane of the commissioner of police because Vorster was angry at Dean's reference to Nazi Germany. Celliers's first question, "Are you a Communist?" would unnerve any ordinary South African. He warned Dean to contact the police immediately if I came to see him.

In due course Dean was charged under Section 44 (f) of the Prisons Act with publishing false information. He had difficulties preparing a defense because the records on which he had relied for his letter had been destroyed, whether deliberately or innocently was not clear. But his stature in the medical world obviously gave him some protection. When the case reached court, a deal had been struck. The prosecutor withdrew the charge and Dean's lawyer told the court, "Dr. Dean has asked me to say that the letter... was written with no political intention whatsoever, nor with malice. It was not meant as an attack on the police, the prison administration, or officials or district surgeons. Nor was it written to vilify the Prison Service of the Republic, of which Dr. Dean is a loyal citizen. If his letter is capable of being construed as such, Dr. Dean expresses his regret."

Some speculation appeared in newspapers that the charge had been dropped because Afrikaans medical specialists in Johannesburg and Pretoria had made representations to the government that Dean had done nothing wrong professionally by writing his letter, and secondly that to put such an eminent medical man on trial would attract worldwide publicity and add to the difficulties that South African doctors were experiencing in international medical affiliations and congresses.

The swift police action against Dean was yet another contribution to ensuring a silent and compliant population. He slipped out of South Africa and went to live in Britain.

The criminal trials tumbled over one another. We faced the wrath of politicians whose already intense hatred for the *Rand Daily Mail* had been inflamed by our prison accusations and the extensive publicity abroad. They had the full power of the State at their command, and we were beginning to experience the implications of this. After van Schalkwyk, each of our informants was picked off, one after the other: Taimo, Theron, Setshedi, and Strachan. We knew Taimo had been arrested because the *Mail's* lawyers could not find him despite their best efforts. Only after a heated argument with Lieutenant Celliers did I learn where he was being held, yet our lawyers were blocked from access to him. When he was finally brought to court, they struggled against the prosecutor's objections before managing to speak to him. Taimo eventually achieved representation.

Taimo, however, insisted that none of what he had

Chapter 14

told us was the truth and that he had no knowledge of electric-shock torture. He said Theron had told him what to say. We were flabbergasted. I had spent most of the day interviewing him, and then Stuart cross-examined him for five hours. It seemed that after spending eighteen days in custody he changed his mind. If that hadn't scared him witless, he was probably also frightened of being returned to Mozambique into the hands of the Pide, the Portuguese secret police whose reputation for cruelty and arbitrary action outdid that of the South African Security Police. And indeed, the more the lawyers spoke to Taimo, the more his version of events swung around to accord with his original statement. He did know about electric-shock torture after all, and he had been assaulted, but he insisted that he had not been shocked. We faced a dilemma: the *Mail* was paying for the defense lawyers, and it was against the newspaper's interests to have one of our informants plead guilty to lying, especially when we were not convinced that he had done so. On the other hand, the first duty of the lawyers was to Taimo. He was their client and the lawyers were obliged to take his instructions and to put his interests first.

After the van Schalkwyk debacle Andrew Brown, the senior partner of Stuart's law firm, arranged the first of what was to become a series of lengthy reviews of our situation with Gandar, Saan's managing director, general manager, a brace of lawyers, and me. This developed into a regular "council of war" led by H. C. Nicholas, a senior counsel reputed to be the country's foremost expert on the law of evidence. It was also in our favor that Brown at that time was chairman of Saan's board and was therefore able to convey to the directors the extent to which we met the requirements of Section 44 (f), and the extent to which the State was prepared to go in order to damn us. The "council of war" decided that the *Mail* had to sit tight and continue collecting as much information as possible about prison conditions in anticipation of the court cases Vorster was promising. On Taimo, it was decided that we had to concede defeat in advance. We could not even contemplate putting Taimo on the witness stand for his own defense. The police had pressured him into signing a sworn affidavit denying his statement to the *Mail*, and any deviation from this while he was under oath as a witness would lay him open to a charge of perjury.

The pressure on Taimo had been overwhelming. His statement was taken by a police lieutenant in the office of the commanding officer at Cinderella Prison, with a head warder interpreting, a Prisons Department colonel present throughout, and a police major coming in from time to time. The only bit of grim pleasure we got out of the doomed trial emerged from the predictable evidence of a black convict who said how well he had been treated in the prison hospital. Cross-examined, however, he let slip that three prisoners had told him they had been "burned," tortured by electric shock. The prisoners were from the ANC, and wanted him to fight the whites. At this stage Yutar was granted a postponement, claiming that the witness was not understanding the court interpreter. When the trial resumed the following day, the witness denied having said that the three ANC men had been burned. He further denied any assaults and instead claimed that the chief warder would laughingly pick up a spade and join the prisoners at their work. With such improbable evidence as this unblushingly put forward by Yutar and accepted by the magistrate without a trace of embarrassment, we thought Taimo lucky to get only six months' imprisonment.

Setshedi was next. We found out that he had been arrested purely by chance. I was arguing with Celliers in his office and saw a clipping of the *Mail*'s interview with Setshedi lying on the desk. Taking a blind stab, I asked, "And what are you holding him for?" Celliers replied, "Murder, robbery, and assault with intent." I nearly fell off the chair. Prison conditions were one thing, but I was shocked to be mixed up with murder and robbery. As it turned out, it was yet another police pressure tactic. Setshedi had in fact been arrested on a charge of robbery, and the police had tried to get him to make a statement against the *Mail* by threatening him with a trumped-up murder charge. The threat failed to frighten him and was subsequently dropped. He was then given treatment probably unprecedented for an accused black person in a South African jail: he was served fried eggs for breakfast and asked to cooperate with the police by testifying against the *Mail*. He refused and stood by his original story. The police interviewed him four times and took four separate statements from him. Setshedi never deviated from what he had told me.

Setshedi believed implicitly in the rightness of what he was doing. Although much of his adult life had been spent as a robber, with lengthy spells in jail, he felt strongly about the inhumanities he had encountered and witnessed there. When I first met him, he confided that he was glad at long last to have found an "ally"—the *Rand Daily Mail*—in his campaign to get the jails cleaned up. He was in his thirties and had a quick, sharp mind. If he had been born into a normal society and had had normal chances, perhaps his life would have been different.

In these fraught days he was in court pleading not guilty to publishing false statements about prisons and making false statements under oath. His story, which we had published, revealed that while he was working outside the hospital section at Cinderella, he heard screams inside. A short while later a convict whom he knew as Dan told him he had been "burned."

Yutar set out once more to prove that the electric-shock machine was totally innocent. One of his witnesses was Head Warder Giliam Malan, who had been working at the prison for twenty-seven years, the last five in the hospital section. He administered the machine under the supervision of another head warder. During the cross-examination, the defense lawyer asked Malan what he knew about physiotherapy. Malan responded that he was reading a book about it, though he could not remember the name of the book, its author, nor did he retain any of its information.

Another, more crucial line of attack by Yutar was to deny that any such person as Dan existed. Warders and policemen described examining the hospital registers and not finding any trace of Dan. They had found someone nicknamed "Long Dan." When confronted by "Long Dan," Setshedi had denied knowing him. They had taken Setshedi around the townships, but he had been unable to point him out. With much passion and rhetoric Yutar said that Dan did not exist; he was a "myth."

However, "Long Dan" was indeed Dan. Setshedi had quickly and shrewdly assessed the situation when the police brought Dan to him: he had just been subjected to threats and blandishments, and he knew what pressures would be applied to "Long Dan" once he was identified as Dan. He thought that Dan might soon be telling a story to the taste of the police and to the detriment of Setshedi, so he calmly denied that "Long Dan" was Dan. The police dropped "Long Dan" and continued their search, naturally without success. Meanwhile, Setshedi kept in touch with Dan, who said he was willing to come forward, if needed, to tell the truth about how he had been shocked.

As the trial got under way, and Yutar committed himself to claiming that Dan was a figment of Setshedi's imagination, the police continued their investigation and became convinced that "Long Dan" was Dan. They extracted a sworn affidavit from him that he had never been treated badly with the electric machine at Cinderella.

Here is where it grew complicated. The prosecution could not call Dan/"Long Dan" as a witness to say that nothing nasty had been done to him because Yutar had said he did not exist. But the prosecution wanted the defense to call him so that they could produce the police statement. If Dan deviated from the statement in any way, he could earn three years' imprisonment for perjury. That was exactly why the defense could not call him. The police brought Dan to court and put him in the public gallery for two successive days, dangling him in front of us. Knowing what the game was, the defense did not take the bait. Dan sat in the gallery while Yutar continued to speak of the nonexistent Dan. Both sides knew that Dan was there, and both sides pretended that he wasn't. Setshedi was found guilty on the fiction that Dan did not exist. The magistrate, in his judgment, found that Dan was "a mythical person," and because Setshedi was untruthful, no reliance could be placed on anything he had said to me. "It is a made-up story," the magistrate concluded. He sentenced Setshedi to six months' imprisonment for making a false statement under oath, and the *Mail*, in turn, paid his bail. The one consolation for us concerned the electric-shock machine because the magistrate said that "it must be conceded that such a machine, if it is misused—like anything else—can cause shocks and burns." This was the first breakthrough for the *Mail* and was a far cry from the findings in the van Schalkwyk trial three months before. But it did little to erase from the public mind the initial impression created so strongly by Yutar in the van Schalkwyk trial that the machines were incapable of causing shock.

The *Mail* lodged an appeal for Setshedi. It was heard three years later. Yutar argued for the State, saying that if no such person as Dan existed, then it followed that what Setshedi had claimed about Dan must be untrue. But the two appeal judges rejected his argument. Although Setshedi's statements were open to doubt, they said, the prosecution had not proven they were false; nor had there been evidence that the hospital registers were accurate. They acquitted Setshedi. It was a victory on technical grounds and not the kind we wanted to vindicate our reports, but at least a brave man was saved from unjustly going to jail.

The van Schalkwyk verdict and the ongoing trials created considerable fear among potential informants. Several ex-prisoners with whom I was in contact immediately refused to have anything further to do with the *Mail*. One man was actually on his way to keep an appointment with me when he bought the *Star*, read the van Schalkwyk verdict, and walked off in the opposite direction. It took several months of patient contact before he could be persuaded to continue cooperating. We needed more informants. The "council of war" debated whether to issue a public promise about paying legal fees for anyone who fell foul of the government because of their dealings with the *Mail*. Arguments in favor of doing this were obvious, but it was also argued that the *Mail* could lay itself open to new attack for appearing to offer financial inducements for information. As we were in an emergency situation, it was agreed that this factor had to be discounted. No one could say how much money might have to be spent, so the agreement of the board of directors was obtained.

An announcement was published on page one:

> The *Rand Daily Mail* wishes it to be known that all necessary legal aid is being provided, at the discretion of the management, to any person who has been or may yet be prosecuted as a result of his

having furnished information to this newspaper in the course of its efforts to secure an impartial inquiry into conditions in our prisons.

Police surveillance was a constant anxiety. Gandar held a meeting in his office with senior members of the editorial staff to bring them up to date on developments on the jails issue, and the next day one of the staff members was approached by a Security policeman who quoted what he had said at the meeting. Within days of the prisons publication Gandar's office was abandoned for any kind of confidential discussions, and instead he took to wandering the corridors whenever sensitive matters had to be discussed, earning the nickname "the editor in the corridor." One night Celliers and another policeman were found in Gandar's secretary's office, claiming that they were looking for Gandar and me. They were asked to leave. Later that night they returned to the office and were again asked to leave. They did not come back.

Various colleagues with whom I shared an office were most unhappy about the company I was bringing into the office. I was finally put into my own tiny cubicle under a stairway. In the interests of security I moved around the building, using free offices to talk to contacts. I used the phone as little as possible and set prearranged meeting places with my regular contacts, usually late at night. I would drive my car into the *Mail*'s basement garage, get into an office car with a driver, lie on the back floor, and direct him to where I wanted to go.

Sadie and George Stegeman in Cape Town were close friends, and I mailed a quick note to let them know I would visit at the end of the week. When I got there, George said to me, "That was a strange letter you wrote us." "What do you mean? It was a quick note to let you know I was coming here." "No, not that one, the other one, where you used those four-letter words about Sadie." I had no idea what he was talking about, but he insisted I had written the letter—my signature was on it. They retrieved the note from the wastepaper bin. It was typed, but the signature at the bottom was a very good forgery. Whoever manufactured the letter had made a revealing mistake, though. They sent the letter to George's post office box, which was the address at the head of his letters when he wrote to me, whereas I always sent my letters to his street address. I was relieved to have come to Cape Town that week and resolved the matter before it festered, but for months afterward I wondered whether any other friends were getting strange and abusive letters and weren't saying anything because they thought I had gone over the edge.

The most sinister episode we learned about involved a white prisoner. On the morning of Monday, August 9, 1965, Gandar arrived at his office to find a phone message taken for him the previous Friday night saying that Paul Putter had called to instruct, "Don't use the story I gave you until I tell you." Gandar knew of no such story, and checked with me. I did not know about it either, but I did know about Putter—he was legendary for his criminal record that spanned two decades. He knew all there was to know about jails, and would be a valuable witness if he was available. He was then a serving prisoner. I had also been warned by many ex-prisoners that Putter was highly unstable and that I should exercise great care in dealing with him. And here we were with this cryptic message from him.

A few days later I was walking to the *Mail* in midmorning and saw a large black car slowly driving down the other side of the street. A man sitting in front turned and pointed to the side entrance of the *Mail*'s building. There were five men in the car, all wearing dark clothes except for one man in a brown jacket. I caught a glimpse of his sharp-nosed face and brush of brown hair. The car carried "GG" (Government Garage) number plates. I wrote down the number and watched as the car halted down the street, with the men still looking back at the side entrance, before driving off. Later I described the episode to a couple of ex-prisoners. They said the description sounded like Paul Putter.

Soon thereafter Helen Suzman visited Pretoria Central Prison—in response to an invitation by Vorster—and reported a bewildering story to us. She was walking through the prison in the company of senior officials when she saw a man standing at the side of the passage, cleaning a door. He turned around and asked, "What are you going to do for me now, Mrs. Suzman?" and "Don't pretend you haven't seen me before. Don't pretend you don't recognize me as the man who Gandar and that other man, Pogrund, brought to see you at your house in Houghton. Don't pretend you don't know me. You all offered me money if I would give evidence against the prison authorities." Suzman had never seen the man before and, as she told us, for once she was struck dumb and almost all she could think of to say was, "This man is totally mad," and walked on. The officers with her were smiling broadly. She asked the name of the prisoner. "Paul Putter," she was told.

We did not know what it meant, but we were uneasy. The answer came in a phone call from Putter himself. He phoned me at the office one morning and I challenged him, saying, "I've been wanting to meet you. What the hell are you involved in?" Putter sounded desperate and afraid. He said he was calling from the pay phone in the cells of the Johannesburg magistrates' courts. He was there on a charge of escaping from prison. He said he had been forced by the authorities to undertake certain actions against the *Rand Daily Mail* and he wanted to tell the full story to a lawyer. Putter begged me to arrange for a lawyer to see him immediately in the cells. My own experience four years earlier as a prisoner in those cells proved useful. I knew that prisoners could reach the pay phone through the bars, and I also knew that the cells were under the control of the police and it was possible for someone being held there to make a phone call without the prison authorities knowing about it. The Putter contact seemed genuine, so I arranged for a lawyer from Bell, Dewar and Hall to rush to see him. The lawyer took down a statement, which immediately resolved the mystery and gave us information about the lengths to which the government was going in order to destroy us.

Putter started by describing his list of convictions going back twenty years for theft of cars and clothing, fraud involving checks, stealing military uniforms, impersonating military officers, and escaping from jail. He had been in prison for the past eight years and was currently serving two consecutive sentences, each between nine to fifteen years, as well as a four-year sentence. He had had fifty-six abdominal operations to remove foreign bodies such as four-inch needles, razor blades, finely ground glass, and poison. In prison he had cut his veins about forty times, and he exhibited the scars to the lawyer. He had once jumped from the third floor of a building and fractured both legs.

Putter said he had escaped on August 6th. That same night he was rearrested at his sister's home in Johannesburg by Head Warder Schambriel and Chief Warder van Zyl of the Fort. "They took me to the Fort and asked me where I had been," he said in his statement. "I knew of the *Rand Daily Mail* campaign against prisons and told them that I had just been to the *Rand Daily Mail*. This was at 9:00 P.M. Van Zyl gave me the phone number and I asked the night editor not to publish anything I had said. I gave this story to the prison authorities just to frighten them. I was then locked up."

That cryptic message received by Gandar finally made sense, but Putter went a lot farther:

> On the Saturday 7 August, van Zyl showed me a pile of blank paper and started sympathizing with my troubles. He said he would try and squash my charges on condition I helped the

department. I said I would think about the matter—I know I can't accept their word. Van Zyl, Schambriel, Colonel Germishuysen and Major Wolmarans questioned me all day on the same lines. They said I could only gain with the department. They said that if I helped the department to restore their good name they would let me out. They said that I must say that the prisoners are being well treated and that no one has any complaints, except malcontents and the really bad class of convict. I was confined to a cell and placed under guard. On Sunday afternoon 8 August I got so despondent that I cut the veins of my throat [and] jumped from the first floor... at the Fort. Europeans can keep razors in their cells. I was taken to the General Hospital and after my throat had been stitched van Zyl came and questioned me further asking whether I would be prepared to take the side of the department. He emphasized that I would only gain by it.

I was then transferred to Pretoria Central Prison where I was placed in isolation cells with no medical treatment whatsoever, despite requests for it... After a few days in isolation I was placed in segregation. Chief Warder Bodoff of Observation Section, Central Prison, Pretoria, told me that if I made a statement saying that Mr. Gandar of the *Rand Daily Mail* knew I was an escaped convict and had given me thirty rand to buy clothing for me at Rosebank, I would have every assistance from the Prison Department and would be released shortly. In fact I purchased clothing on 6 August at Rosebank with money my sister gave me—they wanted to work this fact into my story.

I agreed to give the statement. Colonel Steyn, chairman of Prisons Board, was sent to me. He suggested that I immediately be taken out of segregation because I was prepared to make false statements about Mr. Gandar. I was then removed from segregation and made an ordinary A class prisoner again. They wrote out a statement for me to sign. Main points of the statement were:

1. Gandar gave me thirty rand to encourage me to make accusations against the Department of Prisons.

2. Gandar personally took me to Rosebank to get clothing and a doctor. Gandar also took me to Mrs. Suzman, who was at Gandar's house in Killarney.

3. Mrs. Suzman and Mr. Gandar said they would attack the minister about prison conditions in parliament.

4. Mr. Gandar and his legal advisers would meet me at 9:00 P.M. at Rosebank Hotel to take a statement.

5. Mrs. Suzman promised help.

6. Mr. Gandar asked me to have full confidence in him and he showed me a letter written to the effect that he had supplied assistance to Bram Fischer [the jailed leader of the Communist Party] in Kroonstad [prison].

7. Mr. Gandar has mighty organizations behind him and one of them is the press (I understood that they were getting me to insinuate that Mr. Gandar is a leading Communist in South Africa).

Chief Warder Lombard typed the statement and was instructed by Captain Pretorius to show it to no one. Captain Pretorius read it to me and asked me to take the oath and sign it, which I did. Lombard administered the oath. I signed this knowing it to be completely false because I wanted to stay out of segregation because it was terrible there. I don't know on which date I signed.

At about 10:00 A.M. on 2 or 3 September Colonel Steyn came to me in the Central Prison and said that now they were going to test me. Mrs. Suzman was coming in the afternoon and Steyn told me that when she came round I was to ask her what she proposed doing to help me, as she had previously made promises to me. This was all fictitious and supposed to link up with the alleged events in my false statement discrediting Mr. Gandar. I was told not to talk to any convict about the conversation. Mrs. Suzman came and I attacked her—she didn't know what to say.

The Prison officials brought me to the Fort on 6 September. A few days later Colonel Steyn came and saw me and said I would be taken out of prison with him and Lieutenant Victor of Security Branch and that I would have to show him the places mentioned by me in my false statement. Then he explained that when we drove down Riviera Road we would go slowly past a certain brick house which he described to me, No 6 Riviera Road [Gandar's home]. I must point out that house as being the one I had visited with Mr. Gandar.

The next day Colonel Steyn and Lieutenant Victor and Head Warder Schambriel and myself went to Killarney. I showed them the house. I also showed them the consulting rooms of a doctor whom I was supposed to have visited. I did this on their instructions. I also showed them where I bought the clothing. They took me to the *Rand Daily Mail* buildings, I had never seen before and just showed me the building and explained that that was the building I visited to see Mr. Gandar. They took me back and told me they would take a full complete statement. This hasn't happened yet. We also passed next to a block of flats across from Mr. Gandar's house and Victor pointed out Miss Fischer [Bram Fischer's daughter] to me and told me that I must say that that woman was present there.

With Putter's statement tucked away, we were able to breathe easier. At least this gun could be spiked if the need arose. Whether his statement to us was totally accurate was never put to the test, because he was never used as a witness against us. We never called him, because his instability made him too risky, but his statement tied in so perfectly with the series of episodes that had puzzled us that there was every reason to believe his description of the intended smears. Three years later I heard that Putter had succeeded in a suicide attempt. Much later I heard another whisper that he was still alive and that the suicide story had been passed along to keep us away from him. I never heard about him again.

The public focus on prisons unfortunately took attention away from another set of valuable articles published in the *Mail* at the same time. Written by Allister Sparks, these exposed what the police were doing to rank-and-file members of the ANC in the Eastern Cape, long an ANC stronghold. Over a two-year period, the reports said, the police had not only arrested nearly one thousand people but had split the charges against them into different counts, each carrying a possible three-year sentence. Thus the basic charge of belonging to an illegal organization was split into attending a meeting of the illegal ANC, membership of the ANC, and contributing money toward the costs of traveling to a meeting. In this way sentences of ten, twelve, and fifteen years were secured. People were also rearrested to be charged again, some of them up to four times. To round it off, the trials were held in a string of small towns, so there was little comprehensive coverage in the local press.

The *Mail* reports made the abuses known, and when the cases went on appeal, more than one thousand years were lopped off the collective sentences because of the irregularity of the split charges.

On August 29th, the *Sunday Express* reported, "*Mail* Is To Be Charged." The paper said there would not be an immediate prosecution until all other cases had been disposed of. There would also be three civil actions for defamation by warders named in our reports. Gordon Winter, an *Express* reporter, wrote the story. He was known to have intimate contact with Vorster and the police establishment. We realized that the report was authoritative and as close to an official statement as anything could be.

The *Express* was owned by the same company as the *Mail*, but they were editorially independent. This particular report added to deep resentment at the *Mail* because, throughout the prison turmoil, the *Express* went beyond the straightforward reporting of events and went out of its way to seek damaging stories against us. This feeling was reinforced because the editor, Johnny Johnson, had flatly refused to help us. Winter told me that a black prisoner had been kicked to death at the Fort in February that year during an escape attempt. He said he had drawn the attention of Prisons headquarters to the killing, and until he did so, they had no knowledge of it. The *Express* did not run the story, but Winter was willing to cooperate with me provided Johnson agreed. But Johnson refused, according to Winter, saying, "I'm not allowing my staff to be involved in the *Mail*'s jails bandwagon."

There was a sequel because, shortly after, Winter landed in prison due to a link with a gangland murder. He was friendly with a British gang that was behind the local murder of a prospector, Thomas Waldeck. The killer used Winter's gun, but Winter only learned about it after the killing. Months later the police made the connection, arrested Winter, kept him in the Fort, and gave him notice of deportation to Britain. I met him at a party when he was about to leave the country and asked whether he had learned anything in the Fort about the murder of the convict. He brandished his diary and said, "I've got the name of the warder who did it and even have an interview with him. One day I'll use the story." Winter was an indefatigable reporter, but just about everyone in journalism knew that he was a police informer. He was an obsessive collector of details, an incessant photographer, and kept filing cabinets stuffed with information. Winter left South Africa, but there was a distinct impression that his leaving was a put-up job between him and the police to give him some credibility in trying to penetrate South African exile circles in London. He later returned to South Africa.

If the *Sunday Express*'s attitude was resented, the behavior of the English-language press generally was cause for dismay. After the *Mail* had broken through the silence surrounding prisons, it was hoped that other newspapers would carry out their own independent investigations. But only the *Sunday Times* did so, while the bulk of English newspapers either remained utterly silent or, in a few cases such as the *Star* and the *Sunday Chronicle*, gave support through editorials. The *Daily Dispatch* in East London published the Strachan reports, but because the paper was small and relatively out of the way, it was never prosecuted. When, after the van Schalkwyk verdict, the heat was really on, and wild and heavy threats against the freedom of the press were being aired, support dwindled even more. At the same time two Argus Company newspapers—the *Sunday Tribune* in Durban and the Afrikaans-language *Sondagstem* in Johannesburg—lined up with the government. Both were given access to Pretoria Central Prison and published lyrical accounts of conditions there.

The police came for Harold Strachan one morning, but he was out. He heard they were after him, so he went fishing for the day and returned home at six P.M. to comply with his house-arrest order. Irrepressible as ever, he gave warning of what was afoot by sending me a telegram: "Two gentlemen awaiting me at home probably for six months' vacation." The next morning's *Mail* carried the defiant headline "He Shocked South Africa With His Jail Disclosures—Harold Strachan Is Held—Charges of Giving False Information." He was held overnight before being charged with contravening the Prisons Act and perjury, and was then released on bail paid by the *Mail*.

We welcomed the coming trial. Here at long last, we thought, was a case that could be won. Even if the court judgment went against us, at least the truth could be defended, vindicating what the *Mail* had published. Strachan would never succumb to pressure from the government, and the prospect of him going into the witness box was awaited with keen anticipation. He would be a star witness. The start of his trial in Durban, three months from when the reports first appeared, was greeted with confidence, almost eagerness.

I felt the first tremor of anxiety on the opening morning. H. C. Nicholas had been briefed as the senior counsel for the defense with an extremely capable local barrister, Andrew Wilson, as his junior. When the first Afrikaans-speaking witness took the stand, Nicholas immediately asked for an interpreter to translate his questions and the witness's answers into English. Interpreting was common in South African courts because many blacks who spoke vernacular languages were not sufficiently fluent in the official languages, English or Afrikaans. But it was unusual to have a barrister ask for an interpreter from Afrikaans into English, and it was a poor tactical move because so many of the witnesses in this trial were going to be Afrikaans-speaking. Interpreting would slow down the proceedings and give witnesses, most of whom understood English anyway, precious extra time to prepare their answers. It also confirmed the perception of the *Mail* as an "English" paper.

I was especially dismayed because I had suggested someone else to lead the defense. Vernon Berrange, a former member of the Communist Party, had a fearsome reputation as a tigerish cross-examiner, and it was said that half the defense fight was won when a police witness saw Berrange standing up to question him. He had retired and was living in Swaziland. He sent me a message that he was willing to come out of retirement to defend Strachan, and I conveyed this to Stuart. After the bruising experiences with the first trials, I thought he was exactly what we needed, but Stuart turned him down on the grounds that he was not bilingual in Afrikaans. Here was Nicholas who was not bilingual, and I later learned that Berrange was in fact bilingual. I think that Stuart had been put under pressure inside Saan to brief Nicholas. The lack of proficiency in Afrikaans was only the start of it. Nicholas, a heavily built man, soft-spoken and considerate, was the wrong lawyer for this trial because he did not have the stomach or aptitude for a knockout criminal fight, especially one so political. The chief prosecutor, Cecil Rees, was consistently rude and antagonistic toward the defense. Nicholas took it lying down. At first he believed he should continue to act like a gentleman, as the contrast between him and Rees was bound to impress the magistrate. But as the days passed, it became painfully clear that the magistrate, M. E. Goodhead, was beyond being impressed. He cleverly walked a tightrope, blocking the defense as hard as he could, wherever he could, always stopping short of any action that could provide evidence of partiality in the trial record. We thought that the choice of Goodhead, English-speaking and with an English name, was no accident. It helped perpetuate a superficial impression that all was fair in the trial.

Even when Nicholas realized that there was little prospect of receiving justice at Goodhead's hands, he still refused to slap Rees down. I kept nagging Stuart about it, and he became increasingly embarrassed. He told me he was also urging Nicholas to respond once and for all to Rees's incessant insults. "I don't wish to make enemies," responded Nicholas. I lost all hope of any fight in him during one of our regular Sunday consultations at his home in Johannesburg, where he spent weekends before returning to Durban. Prime Minister Verwoerd had addressed a parade of warders, praising their work and condemning the "lies" published about the prisons service. Even to my nonlawyer eyes it was flagrant contempt of court, and I handed Nicholas a copy of the speech, which had received a great deal of press coverage. I suggested that he might want to raise the matter in court the next morning. "What, do you want me to have the prime minister brought to court for contempt?" he asked. With that his lower lip dropped. "I can't do that."

As it was, the defense faced exceptional difficulties in deciding which witnesses to call. The danger in using serving prisoners was fully realized because they were especially susceptible to pressure from the government. Only too often they were men willing to do virtually anything to curry favor with the authorities in hopes of obtaining some remission of sentence, or even smaller rewards such as an increased tobacco ration, or more letters and visits. We were the most popular show in town. There was a frantic scramble by convicts to offer their testimony for Strachan's defense. Letters reached the different lawyers, the *Mail*, Gandar, and me all the time. Some were sent openly through the prison authorities, while others were probably smuggled out. Prisoners just released from jail would come to the *Mail* to see Gandar or me with messages from inmates begging to be seen as soon as possible. Invariably they claimed to have vital information for the defense. Virtually every one of these leads was followed up, even where it was strongly suspected that the prisoner was a trap.

The bulk of the interviews were carried out at Pretoria Central, and it was generally believed in legal circles that the interview room contained a bugging device. In political trials it had become standard practice for lawyers in pretrial consultations with their clients to discuss the more critical details of the planned defense by exchanging handwritten notes. The bugging was confirmed to me by an ex-warder, who told me that the microphone was in the ceiling above the table and that the recording machine was next door. When the white political prisoners were later moved to a new section, they had bellpushes at their cell entrances in case of emergency. A former prisoner, an electrician by trade, told me he had to repair one of the bells and found a tiny microphone inside for the authorities to monitor all discussions between the politicals as they stood at their cell doors. It made sense, though I was never able to confirm this.

Our lawyers in the Strachan case, already on their guard against treachery, found themselves in a perpetual maze of lies. They would interview a prisoner and he would confirm what Strachan had said, be frank about his criminal history, and give every indication of being a suitable witness. A few minutes later another prisoner would say that the prisoner whom they had just interviewed should not be trusted, as he had been going around the jail telling people that he was going to trick the defense in the witness box, or he had been seen entering the chief warder's office immediately after his interview with the lawyers. In turn, the impressive carrier of this information would be discredited by others. It went on with a considerable number of prisoners being interviewed and discarded.

After this huge effort only two serving prisoners were deemed reliable and subsequently selected: Jewell and Marais, both from Pretoria Central Prison. The day before they were to testify, our lawyers interviewed them in the local prison. Marais said he had reconsidered and would not testify. With the lawyers present, Jewell abused him for being "yellow." Jewell claimed he was not afraid and would still give evidence, and duly went into the witness box, only to turn against the defense, much to the delight of the prosecutors. Later, word leaked out to us: the two of them were a trap set for us by the authorities. Marais was the honest man who had shown rare courage in backing out at the last moment. We tried to find out if Marais suffered any punishment when he was returned to Pretoria Central. It seemed, from our limited information, that he was fine.

We also discovered the impossible odds in taking on the might of the State. The *Mail* was quite a large organization and, with the backing of the management and the board of directors, there was no stinting in the resources put into defending Strachan and the other accused. Lawyers of high repute were hired. For months on end I did little at the *Mail* except track down witnesses for the Strachan trial, shuttling between Johannesburg and Durban, and going wherever in the country a lead took me. One of the *Mail*'s best reporters, Jill Chisholm, was sent to Durban for the two and a half months of the trial to file lengthy daily reports, which took up significant space in the paper. It was a herculean effort on her part, and her articles, each up to a few thousand words long, served to keep public attention on the prisons. But all of it was puny when set against the resources of the State, which was determined to crush us. Apart from the pressure that the authorities could apply to their own witnesses, they needed only a few hours to put together a dossier on anyone whom we put forward, with details of past history, criminal convictions, evidence given in previous trials, and court records. On our side we had to struggle for details, fighting against time and expending extraordinary energy for every scrap of information. We used private tracing agents to track down former prisoners whom we had identified as possible witnesses. But the tracing agents tended to be former policemen, and several times we had reason to worry that some of them were telling the police about the people we were trying to find.

"Fires" van Vuuren was a former prisoner whom I got to know. He had left a criminal past behind and was now living a quiet and sober existence. I was certain he was truthful. I spent hours persuading him to testify for us and he repeatedly said, "Strachan told the truth, I swear to God. But I'm frightened, I'm frightened." Not only did he fear his past being revealed in public and the treatment he would get if he landed in jail again, but the police threatened him with deportation. Despite this he agreed, of his own free will, to testify for Strachan. He was a tall man, and stood in the witness box with trembling hands and sweat running down his face. Early on, he had a mental block about one of his previous convictions involving a relative, and the more he was pressed about it, the more frantically he denied any such conviction. By the time the prosecutor confronted him with the official record of his convictions, proving that he had been untruthful, he was a mental wreck and incapable of offering sensible testimony. Van Vuuren's intentions were of the best, and he was courageous in overcoming his fear to testify, but he was a disastrous witness for us. Goodhead, in his judgment, commented adversely on his anxiety as a sign that he was lying.

We also found that our original legal advice that the State prosecutors would have to take Strachan's entire story into account had been misplaced. They selected words and passages, thus dictating the agenda for the trial. Strachan's story in the *Mail* ran to 11,700 words. He was charged on only 1,389 words, with the prosecution seeking the best of all worlds by noting that this did not signify that the unchallenged words were accepted as truthful and correct. But the trial was locked into those 1,389 words, and only witnesses who could testify about exact incidents on the exact days in the exact prisons referred to by Strachan could be put into the witness box.

My close friend Robert Sobukwe, who was detained without trial and in virtual solitary confinement on Robben Island, wrote to me early in the trial offering himself as a witness. The government was watching Sobukwe and deciding from year to year whether he should still be detained. His letter must have been further proof to the government that he was as defiant and unyielding as ever and therefore should be kept in jail, which is what was done to him for four more years. One of our lawyers went to interview Sobukwe, and he confirmed details of Strachan's statement about the assaults and the treatment of prisoners. But he had not been at Pretoria Prison at the same time as Strachan, so regretfully he could not be called to testify. He was disappointed, and wrote to me in words that were extraordinary in coming from a man who was at the mercy of his captors and which brought out my tears:

> I want to assure you that I am quite aware of the political implications of this case. And I do not wish history ever to record that for some opportunistic reason or other, I kept mum like Br'er Rabbit, when I should have spoken, at the same time being quite voluble when I should have held my peace.
>
> If then, at any time in the future, at any stage of this case, you should like me to testify please don't fear that your calling me as a witness will jeopardize my position. We have become so anxious to shield and spare our friends that we are virtual 'collaborators'!

Our inability to call Sobukwe as a witness reflected the artificial situation created by the State: we could not press forward with our examination of maltreatment and assaults of prisoners, and were confined within narrow parameters. The State could delve into its store of prisoners and put in a few to cover a particular point of evidence. If our lawyers managed to kick holes in their testimony, the prosecution simply put in another set of witnesses primed to close the gaps, now knowing the extent of the defense's knowledge and the questions that would be coming. We were buried under the corpses of the State witnesses; the more we destroyed, the more were put into the witness box.

Some remarkable evidence emerged, though. To counter Strachan's accusation of dirty eating utensils, a warder from Port Elizabeth's North End Prison said that, unfailingly for the past eleven years, three times a day, he had personally picked up and examined 1,200 plates at a time to check that they were clean. In eleven years he had found two dirty plates. Dr. M. J. Odendaal, who had served at Pretoria Central Prison as medical officer, testified that it took him ten to fifteen minutes to examine fifty to sixty prisoners (ten to eighteen seconds each), new admissions who had to be examined in accordance with regulations. He regarded his examinations as adequate. A prison colonel testified that regulations specified a minimum of thirty-six square feet of space for a white man, and only thirty square feet for a black man (though in fact, with three white men to a cell, each white man was getting only sixteen square feet).

Joseph Lelyveld, the resident correspondent of the *New York Times* reported his impressions of the Strachan and other prisons trials:

> Not content with casting doubt on the *Rand Daily Mail*'s allegations of brutality in South African jails, the government seems determined to portray the prisons as pleasure resorts of such exquisite refinement that any normal South African would be tempted to a life of crime... The warders and prisoners called by the State as witnesses in these trials are uniformly astonished by the allegations. Some admit the theoretical possibility of assaults in jails, but hasten to add that they have never seen or heard of such things in South Africa. The prosecutions in these cases have become carefully orchestrated recitals of the idyllic conditions in South Africa's jails... The chorus of happy jailbirds sings of life in walled arcadias.

For Strachan's defense, our lawyers relied on white political prisoners. This decision had its drawbacks. It gave the prosecution a natural opening to attack their credibility because of their opposition to the government, and enabled the prosecution to charge the emotional atmosphere of the court, which could only work against Strachan and the *Mail*. This was all the more so because the bulk of the white politicals were Communists. On the other hand, the politicals had the courage of their beliefs. They were educated, intelligent men and they could be relied upon to tell the court whatever they had previously said in their pretrial statements to our lawyers. The politicals were subjected to fierce barrages by the prosecution, but they stood up to it with courage and dignity.

Dennis Goldberg, sentenced to life imprisonment with Nelson Mandela at the Rivonia trial (and coincidentally, we grew up together in the same Cape Town suburb) was confronted by this question as his cross-examination began:

> Prosecutor: Mr. Goldberg, would we be correct or not to describe you as a master of deceit?
> Goldberg: I would say I have resorted to subterfuge on occasions.
> Prosecutor: Very successfully?
> Goldberg: Well, no, I'm in jail.

Govan Mbeki, also serving life imprisonment for sabotage and a key member of the ANC in the Eastern Cape and of the Communist Party (and father of Thabo Mbeki, who in June 1999 was elected to replace Nelson Mandela as president), faced this:

> Prosecutor: You, who would not shrink from bloodshed in order to obtain your political ends, would, in fact, not print half-truths or untruths in support of those ends?
> Mbeki: I wouldn't print an untruth. There is no relation between telling a lie and bloodshed. Men who conduct wars do not do so because they have abandoned the principle of truth.

Strachan was the last witness. We had high hopes for him. Everyone on the defense team was enthusiastic about his personality, his articulateness, and his keen memory. But he displayed none of these strengths in the witness box, and with a sinking feeling we could see the prison doors opening for him. He explained afterwards that he had been exhausted, but the damage was done. On December 10th, after thirty-seven court days, fifty-nine State witnesses, and fifteen for the defense, Goodhead adjourned the trial to prepare his judgment.

Four weeks later, while the magistrate was still preparing his decision, evidence of behind-the-scenes perfidy emerged, arising from the prosecution evidence given by Raymond Thoms. His appearance in the witness box had been a bombshell. He was serving a twelve-year sentence at Pretoria Local Prison for sabotage. To have a white political prisoner testifying for the State was startling, and what he said had frightening implications for both Strachan and the *Mail* as a newspaper headline that day graphically and damagingly conveyed: "Strachan Conspired To Lie—Witness; Cell Plot To Smear Jails Alleged." Thoms, speaking calmly and confidently, testified that he had at one time shared a cell with Strachan and two other politicals; the four of them had agreed to lie outright about conditions in the prison so as to discredit the system. This was to be achieved through reports in newspapers in South Africa and abroad. Strachan played a principal role in these discussions, he said. The chief topic to be stressed was alleged assaults by warders on black prisoners. They had prepared intensively for Strachan's release. He was to contact Helen Suzman and other members of parliament, the *Observer* newspaper in London, and me. Strachan had said that in the struggle against the government no means must be neglected and truth must take second place. Thoms's claims neatly covered, and undermined, much of Strachan's original statement.

Overnight, we drew on every possible resource to find out as much as possible about Thoms. We learned that he was an unstable personality who had wanted to be more active in left-wing circles than the leftists allowed him to be. He was in jail because he had been caught trying to blow up a police station in Johannesburg and had clearly been set up by an agent provocateur. When our cross-examination began, he agreed that it "could be said" that he was mentally unstable from 1961 to 1963 and had received psychiatric treatment. He had attempted suicide three times, the most recent only two months before, while in jail. Nicholas extracted the admission that he had been a police informer in prison since early that year, 1965, when Strachan was still in jail. But he said he had not told the authorities of the conspiracy to smear the Prisons Department because he thought they were aware of it! He had made a statement to the authorities about the conspiracy for the first time ten days before giving evidence. He also admitted that several times in recent months he had been involved in fights with the politicals who had accused him of being a traitor.

Under rigorous cross-examination he remained unshakable, even on his more improbable claims. We knew that he was a total liar, whether of his own accord or put up to it by the authorities we did not know. But he was effective and did us great damage through the classic use of the "Communist conspiracy" smear.

On January 6, 1966, however, Stuart's law firm received an urgent message to arrange a visit to David Kitson in the political section at Pretoria Local. The next day a lawyer was able to interview Kitson. En route to the interview Kitson was strip-searched. The reason the prison authorities did this was because they had been desperately trying for more than a week to conceal a development of major importance in the Strachan trial, with the political prisoners straining every muscle to out-flank them. The lawyer getting to see Kitson was the breakthrough, and from then on the story came tumbling out.

On December 29th, after Thoms had given his court evidence, a note was slipped under the locked door of the cell of three politicals, Dennis Goldberg, David Evans, and Allan Brooks. The note, in Thoms's handwriting, read:

I have reached the nadir of moral degradation and the only course left to me is to do what I can to vindicate the innocence of an honest and courageous man. From him and from you I shall naturally ask for neither sympathy nor forgiveness, but I beg you to advise me immediately what would be the best means of getting what I have to say into the hands of Strachan's lawyers. What I have to say will be not only a retraction of my own depositions and evidence but information as to the perjurious structure of the whole State case.

There is little doubt that the authorities, if they get any hint of it, will do *all in their power* to prevent me from divulging what I know. I am prepared for any consequences afterwards, but am concerned that everything should be got to the defense first. Whatever comes thereafter will be a small price to pay for a conscience even slightly eased. Please advise me immediately.

—R. J. Thoms.

It may be possible to get a message out via Fr. Magennis [a Catholic prison chaplain] whom I see weekly.

Brooks copied the note and put it inside a book. Goldberg hid the original, no mean feat in jail.

Less than twenty-four hours later Thoms told the authorities what he had done, and wrote another note, this time addressed to the Officer Commanding, Pretoria Prison:

I wish to place on permanent record that the contents of a note which on 29 December I foolishly and hastily put into the possession of the prisoners Goldberg, Evans and Brooks, do *not* represent my true opinions and attitudes, *which remain and will continue as before.*

I would plead in explanation that the note was written in a state of severe psychological disturbance, induced by the continuous and overwhelming consciousness that *every* man's hand is against me, i.e. that I am hateful both to my enemies (my former political associates) *and* also to those whom I would regard as my friends (the loyal servants of their country).

I apologize most profoundly for an ill-considered action, and for the inconvenience it has caused.

Warders descended on the sixteen politicals. They were stripped naked and searched and were kept in the exercise yard while their cells were ransacked. The copy of the note made by Brooks was found and removed. He wrote to the Officer Commanding asking for its return, and the politicals began their struggle to contact the *Mail's* lawyers. While this drama was being played out, the prosecutor, Rees, was seen at the prison.

On January 5th, Thoms passed another note into Goldberg's cell. But a warder saw him doing it and rushed to open the cell door. Goldberg had a quick look at the note, and at Thoms's shouted urging, swallowed it (complaining later that he wished Thoms hadn't used thick paper). He had enough time to see that it was once again a note expressing a desire to help Strachan in his defense. Goldberg and his cellmates were stripped naked and the cell was searched again.

Later still, Thoms tried to speak to one of the politicals but was stopped by a warder. He was moved elsewhere.

On January 7th our lawyers interviewed Kitson. He had memorized Thoms's note and recited it. He said that on his way to the interview he had been completely searched. "I have been deputed to see you because I can draw the fire," he said. "At the moment my cell is most probably being thoroughly searched."

On January 10th the authorities realized the game was up, and a copy of the note was handed to Stuart, who had returned from holiday to deal with the crisis. He and Andrew Wilson went to Pretoria Prison to interview the politicals, and Goldberg at long last produced the original note that he had so successfully hidden. Thoms insisted on having a warder present when the lawyers interviewed him: he told them that he wished to withdraw his notes to the politicals, and refused to discuss the matter.

Within two days all the statements taken from the politicals, together with Thoms's notes, were filed with the Clerk of the Court in Durban with a formal application for the "recall and reexamination" of Thoms. Our lawyers were taken aback when, within a few hours, Goodhead replied by letter: "Kindly inform the attorneys that I have perused these papers and that I do not consider it necessary to recall the State witness Thoms; and that the application for his recall is accordingly refused."

The obvious next step was an immediate appeal to the Supreme Court to order Goodhead to hear Thoms again and probe the strange circumstances of his conflicting notes. The mere fact that he claimed to have information about the "perjurious structure" of the State case seemed to demand that he be questioned. Even allowing for Thoms's instability, the episode surely could not be allowed to pass without action. Nicholas, however, rejected an urgent application to court. It was not wise at that stage, he said, with Goodhead in the process of writing his judgment. Better wait, and perhaps it could be used later as a ground of appeal against the judgment. Nicholas would not budge, and his caution prevailed.

At the *Mail* there was strong belief, led by Raymond Louw, who had become editor at the start of January 1966, that the Thoms affair should be blasted into the open simply because it deserved to be. The authorities were doing their utmost to hush it up, and the *Mail* set out to thwart them. Although the *Mail* had in its possession the formal application lodged by the lawyers, it could not make use of the documents unless it obtained official access to them in the court records. The *Natal Mercury* was asked to send a reporter to the courthouse to obtain access to the documents, but Goodhead refused permission and warned that he would regard any mention of it in the press as contempt of court. Louw felt so strongly that he personally phoned Goodhead, who responded, "Those papers form no part of the record at all. It was merely a letter that was written with some statements attached... and which I dealt with summarily, on the spot, there and then... and it does not form any part of the record at all... It is something which is entirely a matter in my discretion."

Louw wanted to apply to the Supreme Court for permission to publish. Even if the application was rejected, the story could thus be forced into the open. But Nicholas again turned it down, and the *Mail* could not risk going against the advice of an eminent senior counsel. Everyone except Nicholas writhed with fury at the missed opportunity to expose the framing of Strachan and to publish a riveting story.

The one small consolation was that Goodhead could not make use of Thoms's evidence. When he came to give his judgment, he referred briefly to the events and said he had already, before that, decided not to attach any weight to Thoms, so did not recall him. We laughed over that one.

The postscript was that Thoms lost out on all counts. The authorities, probably enraged with him, kept him in jail for his full twelve years. As an act of sheer cruelty he was brought back into the special section in prison with the politicals. They refused to have anything to do with him, especially as he had told the authorities about Kitson's radio, which had been kept hidden for more than a year. Thoms walked around all day with a towel wrapped around his face, not speaking to anyone. That went on for eleven years. He committed suicide after his release.

Late in January, Goodhead gave his judgment. There were no surprises: he found Strachan guilty and jailed him for two and a half years. We immediately lodged an appeal and bail was allowed to stand. Strachan returned to house arrest. Four months later, as the appeal hearing was under way, Strachan faced a decision: the government announced that prisoners who were in jail on May 31st, Republic Day, would be granted a part-amnesty. Strachan did not know if he would qualify for this, as politicals usually served their full sentences, but he decided it was worth taking a chance. On May 30th he asked to be admitted to Durban Prison. He was turned away because there was no committal order for him. Undaunted, he rushed to the magistrates' courts and after some arguing was given a committal order only a few minutes before closing time. He was back in jail that afternoon.

Strachan was apprehensive about the treatment he would get, but the torrent of publicity surrounding him ensured that no one laid a finger on him. Instead, as he later told me, "Everything had the aura of punishment about it. There were no blows or shouting. It was quiet and calculated, petty." He was immediately put into solitary confinement. "I just sat there for about six weeks," he said. "I had nothing to do. I was not allowed visitors. I could stand up or sit down. I was not allowed to lie down on my mat and blankets during the day. I only had the *New Testament* to read. You could not have the *Old Testament* unless you were Jewish, because of its rude stories, which you would use for purposes of masturbation; that's what I was told by a warder." When solitary ended, he was given a bristleless broom and ordered to sweep a courtyard next to a chimney stack. When he finished one end, he had to start at the other to deal with the constant rain of soot. Despite his caution he was trapped into trying to send a message on a scrap of paper to another prisoner and was sentenced to six days' spare diet, getting only rice water in the morning and evening.

Meanwhile the Appeal Court reduced his sentence to eighteen months. Surprisingly he was granted amnesty and was out after a year, back to house arrest. Goodhead and the appeal judges found that Strachan had lied in denying that he had sought me out and that he had made his statement to me knowing it was going to be published. I knew for a fact that this was not the way it had been, yet here was Strachan being jailed for it.

Strachan returned to Durban after completing his prison sentence and built a new life restoring paintings. His banning and house arrest continued for years, and he was kept under police surveillance. He had always been a long-distance runner, and each weekday morning at six A.M., when his night arrest ended, he set off to run for a few hours. The Security Police watching him grew suspicious. One morning Strachan found a stranger, also in shorts and vest, running a few paces behind him. Strachan ran a bit faster and a lot farther that morning, until he heard a groan and looked back. The stranger had fallen by the roadside. Strachan was left to run in peace after that. But he was denied permission to leave Durban's city limits to take part in the annual marathon to Pietermaritzburg.

Strachan was still not out of the woods: two murder attempts were made on his life. One night he opened the kitchen door and a man fired at him at point-blank range and missed. Another time, submachine-gun fire raked through the walls of his master bedroom. No one was ever arrested. Strachan used ship's steel plating for a high garden gate and closed in the veranda with cement breeze blocks. He lived inside with a shotgun always ready and waiting. He created his own prison in his home and in his mind.

The losing battle against the government on the prisons issue triggered an effort to get rid of Laurence Gandar in 1965. It was generally known among the *Rand Daily Mail*'s journalists that the Syfrets people in Cape Town, who controlled the majority shareholding in Saan, did not see eye to eye with him. Conservative in outlook, they remained wedded to the United Party and were dismayed by Gandar's unflagging support for Helen Suzman's lone stand in parliament and her Progressive Party colleagues in the country. But until this point there had been no sense within the *Mail*'s newsroom that the conflicting viewpoints were threatening. Inside the Saan building Gandar had the support of the then acting chairman, Henri Kuiper, as well as Leycester Walton, the new managing director. They consistently believed that the *Mail* was putting forward crucial and cutting-edge analyses. Lunchtimes in the executive din-

Chapter 15

ing room could get somewhat strained, however. Occasionally Kuiper would look across the table at Gandar and say, "That was quite an editorial this morning, Laurie. Could cause trouble, don't you think?" And Gandar would pause for a moment and reply, "I don't think so," or "Do you really think so?" and continue eating, leaving Kuiper speechless.

Outside of South Africa Gandar's stature was high. In 1962 the *Observer* in London published a profile feature headlining him as the "Thunderer Against Apartheid." In 1964 he went to London to receive the first Gold Medal awarded by the British Institute of Journalists. The prison reports climaxed international admiration for Gandar, and the American Newspaper Publishers' Association awarded the *Mail* its World Press Achievement Award.

Gandar could not travel to Atlanta, Georgia, to receive it, because he was still without a passport, so Walton collected it instead.

The citation got to the heart of the *Mail*, lauding "the broad scope of its news coverage and outstanding public service in pressing for improved living conditions, freedom of expression and social justice for all citizens," and, "The *Rand Daily Mail* has frequently exposed unfavorable conditions in South Africa's housing, schools, transportation and prisons systems and has opposed arbitrary laws permitting house arrest and imprisonment without trial... Despite its frequently sharp differences with the present Nationalist government, however, the *Mail* has continued to praise government action where it has believed praise is called for and has maintained balance in its news columns, reporting on all aspects of world, national and community life."

A printed copy of the citation was given to every staff member, and the award seal was carried on the masthead for years after. Johannesburg's liberal community gave its own tribute late in 1965 with a presentation to Gandar at a garden party. The following year he received an Award of Excellence from the Society of the Family of Man, in the United States.

However, the decline in circulation and advertising since Gandar had been appointed editor were adding fuel to Syfrets's disapproval of his political policies. Syfrets worried that Gandar was hurting the newspaper's long-term viability. Circulation had been about 127,000 when he began, and had fallen below 112,000. The daily sales on the streets of Johannesburg, which served as a rough barometer of how the newspaper was faring, had dropped from about 22,000 to 16,000. The gap between the *Mail*'s circulation and that of the *Star* was 60,000. The paper was still showing a profit, but advertising was down and this was having a serious impact. The size of the newspaper had to be reduced: the total amount of editorial space available each day was sixty to sixty-six columns—less than the *Star*'s news section. While the *Mail* had its impressive staff of journalists, their morale was sagging. They were suffering from the worst affliction that can beset journalists: lack of space meant that many articles could not get into the paper. There was the sense that the prisons issue was damaging the *Mail*. Those editorial staffers who were against Gandar at the best of times were muttering, what else could you expect? The counterargument that running a newspaper in South Africa was a high-risk venture in a high-risk society and that setbacks were inevitable, was not well received.

As a sidelight there was also talk that Vorster had an acute personal dislike for Gandar and that this was coloring his responses to the *Mail*. Vorster was saying that Gandar had been rude to him. Gandar was baffled about this, as they had never met nor even spoken to one another. I believe that I eventually stumbled on an explanation. It involved A. B. Hughes, who used to take over as acting editor when Gandar was away and move into his office. Hughes usually had several drinks during lunch, and his tiredness would be evident for the next hour or so. He would slouch over the desk, and didn't treat the world too seriously. The gentle humor in his twice-weekly column showed itself in his conversation. Many years later he told me that during one of his spells as acting editor, the phone rang and a voice announced, "This is John Vorster." Hughes thought it was a prank call, and more or less told the caller to go away and stop bothering him. When the caller abruptly rang off, Hughes went to the secretary's office and asked, "Who was that on the phone?" And she replied, "Mr. Vorster, the minister of justice." When Hughes told me this story, a light dawned: it seems likely that Vorster believed he was talking to a rude Gandar, when in fact he was being ragged by a cheerfully tipsy, postlunch Hughes.

On the morning of November 11, 1965, the day, by chance, that white Rhodesians led by Ian Smith declared their Unilateral Declaration of Independence (UDI) from Britain, Kuiper came into Gandar's office and, in his customary brisk manner, told him that the board of directors had decided that the stresses of running the *Mail* had affected his health, that it was adversely influencing his judgment, and that he should be relieved of his responsibility.

Gandar did in fact suffer from asthma and the dryness of the Johannesburg winter. And, while he believed in what he was doing, he endured bouts of insomnia because of the burden of his responsibilities. He worked long hours, but there was certainly nothing seriously wrong with his health. On the other hand he fully accepted that the board of directors had the right to fire him if they objected to what he was doing. Only when he learned that the *Sunday Express*'s Johnny Johnson was his prospective replacement did he begin to fight back. He objected strenuously. He respected Johnson for his work as a news editor, but believed he would be a disaster as editor. He wasn't up to the task. Johnson's hostile use of the *Sunday Express* in the prisons issue was also a potent factor against him. Instead Gandar recommended Louw. But Louw heard from Walton that he was being considered for the post and asked Gandar about his health and was told, "There's nothing very much wrong with me, they just want to get rid of me."

Gandar asked Louw to take the job. He suggested Louw because he had established a strong reputation in the news editor's job and was not known to have any political affiliations or leanings, and could be presented as a neutral appointment, which could appeal to the board. But Louw was uneasy. He supported Gandar's policies, and felt that editing the *Mail* would be extremely difficult without Gandar there. He urged Gandar to stay on as editor-in-chief and be in charge of policy. The only other choice was associate editor Harry O'Connor, who wrote a weekly political column in sharply antiapartheid terms, and Gandar feared that the board would reject him because of his political edge.

While these discussions were under way, word leaked out that Gandar was being fired. Protest grew rapidly among senior editorial staff. They approached Louw without knowing that he had already been offered the editorship. Louw told them that he had agreed to take the job on the condition that Gandar stayed on. Some half-dozen senior staff members, not including Louw, went to see Kuiper at his home to urge him to keep Gandar on. They threatened wholesale resignations if he was fired. The editors discovered, however, that the full board had not met to discuss terminating Gandar's editorship, which thus strengthened their counterattack. Some members of the board did not know of Kuiper's actions. The initiative had come from Vic White, acting on the orders of Syfrets. White could not have enjoyed wielding the knife, though. He was among the most liberal members of the board, his wife was a strong supporter of the Progressives, and his daughter, Jill, worked for the Liberal Party in Johannesburg and was married to Ernie Wentzel.

As news spread, individual members of the board became targets for lobbying, with *Mail* staff members and well-known members of the public urging them not to give way to Syfrets. The liberal community, admirers of both Gandar and the *Mail*, was composed of influential people in the professional, business, and academic worlds, and they were exercising their power. In the midst of these turbulent days Kuiper was dropped as acting chairman, and attention switched to the new chairman, Cecil Payne. It was widely understood that Syfrets had selected him for the specific purpose of getting rid of Gandar and bringing the *Mail* to heel, and on the surface it seemed that Syfrets had chosen the right man for the job. Payne, aged fifty-nine, had been a senior partner in a leading Johannesburg firm of accountants and auditors, and worked as a financial consultant and company director.

Louw pleaded with Payne, arguing that the *Mail* would be gravely harmed if its policy changed, and insisted that Gandar had to stay on. Anthony Fleischer, the general manager and a liberal, vigorously backed Louw's sentiments. Payne listened carefully and made up his own mind. He decided that the *Rand Daily Mail* was worthwhile and valuable, and agreed that Gandar was vital to the newspaper.

Syfrets decided that Gandar would remain on staff as editor-in-chief, responsible for the editorials projecting the *Mail's* policy. Louw would be editor in charge of the daily running of the paper. This was an unprecedented arrangement at the time, and it suited Gandar, as he found it burdensome to attend to the day-to-day details of running the paper, and preferred the role of a writing editor. The arrangement took effect on January 1, 1966. Gandar and Louw prepared a document for the board, mapping out the *Mail's* policy. They only changed one aspect—to give due recognition to the United Party's role as the official opposition in parliament. Syfrets backed off, for the time being.

Born in Cape Town, Louw had returned from a six-year stint in Britain to work as a reporter for the *Mail*, going on to become night news editor and then news editor. It was unusual for a news editor to be catapulted into the editor's chair, but in this case it was a gifted choice because Louw proceeded to invest in the *Mail* a hardheaded news approach that took the paper to new heights. He was not a political person, which was atypical for an editor in the charged South African situation, but he had an instinctive humanity that more than compensated for it. He also had a formidable energy, innovative spirit, and a ceaselessly inquisitive eye that watched over every detail of the *Mail's* existence.

Louw also had to contend with the ongoing problem of the prison trials, as they affected staff and editorial space. The government was still working its way through our informants, one by one. There were occasional reminders in one or the other of the Afrikaans newspapers that Gandar and I were next on the list. My life was in suspension. Norma Kitson moved to Britain in 1967 out of fear for her safety. I planned to follow, but could not regain my passport. After three unsuccessful attempts, and agonizing over leaving my daughter behind, I applied for an exit permit, which allowed a person without a passport to leave the country at the price of losing South African citizenship. In terms of the law the government was obliged to give an exit permit to anyone who applied for it: the Nationalists were only too pleased to have anti-apartheid opponents emigrate which was why they phrased the law in this way. Only years later did they realize that many of those driven into exile were highly educated and highly motivated and were playing an incalculable role in mobilizing world opinion against apartheid. Gandar worried that my pursuit of an exit permit would precipitate government action against us, so I waited until the conclusion of the last trial of our informants before submitting an application.

Gandar's sense of foreboding proved justified. The night before I was due to leave, the permit had not arrived. I returned to my apartment from a dinner date to hear the phone ringing. It was Louw warning me that the police were looking for me. Within three minutes there was a knock on the door. My apartment was on the twelfth floor and I did not want to be alone with a couple of policemen, so I called Wentzel and kept the line open. But the two detectives had no plans of tossing me out of the window, and merely served a summons under the Prisons Act. Gandar received his own copy. He and I were both charged, along with Leycester Walton, on behalf of Saan, Kelsey Stuart, and Joel Mervis for his articles on Cinderella Prison conditions. Hauling Stuart into court was unheard of: bringing criminal charges against the lawyer who had advised his clients on publication set a worrisome precedent, though charges against Stuart were eventually withdrawn.

My application for an exit permit fell away, one of only two times of which I am aware that the right to go into exile was blocked. But because I had been planning to leave the country, I was singled out for special bail conditions and had to deposit money—which the *Mail* did—and report to the police between one and two P.M. every Thursday. Having to do this every week made travel difficult inside the country, while the lack of a passport halted all external travel. The *Sunday Times* of London, for which I was a correspondent, wanted me to go to Beira in Mozambique to report on the oil embargo against Rhodesia, but my application for a passport was turned down. After UDI, Britain's prime minister, Harold Wilson, was confidently declaring that the oil embargo would bring about the collapse of Ian Smith's regime within weeks. The *Rand Daily Mail* reported otherwise, largely because of investigations by Peter Hazelhurst, who reported that the Rhodesians were deluged with oil from South Africa and Mozambique. Over a period of several days he built up a picture of how many road tankers were going north and how much petroleum they were carrying. In Mozambique he watched trains carrying petroleum products heading toward Rhodesia under cover of night.

I drew on Hazelhurst's findings for my reports to the *Sunday Times*, focusing on the complicity of BP, the oil multinational partly owned by the British government. Ultimately the imperfect but prolonged sanctions proved a powerful factor in ending white rule. But it took many years and lives until Rhodesia became Zimbabwe in 1980.

I spent months working in the copy editors' room. Many of them opposed the *Mail*'s liberalism and blamed Gandar and me for harming the paper. I felt isolated and was the target for a lot of needling. The trials were going on remorselessly. The principal case at this point was against Theron. Yutar prosecuted, but the defense was led by Arthur Chaskalson, a brilliant barrister who, in 1994, was appointed president of the new Constitutional Court in postapartheid South Africa.

I have always believed that Theron was truthful in his statement about the assaults and electric-shock torture at Cinderella. But I did not fully take into account that he had a grievance against the Prisons Department and was venting his anger by exposing conditions, and the odds that, as a warder, he was probably participating in the assaults. He was vulnerable to attack on both scores.

One of the problems was to define "assaults." I asked several warders if they had seen assaults on prisoners. Their usual answer was that they had not, because assaults were not allowed in prison regulations. But, I would ask, wasn't it widespread practice for warders to stand outside cell doors and, as black prisoners emerged, hit them with hand, fist, baton, or stick to make them run faster? And weren't blacks also hit when they were made to run in a long line past a zinc bath, bending down to scoop up sour milk with a mug? Those weren't assaults, the warders replied, but were done all the time to speed things up, otherwise they would be late getting off duty.

This was a period of few heroes among South Africa's whites, but one emerged during the trial: Robin Lazar owned a laboratory that performed chemical analyses, and he agreed to give evidence for the defense about the effect of electric shocks on the skin. There was no reason for him to carry out tests and to testify except to make his expertise available; there was every reason for him not to testify, because he could be imperiling his business through alienating clients and making himself a target for the government. During the trial, Yutar subjected him to an unpleasant, personal cross-examination, questioning his motives for giving evidence. Lazar did not budge, and came through with the utmost dignity. He was an unsung hero.

Theron was found guilty of making false affidavits and causing false information to be published. He was sentenced to a total of four years and four months' imprisonment and a fine of two hundred rand, or one year. We took it on appeal, and the sentences were reduced to twenty-four months, only part of which he had to serve, and a derisory fifty-rand fine.

I had previously sued Yutar for defamation because of his attack on me during the van Schalkwyk trial. I lost, but we went all the way to the Appeal Court and I was awarded damages. It created an interesting precedent, as it was now established that prosecutors did not enjoy total freedom to say what they liked in court about someone who was not party to the case. There was also a wryness to a South African court ruling that calling me "the nigger in the woodpile" was defamatory. Saan had backed me financially, and as the irrecoverable costs were substantial, I handed the damages award to Saan. Right at the start I told Stuart that all I wanted, apart from giving Yutar a good kick, was a shiny half-cent coin, and he sent me one pasted to a sheet of paper with an important-looking, red legal seal and a poem he had written:

> This is a symbol for Benjamin P
> A coining of phrase for his victory.
> His honour upheld by judgement (A.D.)
> he has established his true pedigree.
> The damages prove no African he
> concealed in a stockpile of quondam tree.
> The moral there is (if moral there be):
> In tarring *hamba so very kahle* [pidgin Zulu for "act very carefully"]
> lest, wielding the brush, you slip at the bar
> and find that it's your own name that you tar.

Although summonses had been served on us, the State had yet to set a date for trial. Every few months we appeared for a few minutes in court for remand. While this was dragging on, a brief item appeared on the front page of Johannesburg's *Sunday Times*, saying that the newspaper withdrew the accusations it had leveled at the Prisons Department and apologized for having published them. Gandar, Stuart, and I knew nothing about it. Mervis's betrayal of our joint interests shocked us. We assumed that he had done some kind of a unilateral deal behind the scenes, confirmed in our next court appearance a few weeks later, when the prosecutor dropped charges against Mervis with no reason cited. We worried that Mervis's retraction would be used against us, with the potential to damage us severely, but it wasn't used. Perhaps that was also part of the deal he made. The only explanation Mervis ever offered us was that he could not face the boredom of a lengthy trial.

Waiting for the State to frame the charges put us in limbo. Gandar and I estimated that we were probably facing seven to eight years' imprisonment. When the detailed charges were finally served on us, we were relieved to learn that we faced a maximum of three years' imprisonment. In the meantime I was under pressure to flee the country. Norma was having a hard time in Britain, and became ill. I applied for a passport on compassionate grounds to let me travel to London for two weeks. It was cleared by the prosecutor, the attorney general's office, and the Security Police. The day before I planned to go, an urgent letter came from the minister of the interior turning down my application. Stuart believed that they had never had any intention of letting me travel, but intended to build up my hopes and then dash them. He suspected that they wanted me to run for the border, catch me doing it, and smear me with a charge of trying to leave the country illegally to avoid prosecution. He might have been right: several strange people offered to smuggle me out of the country, for example under the driver's seat of a truck.

There was further confirmation that I was being watched. A new tenant, an Afrikaans man, moved into the apartment adjoining mine, and I went to welcome him to the building. The next evening he came to see me and, laughing a lot, told me he had a cousin in the Security Police and had bumped into him outside the building that morning. His cousin noted that I had called at his apartment for thirty-six seconds the previous evening, and knew this because he was one of the Security policemen stationed at the front and back of the building. That's how I learned I was being watched twenty-four hours a day, and was being followed wherever I went.

At least one encounter seemed to miss the attention of the watchers. Returning to the *Mail* building from lunch, I saw a "GG" car with chauffeur parked outside. Waiting in my office upstairs was an elderly man who introduced himself as a member of the Prisons Board that decided on parole for prisoners. He said he had been given the high-level job because he was a friend of John Vorster; they had been detained together during the Second World War in the Koffiefontein internment camp. That was where those suspected of Nazi sympathies were kept. He was frank: "You know and I know that what you published about prisons was correct. But you cannot prove it. They are preparing cases that are destroying you. I can help you because I can get hold of files at prisons headquarters that will show that what you published was true. I can also get files that show how they are preparing the case against you."

He explained that he had had a son late in life and wanted a nest egg for him: for 5,000 rand he would get us all the files we needed. It was a fairly substantial amount of money, but not all that much. Chiefly, though, I thought that he might be setting me up for a charge of bribing a government official. I said that I would have to refer the matter to others, and we arranged that I would visit him at his home the next week. He was affable and completely relaxed.

We puzzled over it at a meeting of Saan's top management and our lawyers, trying to assess what lay behind the openness of this senior official coming to the *Mail* in broad daylight in an identifiably government car. Was he naïve, or Machiavellian? Everyone agreed that it could be a trap, but on the other hand, what if it was genuine? We agreed that I should see the official again but that it was too dangerous to go on my own. Harry O'Connor agreed to accompany me, and I bought an expensive miniature tape recorder, which fit under my armpit with the microphone in a fake pen. That sort of gadget was still relatively new on the market, and I was warned that the wiretap might malfunction and squeak. The official was as affable as before and did not object to O'Connor's presence. But he said he had reconsidered and decided he did not want to proceed. Then, looking at me hard, he said, "This is confidential between us. If a word of what we have talked about gets out, I will take a gun and come and shoot you." I believed him. Worried that the tape recorder might go wrong, I frantically but as unobtrusively as possible searched in my trouser pocket until I found the control and switched it off. I later wiped the tape clean because there was too much risk in keeping it.

I never again heard from the official—I cannot remember his name—but subsequently learned why he had probably discarded us. An elderly businessman was serving a sentence for fraud, and I heard on the criminal grapevine that his family secured his release by paying off the official and a prison lieutenant.

On November 1, 1968, three years and four months after the Strachan articles appeared, Gandar and I were finally in the Supreme Court in Johannesburg to face charges of publishing untrue information about prisons and not taking reasonable precautions to ensure accuracy. We had the best legal representation, led by a senior counsel, Sydney Kentridge, with John Coaker to assist him and Kelsey Stuart to oversee the daily details of the battle. Kentridge, with his aquiline nose and his deep voice, looked and sounded like a movie depiction of a British barrister; he was already highly regarded and this trial was to confirm him as the country's foremost lawyer. A few weeks before the start of the trial I shaved my beard, as some thought it made me look like an anarchist, and Kentridge thought we had enough trouble already.

A few days before the trial opened, Gandar and I were called to a meeting with our lawyers, senior Saan management, and Cecil Payne to be given an astonishing message: we were told that if the *Mail* published an apology for our prison coverage, the charges against us would be withdrawn. The identity of the person who had conveyed this could not be revealed, but he had given the assurance that he was speaking on behalf of people in high places. Our discussion centered on the idea that the approach indicated a weakness on the part of the government. Perhaps the politicians had decided that the coming burst of publicity would be too punishing. Payne finally said that it was a matter for Gandar and me, as the accused, to decide. We both felt that we were not prepared to throw away all that we had been through. We did not believe that we had done anything wrong, we believed in the essential accuracy of what the *Mail* had published, and we refused to deny it.

Three months later the same message was conveyed again. This time Payne said that Saan would like to see the trial brought to an end. It was costing a huge amount of money and the continuing publicity was not good for the *Mail*. But it was up to the accused to decide, and Payne said he would support us unconditionally. Gandar and I again agreed that we saw no reason to go back on what had been published. Payne sighed, "Oh well, I suppose I had better tell the board about it."

Whatever he told the board, there was never, as far as I was aware, the slightest pressure on us to recant. I have often wondered how many newspaper companies in the world would allow editors the degree of freedom practiced in Saan at that time, which was all the more remarkable for happening during an era of decreasing press rights due to government restrictions. Unhappily, as later events were to prove, Saan did not continue to stand firm on principle.

The trial went on and on and on. There were times that I thought they were trying to kill us with boredom through a procession of witnesses, prisoners, ex-prisoners, policemen, officials, and warders, who droned on interminably through sweltering summer days about the immaculate condition of prisons and the exemplary behavior of warders. As with the Strachan trial, the prosecutors and police determined the agenda, confining the charges to passages, even sentences, of what we had published. I countered the boredom by enrolling for a post-graduate degree at Wits: class times were arranged for me in the late afternoons, after the court sittings.

After a few months Gandar showed me a memo he had received from Tony Stirling, a *Mail* reporter who had spent the previous six months tracking down potential witnesses for our defense. Stirling had been out of the country when my prison articles were published and noted that, "Among the [*Mail*'s] staff there was and still is a great deal of criticism about Mr. Pogrund and the articles, and much of this criticism came from senior personnel. As this criticism was fairly general, I came to the conclusion that Mr. Pogrund's articles might have been somewhat exaggerated." He said he had since spoken to about one hundred former prisoners: "They not only corroborated all that was said in the articles, but spoke of things that went on which they considered to be far worse than was printed." Not one ex-prisoner, he added, had confirmed any of the evidence given in court by warders or prisoners where it conflicted with what had appeared in the articles.

Stirling also said that there was "an immense fear of the authorities. Although most of the prisoners were willing to speak to me about their experiences when I approached them privately, very few were prepared to come and see the lawyers. They stated quite frankly that they feared reprisal from the authorities. Although I never encountered any who had been directly intimidated, they almost without exception were of the belief that the 'government' would get them."

To have a knowledgeable colleague back me in what I knew to be true cheered me enormously. It was also a reminder of what we also already knew—the difficulties we faced in overcoming the charges against us.

The judge for our case, Piet Cillie, was poorly rated in legal circles, but his appointment as judge-president of the Transvaal over the heads of more senior judges took effect shortly before our trial. The joke that did the rounds was that he had received his reward in advance. White-haired and wearing his scarlet, black, and gray judicial robes, Judge Cillie looked benign and avuncular. Closer examination revealed his thin slash of a mouth. We knew from the start that we did not have a chance with him. He tried to present himself as impartial, but when a prosecution witness was being mauled too much, he would intervene to protect him. When Kentridge pursued cross-examination, the judge's face went red, and his head tilted back as he visibly struggled to control his temper. Kentridge dealt with him without ever raising his voice. He would turn sideways, and address Cillie with cold contempt. In Kentridge's mouth the ritual phrase, "As Your Lordship pleases," sounded a total insult, and Cillie knew it and would burst into shouting. Then, realizing he had lost control, he would abruptly adjourn the court, stalk out, and return a few minutes later.

But even Kentridge's cross-examining skills could make little headway against many prosecution witnesses. The reason, as I grew to understand it, turned my ethical world on its head: I had always believed that the truth triumphs in the end. I discovered in the trial that it was the other way around. A witness who has been schooled in a set of basic lies and who sticks to his story is virtually unassailable, even to the most expert cross-examiner. An honest witness, on the other hand, will be open to admitting the possibility of error; once the possibility is revealed, cross-examination can widen the uncertainty, and all it then needs is a judge waiting to seize on the gaps as the means for discrediting the witness.

The only times we were able to undermine prosecution witnesses were when we could show them up as utter scoundrels. Our opportunities were very limited. Without notice the prosecution would put a witness on the stand, and we would postpone cross-examination until the next day. Each such witness required the utmost outpouring of energy and mustering of resources overnight, which meant the diversion of scarce reporters from the *Mail*'s news-gathering. Otherwise, Kentridge and Coaker chipped away day after day, seeking out contradictions and inconsistencies.

Some of the lying by prosecution witnesses was simply inept. John Brooks, an undercover Security Police agent, called Q agents, testified that Strachan had told him he had arrangements with a *Mail* reporter for publication of reports on prisons. Strachan had told him this on June 6th, said Brooks. In fact I had met Strachan for the first time on June 7th, and the first he knew that his story was going to be published was on June 28th.

The most unexpected government witness was Andrew Sacks. With no warning he was on the witness stand. We could not understand it. I was even more puzzled because Sacks kept winking at me from the witness box. That evening the daily consultation with our lawyers went on for longer than usual as we went over my thick file on Sacks. I had first met him about three years before. A former con man and prisoner, Sacks was in hospital at Krugersdorp, forty-five minutes from Johannesburg, being treated for tuberculosis, and wanted to tell me about prison conditions. He was personable, and a fast, glib talker. He said that he wanted to tell the truth about prisons because "Auntie Helen"—Helen Suzman, whom he always wrongfully claimed as a relative—had helped him so much in getting out of prison. Sacks wanted to tape our interview, but the tape recorder did not work during our conversation.

Later that same evening Sacks phoned to say that he wanted to see me immediately. I returned and he told me that he was in fact working with the Prisons Department to trap me. When I had been there earlier, Colonel Steyn, the head of the Prisons Board, had been skulking in the bushes nearby. The idea was for Sacks to give me favorable information about prisons and if I did not write the story, which they thought I would not, they were going to pass this information to other newspapers.

Sacks and I arranged to meet in a hotel room a week later. He arrived with a briefcase given to him by Steyn. Inside there was a tape recorder and a miniature microphone and the driver's license of Steyn's official driver, Head Warder Pieter Aucamp, which apparently had been left in the briefcase by mistake. Sacks and I recorded a statement on my recorder in which he described how he was supposed to trap me, then we switched on the prison tape recorder and taped an entirely fictitious, favorable account of prison conditions. Sacks went off and handed the fictitious tape to Steyn. This time I was the one skulking in the bushes, watching from a distance. In due course I had both recordings transcribed, but could not get Sacks to sign it, succeeding only after a few months. Adding to the farce, the Prisons Department recorder had malfunctioned again, and Steyn asked Sacks to get a copy of the transcript from me. A while later Sacks confessed to me that he had told Steyn he had double-crossed him by telling me the full story.

I was aware that Sacks had a friend in prison, Pat Rafferty, and would stop at nothing to get him freed. He confessed to me that this had been his aim in cooperating with Steyn. He said that Rafferty was also trying to trap me in exchange for leniency. If I phoned the Prisons Department and asked to interview Rafferty, it would be granted immediately. Rafferty would give a favorable interview about jail conditions, it would be secretly taped, and if I did not write it up, the department would publicize my failure. It all sounded silly, but to my surprise I was readily given access to Rafferty, and everyone at the prison pretended that it was the most natural thing in the world. We sat at a desk in an office. A prison official came in and out of the room, and whenever he left, I quickly ducked under the desk and looked in the drawers in search of the hidden microphone. Rafferty did not seem to find my behavior strange, and continued speaking. I could not find the microphone.

I thought I had neutralized Sacks and had protected myself. From then on, Sacks contacted me occasionally. Once he asked me to visit him at an office in the city. I realized things were not quite right, but couldn't figure it out. A few weeks later he confessed it was another trap. A tape recorder, he said, had been hidden in the desk and policemen were in the next office waiting to arrest me if he succeeded in getting me to make incriminating statements.

I did not see Sacks again until his appearance in the courtroom. I knew he had double-double-crossed me and that it might even have been a double-double-double-cross. I had lost count of all the lies. I assumed the Prisons Department was on to him, so why was he a prosecution witness? Had he managed to lay another trap for me without my knowing it?

It turned out that the Prisons Department did not fully grasp the extent of his double-double-crossing, and required him to testify against me. But Sacks realized he was in a corner because I had his full statement. He decided, for once in his life, to come clean. As Kentridge began his cross-examination next morning, and the truth of Sacks's betrayal of the Prisons Department emerged, there was consternation. Judge Cillie went turkey-red in the face, threw back his head, and vented his rage.

In practical terms Sacks faced charges of perjury because of his sworn statement to the Prisons Department, his contradictory sworn statement to me and our lawyers, and his contradictory evidence in court. But without anyone noticing, he managed to retain the main incriminating document, a court exhibit, which the prosecutor handed to him to identify. During a break, he flushed it down the toilet. He fled the country later that day.

In one of the more bizarre aspects of Cillie's judgment, when he gave it, he condemned me for using Sacks as the means of entrapping the Prisons Department. He brushed aside that I had been the target and resented only that I had succeeded in reversing the trap.

About three quarters of the witnesses for the prosecution were clearly organized perjurers. I felt tainted by the filth that was raining on us. There were days when all I wanted to do was rush to my apartment and get into a bath to wash it off. The prosecution was twisting and turning because substantial improvements were made inside prisons as a result of our disclosures. The government took note of what we exposed, but in the interests of crushing us was not willing to admit to it. The biggest change was the clothing for black prisoners: They were given long trousers instead of the traditional *tsotsi* (gangster) knee-length shorts, as well as shoes and socks instead of rubber sandals or going barefoot. These changes transformed utter misery into a more tolerable existence. The conditions of white political prisoners also improved dramatically after Strachan's statements: they were allowed hot water for bathing, warders shouted less, there were fewer difficulties with studying, and they could borrow books from one another and the outside world more easily. They had extra blankets, more exercise time, could buy games such as chess and checkers, and could play with a ball in the yard. Their complaints received more attention than before.

Although our reports had not covered Robben Island Prison, and little information came out, improvements were also under way for Nelson Mandela and his fellow inmates. When Mandela and other black political militants first got there in the early 1960s, they were forced to sit in long rows on the ground in the open, breaking up stones, or they worked in the quarry, mining limestone. Many years later the powdery substance resulted in Mandela suffering serious eye trouble. Those were the days of the three Kleynhans brothers, warders with an unsavory reputation for brutality on Robben Island. One of their deeds was to bury a prisoner in the ground up to his neck, and urinate on his face. This was reported in the *Observer* in London, and seemed so outrageous that I did not believe it. Only years later did I get confirmation that it had been true. Conditions for the politicals on the Island, although still rigorous, improved considerably after our prisons coverage.

Johnny Scholes was the star witness. Virtually every ex-prisoner I knew advised me to get Scholes to testify for us. He was a legend in underworld circles for having spent more than half of his life in prison. He was respected by his mates for refusing to defer to authority.

When I finally met him, his lined and battered-looking face matched the life I had learned about. He told me that he had used practically every known means of assaulting other men—guns, knives, bicycle chains, knuckledusters, yet his face was devoid of brutality, and his dark, shining eyes seemed to reveal a different person. There was indeed an inner soul who believed in justice, or what he believed to be justice. His problem was that he had a violent way of conveying his commitment. He told me how a warder had seen him smoking a cigarette and had rushed to seize the evidence, but Scholes managed to drop the stub into a drain. The warder lay a charge against him. He said to the warder as they went into the prison court, "Make sure you tell the truth" and the warder drew himself up and replied, "I will do my duty."

The warder proceeded to lie, claiming that he had found the cigarette stub in the lining of Scholes' hat. Scholes was found guilty and sentenced to "three meals"—no food for thirty-six hours. He bided his time. Several months later he was using an axe for work and the warder happened to walk past. Scholes went for him with the axe, inflicting head injuries. He was charged with attempted murder and his sentence was extended, but he did not mind because he had ensured that his justice was done.

Scholes was not always a coherent witness, but it was worth the effort because—in my judgment, not that of Cillie—he provided unvarnished truth and supported the essentials of Strachan's accusations. As his cross-examination neared an end, the prosecutor sneered at him, "You were probably one of the toughest prisoners that the Prisons Department had to deal with in the twenty-eight years that you were in prison?"

Scholes replied, "Well, the difference was that I wasn't a rat and I tried to be a man."

Finally, in July 1969, eight months after it began, the trial came to its weary end. A total of 105 State witnesses and sixteen for the defense were recorded on 4,974 pages of evidence. We were moved into a larger courtroom to accommodate the crowd, and Cillie began reading his judgment. He started by calling me a liar for the evidence I had given. One of the issues for this condemnation concerned Mandela. While I was in the witness box, the prosecutor asked whether I had ever sent money to Mandela on Robben Island. I replied that I could not remember doing so, but would not deny it if I had done it. The prosecutor was holding a sheet of paper and I realized he seemed to know more than I could remember. He kept pressing me, and finally handed me the piece of paper. The moment I saw it, I remembered. It was a letter I had sent to the Officer Commanding, Robben Island Prison, enclosing money to pay for study books for Mandela. Ah yes, I said, now I remember and of course I did send money. From the prosecution's perspective this was meant to convey that I was supporting efforts to overthrow the government. Cillie decreed that I had deliberately lied in an effort to conceal my contact with Mandela.

As much as I despised Cillie, I still felt bad about being dubbed a liar. I glanced at Gandar next to me, who was glaring at Cillie. He leaned forward, and in a whisper that went around the courtroom, hissed, "Fuck you, you bastard." That, coming from Gandar, was amazing. I had never heard him utter even the mildest obscenity, and to have this outraged reaction on my behalf lifted my spirit. The six-hour judgment was so divorced from the reality of the evidence that we did not take it seriously.

It was obvious that it would be impossible for Cillie to send us to jail. Our lawyers had cast too much doubt on too many of the prosecution witnesses. The public spotlight had remained on the trial. Apart from the daily presence of South Africans like Helen Suzman, Black Sash members, and other friends, there was also a flow of visitors into the courtroom from abroad, including the venerable British judge Lord Devlin, who came as the representative of the International Press Institute; the British political leader Lord Butler; and William Rees-Mogg, the editor of the *Times*, who testified for us in brilliantly incisive language about the function of the press in exposing wrongdoing.

As expected, Cillie found both of us guilty. In the hushed courtroom he waited expectantly for us to plead in mitigation of sentence. But Kentridge rose to his feet and uttered the few words that Gandar and I had drafted, "Both the accused gave evidence in the case and do not wish to say anything further." It was, for me, one of the best moments in the trial, as I thought that Cillie would get our message of how we viewed him and the trial. Gandar and I had agreed not to give an inch. To put in a plea in mitigation of sentence, which was often done at the end of trials, would amount to an admission that we had done something wrong. We also agreed that if we were fined with the option of imprisonment, we would go to jail. Cillie realized what we had in mind, and separated us. He sentenced Gandar to a fine of 200 rand, with imprisonment of six months if he did not pay, and gave me six months' imprisonment suspended for three years. He imposed a small fine on Saan.

That we had not gone to jail was greeted as a great victory by our supporters, and we emerged from the courthouse to a cheering throng of hundreds. The government was sour: its *Transvaler* newspaper showed photographs the next day of us surrounded by crowds, with a caption that made a point of drawing attention to the fact that a *Bantoevrou* (a black woman) was holding my *linkerhand* (left hand).

Gandar considered whether he should opt for prison, but the decision was taken out of his hands when an unknown person paid his fine. We had a few weeks to decide whether to lodge an appeal. We were both exhausted, and wanted to get on with our lives. We finally agreed to appeal, if only to keep pushing away at the Prisons Act. However, when Gandar took this back to Payne, he was met with astonishment. "But you've won. Why do you want to appeal?" So we decided to leave it at that.

As convicted people, our fingerprints were taken. The officer in charge of our case, Major Johan Coetzee, who would later become the head of the Security Police and then the commissioner of police, said he would come to the *Mail* to do it—an unusual courtesy. As he pressed my inked fingers on to the official forms, I commented on the lengths to which the government had gone to get us convicted. Coetzee, still holding my hand, looked at me and said, "You're the enemy. We'll stop at nothing to get you."

The prisons issue had taken four years. It had cost Saan upward of 350,000 rand, a great deal of money at the time; the *Rand Daily Mail's* annual profit was 300,000 rand.

Syfrets moved again to fire Gandar soon after the end of the trial. The first fumbling initiative was taken at a Saan board of directors meeting by G. K. Lindsay, a member of the Abe Bailey Trust, controlled by Syfrets. He said the Bailey trustees had discussed the *Rand Daily Mail's* editorial situation and felt it was finally time for Gandar to go; he should be provided with a good settlement. Raymond Louw was doing well, and there was no reason why he shouldn't be editor. When was this decided?, asked Jim Bailey, also a trustee in his late father's estate. At the last meeting in Cape Town, said Lindsay. You were there. That's what the trustees decided. Bailey denied it and Lindsay backed off. They would have to go back to Cape Town and find out just what the situation was, he said.

Syfrets's boss, Clive Corder, came from Cape Town for the next board meeting to get his representatives out of the mess, and was formally invited to take part. He said the Cape Town people had thought about the matter for a long time. They recognized Gandar's prominence, but they really did not think he should continue as editor-in-chief. They had come to the conclusion that his bitterness against the Nationalist government was too great for him to run a balanced newspaper. Corder said that Gandar's anti-Afrikaner stance was not compatible with his position, and claimed once again that his health was suffering.

These remained untrue claims. Gandar was not anti-Afrikaner, and he wasn't sick, save for his understandable exhaustion from the trial. But Syfrets had made up their minds and Gandar was fired. He accepted a job in Britain as the first director of the Minority Rights Group, which investigated and publicized the plight of minorities around the world. He returned to South Africa after two years and half-jokingly said he had reached the conclusion that at any given time half the world's peoples were being "beastly" to the other half—the proportion always remained exactly the same and only the victims changed. He no longer wanted to write about South Africa, and sheltered himself behind a cloak of cynicism. I think he was a badly hurt man. At the *Mail* we tried to coax and prod him into writing, but only an occasional analysis, always insightful, emerged from him.

Our friendship deepened, but only after many years did I pluck up courage to write and ask whether he had any regrets about having published my reports on prisons. They had, after all, fundamentally changed his life. He replied that if he had been able to forecast the extent to which the government would go to destroy us, and what we had to endure, he would not have published. But having published, he had no regrets.

Part III

The War of Words

It was an enduring myth perpetuated by the government that the country was democratic and the press was free, and both claims were widely believed by many whites and by the Nationalists' friends abroad. In fact, after more than two decades of the Afrikaner Nationalists, the press was fettered to an extent that few realized or, more accurately, wanted to realize. Even many journalists were unaware of the full ramifications. Many of the restrictions came about because of the cramping of personal rights; as the press is part of society, it enjoys the same rights as ordinary citizens, which, in the skewed South African situation, meant whites. Each attack on individual liberties therefore reduced the rights of the press. Some laws were specifically intended to restrict the press while others played their part by creating gray areas into which it was dangerous to tread. By the 1970s the press was choked by a wide range of laws that gravely

Chapter 16

impeded the public's right to know what was happening.

Apart from the knowledge of restrictive laws that I gained from reporting black and radical politics, and my close experience with the Prisons Act, I had to deal with these problems on an everyday basis as the *Mail*'s night editor, to which I was appointed in late 1969 after the Prisons Trial. My job was to supervise the content and quality of the paper.

A formidable range of laws was in place:

> ► The Official Secrets Act sought to protect information affecting the security of the State. In 1965 the Nationalists added the phrase *police matter*, defined as "any matter relating to the preservation of the internal security of the Republic or the maintenance of law and

order by the South African Police." This was a blockbuster law, and we were never quite sure what to do about it.

➤ The Native Administration Act, first enacted in 1927, was extended by the Nationalists thirty years later, making it a crime to "promote hostility" between whites and blacks.

➤ The Riotous Assemblies Act of 1956, similar to the Native Administration Act, gave the government the power to ban any newspaper or any other "documentary information" that was "calculated to engender hostility" between blacks and whites.

Laudable as these words seemed in theory, in practice they were used as a weapon to maintain white rule. Nationalist leaders and politicians beat the racial drum as hard as they could to whip up white emotions for racist policies. They were immune to the law. Antiapartheid militants and newspapers had to be careful. How were we to decide what "promoting hostility" meant? If a prosecution followed, what might the political climate be like in the trial that would ensue three or six months hence? How to take account of that? Most editors, in this sphere and elsewhere, applied the newspaper adage: When in doubt, leave out.

There were other laws that were more explicit in their repressive nature:

➤ The Criminal Law Amendment Act, passed in 1953 during the early years of Nationalist rule, took *incitement* a great deal farther by making it an offense to use language or do anything calculated to cause anyone else to break the law by way of protest. For example a newspaper could campaign for the repeal of a law, but it faced punishment if it "advised, encouraged or incited" its readers to break the law as part of the campaign. If a newspaper published news of an illegal strike planned against apartheid, it was in danger of being charged with incitement. The penalty for a transgressing editor included jailing for up to five years and/or a whipping of up to ten strokes. Whipping was mandatory for a second offense, but did not apply to those who were past their mid thirties.

➤ The Public Safety Act of 1957 stated that if the government declared a State of Emergency, (as it did in 1960 and was to do again from 1985 onward), its absolute control included the ability to close down newspapers and forbid the printing or distribution of any material.

➤ The Pass Laws restricted the right of black journalists to live and work where they pleased, and the right of newspapers to employ whom they wanted. We could not, as a matter of course, hire a black reporter living in Cape Town. He/she had to apply for permission to live in Johannesburg and was at the mercy of capricious officials. Travel was also difficult. Asians, for example, were not allowed to travel through the Orange Free State province without permission. On the other side of the color fence, the access of white journalists to news was restricted, as they needed official permits to enter black townships outside cities and the rural "reserves" set for blacks.

➤ The Suppression of Communism Act dated back to 1950 and had been extended many times to give the government draconian power and to close loopholes opened by court decisions. Newspapers could be banned if they were "deemed" to be spreading Communism. The ideology was so broadly defined that virtually anyone opposing the government could be slapped with it. The earlier prohibition on banned people attending meetings—which in practice meant not being with more than one other person at a time—was expanded to include a bar on publishing anything said or written by a banned person.

The effects of this law on newspapers, and on the country, were far-reaching. First, we had to exercise great care not to propagate "Communism" in reports and commentaries. Second, more than six hundred people had been banned under this law and care had to be taken not to quote them in any way. And there were many other people who could not be quoted because of other laws, such as blacks banished to remote areas under the Native Administration Act. The effect was to exclude a wide spectrum of opinion from the public arena: the views of the banned ranged from Communism through African Nationalism and pan-Africanism to liberalism and less. To help newspapers steer clear of danger, Sapa supplied and updated the names of banned people on index cards in a variety of colors to differentiate between the banning laws. Even then, checking someone's status was not always easy because of the uncertainty about the spelling of black people's names.

One night I spotted a statement by a banned person that had slipped into the paper. I ran down six flights of stairs, burst into the machine room, and yelled, "Stop the presses!" I ordered the already printed copies to be dumped. New plates were hurriedly made, and printing resumed. It was better to waste some money and run late than expose the paper to a criminal charge. Of course it was better to ensure that "wrong" names did not get into the paper at all, but despite utmost vigilance, mistakes like this could happen under the pressure of producing a daily newspaper. It happened another time, too, and again I halted the presses and dumped newspapers. We always assumed that the government was paying more attention to the *Mail* than to anyone else, so we had to be extra-careful.

> The Unlawful Organizations Act proscribed the ANC and the PAC in 1960, and was a warning to newspapers not to publish any views of these organizations.

> Prisons Act of 1959—Our prosecution and conviction under ensured that no one published any news about jails. No one dared do so because the effect of the judgment against us was that the only way to ensure that information was publishable was to submit it to the Prisons Department. If a newspaper learned that warders were savagely beating up prisoners, it had no choice but to go to the Prisons Department. Only in the unlikely event of the department agreeing that the information was true could it safely be published. If the department denied it, then to publish was to publish information you had been told was inaccurate and therefore you were guilty.

> The Sabotage Act of 1962 extended the definition of sabotage to include anyone who "incites, instigates, commands, aids, advises, encourages or procures" any other person to commit acts of sabotage. Penalties included hanging. The same applied to the Terrorism Act of 1967, again with a wide definition of terrorism, and with penalties that could range between a mandatory minimum of five years' imprisonment to hanging. Lawyers told me that creating a traffic jam to oppose the government could be considered "terrorism."

> The Extension of University Education Act of 1959 led to regulations that prohibited students from giving statements to the press without their rector's permission.

> Section 205 made it a crime to refuse to disclose a source of information to the police. It was originally Section 83 of the Criminal Procedure Act, and became a lot tougher than when I had been jailed. It provided for imprisonment for up to a year, to be repeated if necessary, and was later increased to five years. No editor in his right mind was going to risk losing a reporter to jail through publishing a report likely to lead to a demand for the source.

To add to this worry, publishing any information with sensitive sources could lead to incommunicado detention without trial. When first enacted in 1963, detention was for up to 90 days, renewable indefinitely. In 1965 it was extended to 180 days, renewable indefinitely. In 1967 it became indefinite detention.

➤ The government could declare any place or area "protected." The press was debarred from identifying these places. How to know what was a protected place? When we asked officials in Pretoria about it, we were told, "You will know that a place is protected when you identify it."

➤ The laws of defamation under common law were a major factor in discouraging investigation. This grew more serious over the years because the longer the Nationalists were in office, the more corrupt they became. Only occasionally was it possible to put together sufficient evidence to expose profiteering by the Nationalist elite.

➤ Seditious libel could be committed by publishing words directed against the authority of the State with the intention of stirring up and exciting discontent, disaffection, and sedition among the citizens of the country and causing them to withdraw their allegiance from, and to oppose, the government. We were able to draw comfort from knowing that the frightening vista of no-go areas this opened up was qualified because the prosecution had to show that publication was followed by seditious conduct by a number of people. On the other hand, anything calculated to violate the dignity or injure the reputation of the state's president could draw a heavy fine or five years in jail.

➤ Blasphemy, in a country ruled by Calvinists, covered contemptuous references to God and Christ and the mocking of public divine worship.

➤ The General Law Amendment Act of 1962 meant that anyone who wanted to start a newspaper faced the hurdle that the government could demand a hefty deposit, which was forfeited if the government later decided to ban the newspaper. This was the device used to eliminate left-wing newspapers. To pay a deposit of twenty thousand rand might be possible, but to contemplate having to do this every time a banning was decreed made going into the newspaper market hazardous.

➤ The Atomic Energy Act declared that not a single word could be published about South African atomic energy without permission. Anything to do with atomic energy was forbidden. The seriousness can be gauged by the penalty, with offenders facing a fine and/or twenty years' imprisonment.

➤ Censorship was a whole other area. Newspapers were exempted from the Publication and Entertainment Act because they had their own rules to which they had to adhere, but the official censors had wide powers to prohibit or alter any publications or films they considered "indecent or obscene," or "blasphemous or offensive to the religious convictions or feelings" of any section of the population, or harmful to relations between people, or "prejudicial to the safety of the State, the general welfare or the peace and good order."

➤ The Defense Act made it an offense to publish any information about military matters without permission, except in defined cases such as if the details came via a foreign parliament. At the end of 1975 this law was used to conceal South Africa's invasion of Angola. An army was sent across the northern border of South-West Africa—illegally, because the government had no right to send conscripts out of the country without their agreement—but the public knew nothing about it. Each night, as required, we read the reports received from Reuters and Associated Press to Defense Force officials; each night they canned the reports. No information about casualties was released, but we were picking up details from death notices placed in the newspaper by bereaved relatives.

Even this plethora of prohibitions was not the end of it. There was also the Press-Police Agreement, which had been renegotiated in 1967. The NPU, representing newspaper owners, and the commissioner of police together created a framework for relations. The press promised not to hinder or embarrass the police in their duties and the police promised reasonable cooperation in news reporting. This was cause for unease because the press has no business promising not to embarrass anyone. But it went even farther, with an undertaking by the NPU: editors were obliged to communicate, "before publication," to a senior officer, "information concerning crime or State security which has been obtained by the newspaper independently of the police, to enable such officer to advise whether the information should be published where such publication may interfere with the investigation of any crime." And still more, where information related to "a crime of extraordinary seriousness or to State security or where the publication thereof may defeat the ends of justice," the police could "request" an editor not to publish or to delay publication. Finally, the agreement promised that if a newspaper attributed a report to an unnamed policeman, his name would be divulged if the commissioner of police asked for it.

It is a moot point whether the NPU could have refused to cooperate in the security climate which grew and was fostered in the aftermath of the Sharpeville shooting, the banning of organizations, and the start of sabotage. To what extent the NPU willingly entered into the agreement is yet another issue: its members included the government's loyal Afrikaans newspaper groups while the English-language owners were not immune to pressures to stand with the government against the enemy at the gates.

Ominous as the agreement was, in practice I do not know of any instance where it was directly used to dragoon the *Mail* into cooperating with the police. It might have caused problems for other newspapers, but the police did not really need to wield a big stick because many journalists would have considered it their patriotic duty to inform the police about anything they saw as a threat to national security. This does not mean that the agreement had no effect. It did, because it was hanging over us all the time, instilling caution to avoid situations where its provisions might be invoked. Its effects were hidden. Any editor who was not going to cooperate with the police would simply have dumped stories that could have fallen within the scope of the agreement.

We found that the restrictive laws, together with the never-ending attacks on the English-language press, had predictable effects on government officials. By the end of the 1960s we were finding that news was harder to get, even straightforward, everyday information. Officials thought they could get into trouble if they spoke to the press, and their concern was probably justified. We seldom gained from that important element of democracy, the leakage of information from inside the system by officials moved by their conscience. The generalized fear spread to the public. People were less and less willing to give information about anything.

"The total result is that South Africans can no longer be certain that their newspapers are telling them all that they should know or might want to know," was my summation in an article I wrote at the time. "Their newspapers are either forbidden to tell, or are afraid to find out—or even if they do find out, are afraid to tell."

The *Mail* worked hard to climb over these hurdles. The impulse to publish the maximum amount of information was by now ingrained, but how to ensure enough editorial space for the information? Underlying all else was the newspaper's weak position in the marketplace, and how to resolve it. Even while Louw was only acting editor, a briefing meeting was arranged with the circulation and advertising managers to describe the *Mail*'s shortcomings. They told him they could not sell advertising or get readers because of the political policy.

Louw listened patiently to the two-hour presentation, and thanked the managing director, Leycester Walton, for arranging the meeting. But he did not believe that what they had told him was accurate and he set out to prove that they were wrong. He argued that the *Mail* was being held back because of the newspaper's limited space. It did not publish reports that had appeared in the *Star* unless they were of special importance. It was not providing comprehensive news coverage. The public did not have to buy the *Mail* to find out what was happening, and that had to change, said Louw. The *Mail* had to be an inclusive package covering a wide range of activity, even if some of the reports were brief. More editorial space was crucial.

Louw did not get what he wanted right away. It took many discussions and meetings before he was given the green light for what was clearly a risky step. The winning concept sold to advertising agencies was that the *Star* was so large that advertisements were lost in it; the same advertisement in the thinner *Mail* would enjoy far more exposure. Simultaneously the *Mail*'s advertising rate was considerably increased to bring it in line with that of the *Star*, which was cheeky because the *Mail*'s circulation was much lower. But the agencies liked it because they would receive the same commission and they could choose between the two newspapers without affecting their pockets. The concept took off with the redesigned *Mail* in 1968, and was an instant success. It gained more advertisements and revenue, and provided more editorial space—up to 45 percent of the total pages each day. Circulation rose a phenomenal 14 percent a year.

The additional editorial space and Louw's hands-on style unleashed energy and initiative. He turned the *Mail* into a hybrid newspaper: the news section was hard-edged with strong headlining and bright presentation. The feature pages were elegant and in serious mode. The financial pages, which drew substantial advertising, were sober, authoritative, ahead of anyone else in quality, and broke new ground by publishing a full page of stock market prices each day. And the sports pages were sparky and brash. It was a giant leap forward for the *Mail*, at a time when the paper required new life.

When I took over as night editor, I was physically, mentally, and emotionally exhausted from the Prisons Trial, and the last thing I wanted was a taxing job, but there I had it. It proved to be what I needed because there was no time to brood. The copy editors' room was in bad shape. Night work was unpopular and we struggled to find competent staff. Drinking was rampant: some copy editors often worked with a glass of whiskey on the floor next to them. The moment the first edition was put away, there was a rush to the "Fed," the tasteless Federal Hotel bar a block away. After the late-night break and an hour in the Fed, production and accuracy fell off at alarming rates.

Anyone who wanted liquor could also get it inside the building through the service run by Hymie Snoyman, known to everyone as "Fish," who also did chores for the sports department and was paid a small retainer. At any time of the day or night, whiskey or brandy could be ordered and Fish would disappear for a short time and produce however many bottles were needed, all at normal store prices. Fish was always unshaven, shabby, and unkempt but was said to be extremely wealthy because he owned a cinema for blacks a block away from the *Mail*. It looked seedy, but it was valuable for being the only one in the city center. On the news side, Fish was responsible for the vital Wall Street share prices: because of the time difference between South Africa and the United States, a paragraph about the prices was usually the last item to go into the paper at around 1:30 A.M.

The Snoyman family was well known in Johannesburg: they were reputed to be ten brothers and one sister. When they were younger, they had made up a soccer team, with the sister as goalkeeper. One brother ran a car-tire business, another a cartage company. Through Fish, *Mail* people had access to their wide range of businesses, always at favorable prices.

As the night editor I had to get the staff to reduce the drinking to manageable proportions, and upgrade the quality of work. I wasn't always popular: I had been leapfrogged into the job, and did not always act wisely in dealing with the clannish copy editors. I spent countless hours after the paper had been put to bed, until three, four, or five A.M. talking to staff members and drinking Scotch to sort out personal and work problems. Louw was a tough editor. Late each night I called him at home to report on the next day's paper, waiting with trepidation for him to zero in on mistakes and misjudgments that required frantic repair.

It was all the more difficult to find copy editors because it was still an all-male preserve, and white to boot. We hired David Farrell, a poet of some note who had never done any editing. I thought that anyone who wrote poetry must have possibilities, and he proved to be outstanding when he wasn't drunk and high. He was all right if he was doing one of these, but when he did them together, strange things happened. It came to a boil while I was away on leave. I returned to find my stand-in, T. J. Botha, beside himself with fury. Farrell had had one of his bad nights, and during an argument he called Botha "a mustachioed hairyback bastard" (*hairyback* was a derogatory word for Afrikaners). T. J. was, in fact, Afrikaans and did have a mustache. An assistant editor, he was liked by everyone and was devoted to the *Mail*. Abuse across group or color lines was not tolerated, and Farrell was fired. A few years later he returned to the *Mail* a changed man, and was the finest copy editor on the paper.

Despite all the problems and shortages, the *Mail* was humming along. Our people, both reporters and copy editors, poured out quality articles day after day. The paper looked good and read well most of the time. But I learned to mistrust my own feelings of satisfaction at the end of a heavy night because only too often I would wake up in the morning, take one look at page one and immediately spot a horrendous error that I had let through. We had a particular jinx in regard to the company's board of directors. Everyone knew that we had to be extra-careful about any references to them, but somehow, despite our best efforts, we regularly screwed up the spelling of their names and the names of their families. Once we gave the chairman of the board a son he did not have.

Errors were inevitable. They had to be when each day saw the start of a new process to produce a book full of words by that night. The aim was to keep errors to a minimum. The final precaution for each page was that I approved the proofs for printing. One night a proof slipped through the net, and just as the presses were about to start, I spotted a headline on page three that read: "Vorster Is A Liar," with the text filled with defamation. I ran to the machine room and delayed the printing. The production staff climbed into the machines to attack the printing plates with hammer and chisel, hacking out the offending words—better blank spaces than libel, I thought. Only when the first edition printed did I realize what headline I had perpetrated: "Vorster Is A..." Everyone had fun choosing their own word.

Vorster featured in another error of judgment that wasn't caught in time. A columnist, Kate Lee, was suffering from a shortage of ideas, and wrote, "A is for Another Day, another column, another attempt to amuse with an alphabet of topical news, an A to Z of what's going on." It was innocuous stuff, until she reached "V," when she wrote, "V is for Venereal Disease, which isn't nice; and for Mr. Vorster." She did not intend to link Vorster with venereal disease, nor did deputy editor Rex Gibson make the connection when he read the column and passed the page proof for printing. Late at night the chief copy editor realized the implications of the juxtaposition, and the item was hurriedly excised.

But the damage was done. It made the early editions, and an angry private secretary was on the phone from Pretoria first thing in the morning, conveying the feelings of the prime minister, who took it as a deliberate, personal insult. That evening the *Mail*'s political correspondent, Bernardi Wessels, received a message telling him that an invitation to dinner at Vorster's official residence an hour later had been withdrawn because of the "exceptionally filthy article," and that the *Mail* would never be welcome. An abject apology was subsequently published in the newspaper, but without effect. The invitation had been a breakthrough because, until then, Vorster had refused to speak to the *Mail*; the contact was broken before it was established.

My private passion was the preservation of documentary material and records of radical and black political movements from which complete histories could one day be written. People were scared to keep documents because it became a criminal offense to do so after the banning of organizations. I wanted the originals to remain in South Africa but to be safeguarded by being put on to microfilm, with a copy sent out of the country. Initially, in 1963, I worked on a grant from the Africa Collection at the Hoover Institution for War, Revolution and Peace at Stanford University, and later with the Center for Research Libraries in Chicago, a cooperative project comprising over thirty major American university libraries.

I met Dr. A.B. Xuma's widow at a conference early in the 1960s. Xuma was the ANC president until 1949, and was responsible for modernizing the organization. I learned from her that his papers were lying in a garage in Soweto under attack by damp and mice. She said that she did not know what to do with them, and was only too glad to donate the papers to the South African Institute of Race Relations. The institute's library became my repository for original documents and especially for the court records of political trials, which defense lawyers gave to me. Everything I could lay my hands on was preserved, and in return for access to documents I gave the owners a complimentary copy of the microfilm, which could be easily hidden. The Black Sash, Nusas, and the Garment Workers Union were some of the groups whose records were preserved. A friend in the banned COD literally dug up a box of papers and gave it to me for a swift overnight filming. I did the Cape Town's NEUM papers the same way. Tucsa had the accumulated papers of the trade union movement dating back to early in the century, and I raised money to hire two librarians for a year to sort out and prepare the documents for filming. A strongroom full of paper was reduced to ninety-seven reels of microfilm, each one containing 1,000 to 1,300 pages. Once filmed, the originals were to be presented to Johannesburg's city library, but at around that time I wanted to research Communism, and the library refused access to its material. That set off warning bells: this was not a library to be trusted, I told Tucsa, and the papers went instead to Wits.

Every once in a while I lost sleep wondering how many thousands of years of possible imprisonment I had earned by having had all these underground documents filmed. I was also worried about what effect a prosecution arising from my personal life might have on my position at the *Mail*. But I got away with it and the Center for Research Libraries named its Southern African collection of documentary materials after me.

Some papers were lost forever, though. Several years after the banning of the PAC in 1960 I heard from exiles abroad that the headquarters files had been hidden in the roof of a house in Soweto. For months I worked carefully and surreptitiously to gain access. When I finally was able to send someone to collect the papers, we found that a new tenant had found the papers and, frightened, promptly burned them.

On September 6, 1966, the father of "granite apartheid," Prime Minister Verwoerd, was stabbed to death by a parliamentary messenger, Dimitri Tsafendas, as he sat in his seat in parliament. The news of the assassination took up the *Mail*'s front page, and that was obviously the way to handle the story. But a heavy black border surrounding the page drew mixed reactions, with criticism from both staff members and the public. They felt it looked as if the newspaper that attacked Verwoerd more vehemently than any other during his lifetime, was now fawning and hypocritical. A court judged Tsafendas insane and he was locked away for life. For the first twenty-five years he was kept in a cell next to the gallows chamber in Pretoria Prison where prisoners were executed in batches week after week; another prisoner described him as "howling like a dog" at the sound of the

Chapter 17

trapdoors being sprung. Later he was placed in a mental asylum and died there, aged 81, in October 1999.

With Verwoerd's death the government's authoritarian face did not change, and indeed John Vorster was chosen to succeed him precisely because Afrikaner Nationalists believed that that is what he embodied. Yet while Vorster pressed ahead with separate development at home, he did start to move in new directions, and for a time sought to end South Africa's isolation by making friends in Africa. He sent emissaries and visited countries such as Zambia, the Ivory Coast, and Malawi. Within the National Party he was accused of moving away from Verwoerd's policies, and the conflicts led to the breakaway of an extreme right-wing group led by Albert Hertzog to form the Herstigte Nasionale Party (Renewed National Party).

How was the *Mail* to cover the HNP? The new party was a total denial of all that we stood for. The racial utterances of its leaders were offensive, and took the country back to the rawest days of the Afrikaner government. We agreed that we were obliged to report the HNP as part of the shifting political scene, but that we would strive to maintain a balance. Meanwhile the rest of the media downplayed the HNP. The *Star* paid them little attention, and the Afrikaans newspapers and the SABC generally ignored them altogether. Like it or not—and we didn't like it—we ended up giving the HNP the most coverage, sometimes with unexpected consequences. Bosman Swanepoel, in the *Mail's* Pretoria bureau, told me he reported an HNP meeting that was broken up by Nationalists. It was the usual sort of political rowdiness, with men punching each other and chairs flying around. Swanepoel sat at the press table at the front of the hall pretending he wasn't there. A burly HNP man rushed up, leaned over the table, grabbed him by the shoulders and hoisted him into the air. "*Wie is jy?*" (Who are you?) he yelled. "*Rand Daily Mail,*" replied Swanepoel. The man let go and, as Swanepoel fell back into the chair, said, "Sit, friend."

Vorster's "outward " policy took him to Malawi in 1971, the first visit by a South African leader to an independent black state. The following year President Hastings Kamuzu Banda returned the favor, and South Africa was agog. I walked to the President Hotel in the city center, where Banda was staying, to watch the crowd of hundreds, people of all colors, standing outside waiting to catch a glimpse of him. Walking back to the *Mail*, I passed the Langham, faded, but still one of Johannesburg's premier hotels, and was surprised to see a long line of black "GG" cars outside. Chief Gatsha Buthelezi, the leader of the tribal "homeland" for Zulus and a friend of mine, emerged as I passed the entrance. "You're staying here, at the Langham?" I asked incredulously. Banda was one thing, but local blacks checking into the Langham was unprecedented. "Yes, and I'm on my way to have tea with the mayor," replied Buthelezi, echoing my astonishment. "It's a revolution."

As part of the ceremonies, Banda arranged a formal dinner for Vorster. The *Mail* duly made up page one with photographs and reports of the speeches. Late that night, after our usual deadline for the final edition, another set of photographs came in showing the guests at the head table with Vorster sitting between two Malawian women. It was a unique sight. I put my hands on the picture to screen out everyone except Vorster and the two women and ordered a remake of page one to accommodate the image. As I walked back to my office, I joked, "How many bets the HNP buys five thousand copies of the paper?" To my embarrassment that is exactly what the HNP did, and distributed our front page to attack Vorster for socializing with black women.

Even while Vorster was looking beyond the borders, he pressed down on his opponents at home. As his policy unfolded into the 1970s, he relaxed some apartheid but was inflexible in seeking to dictate the pace and direction of change. The police were fundamental in maintaining control, and no one more so than Hendrik van den Bergh, the detective who had arrested me for the Damp Squib article. With the ANC, PAC, and others turning to sabotage, Vorster put van den Bergh in charge of the Security Police in January 1963. They were friends from Second World War days, when both were interned as suspected Nazi sympathizers.

As luck would have it, I learned about the appointment even before it was made public when I ran into van den Bergh outside Parliament in Cape Town. It was the first time we had seen each other since he had escorted me into jail eighteen months before, and he told me the news. He invited me for lunch, told me that the country was in peril from Communists and that he was recruiting a range of people, including psychologists in universities, to fend off the danger. He offered me a full-time job. I laughed. "You're like a man with a spade walking behind a team of oxen and cleaning up their mess," I said. "You are cleaning up the mess made by your political masters. There is not the slightest chance of my getting involved."

Van den Bergh and I continued meeting for an occasional lunch over the years. He used to tell me indignantly that he had been wrongly interned because police raided his home and found a wooden carving of a submarine made by his young nephew. I thought there must have been more than that but never got to the bottom of it. During one lunch he told me that if I knew John Vorster as well as he did, I would become Vorster's greatest supporter. Vorster, he said, believed that South Africa would become a nonracial country—not during his lifetime nor that of his children's or grandchildren's, but one day. That was a startling statement, especially during a time when Vorster's security forces were straining themselves to destroy extraparliamentary opposition. At the *Mail* we looked for evidence to support van den Bergh's statement, but never found any.

At the end of the 1960s van den Bergh set about extending his empire, proposing a new agency that would be like a combination of the CIA, FBI, Mossad, MI5 and MI6. This new agency's role would include supervising the army, he told me. The military people, he said heatedly, were getting away with whatever they wanted by exaggerating the country's defense needs. The new agency, named the Bureau for State Security—or BOSS, as it was promptly dubbed by the press—would bring them under control by screening their intelligence assessments and requests for money to buy arms. Inspired by my friend Ernie Wentzel, the *Mail* quipped that *BOSS* actually stood for *BO* and *SS*.

BOSS was indeed established, but did not receive the power to supervise the military. A diplomat told me that the attempt to invest BOSS with the control van den Bergh wanted had set off a titanic power struggle in Nationalist ranks. Military leaders had gone to Vorster to tell him that, although they supported him, shared the Afrikaner Nationalist cause, and did not want to see the HNP's Albert Hertzog as prime minister, they insisted that he leave the army alone. They said they would tell Vorster what they needed; he would continue to make speeches to keep the public in line and ensure that parliament voted for the money. The threat succeeded, and Vorster backed down. It was, however, by no means the end of the conflict, as events unfolded the following decade.

The occasional contact I had with van den Bergh gave me insight into the power elite. I enjoyed my liberty as a journalist, and the fact that I could ignore barriers and meet and cross mental swords with whomever I pleased. But it is also dangerous because contact with someone, whether a policeman or politician, can lead you to feel protective of him. A wise friend, the late Leonard Silk, who was the *New York Times* economics columnist, told me that he derived his approach from Machiavelli's *The Prince*: to get close enough to the fire to enjoy the heat but not close enough to get burned. With regard to van den Bergh, another factor was at work for me: the excitement in riding the tiger.

I knew that van den Bergh wasn't always truthful with me, although there were times when I thought his attempts to mislead me were insultingly simple-minded. For example, I asked him how John Harris—who set off a murderous bomb at Johannesburg's railway station in 1960 and was hanged for it—had come to suffer a broken jaw after his arrest. Van den Bergh said that his personal intuition had led to Harris' arrest only a few hours after the blast, and he had been at Security Police headquarters in Johannesburg when Harris was brought in. "When I left late that night I walked down the stairs," van den Bergh said, "there was a light missing. I told them they should put in a bulb otherwise someone was sure to trip in the dark and hurt himself. That's exactly what happened to Harris. After he had confessed, he was being brought down the stairs and he slipped and fell and broke his jaw." In fact, a Security policeman broke Harris's jaw. Another time, van den Bergh said that he had personally exposed a Soviet spy, Yuri Loginov, who was operating in South Africa. He said Loginov had been arrested on suspicion and was sitting in his office when van den Bergh suddenly threw a question to him in Russian and drew an involuntary reply in Russian. Loginov smiled, he said, and immediately confessed. However, another version that emerged in due course of time was that the United States learnt about Loginov from a Soviet defector and exposed him to the South Africans.

Van den Bergh transformed the security apparatus. After he took over, many of the Security policemen were zealots. They were not merely policemen upholding law and order but were defending Afrikaner Nationalist rule. The laws enacted by the government let them do as they pleased: no habeas corpus was allowed, and they could keep anyone in jail incommunicado and indefinitely so that any marks of torture would disappear. The no-holds-barred treatment of detainees began in earnest, starting with torture and going on to deaths—probably accidental at first or suicide through being driven too far in interrogation—and fast turned into a process that led to the murder squads that became a feature of South Africa from the mid 1980s onwards.

It is not known when government spies began to infiltrate the *Mail* and other newspapers. The first known spy was Gerard Ludi in the early 1960s, and used his newspaper job at the *Mail* as a base to penetrate the underground Communist Party.

John Horak, who worked in the copy editors' room, was for many years also suspected of being a spy. Raymond Louw told him that his colleagues were claiming he was a spy. Horak denied it and said he was prepared to swear that he was not.

My argument to my colleagues was that Horak was too obvious to be a spy. He was also conscientious and worked hard for the *Mail*, so I defended him. I felt sorry for him for being targeted when there was no hard evidence. After a few years one of my former prison contacts phoned to tell me that he and Horak attended an Afrikaans fundamentalist church every Sunday and stood around chatting after the service.

Horak did not know that his fellow churchgoer was my friend, and revealed that he was a Security Police agent at the *Rand Daily Mail*. The next morning I did the rounds of my senior colleagues, beating my breast and saying "mea culpa." We did not act against Horak. He continued his work in journalism and later moved to a Sunday newspaper in the building. I think we agreed that it was better to know who our spies were.

Horak was a police agent for twenty-seven years, and reported to Johan Coetzee, who had been in charge of the Prisons Trial. His curriculum vitae (he showed it to me because he wanted me to write a book with him) was divided into two sections, dovetailing with each other: "Journalistic career" and "Police/Intelligence/Military Career," which included work for the Security Police, BOSS, and sundry branches of the security agencies. While working in 1985 as manager of Saan's Morning Group, he emerged from under cover and worked full-time with the police with the rank of major.

In 1970, when I was night editor, a reporter X phoned me at home and asked to see me. After he arrived, he suggested we walk around the block, as my home might be bugged. He revealed his suspicion that a colleague, Y, was a police agent. He had seen Y going through desks in the newsroom, and said that Y was always asking what was going on. X urged me to expose Y. I counseled patience. It was better to know who the spy was than risk having a new one put in his place. The next night at the *Mail*, Y asked to speak to me privately. He said we should stroll along the corridors, as my office was probably bugged. He revealed his suspicion that X was a spy because he saw him going through desks and he was always asking questions.

At that stage I did not have the slightest idea whether either, neither, or both of them was a police agent. I later learned that it was X.

The three security services—BOSS, the Security Police, and Military Intelligence—operated independently, but could ask one another for information. Each thoroughly mistrusted the other, not unusual in intelligence circles, and especially in authoritarian societies. I surmised that, in our editorial staff of some 130, each agency had at least one informer and probably two to allow for illness and holidays. The number was probably even greater to ensure penetration into different editorial departments. The chief anxiety, as far as I was concerned, wasn't so much what information they might carry back, but the threat to morale. Suspicion about spies could poison editorial relationships. Sometimes allegations were made with good reason; at other times, with only the slightest excuse.

It was even worse in left-wing circles outside the newspaper. Paranoia was understandable because it was well known that the Security Police were infiltrating underground movements, and life and death were at stake in resistance politics. Added to this, anyone who did not fit into the known mold aroused suspicion. I started running into this problem early on, when the ANC was still legal. Myrtle Berman, who was on the Left, told me that Duma Nokwe, then the ANC's secretary-general, believed that *Mail* reporter Oscar Tamsen and I were British MI6 agents based on the fact that we had each been on a trip to Britain. This was ridiculous, I protested. Tamsen had a Kemsley journalist's study scholarship, and I went there as an Abe Bailey Fellow from the University of Cape Town before I became a journalist. I confronted Nokwe, but he denied making these allegations to Myrtle Berman; she had made them to him, he claimed. Tamsen and I decided to shrug it off.

My close friendship with Robert Sobukwe, in the fevered atmosphere of the time, also gave rise to talk in ANC circles that I was a PAC supporter. I knew about this and believed there was nothing I could do about it except to continue to be as evenhanded as possible in my reporting. Only thirty-five years later, in a letter from Walter Sisulu, did I learn that the rumors had included the belief that I had a hand in drafting the Pan-Africanist statement of independence. It was a power and influence I never possessed.

As the years went by, I was alleged to have been alternately an agent for BOSS, the CIA, Mossad, and MI6. Those were the ones I heard about. When I wrote the Strachan prison reports, someone spread a rumor that I had deliberately misquoted Strachan to get him prosecuted in order to discredit the Left. On the police side, van den Bergh revealed that he had suspected I was a Communist Party leader. Johan Coetzee waged a personal campaign for some years: Winnie Mandela told me that while Coetzee was interrogating her during one of her detentions, he said that he was convinced I was a secret ANC member. Several other detainees passed word to me that Coetzee told them he would not regard his police career as complete until he had me behind bars. To add insult to injury, when he was appointed chief of the Security Police, he described me as a "friend" in an interview with the Afrikaans newspaper *Beeld*; I assumed he was trying to show that he moved among a wide range of people.

Many of these swirling currents suddenly came together when I received a letter from Gordon Winter in 1981. He had come into the open with his book *Inside BOSS*, in which he admitted, in copious detail, what everyone had believed: he had worked as a spy for van den Bergh for years. Winter sent me a five-page letter from his place in hiding—it was Britain or Ireland—and assured me he was telling me the truth when he claimed the following:

> I was guilty of smearing you (in journalist circles) of being a CIA sub agent, used to sluice money from the CIA for Mrs. Sobukwe's upkeep, while Mangaliso was in jail. Don't blame me for that. As Eichmann said: "I was only doing my duty. My superiors ordered me to do it" etc. I also rumored it round town that HJ [van den Bergh] had recruited you when he discovered your connection with the "CIA" re: Sobukwe funds etc. All this must have damaged you. But that's what the game is all about. Character Assassination. Again, I throw up the same lame excuse. "I did as I was told."

It was uncomfortable to have to be on guard so much of the time, wondering which casual phrase might be seized upon and reported by whichever spy of whichever security agency. My one hope was that whoever reported me should do so accurately, and in context.

Spy recruitment went on all the time. We were aware of it because, every once in a while, a staff member would report to the editor that he had been approached by a government agent who wanted him to become an informer at the *Mail*—and who had even quoted something the staff member had said at an editorial meeting. A secretary of mine was courted for six months by a man—and he then revealed he was a Security policeman and wanted her to spy on me; she was shocked to realize there was no love, only a setup. And these were just the ones we knew about. We did not know who had accepted the offers.

At an entirely different level was a middle-ranking leader of the PAC who was a friend of mine. After the organization was banned, he came to see me now and again. Sometimes he said that the Security Police had pulled him in and during the questioning had asked about me. One day he said he needed my advice. The police had ordered him to be an informer. The carrot was the money they would pay him, which was substantial in terms of what he was earning. The stick was that if he did not cooperate, he would be "endorsed out"—ordered to leave Johannesburg to go to live with his family in rural poverty. "What must I do?" he asked. I could not look him in the eye. I stared down at the floor and said, "That's not a question that one human being can answer for another." There was a short silence and he got up and left. He did not say a word. He never came to see me again. I took that as an act of friendship because it meant he would not be in a position to answer any police questions about me.

Riding the tiger, I told van den Bergh that it had become a *Mail* tradition that whenever someone said anything nasty about BOSS or the Security services during editorial meetings in our conference room, the speaker looked up at the ceiling and called out, "Sorry about that, General." Van den Bergh, who was not given to making jokes, gave me a thin smile and said, "Yes, I've heard those discussions. And it's not in the ceiling."

Anthony Holiday was told by a friend at the *Rand Daily Mail* that, in the past year, there had been three broken marriages, one nervous breakdown, and two suicides among the editorial staff. "I thought," says Holiday, "that's the sort of newspaper I want to be part of, that's living!"

It was a quirky reason for joining the *Mail*, but it did reflect a reality. In 1970 the newspaper was crackling with energy. It was also operating within a hostile environment, and the physical and emotional strains took a heavy toll on staff. You had to be a bit odd to want to be part of it, and eccentrics flourished. Holiday was one of them, his long brown hair flying, his hands weaving, words falling out of him excitedly. He had a habit of pacing up and down, silently addressing the air, pen clutched between his teeth and fingers flicking. One night I watched him in the newsroom and quietly asked, "Tony, who are you

Chapter 18

speaking to?" He looked at me with surprise, "To myself, of course," and went on with his conversation.

It was also a time of intense political activity. Although white power was at its zenith, there were shifts and the possibility of shifts. At the start of the 1970s John Vorster led the National Party to its sixth electoral victory, but for the first time since 1948 the party lost ground to the United Party. The HNP polled a measly 3.56 percent of the vote and didn't win a single seat because Vorster demolished most of their extreme right-wing demands with his own right-wing toughness. He pushed ahead with "Grand Apartheid," the territorial dismembering of the country by creating tribal ministates; initially refused the U.S. black tennis star Arthur Ashe permission to visit South Africa; told England that its touring cricket team could not include Basil d'Oliviera, the South African–born colored who had emigrated to Britain (and Vorster thus destroyed cricket links with the world); propped up Rhodesia's white government in defiance of the world; and refused to yield control of South-West Africa.

On the other hand, on March 30, 1971, Vorster held a press conference, the first time that a South African prime minister had done so. And the first steps were taken to reduce what was called "petty apartheid," the much-used phrase for the "smaller" aspects of apartheid, although I avoided the term. How could any apartheid be "petty"? But as a sign of the times, Johannesburg's city council opened public parks, public benches, and libraries to people of all colors. With world economic sanctions spreading, and public and shareholder protest building, the U.S. Polaroid Corporation launched a program to improve conditions for the black workers of its South African agent. (Polaroid later became one of the early U.S. corporations to divest from South Africa.) In 1974 Vorster won another general election, this time increasing the Nationalist majority, while the Progressives finally made some headway in persuading more whites to accept their policy of a qualified franchise to apply to everyone in a multiracial South Africa. They won 7 seats out of 170, giving Helen Suzman company in parliament after thirteen lonely years.

The *Mail* thrived because it had adequate "space between the advertisements," as the Canadian-British press baron Lord Thomson half-jokingly described his own newspapers' editorial columns. We also had enough talented writers eager to fill the space. Holiday speaks of the "exhilarating sense of critical freedom." He says that "a lot of the fun of the *Mail* had to do with the stress of being there—we worked hard, played hard and drank a lot." It was "tense because with every story, with everything you did, you felt you were on trial as a journalist, in terms of professional standards." In the nature of the politics that he was writing, there was a good deal of interpretation, and he was often challenged by the editor or an assistant editor to validate his views. "There was fierce disagreement about the handling of my reports—I was writing sensitive political stories—but I never felt oppressed."

But Holiday had a hidden side. Unknown to most at the *Mail*, he was a member of the underground Communist Party. Belonging to a secret organization doesn't square with covering the daily political scene, and had it been known, he would not have held the political reporter's job. If the police had uncovered his political affiliation, it would have seriously damaged the *Mail*, and would have confirmed the government's darkest suspicions about the newspaper's agenda. After hours Holiday was writing and printing three to five hundred copies of an underground news sheet, *Revolt*, and distributing copies at Wits and in telephone booths, as well as mailing out thousands of ANC leaflets smuggled to him from Britain. Holiday insists that he never felt any clash of interest. "The CP never required me to abuse my position and I would never have done it even if they had asked me to do so. There was never any question of slanting my copy." He was not the only secret Communist on the *Mail*. His cell included Paddy Weech, a reporter, and Rosemary Arnold in the Saan library. Holiday left the *Mail* late in 1975 and went to the *Cape Times* in Cape Town. A few months later, the Security Police intercepted a communication with London and arrested him. He was tried and imprisoned for six years, completed a university degree while in jail, went on to do a doctorate at Oxford University, and returned to teach in South Africa.

For all his eccentricity Holiday did succeed in keeping his political views separate from his work. His *Mail* colleagues were taken aback when his underground links became known because he had a reputation for fairness and accuracy in reporting.

Years later, in April 1994, Holiday and I sat in a coffee shop in Cape Town and talked about the strange people who had inhabited the *Mail*. It was the month of the elections for the new democratic South Africa and it was the first time we felt able to speak freely. We had even outgrown the nervous habit of glancing over our shoulders—the hallmark of South Africans—and paid no attention to the man at the next table. After nearly two hours of conversation the man came to our table. "I hope you will not mind but I've been listening to you, and I want to thank you," he said. "I don't know when I last heard such an interesting discussion."

One of the big news stories was the siege of the Israeli consulate-general in April 1975 just a few blocks from the *Mail*'s offices. Israel was a target for hijackings in that era, so the first message out of the consulate from a security officer, David Protter, that Red Army terrorists had taken over was accepted without demur. A wild burst of gunfire from the police on the ground, which they said was aimed at the hijackers, caused much damage to surrounding buildings in the narrow street. Every possible *Mail* reporter and photographer was rushed to the scene as the drama went on throughout the night. Shortly after four A.M., Syd Duval, the religious-affairs reporter, phoned in from the scene: he had learned that no terrorist group was involved. Protter, a South African Jew, was himself the hijacker. The *Mail*, in one of its great feats, published a series of special editions to give the latest news. When the presses finally halted after ten A.M., 250,000 copies had been printed and sold, compared with the normal day's sale of 140,000.

Protter had killed one of the consular officials, and several people were wounded. He agreed to let a doctor treat them, and Solly Gottlieb volunteered for the dangerous duty. He went upstairs dressed only in his underpants and took a mobile phone so that proper contact could be made. Van den Bergh spent the night talking Protter into surrendering. At dawn Protter came down the stairs carrying a gun, and van den Bergh walked forward to meet him and accept his surrender. Israel's ambassador, Yitzhak Unna, was there and told me later that van den Bergh displayed total courage because no one knew whether Protter, deranged and unstable, might not simply shoot him down. After arresting Protter, van den Bergh drove him to Pretoria, took him to his own home for breakfast, and then put him in jail. He explained that he knew this would be the last normal meal Protter would eat for years.

The *Mail* was once again forced to come up with a strategy for boosting circulation. The first aim was to make the *Mail* a comprehensive daily package of news. Getting the "mix" right was the nightly obsession: to strike a balance between significant news, news of interest to readers, and news it was believed readers should know, with a dollop of human or humorous stories for a change of pace. As night editor I had a report on my desk one night about the deficiencies of black education—important but unlikely to attract the bulk of white readers—and another report of little enduring importance that I knew would likely draw readers. After agonizing, I placed the report of little consequence as the lead story on page one and the education report as number two, thinking that the information about education might get more attention than if it was in the number-one spot. Louw approved my decision, though I continued wondering whether sugarcoating was the way to treat significant information. But it was the sort of decision that was not uncommon.

Now and again a link was discernible between what we published and public consciousness. We repeatedly published reports about "poverty pay"—the wretchedly poor pay of untold numbers of black workers—

but to little effect, it seemed. Then, in the early 1970s, an outbreak of strikes by black workers in Natal province set off a wave of public concern about low pay. The screeds of material we had been publishing over an extended period of time—articles providing facts, examining the effects of poverty pay, describing the human suffering, reporting the pleas and warnings by politicians about the need for change, plus our own editorials—had been seeping into the public mind, lying dormant until the trigger event of the Natal strikes.

After more than two years as night editor, in 1972 I became an assistant editor in what reporters called "mahogany row," a bit of a misnomer for the simple offices that were home to the newspaper's executives.

Among those I dealt with was Dirk Rezelman, a columnist hired to write about politics from the Afrikaner Nationalist viewpoint. It was a worthy idea to give the other side a voice on the paper, and Rezelman had the necessary credentials: he was a good writer, had worked for the National Party, and had served as Prime Minister Vorster's first press secretary. The only trouble was that he seemed to have grown disillusioned with the National Party, and the more he wrote, the more his sympathy with the Progressives became apparent. He finally left to handle press relations for the Maize Board, which represented corn farmers, the most powerful agricultural lobby in the country. He told me about an earlier job, as an information officer in the South African embassy in Washington, D.C. He gave lectures on university campuses and one day received a sharp message from his bosses in the Department of Information in Pretoria, quoting what he had said at a lecture and pointing out that his view was contrary to government policy. Rezelman, angry, went to the Security officer in the embassy and demanded to know who was spying on him. The officer, although embarrassed at being confronted by a colleague, refused to reveal the person's identity. Rezelman used his political contacts at home to ferret out the name of the spy and it turned out to be a black exile who attended many of his meetings and always stood up and furiously condemned him.

Rezelman's way of dealing with this situation illustrated the lunatic nature of South Africa. For, as he told me, the next time he spoke on a campus and the exile made his usual attack, he, Rezelman, an official spokesman for the South African government, dramatically accused the exile of being an agent for the South African government. The exile hurriedly left and wasn't seen again.

A lot of time and space were invested in projecting the *Mail* into the community in order to help people. The Christmas Fund, started in the earliest years of the century by Edgar Wallace, became an annual fixture and always drew strong support from the public. Eventually it extended its aid beyond the white community. A complementary midyear fund sprang into existence in the winter of 1964 when Johannesburg had one of its rare snowfalls. It was bitterly cold that year and a businessman, Errol Pappert, phoned Louw to suggest that the *Mail* collect blankets for people in need. Louw did one better by launching a full-blown Operation Snowball campaign, which became an annual event, collecting money, blankets, and clothing. Several dozen collection depots were opened during the winters and run by such volunteer groups as the American Women's Club and Jewish women's organizations. The appeals were so successful in drawing donations, and the need so great among thousands of people, that distribution in Johannesburg was turned over to the Non-European Affairs Department.

Another social promotion grew out of a news item I read in the *Star* that teachers and principals of Soweto high schools had formed the Rand Bursary Fund to help keep promising youngsters in school. The government provided white children with free, compulsory schooling all the way to matriculation, but the amount of money provided by the government for black education was a paltry six million rand a year. It had been kept at that level in spite of soaring numbers and inflation. Black parents made up for the reduced government spending through a compulsory local tax plus levies imposed by schools to buy basic items like chalk, blackboard erasers, and toilet paper. Parents also had to buy the books their children needed in high school. Given the widespread poverty, many parents could not keep their children at school because they either could not afford the fees and books or they needed the children to work.

The article in the *Star* described the efforts of the Rand Bursary Fund to raise money for scholarships. The bursaries were modest at twenty rand each. It was ridiculous that the amount of money it took to pay for dinner for two could also cover most of a year's school fees and books, and could mean the difference between a youngster continuing high school and dropping out. There was immediate agreement at the *Mail* that this was a project we should support and I was given all the space and facilities needed to launch a campaign. Somehow we struck a chord among the public, because within days enough money poured in to enable the Rand Bursary Fund to give immediate scholarships to more than 700 children. The following year the number shot to 1,100. We had to keep raising money to keep them at school.

I didn't like to use photographs of the youngsters on whose behalf we were appealing, but using them was like pressing the keys of a cash machine in drawing money from readers. I compromised by not using surnames. Every story was a tale of acute human distress, a community and families in poverty and social disarray. Each story also revealed hope and aspiration.

There was no shortage of material. The education system for blacks was a mess. Each time I went to Soweto, I returned with a clump of emotional stories. Pupils preparing for their final examinations often only had one textbook, if any at all. Most teachers were underqualified and badly paid. Home conditions were crowded. Because of the distorted educational system, untold numbers of children had to wait a year or so before they could enroll, then face the same hurdle when they went into higher grades. Less than 4 percent of children were enrolled in high schools, and the schools were often populated by young men in their early twenties, causing severe discipline problems. "Bantu education," as the government called it, was notorious for its thought control. The declared intention was to teach blacks that they had no place in "white" South Africa, and any teacher who protested was fired.

The fund's chairman, Wilkie Kambule, was headmaster of Orlando High School, the second biggest high school in the country. Kambule contradicted the belief among whites that blacks could not do mathematics: he was a gifted mathematics teacher and his school produced several students who went on to study nuclear physics. He used unusual methods to teach broader lessons of life. On a visit to Orlando High, Kambule took me into a laboratory where pupils were at work. They looked at me curiously from across the room. Kambule beckoned to one, calling out, "Hey boy, come here!" To be called "boy," as whites often did to black men, however elderly, was humiliating, especially in front of a stranger. The youngster stood his ground. Again Kambule called out, "Hey boy, I am telling you to come here!" The youngster reluctantly walked toward us, glaring at Kambule. As he reached us, Kambule softly asked him, "Since when do you come when someone calls you 'boy'?" It was a hard way to give a lesson, but I doubt that the young man was ever servile to anyone again. Because of Kambule's enthusiasm and drive, Orlando High had reasonable facilities and even boasted a fine library.

Across the street from Kambule's school was a higher primary school whose principal was the Rand Bursary Fund's secretary. His pupils were supposed to get free textbooks, but the government met only 20 percent of their needs each year. The books were flimsy and did not last the decreed five years before replacement, so there were never enough books. Pupils in some classes kneeled on the floor, using long benches as desks. I found pupils sitting on rocks on the earth floor at a school in Alexandra township on the other side of Johannesburg.

The *Mail*'s support for the Rand Bursary Fund extended beyond publishing articles. It seemed to me that the cause lent itself to teaching whites about black lives, and I set out with the Fund's teacher-committee to involve as many members of the public as possible. One method was to "adopt a child." We offered donors the chance to increase their contribution by "adopting" a child, hoping that personal communication would develop between donor and bursar, but most of the money that came in consisted of small amounts.

We hoped for really substantial donations from business corporations, but few arrived, so I was delighted when the local branch of the U.S. company Cyanamid offered one thousand rand. They wanted publicity in return, to which I agreed. I went to collect the check from Cyanamid's local boss, an American. He made it clear that his contribution was donated for the sole purpose of showing his head office in the United States that he was doing something to get antiapartheid shareholders off their back. His attitude as an uncaring outsider upset me, and I was so angry that I thought of tearing up the check. Then I thought of the fifty children who could stay on at school and resisted the temptation. At least he gave the one thousand rand, which was more than what most South African business houses were willing to do, as they claimed they would not get involved in "politics." It was only after the "children's rebellion" in June 1976, when commerce and industry suddenly awakened to the prospect that everything could be going down the drain, that their attitudes changed and they began to push for improvements in black education and living conditions.

Until the early 1970s, contact with Nationalist leaders was extremely rare. Bernardi Wessels, who covered parliament, invited Dr. Connie Mulder, the Minister of the Interior, to an off-the-record lunch at the

Mail. Mulder, who was known for being outgoing and friendly, was on his way up the political ladder. It was a successful exchange of views for everyone, and also proved helpful for me in regaining my passport.

A few months later I was invited to London by Harold Evans at the *Sunday Times* for a conference on cities organized with Unesco. I applied for a passport but after six weeks had passed, I asked Wessels to approach Mulder's office. The next day Mulder himself phoned to tell me that he would give me a passport for three months so that I could attend the conference. The passport was restricted for travel only to Britain but I didn't care. All that mattered was that I could escape for a few weeks, after being caged-in for more than five years.

For the next ten years, a pattern was established: passports were issued to me for six months or a year at a time, and were gradually extended to other parts of the world. Each time I applied, I would repeatedly go to the passport office, stand in a queue, only to be told that it wasn't ready. After six to eight weeks, I would write to the Department of the Interior to ask about the delay, and the passport would arrive a few days later. It was a waste of time and I could never be certain whether I was going to get the passport. Each time, sitting in the plane waiting for take-off, I wondered whether they were going to haul me back, and was quickly relieved when we ascended into the air.

Dr. Piet Koornhof, then the Minister of Sport, was also a lunch guest at the *Mail.* His large ears and long nose made him a natural target for cartoonists, especially as the gloss he put on government policies earned him the nickname of Piet Pinocchio, with his nose drawn longer and longer. He had recently allowed the first nonracial boxing tournament. He confided how worried he had been at the ringside about the possible reaction of the crowd as blacks and whites battered each other inside the ring, but all had gone well. He assured us that he wanted to increase nonracialism in sport, but that he was having trouble because the Aurora cricket club in Natal was insisting on playing nonracial cricket in defiance of the laws prohibiting it. He asked for our support. "Please help me to further nonracial cricket by telling Aurora they must stop playing nonracial cricket," was his bewildering message.

These off-the-record and unreported contacts with government members grew stronger because, not only did the editor continue the traditional practice of spending a week at parliament each year, but Rex Gibson and I also started doing it, each year meeting a score or so of cabinet members and backbenchers. The novelty of the encounters never wore off for either them or us. They were fascinated to be talking to executives of the despised English-language press and many were eager to explain their doings to us. We were equally interested in looking at them close-up and the contact helped us to assess government policy. The Nationalists were always friendly and discussions were open and tough, save for one time when I met P.W. Botha, then the Minister of Defense and notorious for his bad temper. Wessels took me to the meeting and walking through the corridors to Botha's office, frantically advised me, "Please don't say anything to him that will upset him because he will lose his temper and shout at you and then I will have a miserable time for the rest of this session of parliament. Please just be nice to him, smile at him and don't upset him."

I had a half-hour meeting during which I asked polite questions, and Botha gave me his wolfish smiles and spoke pleasantly. We parted amicably to Wessels' great relief when I reported to him afterwards.

Alwyn Schlebusch was a cabinet minister and leader of the party in the Orange Free State, the smallest but most agricultural province, thus tapping the deepest roots of Afrikaners. He was admired by his fellow-Nationalists for being a God-fearing man of integrity and honesty. Schlebusch was one of the more than a dozen cabinet ministers with whom I met during my visits to parliament in the early 1980s. On one trip, we spent an hour together in the morning, and he asked me to come back later in the day and then again after that. We spent a total of nearly three hours talking. Nationalist policy at that stage was undergoing change and it wasn't clear where it might be heading so I asked Schlebusch if he could sum up policy in one word.

Schlebusch treated my question seriously. He sat and thought for some time and then said, slowly and heavily, "If you want me to sum up our policy in one word then the word is compassion." As it happened, the day before I had gone into District Six in Cape Town where the government's racial clearance of 35,000 people was nearing its end, and my mind and emotions were filled with the sight of the vast wasteland of the rubble of destroyed houses and the bitter, hopeless talk of the few people still there. I replied, "After what I saw and heard yesterday in District Six I have great difficulty in understanding that word when it comes from a member of your government." It was a meeting of long pauses because we again sat and looked at each other and he then changed the subject.

Not long after, he sighed and said, "It's been very interesting talking to you but I haven't changed your mind and you haven't changed my mind so we had better stop."

Schlebusch's claim to "compassion" was bizarre. Yet there wasn't the slightest doubt that he believed it to be an honest statement and that is how he saw himself and his government's policies. There were many Nationalists I met who were like him and I was never sure if that made it easier to be friendly with them and to exchange views or whether it was pointless to talk to them because, armored by belief in their righteousness, they were impervious to argument; at least with the political cynics like Connie Mulder you could argue power realities with some hope of getting through to them.

There was little long-term planning in the *Rand Daily Mail*'s move away from its traditional role as a newspaper written by whites for whites. Getting into the black market was viewed by Gandar and then by Louw as desirable for both commercial and political reasons. But what should have been normal for a newspaper—chasing news and readers—was deformed by apartheid and was filled with never-ending doubt, angst, and contradictions. My work as African-affairs reporter showed that significant and interesting news was available, and the first two reporters who were not white were hired in 1963. Initially they were only on retainers plus payment for however many words they got into the paper. Lawrence Mayekiso and Sydney Hope were selected from among the freelance journalists earning tip-off money. Hope was colored under the Nationalists' Race Classification laws, but had volunteered for army service during the Second

Chapter 19

World War and served in the Transvaal Scottish regiment. He spoke with wry amusement and some cynicism about those years when he was accepted and treated as white. Mayekiso was a solid reporter, reliable and accurate. Later, during the years of the Prisons Trials, he was also outstandingly brave: he did one investigation after the other, hunting down former prisoners whom our lawyers wanted to interview. He knew that the police were watching him and that he was risking punitive action; he could have refused to do the jobs, but never did.

Black readership of the newspaper at that stage, inasmuch as anyone could estimate it, was probably very small and confined to an elite. I was aware of our growing number of readers because they were the people I was reporting about. They liked the *Mail* because of Gandar's editorials and articles and because it was the only mainstream newspaper making an attempt to publish news about black existence. Page three was corralled off for news about blacks, and soon a special edition, known as a slip edition because only one page was changed, was being run under the title of *Township Mail*. Within two years, as the volume of news increased and the potential for readers became more firmly established, black news was given a full page. The number of reporters, full-time and part-time, grew and they occupied a separate room with a white news editor. What they lacked in training and skill they made up for in enthusiasm. The general, all-white copy editors' desk handled their reports with some acerbity because of the racy style of writing and often contorted grammar. The racial factor added to the usual tension between copy editors and reporters.

The newspaper industry started waking up to the possibility of adding to circulation. A new government-supporting Afrikaans Sunday newspaper, *Rapport*, published an *"Ekstra"* (Extra) edition aimed at coloreds in its Cape Town home area. The *Sunday Times*, alive to the threat to its dominance as the circulation leader, launched its own *Extra* editions aimed at black, colored, and Asian readers. The *Mail's* Township edition flourished, and by 1970 was selling about twenty thousand copies a day. The journalists writing for it became part of the general newsroom.

In 1972 Louw asked David Hazelhurst, formerly the deputy editor of the weekly *Post*, to investigate the possible expansion of Township edition. Hazelhurst recommended more space and a news editor to supervise production to get away from the copy editors' desk. Louw enthusiastically went along with this, and appointed Gavin Stewart, another journalist from the *Post*, as news editor. Mondays had an additional forty columns of space and was grandly called *Rand Daily Mail Extra Extra*. The *Mail* became an aggressive contender for black readers and was locked in combat in the daily market with the *World* newspaper meant only for black readers, which was owned by the Argus Company.

One of the breakthroughs in internal work patterns came about through hiring a top photographer, Peter Magubane, as a *Mail* staff member. He was responsible for many of the images that made the Rand Bursary Fund and Operation Snowball money-raising campaigns so successful. Magubane was friendly with the Mandela family, which led to his harassment and detention without trial. Between 1969 and 1971 he was held in solitary confinement for 586 days, and was the only *Mail* staff member ever banned. The banning not only made it a criminal offense for him to be with more than one person at a time, but it further prohibited him from entering the newspaper office. Louw went to see the chief magistrate in charge of banning restrictions to request easing Magubane's banning orders. Instead of agreeing, the magistrate reissued and tightened the orders. The *Mail* paid Magubane's salary throughout his detention, but halted it when he was banned. Magubane eventually had to become a door-to-door carpet salesman to make a living.

How those of us who were under threat might be treated by Saan if we were ever banned was always a nagging worry. I assumed that if a banning was imposed as a discernibly direct result of our work for the *Mail*, Saan would look after our families financially, but not if it was a result of actions in our private lives. Banning was usually for five years, and was frequently renewed for further periods, so it could land a com-mercial company with a considerable responsibility.

Even before Magubane was banned, the segregation laws prohibited him from using the *Mail's* darkroom in the Saan building, so a special darkroom was created for him in a nearby building. Security policemen came several times in search of him, but he was able to evade them until they sent a black policeman posing as a minister of religion. When the unsuspecting Magubane emerged to see him, the "minister" produced his police identity card. Soon thereafter two Group Areas inspectors visited Louw to point out that Magubane was occupying premises in contraven-tion of segregation laws: they said that he could work inside the *Mail's* building but could not use the darkroom and that whites had to develop his pictures. The Security Police suspected that he might use the photo-graphic chemicals to make bombs—it was as far-fetched as that.

By the time Magubane was able to return to work, the newsdesk need-ed him for general assignments, as there were too few staff photographers for him to be confined to the *Extra* edition. In 1969 Saan newspapers, including the *Mail*, had moved into a new building across the street, and by then the darkroom problem had disappeared. One of Magubane's first assignments was a presentation at the all-white and heavily Afrikaans Randpark Golf Club. We were worried that he would have a rough time, but there was nothing of the sort: he was offered a seat and a drink when he arrived and suffered only a bit of mild teasing. This was at the start of the 1970s, and this was one of the early straws in the wind indicating a move away by whites from the rigidities of Verwoerd-era apartheid.

The blossoming of *Extra* was not universally welcomed. Among *Mail* staff there was unease about the anomaly of denouncing the government's racial segregation in daily editorials while pandering to it, even reinforcing it, with a special edition aimed at blacks. I shared that feeling, but expressed it chiefly through handwringing as I argued that *Extra* was not so much a racial edition as one that catered to a geographical area of interest. The *Mail's* first edition circulated in the country areas and throughout the towns on the gold-mining strip that stretched east and west of Johannesburg. Then came *Extra*, followed by a slip edition with a smattering of news for Pretoria, and two to three hours after the first edition, the main *Morning Final* edition for Johannesburg and its suburbs. I would have preferred a unified Johannesburg-*Extra* edition, but accepted that it was not practical: we had limited space and could not carry all the local news of interest to the separate audiences in the suburbs (who were mainly whites) and the townships (who were blacks) in a single edition. As it was, the continual problems about how best to serve the smaller colored and Asian communities were never resolved. Sports, vital for circulation and the source of unending stories, illustrated some of the dilemmas. Soccer was the big game for blacks and was played throughout the year, while rugby was the stuff of religion for whites, so *Extra* played up soccer and downplayed rugby, while the other editions did the reverse. We had to live within the circumstances and constraints, the results of the government's success in dividing people. We had not created the apartheid townships and the different lifestyles between blacks and whites, but we did have to adjust to their existence.

Black journalists came into their own in the turmoil that followed the "children's rebellion" on June 16, 1976, the day the police opened fire on high school pupils taking part in a protest march in Soweto. Although no one knew it at the time, it was the beginning of the end of apartheid, while also serving to open a new chapter in journalism. Until that moment the Afrikaner Nationalist grip seemed beyond challenge, even though changes were rippling through the country. Vorster was proving to be a mainspring of change. Given his authoritarian background, it was surprising, but he felt he had to get away from the unyielding apartheid inherited from Verwoerd.

There was a spate of what I called "significant insignificant change," such as legislation to ensure that white soldiers saluted black officers, the ending of apartheid in dining and lounge cars on luxury trains, and allowing leading hotels to admit more black guests. At the heart of it, though, the government was holding on to white power. Blacks were hostile to the government insistence on greater use of Afrikaans in teaching. Black teachers, pupils, and parents wanted English because it was a language for the world, plus few black teachers were trained to teach in Afrikaans, the language of the oppressor. They were aggrieved already because of the sub-standard education given to their children. The government was spending 605 rand a year on each white child's education while spending less than 40 rand on each black child's. The teacher-pupil ratio in white schools was 1:20 and in black schools 1:54. The facilities, teacher competence, and examination results reflected the disparities.

"African schools in the white areas are reluctant to have important subjects like mathematics and physical science taught in the medium of Afrikaans because there are no African teachers proficient in teaching these subjects in Afrikaans, say African educationists," reported the *Mail* in late April 1976. Alongside the report we published the minutes of a meeting of the Meadowlands Tswana School Board held on January 20th that year. The minutes laid bare how white officialdom enforced its racial writ through arrogance and threat of sanctions. The circuit inspector who attended the meeting was white and the board members were black:

> The circuit inspector told the board that the Secretary for Bantu Education has stated that all direct taxes paid by the black population of South Africa are being sent to the various homelands for education purposes there.
>
> In urban areas the education of a black child is being paid for by the white population, that is English- and Afrikaans-speaking groups. Therefore the Secretary for Bantu Education has the responsibility towards satisfying the English- and Afrikaans-speaking people.
>
> Consequently, the only way of satisfying both groups [is that] the medium of instruction in all schools shall be on a 50-50 basis.
>
> The circuit inspector further stated that where there was difficulty in instructing through the medium of Afrikaans an application for exemption can be made. He stated that if such an exemption is granted by the Department of Bantu Education, it shall be applicable for one year only.
>
> In future, if schools teach through the medium not prescribed

by the department for a particular subject, examination question papers will only be set in the prescribed medium with no option of the other language. The circuit inspector stated that social studies (history and geography) and mathematics shall be taught through the medium of Afrikaans, physical science and the rest through the medium of English.

Asked whether the circuit inspector should not be speaking at the meeting in an advisory capacity, the inspector stated that he was representing the Department of Bantu Education directly.

The board stated that they were not opposed to the 50-50 basis medium of instruction but that they wanted to be given the chance of choosing the language for each subject.

The circuit inspector stated that the board has no right to choose for itself, but should do what the department wants. He suggested that the board could write to the department via himself and the Regional Director on this matter. At this juncture the circuit inspector excused himself and left the meeting.

The board was not happy about the statements of the circuit inspector and felt that to write a letter would not offer any favorable reply.

The board unanimously accepted a motion moved by Mr. K. Nkamela, and seconded by Mr. S.G. Thwane, that the medium of instruction in schools under the jurisdiction of the Meadowlands Tswana School Board from Standards 3 to 8 should be in English. The meeting further resolved that the principals be informed about the decision.

Retribution followed. Within a fortnight the Department of Bantu Education dismissed two members of the board. No reason was given, but the link with the rejection of Afrikaans was plain. The board's other seven members resigned.

Opposition to Afrikaans spread, leaping from one Soweto school to another. Pupils began to boycott classes and stayed away even when threatened with expulsion. There were some skirmishes with the police. The deputy minister, in charge of black education, Andries Treurnicht, refused to yield on the use of Afrikaans. He was a former Dutch Reformed Church minister and led the ultraconservatives in the National Party who opposed Vorster's pragmatism. Tension was building up during the first half of the year. Treurnicht and his officials felt that "agitators" were to blame for everything. On June 14th a remarkably prescient warning came from Leonard Mosala, a community leader in Soweto, who said that the children "won't take anything we say because they think we have neglected them. We have failed to help them in their struggle for change in schools. They are now angry and prepared to fight and we are afraid the situation may become chaotic at any time."

Two days later ten thousand pupils joined in a march that converged on Orlando. The police threw tear gas at them. The pupils, in turn, flung stones, and the police opened fire, killing a sixteen-year-old student, Hector Petersen. All the underlying frustration and resentment bred by the deprivations of black education and the harshness of life under apartheid burst out and set off a tide that threatened to overwhelm white control. As the insurrection by pupils spread to cities and villages throughout the country, the police shot them down. The official death toll during the next few months rose to more than six hundred, but there was strong belief that the real number was much higher, with rumors of corpses being removed under cover of night. Hundreds of schoolchildren disappeared. Were they among the dead? Among the thousands detained? Or were they among those who fled the country to join the ANC or PAC as fighters? Parents did not know.

Many years later I happened to buy a car from a former policeman and gained an astonishing bit of information about police behavior. He told me how puzzled he was when he watched riots on television, and saw policemen throwing tear gas at the front of a crowd. "That's the way to do it," I said. "No," he replied, "when I was trained at the police academy in 1976 we were taught to fire teargas *behind* the crowd, and when they ran towards us we shot them."

During that year, I watched the agony from the *Boston Globe*, where I had been sent on a work exchange for six months. On the afternoon of the "children's rebellion," I read the news agency reports flooding in from South Africa and was shaken up by the fury. My first article that sought to explain and analyze the situation appeared in the *Globe* the next day. Within two days the death toll was up to sixty, and the turbulence was unprecedented. More had died than in any earlier interracial clashes, and the disturbances were spreading among more blacks than ever before. And soon I learned that Americans generally knew little about South Africa. When a *Globe* reporter asked me to explain the difference between an Afrikaner and an African, I realized that I had a role as an educator. From then on I poured out articles for the *Globe*, magazines like the *New Republic* and *Atlantic Monthly*, and appeared on radio and television, telling America about apartheid in South Africa.

I was able to assess what was happening in South Africa for Americans because of the wealth of information that I received. Even from the United States I saw a shift in people's minds at home. I saw a photograph taken early in the uprising that showed a line of policemen with rifles and machine guns, and facing them was a young black man holding the small lid of a trash can as an inadequate shield. It revealed a new defiance, a contempt for authority, a disregard for danger. This was no longer the cowed black person of the past. This was a new generation.

Only at the start of the rebellion were the *Mail*'s white journalists directly able to report the townships. Within minutes of the first shots, two *Mail* reporters were on their way to Soweto with a photographer. It was deathly quiet there. Mervyn Rees and Clive Emdon were stopped by a black man who warned, "Don't go farther, they'll kill you." Rees found a house facing the Orlando police station with a telephone line (phones were rare in the townships) and the two went there. It was the home of a black priest and his wife, and they provided the *Mail* reporters with shelter. Throughout the night, as violence spread through Soweto, Rees hid there, and phoned in reports to the *Mail* describing the trucks pulling into the police station and dumping bodies.

Whites thereafter had great difficulty reporting because they could only enter the townships safely with police protection, and that meant seeing what the police wanted them to see. They could not report from the black side—racial passions were too high. Black journalists had to do the frontline job, risking their lives with both the police and the mobs. On the first day, marching students warned Magubane not to take photographs. He tried to sneak some shots, but his camera was grabbed from him. A photographer from the *Sunday Times* was dragged down by students as he tried to take photographs, and the car of a white photographer from *Beeld* was stoned. On another occasion, while Magubane was photographing a roadblock in Alexandra township, a black policeman halted him at gunpoint and took him to a white captain, who demanded to know who he was and whether he had a press card. "I produced the card, and while he was holding it, he hit me across the face with a truncheon. I fell down, bleeding. When I got up, he ordered me to take the film out of my camera, which I did. 'Expose it.' I just looked at him and the man kept on saying, 'Expose it.' Finally I exposed it. That hurt more than the blow from his truncheon, which fractured my nose.

In fact in all the years that I have been photographing, I have never been hit as hard. I knew my nose could be fixed, but I knew I couldn't replace what I had on record on my film."

As copies of the *Rand Daily Mail* reached me in Boston, I was filled with admiration for the *Mail*'s coverage. Bylines were soon dropped: it was considered dangerous to identify reporters and photographers, whether black or white, and this rule became standard in the future coverage of disturbances.

Two *Mail* journalists, Jan Gabu Tugwana and Nat Serache, uncovered a behind-the-scenes cooperative effort between the police and elements of *Inkatha*, the Zulu nationalist party. In the years to come the cooperation would eventually prove to have devastating effects, leading to the deaths of many thousands. On August 25, 1976, the link between the two was still unknown when Zulu male migrant workers from the Mzimhlope single-sex hostel in Soweto went on the rampage. That night, as they sallied forth to murder and destroy, Tugwana hid in a coal box six hundred feet (200 m) from the hostel. Peeping through the holes in the box, he spotted a man in a camouflaged car, one that resembled the kind used by the riot police. He heard him tell the *impi* (war party) in Zulu through a megaphone, "We didn't order you to destroy West Rand Administration Board [the local authority that owned all the houses] property. You were asked to fight people only." At daybreak Tugwana emerged from his hiding place to find three corpses nearby, and still more elsewhere, the victims of the *impi*. Meanwhile Serache followed a crowd of local residents intent on raiding the hostel to rescue women whom they believed were being held hostage. He heard a policeman warning the Zulus in the hostel, "If you damage houses, you will force us to take action against you… you have been ordered to kill troublemakers only."

As always, the government's attempt to terminate resistance included mass arrests under the Terrorism Act and the Internal Security Act, which were essentially the Suppression of Communism Act in a new form. It wasn't easy to know who had been arrested, as the Security Police refused to disclose details. Among the school pupils, university students, churchmen, teachers, black-consciousness and trade union leaders, there were at least fourteen journalists, all of whom were black. Seven were from the *World*, and four were from the *Mail*: Tugwana and Serache, photographer Willie Nkosi, and Magubane. Magubane had seen police talking to men at the Dube hostel; he heard shots nearby and found two young girls with their stomachs ripped open. "It was now becoming tenser and tenser," he later said. "I called the office and told the editor, Raymond Louw, that I was beginning to get scared for my own life. He told me to come back. But as I left the house where I had been phoning, more shooting started. Now, do you think I could go back to the office and leave the action? No. I went straight back and started photographing." He finally pushed his luck too far because he returned to Dube hostel and was seized by the police. He was detained without trial for the next four months.

His *Mail* colleagues tried to get access to him so that he could enter the annual Stellenbosch Farmers' Winery Journalism Awards. They were not allowed to see him, but Magubane put in a late entry after his release and his photographs of the protests and killings won the top award. It was presented at a banquet in a five-star hotel in Johannesburg and I was with him when one of the guests, a white man, came up and said, "Mr. Magubane, I have never shaken hands with a black person before but I want to shake your hand to congratulate you." Magubane politely shook hands. I told him I wasn't sure that I would have responded with his tolerance if someone had spoken to me like that, using "Jew" instead of "black." Magubane merely laughed.

The public's thirst for news during these traumatic times and the quality of the *Mail*'s coverage drove up circulation. Shortly after the unrest began, the *Mail*'s monthly average reached 166,000 copies a day, the highest in its history; yet despite this, the board of directors decided to sack Louw. On Louw's birthday, October 13, 1976, the managing director Leycester Walton reminded him that when he was appointed, they had agreed that the editor should hold the job for a term of ten years, and that time was up.

With the *Mail* at the peak of its strength, and in the midst of brilliant reporting of the unprecedented challenge to white authority, it hardly seemed sufficient reason to get rid of him. But other forces were at work and, taken together, were in due time to prove fatal for the *Mail*. The first, which had already been in place for the past two years, was Syfrets's replacement of Cecil Payne as chairman of the Saan board. Until then Louw had had a virtually clear run. He could not recall Payne ever complaining to him directly about anything; the most he had to endure, and it was little, was an occasional visit from Walton, who in a polite and circuitous way would mention some anxiety about something the *Mail* had or hadn't done. Only once did Payne ever indicate to Louw the pressures on him. "It is never-ending," he said. "Wherever I go in business circles it is never-ending, this complaint about the *Rand Daily Mail*."

The replacement chairman was Ian McPherson, a director of companies and former stockbroker in Johannesburg. Syfrets believed Saan needed solid commercial backing, which would give the company standing in the business community and that McPherson could do this. As events were to prove, the results were questionable.

As Louw saw it, the first moves against him began at around the time that McPherson took over. It was proposed that he direct Saan's moves into the newfangled world of computers. Saan believed it was the road to economic survival since typesetting and printers' skills were in white hands and the Typographers Union was determined that it remain so. The newspaper industry suffered from the same shortage of white workers as everyone else, but the union would not allow blacks to be trained for skilled work. So Saan was caught between not being able to get enough skilled workers and not being allowed to train blacks. Computers offered the way out of the impasse.

Louw wanted to remain editor of the *Mail* while overseeing the investigation into computers. After the initial hiccup, when he had the impression that his editorship was under threat, this was agreed. Payne, now deputy chairman of the board, was still a guardian angel and helped to bring it about. But McPherson was a different person to deal with. Every few months Louw found himself summoned to the chairman's business office in the city to be questioned about the *Mail*'s editorial decisions. Louw would explain and defend his work, but invariably came away wondering whether McPherson had understood what he had said. Only after he had been fired did he think that the scrutiny had been part of a prolonged softening-up process in which nothing he said mattered.

To this day former Saan executives claim that Louw was not fired but promoted, a view that has never carried any weight because the substitute job he was initially offered was as a lowly manager of the Morning Group. He was soon after appointed general manager of the company, but subsequently dumped five years later. McPherson felt too challenged by him, and shared the board's dislike of the newspaper's strong liberal stance, an extension of Gandar's vision.

Walton wanted out, and McPherson approached the Argus Company in search of a new managing director. It was peculiar given that Argus was Saan's biggest competitor. They suggested Clive Kinsley, who was then manager of the Argus newspaper in Cape Town. Saan's board accepted him. His origins put him under a cloud inside Saan, with some viewing him as an Argus man planted in their midst, although there was no basis for believing this. It was more likely, as others speculated and as his later track record indicated, that Argus took the opportunity to pass him on and that, if anything, he was resentful of his former employer.

Between McPherson and Kinsley the *Mail* moved into an era where not only was it in conflict with the government but the hostility of Saan's board of directors increasingly extended into the topmost ranks of management, the people with whom editorial dealt each day and in whose hands laid the commercial decisions that determined the life and ultimately the death of the newspaper.

Louw was still in charge when I returned from Boston in January 1977, and he remained for several months while editorial musical chairs were played out. His replacement was Allister Sparks, editor of the *Sunday Express* and onetime deputy editor of the *Mail*. Rex Gibson, the *Mail*'s deputy editor, was going to the *Express*. Sparks asked me to be deputy editor of the *Mail*. All three of us had worked under Gandar, so the *Mail*'s modern tradition was maintained and spread.

The township turbulence had died down temporarily when I got back, but the *Mail* was getting letters and phone calls from whites berating us for having failed to alert them to the poor state of black education which had triggered the uprising. These were routed to me. I was usually choleric in dealing with them, pointing out that I had personally over the years written thousands upon thousands of words about the ills of black education and how dare they say they had not been warned.

Nat Serache was still in detention, held without trial for three months under the Terrorism Act. Released in February, he was taken straight from jail to the magistrates' courts and charged with possession of banned literature: a pamphlet on detentions and bannings recently published by the Rev. C. F. Beyers Naude's Christian Institute.

The *Mail* had two particular entanglements with those in power. The first was with Cillie, the judge in the Prisons Trial, who was now heading a commission of inquiry into the unrest, with Percy Yutar leading the evidence. At best it was an inquiry into the obvious, and at worst an effort to find someone to blame—anyone except the government. Cillie took his time, and when his report did finally appear three years later, it had been overtaken by events and was bereft of substance. I went to the hearings when Sydney Kentridge appeared for various witnesses. It was Kentridge at his cool and masterly best, making Yutar stutter and scramble and Cillie red-faced with impotent rage. I sat with a hand covering my mouth to hide the grin of pleasure, feeling some recompense for the pain I had suffered from those two.

But serious issues were at stake in the way the commission was running. We weighed in with an editorial, carefully written because we were risking contempt of court and published only after getting it cleared by Kelsey Stuart. But our meaning was clear: "A fundamental tenet of our system of justice is expressed in the legal maxim that the other side must be heard," it began, going on to note that unfortunately there had been a trend in the courts that ran counter to the maxim, such as when someone not a party to proceedings was unjustly attacked. As an example we referred to "a celebrated Appeal Court decision ordering a State prosecutor to pay damages because of his defamatory and wrongful attack on someone who had not been part of court proceedings," a reference to my lawsuit against Yutar.

It continued:

> When it comes to commissions of inquiry the essential maxim is even more open to erosion. While commissions can serve an invaluable purpose there is need to guard against assassination of character and a great responsibility rests on those conducting the inquiry to protect uninvolved and innocent people. This kind of erosion, we believe, has been manifesting itself this week in the Cillie Commission. A number of people have been named by witnesses, sometimes in relation to specific events of last year, and at other times seemingly in a more passing way. The witnesses concerned are current Terrorism Act detainees, freed only temporarily and in a formal sense from their incommunicado detention where they are wholly at the mercy of their captors. As their names are concealed by order of the commission, it is difficult to evaluate their testimony and anyone who considers himself injured certainly faces obstacles in seeking redress. The problem is aggravated because of the absence of normal court safeguards where evidence can be challenged by defense counsel. Thus the way could be opened to character assassination. That, of course, cannot be the commission's intention. But the situation must cause disquiet.

Cillie immediately summoned Louw to tell him that he believed the editorial was calculated to bring the Commission into disrepute. The *Mail* carried his statement in full, including his assurance that anyone could give evidence, and Cillie took it no further. But Cillie and Yutar got our message, and perhaps it caused them to tread a bit more cautiously.

Another area of growing concern was deaths in detention. All the reports and editorials published in the *Mail* and other papers had no effect. The death toll steadily increased, and the government brushed aside all demands for a judicial commission of inquiry. Suddenly, in 1977, Minister of Justice Jimmy Kruger announced that he would hold a press conference on the issue. It was a most unusual step for a Nationalist leader, and probably had more to do with Kruger's cockiness about the power he commanded than the belief that he owed anyone any explanation. We welcomed his announcement as "a sign that the authorities have finally become aware of the huge public concern that has built up," and quickly put together all the unanswered questions and concerns we had been expressing over a long period. The editorial, "Thirteen Questions for the Minister," included, why is there apparently so little supervision over detainees as to allow suicides to occur with such regularity? Why is there apparently so little supervision that detainees are able to jump to their deaths down stairwells or out of buildings? To what extent are the circumstances surrounding deaths investigated by external, independent authorities rather than by the police and prison officials in whose custody the detainees were when they died?

Kruger replied to twelve of our questions, and promised a reply to the remaining query. "It is a sobering reflection on the state of South Africa that we should feel the need to thank the Minister for giving information about a matter of acute public concern. But there it is, and in expressing appreciation to Mr. Kruger we must hope that this is the herald of greater openness on the part of Cabinet members," replied our editorial. The "thank the Minister" was meant ironically, referring to Nationalist MPs' servile speeches in parliament. We said we found Kruger's answers "sadly deficient" because his responses were mostly, "The police deny that there was 'little supervision' over detainees."

He was especially evasive in dealing with our questions about the death of Joseph Mdluli in police custody in Durban the previous year, on March 19, 1976. Mdluli, aged fifty, had been detained during a crackdown on an ANC recruiting network. The police said they found him dead in his cell the next night. They refused to tell his wife and the press about the cause of his death, but when the family saw the body, they reported swellings and bruises. Photographs of the body, taken in the funeral parlor, ended up in Britain and were displayed by the ANC there. The Mdluli family's lawyer was detained for three months, and a barrister engaged for the case had his passport withdrawn. In October, four policemen were charged with culpable homicide—in the United States, that's manslaughter. The prosecutor said that all four men struggled to subdue Mdluli when he apparently attempted to escape during his interrogation. The incident was reported to a senior officer who felt that Mdluli was not injured. Subsequently, according to police witnesses who were in the room where Mdluli was held, he suddenly got up, staggered, and fell, with his chest or neck hitting the back of a chair.

That was the State's story, but its own witnesses in the court case contradicted it. The government pathologist who examined the body on the night of March 19th testified that Mdluli had been dead for longer than he had been told. He and a colleague who conducted a postmortem said that Mdluli's injuries were too diffuse to have been caused by a single fall over a chair, and believed that the death was the result of the use of force to the neck, perhaps a karate blow.

Mdluli's injuries included three distinct areas of bruising on the neck, a fractured thyroid, and extensive deep bruising on his scalp, abdominal muscles, and his lower rib cage. He also hemorrhaged in his left lower rib cage, and had three rib fractures. His brain was extremely congested with blood. It was clear that he had been beaten to death. A cover-up was obviously under way, but it was full of holes.

How could the official explanation be so unconvincing in a society where authoritarianism was so well entrenched? It was probably ineptitude. Accompanying this was an arrogant belief that they could get away with anything. There had been so many deaths in detention, so many people tortured or detained, that the Security Police felt immune. This outlook was bolstered by the public, uncritical support they got from their political masters, as well as their knowledge that they could generally rely on a compliant judiciary to swallow whatever story they put forward.

Their formula for success seemed to be working because Judge Neville James acquitted the four policemen. There was a difference this time, though, because the judge did not leave it at that. "On the evidence before the court I was not satisfied that the four accused were directly involved but medical evidence cast grave doubts on the evidence of the policemen who gave evidence for the State," he said. How Mdluli had met his death was of the greatest importance and should be solved, added the judge. Most unusually for a judge of that era, he urged an investigation. I later learned, but was unable to prove, that the four policemen who were prosecuted had not been involved at all. They were selected for prosecution because of this, thus ensuring their acquittal.

It was against this background that Question 7 in our editorial asked Kruger to explain Mdluli's death, and when he failed to do so, we came back to it. "Mr. Mdluli died in circumstances which remain a mystery... So how did Mr. Mdluli die?"

We never had an answer and were never able to get any further information about the death. But we never stopped asking about it. Every now and again we carried another editorial, always listing Judge James's comments and always asking, how did Mr. Mdluli die? I wrote the editorials and, I suppose, I became obsessed with it. If, on a Sunday, I was short of subject matter for an editorial, I wrote about Mdluli. If I was feeling especially angry about the latest government outrage, I wrote about Mdluli. I felt that among the many deaths of detainees, here was at least one, of a person little known outside his hometown who must have suffered cruelly under interrogation, who should not be forgotten. It was pointless in the sense that we never had an answer and no one was ever brought to account for the crime. But there was no other way to do it in the South Africa of that time, and perhaps possibly the repetition did achieve something behind the scenes—while also helping to remind the public that this was unlawful behavior by the police.

Mdluli's widow sued the government and was eventually paid 15,000 rand in compensation. The police refused to admit any culpability, but they wanted to avoid the publicity of a court case. It provided scope for more questioning editorials, and Helen Suzman joined in by once more raising the matter in parliament. Kruger accused her of posing as a "front" for me. "The people overseas tell them that the matter must be kept going," was his charge.

Government censors never actually sat in newspaper offices to approve every word before publication. But when Nationalist condemnation and threats rose to a crescendo, the censors might as well have been there because we were ensuring that we stayed inside the ever-increasing spiderweb of laws. For the government it was free censorship. It went together with never-ending public battering, with Prime Minister Vorster leading the pack. Bernardi Wessels told me that there was no let-up during the seven years, up to 1977, that he served as the *Mail*'s political correspondent.

"It was a sustained thing. He spent the first twenty minutes of just about every speech attacking the *Rand Daily Mail* and the English press, but particularly the *Rand Daily Mail*. He would be very funny and witty at the expense of the *Mail* because of its liberal stance. He went right across the country giving speeches and especially

Chapter 20

during the National Party's congress season when each province had its own conference. He would take an editorial of ours and rip it to shreds. He was giving us a reputation, which suited him. He was getting it through to vast audiences, high and low, from every walk of life, but especially from the top echelons."

At a party congress in the city of Bloemfontein, Wessels remembered, Vorster was blasting away as usual and arousing the crowd so much that a voice yelled out from the back of the hall, "*Gooi the* Rand Daily Mail *se man uit, smyt hom uit!* (Throw out the *Rand Daily Mail* man!)."

"One of my colleagues said to me, 'Bernardi, there are four huge chaps coming,' and I looked around and saw this huge beer-belly brigade coming to throw me out. They were halfway down the aisle when Vorster stopped them, calling out, '*Nee, wag kerels, ek sal die* Rand Daily Mail *man selfs regsien.* (No, wait fellows, I'll attend to the *Rand Daily Mail* man myself)', and they turned back."

In contrast, cabinet minister Piet Koornhof was affable and approachable, and constantly referred to the *Mail* in his speeches. His style was to emphasize a point by saying, "*Selfs Bernardi Wessels van die* Rand Daily Mail *sal my saamstem* (Even Bernardi Wessels of the *Rand Daily Mail* will agree with me)," leaving Wessels embarrassed for being identified with the views of a Nationalist.

Early in 1977, with the government on edge about the resistance in the townships, there was every indication that Vorster's verbal onslaughts were at long last to be translated into statutory control of the press. Pressure was applied to newspaper owners through their NPU to toughen their Press Code, so as to broaden the definitions of the kind of language a lot of journalists had to avoid. But negotiations broke down, and in March, Interior Minister Connie Mulder gave notice of a Newspaper Bill to create a government code and a council to enforce it with penalties of a fine or imprisonment up to a year. It was necessary, said Mulder, because some unnamed newspapers had continued reckless and damaging reporting despite warnings.

It was always difficult to decide how to handle these threats. Some argued, "Don't feed the crocodile" on the basis that the Nationalists' appetite for power and control was insatiable. Others said that freedom had to be fought for at every step, and it was better to compromise and retain something than to risk losing everything—a valid argument, but one that provided cover for those who were unwilling to fight too hard against the government. The NPU continued negotiating until it satisfied Vorster. He agreed to give the NPU a year to discipline itself effectively under its own code of conduct for journalists. Within a few weeks the NPU produced its own code. Journalists had not been consulted, and had mixed feelings. The *Mail* felt that although the code was less noxious than Mulder's bill,

> this was not a genuine code of professional conduct drawn up by the newspapermen themselves for their own guidance and self-discipline. It is a list of restraints drawn up under duress in a desperate attempt to appease a government that was bent on brutalizing us. And even though much of it is vaguely worded and may sound unexceptionable—who, for example, can object to an injunction not to distort or publish untruths?—that is not the point. The

point, quite simply, is that the government has demanded "self-discipline" and "responsibility" by which it means that the newspapers must report events not as they see them but as the government sees them. And if the new Press Council with its new Press Code fails to bring this about to the government's satisfaction, why then Mr. Vorster will be back next year with his Bill.

Vorster didn't wait that long. Six months later, in October, the government banned the *World*—it reemerged within a few days as the *Post* and later as the *Sowetan*—after Vorster had attacked it for advocating "majority rule." Donald Woods, editor of the *Daily Dispatch* in East London, was banned. This was the first time it happened to a mainstream editor. (He escaped from the country soon after, and wrote his biography of Steve Biko while in exile in England.) In case these actions were not warning enough, Jimmy Kruger threatened to close down any newspaper that incited people "to overthrow law and order." Government action went even farther with the banning of eighteen anti-apartheid organizations and the banning or detention of some fifty people, among them, the *Mail*'s Gabu Tugwana again (apparently in connection with activities outside the office).

A different ethos was creeping into the Afrikaans press, however. They were asking questions and sometimes coming up with different answers from Nationalist political leaders. Where previously the Afrikaans newspapers in our circulation area had been largely irrelevant in news terms, *Beeld* was starting to develop as a news-driven newspaper. The professional gap was still large, and the Afrikaans newspapers were hardly free spirits, but change was under way. Only a year later the unthinkable happened: a Nationalist MP lodged a complaint with the Press Council about the Afrikaans newspaper *Rapport*'s presentation of his views. As Afrikaans journalists began to go on voyages of discovery about their own country, examining issues they had previously scorned, they began to prize press freedom. How much moderating influence they were willing and able to exert on their Nationalist leaders was uncertain, but we hoped that they were doing it.

Steve Bantu Biko was well known in black political circles from his leadership of the Black Consciousness Movement. He was little known among the vast majority of whites but had a significant friend in Donald Woods. I never got to meet Biko, but we knew of each other via our mutual friend Robert Sobukwe, whom Biko secretly and illegally visited in Kimberley. Sobukwe was confined to that town, but Biko traveled across half the country to see him, breaking the banning orders restricting him to the town of Kingwilliamstown. On August 18, 1977, while Biko was returning home from an undercover organizing trip, the police caught him at a roadblock. He died in detention as a result of head injuries and medical neglect less than four weeks later.

At first the government was dismissive. Kruger implied that Biko had starved himself to death. He drew laughter at a Nationalist Party congress when he said Biko's death "leaves me cold." Woods was indefatigable, making speeches, demanding investigation, and going for the government's throat in his weekly column, which had a national audience far beyond out-of-the-way East London because it was syndicated in the *Rand Daily Mail* and other morning newspapers.

The *Mail* worked hard to help search for the truth about Biko's death, and day after day banged away with reports. We were aided by having an inside track through Dr. Jonathan Gluckman, a partner in a private pathology laboratory in Johannesburg and longtime friend of the newspaper. He regularly gave us information behind-the-scenes about the maltreatment of prisoners and detainees. At the request of the Biko family he attended the autopsy. Two weeks after Biko's death Gluckman asked to see the *Mail*'s editor, Allister Sparks. He showed Sparks the postmortem report, which put the cause of death as brain damage. The trail led to the three doctors in Port Elizabeth who had dealt with Biko in detention. The *Mail* broke the story with a report: "No Sign of Hunger Strike—Biko Doctors."

The next day Kruger attacked the report as false and demanded an immediate hearing of the Press Council. NPU members and Saan's management pressured Sparks to agree to this, warning that refusal could precipitate direct government action against the press. The hearing was held that night, and the *Mail* could not cite Gluckman as a source. The Press Council's chairman, a retired judge, Oscar Galgut, severely reprimanded the *Mail* for what he said was its "misleading and tendentious" report. This damning finding against the *Mail* stood, even though everyone connected with Biko's death knew that the report was accurate.

By the time the inquest was held, the extensive press attention had created a fever of public anticipation, both in South Africa and abroad. As with the death of Joseph Mdluli the previous year, the Security Police and their government lawyers probably believed that they did not have to worry too much, and behaved accordingly. They did not even bother to ensure that their lies tallied, but they had a shock. Sydney Kentridge led the legal team for the Biko family and he ripped into the Security Police witnesses, accusing the three doctors who had dealt with the mortally wounded Biko—one of them had signed a certificate that there was "no evidence of abnormal pathology"—of "subservience, bordering on collusion" in their relations with the police. The magistrate, Marthinus Prins, seemed to listen attentively to the fifteen days of evidence and intensive cross-examination. Many thought there might be a different outcome, especially with so much attention fixed on the hearing, but it was not to be. In the end Prins ignored Kentridge's arguments, and took only three minutes to exonerate the police. "The available evidence does not prove that the death was brought about by any act or omission involving or amounting to an offense on the part of any person," he ruled.

Going up against the government and its Security Police was once again shown to be like spitting into the wind. Yet within less than eighteen months the press, with the *Mail* playing a leading role, was to shake the government to its foundations. Although no one at that time could possibly realize the magnitude of what was coming, the first step had already been taken in August 1977 when Mervyn Rees received a phone call from a friend who asked him to come and meet "Daan," a highly placed civil servant. Corruption existed in high places in the government, Daan said, and it centered on the Department of Information. Much money was involved. He was frightened to say more. Rees began to investigate. He had been a crime reporter for twelve years, and his integrity was so apparent that he disarmed the police, persuading them to hand him many scoops.

The Department of Information story had roots going back to the start of the 1970s, when undercover projects were set up in response to the hostile international press that the Nationalists were getting. In 1972 it became more focused when Dr. Eschel Rhoodie was appointed secretary for information, and made the *Rand Daily Mail* a specific target. For most of that decade we were blissfully ignorant of the extent to which government leaders—notably John Vorster, Connie Mulder, and Hendrik van den Bergh—were scheming behind the scenes to destroy us. They were prepared to lie, cheat, and secretly and dishonestly invest huge amounts of public money to accomplish this. In 1975 they began to use a front man, Louis Luyt, who came from a poor background, had worked as a railway clerk, and had built up a successful fertilizer business. A former rugby player, he was a large public presence, and caused a great stir when he went after a majority shareholding in Saan.

Where did his six million rand come from? Luyt was a known Nationalist supporter, and government money was suspected, but he vehemently insisted that he was wealthy enough to buy into Saan. He was promptly beaten off by Max Borkum, a leading stockbroker in Johannesburg and a key strategist and fundraiser for the Progressives. Borkum went to Gordon Waddell, chairman of Johannesburg Consolidated Investment Company (JCI) and former son-in-law of Harry Oppenheimer, the head of Anglo American Corporation, and money was rapidly put together to buy 20.3 percent (later it was said to be 17.6 percent) of Saan shares. Because the Luyt bid was reported as six million rand, it was always assumed, and never denied, that Borkum matched him.

As Luyt later disclosed, when his bid for Saan failed, he and his government backers discussed starting a new paper. He offered to return the six million rand given to him for the bid. "But they said no, we had to go ahead and should start the paper as soon as possible to counteract the *Rand Daily Mail*." The *Citizen* came into being in September 1976. It was greeted enthusiastically by those who disliked the *Mail*, among them Gary Player, the internationally renowned golfer. Johnny Johnson served as editor after quitting Saan and the *Sunday Express*. The *Citizen* recruited among *Mail* staff, offering high, unmatchable salaries, but few people took the bait.

Soon the *Citizen* was claiming a circulation of more than seventy thousand a day. Louw did not believe it, and set up an investigation team. Two months of watching the *Citizen*'s printing plant uncovered the fact that up to thirty thousand copies a day were being trucked away to be incinerated. But even the public disclosure of this did not halt the newspaper, with its daily sneering editorials that railed against those who opposed apartheid. The mystery about who was footing the bill continued.

Vorster was riding high. An early general election in November 1977 gave him the biggest victory in Nationalist history: a swing by the English-speaking public ensured him 65 percent of the vote, with 134 seats out of 165 in parliament. The only bright spot was that the Progressives, now the Progressive Federal Party (Progfeds), took 17 seats and became the official opposition. The United Party disbanded after twenty-nine years of existence.

Mervyn Rees continued burrowing away, working with Chris Day, an assistant editor. The investigation was widening every day, if only through a search of company records. One trail led to another, until a wider web of names emerged, stretching well beyond South Africa. Bits and pieces of information were also beginning to come into the open. The men in charge were confident they had nothing to fear. Mulder dismissed the publicity as "nothing more than a storm in a teacup." Rees sent a mutual friend to see Rhoodie to tell him the press were on to him and knew that millions of rand were missing. As Rees and Day reported in their book, *Muldergate*, Rhoodie responded, "Tell those bastards I know about them. Tell them I have tape-recordings of them. Tell them I know what they're trying to do. Tell them to go to hell."

But in the odd society that was South Africa, where corruption ran to the highest levels of government, some officials retained their integrity and the truth began to seep out. On February 1, 1978, the auditor-general, F. G. Barrie, handed a report to parliament with criticisms of unnamed Department of Information officials for unauthorized spending and expensive junkets abroad. In April, Kitt Katzen of the *Sunday Express*, pursuing his own trail, reported the high living and secret operations, naming Rhoodie as the principal culprit. Katzen only knew the bare bones of the story, and sought out Rees to ask how safe it was to go into print. "I thought it only fair to say, 'If you were to publish that stuff, you wouldn't be far wrong,'" Rees responded. The day after the *Sunday Express* report, Rees opened up in the *Mail* with all that he had. With the investigation widening into the Americas and Europe, Saan's morning newspapers came together, pooling finances and resources. Mulder and Luyt denied that the *Citizen* was funded by the government and clung to this until the *Sunday Express*'s October 29th exposé: "The Citizen Secret Revealed," reporting that it was financed by secret State funds. The next day, fourteen months after Rees had begun investigations, the *Mail* crashed in with the full story: "Missing Millions." Millions of rand of public money had been spent on the *Citizen*, more than thirty million rand altogether. Day after day, Rees revealed the corruption and deception. A rash of car bumper stickers proclaimed, "Pay Your Taxes, Buy the *Citizen*." Rees had a secret contact, code-named Myrtle, and Katzen had a Deep Throat. Whether it was the same source was never clear, as the journalists worked independently of each other.

The month before the full disclosure, Vorster had resigned as prime minister due to poor health. His Nationalist colleagues elected him state president, a ceremonial role at the time. As his successor, the party's parliamentary caucus chose Defense Minister P. W. Botha. They discarded Mulder because they feared what revelations might come, and they were right because Vorster, Mulder, and van den Bergh were identified as the ringleaders. Along the way van den Bergh retired. The full story was in the open: the original attempt to buy Saan had had government money behind it; the *Citizen* was a government operation; Luyt had been a front for the government. Millions of dollars had also been given to John McGoff, a Chicago-based publisher of small newspapers, to buy the *Washington Star* so that the South African government could secretly have a mouthpiece in the United States. The attempt failed, and difficulty ensued in recovering money from McGoff.

A special bit of cynicism also came to light. A few months before, Vorster had appointed van den Bergh to investigate the Department of Information's secret projects, knowing of course that he was deeply implicated. The idea was that once van den Bergh took over the investigation, it would fall under the Official Secrets Act, with the threat of draconian penalties for anyone who revealed the details. When the disclosures first emerged, van den Bergh was quoted in the *Citizen* as saying, "I did not channel a single cent to the *Citizen*. Anyone who says so, or has prompted others to say so, is a liar. I'd like him to prove, and dare him to prove, that I channeled a single cent." But the tide could not be held back, and in a swift sequence of events Mulder quit the cabinet and the Transvaal leadership, and the following June, in 1979, Vorster quit the presidency. Both of them were disgraced.

Late one night, I was working in my study at home when the phone rang. The voice said, "You won't recognize who this is." I told the caller I knew he was van den Bergh. He said he was phoning to tell me that his passport had been seized. I assumed it had happened earlier in the day, and asked why he was phoning so late. "My passport has just been taken. They've just left. You are the first person I am phoning," he told me. "They've taken *your* passport?" I asked. "Yes," he replied, "it shows you what the country has come to." I phoned the story to the *Mail*. Only in the morning did I discover that van den Bergh had given me an exclusive.

There was another weird episode. Sparks was away and I was acting editor when a telex came in on a Friday night from Rees who was conducting investigations abroad. He had learned that some years earlier van den Bergh had discovered that the army was planning to invade a neighboring country, but Vorster and the cabinet did not know about it.

He reported it to Vorster who called in P.W. Botha and ordered him to rein in the army. I discussed the report with David Hazelhurst, then managing editor, and we agreed that I should see van den Bergh. I drove to Pretoria and was cordially welcomed. We sat down and I gave him the telex, asking for his comments. As I waited for his reaction, his face suddenly crumpled. I have never seen anything like it, before or since. His features seemed to disintegrate. "Bennie, promise me you won't put this in the newspaper," he pleaded. "P. W. doesn't know about this. If he sees this he will have me killed. Please Bennie you must promise me. I will have to leave the country," and as he grabbed his head with both hands he cried out in the same desperate way, "I can't leave, I haven't got a passport. I'll have to kill myself!"

I struggled to understand what I was witnessing. Only a few months earlier, he had been the most powerful man in South Africa. I said I would have to return to Johannesburg and see if the story could be kept out of the next day's paper. I told him that the decision wasn't mine to make, even though it actually was.

Hazelhurst thought we should publish it, but since it was late in the night and I did not want to rush into publication, I decided to hold the story. I took van den Bergh's talk of suicide seriously, and did not want to have the weight of his threat on my shoulders. At around 1:30 A.M., I phoned van den Bergh to tell him the story was being held over for the meantime. Amid his repeated thanks were the continuing entreaties that it not appear at all. Later in the day, I went to see Kelsey Stuart, who read the telex and asked, "How can you think about publishing this? It falls right under the Defense Act." The story never appeared in our pages.

Rhoodie roamed the world looking for a place to hide. He was extradited back to South Africa, tried for embezzlement, convicted, and acquitted on appeal. He went to live in the United States, creating a little mystery because an Information Department partner in crime, Les de Villiers, had also left South Africa to live and work in the United States. Why did the United States let them in? Rhoodie eventually died in 1993 while playing tennis. Mulder did not live long after his fall from grace. Van den Bergh was never tried, despite challenging the government to charge him. In the next general election he stood as a candidate for the extreme right-wing Conservative Party. I did not believe this reflected his views. I thought this was his way of lining up against the shared archenemy, State President P.W. Botha. Two weeks before the election he had an operation to remove a brain tumor. He was not elected.

The *Citizen* survived, despite what had been exposed. In 1979 the Afrikaans newspaper company Perskor bought it. We learned the details through an anonymous person inside the organization, who sent the documents to the *Mail*. Perskor took over the *Citizen* and acquired its printing press for 375,000 rand. The press had been bought with taxpayers' money and the installed book value was 1.2 million rand. The independent valuation our informant sent us put the value at between 850,000 to 1 million rand. It was a steal for Perskor.

What if the Mulder–van den Bergh–Rhoodie axis had triumphed? What sort of South Africa might have emerged? Each of them was ruthless. Authoritarianism would have undoubtedly flourished even more under their rule. On the other hand each of them believed there had to be a change of course in South Africa. Vorster had grown old and tired in office and was unable to pursue the change he had initially generated. Extreme right-wingers, led by Albert Hertzog, had broken away during his leadership, and the division was a heavy cross for an Afrikaner leader to bear. There was every indication that he could not face taking any action that might precipitate another split in Afrikanerdom. While inaction became the norm, the students' eruption in 1976 demanded fresh thinking.

Mulder's particular strength was that he was more likely to be guided by pragmatism than by ideology. Two conversations with him stuck in my mind. One was a few days after he had made an outrageously right-wing speech in which he said that there was not the slightest chance of the colored community ever being accepted as part of the white group. Sitting in his office during one of my annual visits to parliament, I asked him about his controversial speech. A cunning look crossed his face as he said, "On the other hand, of course, you could have total integration of coloreds with whites." I burst into laughter listening to a political chameleon. It cheered me. The less ideology inflicted on South Africa, the better.

Another time he told me, "I know my people. They understand that a leader is going to be pushed by events toward the center. They accept that it is going to happen. But it means that if someone wants to be the leader, he must not be seen to be too much in the center to start with. He must be on the right."

P. W. Botha was grateful neither to the *Rand Daily Mail*, the *Sunday Express*, nor the other English-language papers for opening the leadership door for him. He did not appreciate the exposure of the Nationalist government's rottenness. Instead, he and his party railed against "irresponsibility." Botha told parliament in 1979 that press freedom was being grossly abused and that the press had engaged in an unbridled campaign of insinuation, suspicion, mistrust, and disparagement to destroy the political system. He promised a "clean administration," but proceeded to do his best to impede the emergence of more information about the misuse of public funds. Court cases abounded, with government writs to prevent publication, counterwrits by Saan, and the prosecution of *Mail* people for contempt of court. Even while the "Infogate" scandal was still coming into the open, delegates to the National Party's congress in the province of the Orange Free State

Chapter 21

were demanding strong action against any newspaper that published articles threatening "national security." Justice Minister Kruger told them that he was watching the press very closely and would not hesitate to clamp down if necessary. At the party's congress in the Transvaal province, delegates urged that areas of unrest be declared out of bounds to the news media, as they felt the purpose of unrest was to create propaganda against South Africa.

These were not idle words. Their spirit was expressed in the further stamping on personal liberties in the government's effort to thwart black militancy. A *Mail* editorial late in the year conveyed a sense of the times in its dealing with detention without trial, always trying to find new ways of focusing on it so that readers might read and heed.

Mrs. Sally Motlana was arrested on 25 October and detained under the General Laws Amendment Act so that no bail or court appearance were required for 14 days. The 14 days have ended but Mrs. Motlana has remained in detention.

As is depressingly usual in these matters, no explanation has been given. Yet here is someone who is a community leader, a person widely known and respected and who happens, too, to run a business in Soweto.

If it was believed that she had transgressed any law—even one of the Nationalist-made 'security' laws—why couldn't normal police investigations have been undertaken, and whatever evidence was available placed before a State prosecutor for decision? And if the prosecutor thought the case was well-founded why couldn't charges then have been brought?

That is the way it should be done and the way it was once done in South Africa.

Instead, Mrs. Motlana's detention illustrates what is now a frighteningly common practice: detain on some suspicion, fish around for evidence that could stand the light of day, and then at a later stage, whether weeks or many months later, bring charges or release the victim without so much as an apology.

Life grew more difficult because of a law enacted during 1979 giving police the same protection as prisons. Anyone who published "incorrect information" about the police could be charged, and the onus rested on the accused to prove that he or she had taken reasonable steps to ensure accuracy. It had more of a bite than the prisons law because it provided for a heavier fine and/or up to five years' imprisonment. It came in when the violence of police action to suppress protesting school pupils was escalating.

As the police grip tightened, they played games with the press. At the best of times the Security Police were obstructive in confirming information on detainees. They refused to take requests for information over the phone. The family had to ask for information in person. We had to submit requests by telex, and supply the name and date of birth of the person believed detained (which was often difficult because of the varying spellings of black people's names, and the problem of getting birth dates from family members who were too frightened to speak to the press).

The *Star* once requested confirmation of the detention of a young black woman. The Security Police denied all knowledge of her. The *Star* believed she was being held incommunicado and went on pursuing the information, only to be told that no such person was in custody. Finally, the *Star* took steps to seek a court order, difficult as that would have been to obtain. Only then, faced by the publicity, did the police confirm the detention. They had stonewalled based on the fact that two letters in the young woman's name as submitted by the *Star* were different from what they had put down in their books.

The new police law was only part of a heavy year filled with new restrictions placed on the press. There was also the creation of the office of advocate-general to investigate suspicions about dishonesty in the use of State moneys. However, it was not meant to facilitate exposure, but was instead a device to block press investigations and the reporting of corruption. The Afrikaans press joined the English press in objecting to it, but to no avail. There was the Inquests Amendment Act prohibiting advance publication of information about inquests. This was intended to prevent a repeat of the aggressive investigation into the death of Steve Biko. There was also the National Supplies Procurement Amendment Act, making it an offense, punishable by up to seven years' imprisonment, to disclose any information or circulate rumors about the stockpiling of strategic materials.

In September, Alwyn Schlebusch, now a senior cabinet minister close to the prime minister, went to an NPU congress to complain that the Press Council was not doing enough to control newspapers, and threatened statutory control. This blunt warning surprised the NPU because, as we later learned, there had been ongoing contacts behind the scenes between the government and newspaper managements with indications that Botha wanted to make peace with the press. The flurry of management contact with the government led to a meeting of the NPU with Botha and other cabinet members in early October. Sparks heard the details and told the *Mail*'s executives that the government leaders had been conciliatory, and in response the NPU delegates suggested that if the government would lay off the press, the press would go easy in return. Sparks advised us that while he would not dilute the strength of our standpoints, we would henceforth avoid "knee-jerk" emotional responses to situations, using a "quieter voice," especially with regard to editorials; we would cut down on adjectives and let the facts speak for themselves. He also told us that Saan board members would attend a broad-based conference called by Botha the following month—it was the start of his drive to co-opt the business community and especially the dominant English-speaking businessmen—where he would pressure us to tone down the *Mail*. We had to anticipate this and protect the paper.

I expressed my unease about the new direction the *Mail* was taking. The whole point of an editorial was to go beyond the facts and offer commentary on a situation, the more trenchantly the better. There was no further discussion. Ominous as the development was, it seemed to me yet another price to pay for survival. The thought in my mind was that we could be passing another significant milestone in the curtailment of our remaining freedom.

Not only had black journalists come into their own in June 1976 but they were part of the mood change happening outside the building. Zwelakhe Sisulu, a son of ANC leader Walter Sisulu, exemplified the change. He was a reporter from 1975 to 1980 on the *Mail* and other Saan newspapers, and served as president of the black journalists' trade union, the Media Workers' Association of South Africa (Mwasa). As he recalled in an interview in *Weekly Mail*, he led a group of black colleagues on a protest march to police headquarters at John Vorster Square in Johannesburg, where they were arrested. After their release, he said, a *Mail* senior editor bawled them out, saying, "How could you do this? It's a discredit to the paper!" Sisulu said he challenged the editor: "I'm baffled. What we did was a concrete expression of the *Mail*'s editorial policy." "Ah, this is where you don't get it," the editor responded. "You don't march. You write!"

Sisulu remembered that as a watershed in his life. "For me it showed the thin line that, in a sense, was beginning to define me out of South African journalism; that I was now, in a sense, a black activist... I did not set out to be an activist. My activism began with my journalism." The activism landed him in solitary confinement, without trial, for two years. Eventually the coming of freedom led to his appointment as chief executive of the SABC, after which he went into private business.

Black journalists saw themselves as blacks first and journalists second, and that view ran counter to the ethos of the paper. They argued that they had to fight for their own interests and that these were beyond the ken of white journalists. That was a familiar argument, and took me back to my discussions twenty years earlier with Robert Sobukwe. Black journalists had to free themselves as blacks, but I was as worried as before about the potential for future racial divisiveness.

The new thrust showed itself among black journalists in a strike late in 1980. It began as a sympathy strike with colored journalists protesting about pay at the Argus-owned *Cape Herald*. Saan was an incidental target initially, and when I came to work and found a picket line outside the building, I lost my temper. The *Mail* was under such pressure that I took it badly that our own journalists were hurting us with a protest aimed at others. I swore at one of our staff members, the chairman of the Mwasa local chapter, and this inflamed feelings. I immediately regretted my anger. The strike grew into a Mwasa countrywide battle for recognition, and the managing directors of Argus and Saan took charge. It dragged on for six weeks and was only resolved, with recognition for Mwasa, after a leading black businessman, Sam Motsuenyane, was called in as a mediator. The *Cape Herald* journalists meanwhile had returned to work after three weeks.

Even while attitudes were changing, the upgrading of black journalists was a growing concern. Saan ran a company-wide, nonracial training course, but most of the trainees were whites. Saan's personnel manager, Laurie Hall, was well aware of the deficiency but protested that he had huge problems overcoming it because of the difficulty in finding suitable black applicants. The poor quality of schooling for blacks was resulting in trainees who struggled to keep up with whites in the classes. Sisulu was one of the exceptions. The need for training was gaining recognition, and courses for reporters were organized in Johannesburg by Britain's Thomson Foundation and Boston University's journalism department. Some of our black journalists also received grants for trips and seminars abroad. It didn't always go smoothly. The British government sponsored a Thomson Foundation course and we made facilities available in Saan, but Mwasa objected, insisting on a "neutral" venue, despite the fact that many of their members worked for Saan. The British consulate gave in, and the course was transferred to a bank's training premises. We bit our tongues and provided the needed back-up services. All the training, whether local or abroad, was only for one to three weeks at a time.

I thought the money could be better spent. We had excellent reporters, but I was sure that several could do better if they had more extensive training. Better groundwork had to be put into place, with far more intensive, specialized training to overcome the shortfalls. We prepared a six-month training course for twenty people to upgrade their English language skills based at Wits' Business School. The 100,000-rand cost ($16,000) for the initial course was high, but Saan and Argus agreed that it would be money well spent, and each invested 25,000 rand. I applied to the Konrad Adenauer Foundation in Germany for the remaining balance because of its conservative political connections, believing that this would keep the South African government off our back. After months of negotiation they turned me down without giving a reason. I later learned that a senior member of the foundation had put our training proposal before the South African ambassador in Bonn and was told it was "subversive." I did not feel I could push Saan and Argus to put in even more money, so our plan collapsed.

The *Mail* was also struggling to maintain quality. Senior reporters were hard to find and those few we did have either were grossly overworked or were lost to reporting because they were promoted to executive posts. Experienced journalists were drifting away from newspapers, and the talented younger reporters who replaced them were promoted too quickly for their own, or the paper's, good. We were not the magnet for top journalists that we had once been.

Apartheid could not be avoided, even in our offices. Because the printing plant was in the basement, the entire building was subject to the Factories Act, which laid down strict rules for racial segregation. The Saan toilets had to be segregated by law. On the editorial and management floors, little attention was paid to the segregation signs, until government inspectors came on their periodic visits and ordered them put up. On the *Mail*'s floor the toilet signs for "White Males" and "White Women" were in plastic lettering stuck onto the doors. The elevators were slow, so journalists waiting on the landing spent time picking away at the lettering until it was gone. Men and women of all colors wandered into the wrong bathroom as a result.

Separate cafeterias were also required by law, and their existence was reinforced by the white production workers. Saan was among those companies that pushed against internal segregation, and the cafeterias were nonracial by the late 1970s, with separation only between those who wore oily overalls and those who didn't.

The government harassment never stopped. An Air Force Buccaneer bomber crashed, and we had a letter from the chief of the Defense Force criticizing us because we had published the statistics of Buccaneer accidents, reminding us of a previous "friendly request" not to carry such details. We pointed out that it had been merely a "request" and that previous Buccaneer crashes had received extensive publicity, including the statistics. We could win only up to a point, because the "request" was "confirmed" at the next monthly meeting of the liaison committee of the Defense Force and the NPU, and we were bound by that.

There were also repeated problems because the police demanded that every journalist produce an official Press Identity Card before they would speak to him or her, or allow admission to police-controlled areas. In a Terrorism Act trial the judge ordered that only journalists holding a card could enter to report the proceedings. The police issued the identity cards in terms of the agreement with the NPU, but arbitrarily refused to give them to some reporters, especially black reporters.

The spreading resistance among blacks to the government gave rise to so many political trials that it was impossible to cover them all. The problem was compounded by the fact that the government moved the bigger trials to country towns, supposedly for security, though there was little doubt that a primary aim was to add to the defense's strains and costs, cut down families' and friends' ability to visit the accused, and dim the publicity spotlight. For example, a trial of eighteen members of the underground PAC on charges of conspiring to overthrow the government went on in the country town of Bethal, two hours' drive from Johannesburg, over a period of eighteen months. Sapa said it could not afford to provide coverage, so we put in our star political trial reporter, Pam Kleinot. She was the only reporter at the trial, and had to live in Bethal. This trial was so important that we were able to get Sapa to subsidize the cost of reporting it in return for handing over our daily report. We had to suffer the indignity of having the *Star* using our reports at greater length than we were able to do.

The Security Police also played their usual games. One of them joined Kleinot on the press bench and "said enough to indicate to me that they knew my background," recalls Kleinot. "He said it very pleasantly, as chit-chat. I felt it was intended to scare me."

The main person accused in that trial was Zephaniah Mothopeng, known as "Uncle Zeph." He was a mild-mannered, diffident man. Yet his life was an epic of suffering and endurance. He had been a teacher, but was fired for leading his colleagues in opposition to Bantu Education. He followed Robert Sobukwe into jail on March 21, 1960, in protesting against the pass laws, and served two years for "incitement." A year after his release, while studying law, he was detained incommunicado: his treatment included being forced to wear a canvas bag over his head and endure electric-shock torture. While Harold Strachan was in

Pretoria Prison, he saw Mothopeng in an inner courtyard, tied inside a straitjacket and rolling around on the concrete floor, screaming at the top of his lungs. He was later tried and sentenced to three years' imprisonment for working underground for the PAC.

On the day his jail sentence was completed—with no remission—he was secretly taken to a remote place in the countryside and ordered to stay there. He was given an unfurnished shack and work as a laborer at a starvation wage. His family had not been advised of his whereabouts. After six months he was allowed to return to his home in Soweto, but stringent banning orders were imposed. When the bannings lapsed, he had five years of normalcy. Then, in 1976, when the "children's rebellion" erupted, he was accused of inciting them and was detained incommunicado for many months before being charged in the Bethal trial, ending with a jail sentence of fifteen years—he was sixty-six years old. In a smuggled note he wrote, "As the doors of prison lock us in, this time our spirits are very high because we realize that victory is in sight and freedom is on our threshold." He was freed nine years later because he was dying of cancer.

Our own errors landed us in trouble, too, such as a front-page report that tears rolled down the face of a Security policeman while he was under cross-examination during a Terrorism Act trial. It was such an inherently improbable scenario that our copy editors should not have allowed it into the paper. That morning we had a furious complaint from the Security Police about what they saw as an affront to one of their men. The commissioner of police lodged a complaint with the Press Council. The lawyer responsible for the cross-examination was George Bizos, one of the leading defense barristers in political trials and an old friend of mine. I phoned him and he said that much as he would have liked to reduce a policeman to tears, it had not happened. The reporter could not offer any explanation, and was fired. The police, mollified, dropped their complaint.

We tried to be as careful as possible in picking our way through the myriad laws. There were now at least one hundred laws that infringed press freedom, and the production line was still churning them out. There was always a new problem, such as the case of the man accused of murder who was committed for mental observation. We had a photograph of him and thought we could publish it since he was not actually in a prison or police station and thus did not come under the prohibition of photographs. We consulted our lawyers who advised that although he wasn't actually in prison, he was considered to be in prison for our purposes and we should not publish. We took the advice.

There was also the day that we carried an interview on page one with a cabinet minister, Chris Heunis, about the price of gas, a very sensitive issue because of the international sanctions that were building up against South Africa. It was a good interview and quite informative, or so we thought until we had an outraged call from the minister's office denying that he had spoken to any of our reporters and threatening us with every possible unpleasantness. It turned out that our reporter had looked up Heunis in the Pretoria phone book and the person he spoke to was not Heunis the minister, but Heunis the plumber, who had gladly given his views on the crisis when asked.

After 1976, the *Mail* was said to be consistently losing money and the annual debt climbed into the millions. Certainly the *Mail* was badly off in its share of the advertising market compared with the *Star*. In 1980, in appointments, the *Mail* had 21.5 percent against the *Star*'s 36.7 percent; national, 15.5 versus 37.3 percent; retail, 9.7 versus 41.8 percent; small ads, 12.2 versus 58.4 percent. Only in financial advertising was the *Mail* ahead, because various kinds of company notices were compulsory, and the business pages enjoyed a strong reputation.

There was also a sharp fall in the number of white readers and a sharp rise in black readers. Between 1977 and 1980, surveys showed the following contrasting pattern between the *Mail* and the *Star*:

READER PROFILES IN PERCENTAGES

	Rand Daily Mail		The *Star*	
	White	"Nonwhite"	White	"Nonwhite"
1977	48.8	52.2	57.9	42.1
1980	30.6	69.4	49.6	50.4
% change	37.3	+33.0	-14.4	+19.7

In fact a countrywide trend was under way, in Cape Town and Durban as much as in Johannesburg. From 1976 to 1980 the *Mail*'s 30.7 percent drop in white readers was the biggest among newspapers, but the *Cape Argus* and the *Cape Times* were not far behind with 25.7 percent and 26.0

percent respectively. Inside Saan's management the loss of the *Mail's* white readers was blamed on the newspaper's policies—with the repeated and heavy reminder that black readers were not of commercial benefit because they did not draw advertising. Every newspaper they bought was eating up money, as the paper's selling price did not cover costs, management noted.

For a time the Saan management sought to make a virtue of the rapidly growing black readership. The marketing department developed the concept of "The New Consumer," which transcended racial barriers. There were good grounds for believing that this was a jump into the future, where South Africa was heading. Saan organized a conference at the end of 1979 for businesspeople and advertising executives. The head of a university bureau of market research advised that, from 1970 to 1975, the market share of blacks (excluding coloreds and Asians) had risen from 20.6 to 30.7 percent for clothing and footwear, 17.4 to 26.3 percent for washing and cleaning materials, and 7.3 to 15.3 percent for reading-matter and stationery. Whites, despite their far smaller number, were still the dominant consumers, but the figures demonstrated that change was happening fast.

The message did not hit home, partly because so many in business and the advertising industry remained stuck in the past and had a one-eyed view of the numbers that surveys produced, seeing the drop in white readers but without looking at the bigger picture. They were generally behind in their political views, and it wasn't surprising that they were the same way in business.

The other factor at play at the *Mail* was the hostility in Saan's management ranks. It was evident to us in editorial and was to grow a lot worse, especially after 1982, when Clive Kinsley got rid of Raymond Louw and surrounded himself with a small group. By then, too, Saan's group advertising manager, Gerry Swanepoel, had resigned because he did not find the atmosphere in the company to be congenial.

Swanepoel did not share the *Mail's* political outlook but he admired the newspaper and liked the journalists. Going against the conventional wisdom, he did not believe that the political policy was keeping away advertisers. When Louw was editor, the two had proven that the *Mail* could overcome the prejudices against it while being both profitable and saleable. Then Swanepoel was promoted to group manager, thus removed from direct involvement in selling space. Worse still, centralization was introduced, and the *Mail* was deprived of its own advertising salespeople. The idea was that sales representatives would sell space in the *Sunday Times* and the *Mail* as a package to the benefit of both, but it was not a success. It was easy to sell the Sunday paper and hard to sell the *Mail*, so once sales quotas were achieved, the sales people did not bother with the *Mail*.

Kinsley had been totally supportive of editorial during the Information Department scandal, helping to coordinate the countrywide efforts, approving the spending of large amounts of money on the investigations, and even on one important occasion urging an editor who was holding back to go ahead with publication. He was also scrupulous in not interfering with editors in day-to-day operations. I saw that myself in my spells as acting editor. Very occasionally he came down to my office, sat and chatted for a while, and then diffidently told me that something that had been published bothered him, and a frank exchange ensued between us in which I either agreed or disagreed with him. But in dealing with the changing demographics and in facing up to the *Mail*'s weaknesses, he and others in management lacked the imagination and courage, never mind the will, to break out of the white mold, despite what Louw and Swanepoel had achieved not all that long ago. *The New Consumer* tailed off as another failed initiative. Kinsley went on speaking hopefully about advertisers coming to recognize the need to reach for black consumers, which would transform the *Mail*'s fortunes. But to say it was one thing, to pursue it another, and that did not happen. The newspaper's price was increased twice within not much more than a year, making it the most expensive daily in the country. The drop in circulation that followed was even worse than expected: sales plunged from 131,944 to 109,819 a day from 1980 to 1981, before beginning to pick up again. Panic was in the air, and the building was awash with rumors that the *Mail* was either going to be closed or that Sparks was to be fired.

The *Mail* was looking for readers, especially white Afrikaners, by providing a heavy diet of politics, and I thought we needed to look at where we were. I had been on the newspaper for more than twenty-two years and had heard every possible argument for and against what the *Mail* had been and was. Alarmed about what the pressures from management might lead to, in February 1981, I wrote a memo to Sparks with the idea of pushing forward our internal debates. The memo encapsulated the basics that I had grown to believe about newspapering, and began:

It's not our editorial policy, I believe, that is the major cause of our difficulties. Provided our editorial policy is not overextreme and hence totally alien to most of the public, there is no reason why we should not have views that run counter to prevailing wisdoms. I do not believe that we are overextreme; out of step with the bulk of the white community, yes, but not to the extent that we are dismissed as weirdoes or crazies. Indeed, to have a different, robust policy is a distinct plus. It is what gives the paper its specific character. Attempt to remove it, or to alter it fundamentally, and we will lose our loyal readers, both white and black.

The *Mail* has particular difficulties because in many ways we stand in the middle. We are thus open to rejection by both whites and blacks. We have to walk a tightrope between the groups. This is a difficult task and it cannot always be successfully achieved. We have, however, to aim at staying on the tightrope as much as possible, catering to all sections of the community.

But, I argued, we suffered from a large credibility gap which was closely tied to a lack of balance. "This, to me, is the paramount exercise we have to carry out in insisting to reporters and subs [copy editors] on fair reporting and headlining. We have also to look at each page, from day to day, to ensure that a proper 'mix' of stories is carried so that there is a blending of all the aspects that must be covered."

The memo went on: "We have also to strive for a different image in a number of areas—to show, in regard to hospitals, teachers, etc. that we are not merely intent on exploiting crises for some obscure propaganda purpose, but that what we are doing stems from a concern for the community. Perhaps we need to think about saying things in a rather quieter way, with fewer banners, and fewer sounding of alarm bells." I worried that we were missing too many stories because of poor tracking of events, and that reporters were not sufficiently called to account for their whereabouts and productivity. "There is no short-cut to gaining increased advertising and transforming the paper's financial position. It can only come when we have readers and when our reputation is good."

At management level, Group Advertising produced a proposal, "The *Rand Daily Mail* Alternative," which urged the destruction of the newspaper as it then was by terminating the *Extra* edition for the townships, reducing the amount of editorial space, and ending the uneconomic daily circulation, a 280-mile radius (450 km) surrounding Johannesburg. It would be a newspaper aimed at whites.

Sparks wrote a memo for the board arguing that the loss of white readers was due to the fact that Johannesburg had five newspapers competing for them, while the increase in black readers was natural because some black newspapers had been banned and these readers would be profitable consumers in the future. He asked for a year to make changes. He gave the memo to Max Borkum before submitting it to the board. Borkum consulted Gordon Waddell, who said he told Sparks, "'If you give that to the board, they are going to fire you.' Frankly, if you gave that to any board, they would fire you. He was asking for things that no board in its right sense would have contemplated." On a Monday in late May 1981, Sparks set out his memo in an address to the board. On Friday Kinsley told him the board had decided there should be a new editor.

Tertius Myburgh, editor of the *Sunday Times*, was appointed editor-in-chief of the *Rand Daily Mail*, with Ken Owen as editor. That meant my automatic demotion. Myburgh was extremely successful as editor of the Sunday paper, and circulation and advertising boomed. He was described as a "*verligte*" (enlightened) Afrikaner, and the *Sunday Times* criticized apartheid, but there were rumors that he was a government agent and that he was trying to give white rule a more acceptable face through the newspaper. The story about him went on to gain greater substance. Sparks said that two of those deep inside the Information Department scandal, Eschel Rhoodie and a businessman, David Abramson, told him they had been advised from their side that they need not worry about the *Sunday Times*, as Myburgh was a government man. Sparks sent Kinsley a tape recording in which Myburgh was named for having surreptitious meetings with a member of the Information Department. "I then challenged Tertius," says Kinsley. "He denied it, so what could I do?"

John Horak, the police spy working at the *Sunday Times* at this time, explained that when these Myburgh stories were circulating, he was phoned by his handler, Johan Coetzee, and was ordered to offer protection for Myburgh, even at the risk of blowing his own cover. He went to Myburgh's office, telling him that Coetzee had sent him. He says that Myburgh replied, "I knew you would be coming to see me, but everything is under control."

Myburgh and Owen moved into the *Mail*, changed the typeface of the masthead, jazzed up the newspaper's appearance, and went for the trivial and the shallow, turning the paper into a low-grade product. They never understood the *Mail*, nor did they care to. The paper shed old readers, but failed to attract new ones.

I was given little work to do. Day after day I sat in my office staring out the window. They probably didn't fire me outright because I was so identified with the *Mail* that it might have led to undesirable publicity. Instead, the game seemed to be to push me toward the edge of the branch until I jumped. I wrote a few feature articles and filled in as night editor. Every once in a while I was given an editorial to write.

After a few months, I went to see Kinsley and told him that I was having a difficult time, as it was clear that I was not wanted. After more than two decades of work in Saan, what was my future? Kinsley replied, "Oh, yes, Tertius has been complaining to me about you. He says that you never smile."

Most of the *Mail* staff was desperately unhappy about the Myburgh/Owen rule. Several times a week editorial people, including some of our key reporters, came into my office to tell me they intended to resign. Each time I urged them to hold on because it would not last forever. I was a lot less confident than I let on. I had lunch with Rex Gibson from the *Sunday Express*. We could see that the *Mail* was dying. Circulation was dropping fast. He believed that he was the person who could save it; I thought I was the one who could do it, and we had a friendly disagreement. Less than a week later I was sitting in my study at home having breakfast and was feeling very low as I tried to muster the strength for another day at the *Mail*. I told Anne, "I've reached the end of my tether. I can't go on." At that exact moment the phone rang. It was Gibson telling me that Myburgh/Owen had been fired and that he was the new editor. I let out a great shout of joy. Gibson asked me to resume as deputy editor. When the news about the departure of Myburgh and Owen flashed around the *Mail*, cheering reporters danced on the desks. Gibson took over on February 1, 1982.

Myburgh supposedly decided that the *Mail* was past saving and, as he could not get the board of directors to agree to fundamental changes, he would return to the *Sunday Times*. The story as we knew it was different. He had asked the board for some 33 million rand to save the *Mail*, knowing that it was an impossibly high sum and the board would not agree to it. His strategy, it seemed, was to kill off the newspaper, but to his surprise the board decided to persevere with the *Mail* and get rid of him and Owen instead.

When McPherson offered Gibson the editorship, he wanted me fired. Gibson refused. I did not know about this, as Gibson only let me in on it a long time afterwards. What friends told me at the time was that a frisson ran through the Jewish community, or at least some part of it: there was concern that I had been passed over as editor because I was

Jewish. I might not have been the community's pinup boy, but it was a different matter if I was the victim of anti-Semitism. Nor were Jews being oversensitive because the fact that there had never been a Jewish editor of the *Mail* was openly referred to inside Saan before, then and later, but without any explanation.

For my part, I thought it a modern miracle that I was as senior on a mainstream newspaper as I was. I joked that I was one criminal conviction away from being editor. And however true the Jewish factor may have been, McPherson's chief stated objection to me was that I should not put my "political stamp" on the paper, by which he presumably meant my liberal outlook. But not knowing how close I had come to being thrown out, I continued doing what I had been doing for years—pushing for a journalism that took account of the entire South African population in our coverage and editorial stance.

It meant, too, ensuring that all South Africans were referred to with equal respect. This was more difficult than it sounds, and for the same old reason: many of the *Mail*'s staff were whites and many unthinkingly shared the prejudices of most whites. Getting reporters who covered accidents to chase after the names of black victims in the same way they did the names of white victims took a long time to accomplish, if only because the reporters in their turn had to persuade and educate the ambulance attendants, hospital officials, and policemen from whom they got the information. Getting copy editors to follow these nonracial rules was a prolonged battle, with a mixture of requests, orders, recrimination, and finally angry attack.

Gibson's belief in balance and a mix of stories was exactly what the *Mail* needed, and editorial people perked up and circulation began to recover. Myburgh/Owen had inflicted a lot of damage in their eight months at the *Mail*. Very occasionally Gibson and I were at odds because he thought that I was unrelenting and overly harsh in my assessments of the Nationalists. Kelsey Stuart used to ask me, "Won't you people please, for a change, say something good about the government?" He was an alternate member of the board of directors and he said he always had to defend the *Mail* against the charge that it was unfailingly down on the government. Every now and then I would phone him and say, "Kelsey, I started writing an editorial this afternoon praising the government. Then I took a deeper look at what they are proposing and saw the crookery in it and I got mad, so I am sorry but I've felt obliged to write a leader attacking them."

Under Rex Gibson's editorship, devotion to the *Mail* among staff members ran deep. The *Mail* reemerged as the pace-setting newspaper in the country. But in the 1980s it was not the newspaper it had been a decade before. It couldn't be. Circumstances had changed too much. There had been a quantum leap in limitations on what we could publish through the restrictive laws enacted without end, the browbeating and threats. Yet the press was being expected to do more than ever before because the public silence was greater than ever.

As the level and vigor of political opposition among whites sank, friends chided me about the *Mail.* I reacted testily. You tell me we must do more to oppose the government, I would say, so go and do something brave and we'll be more than pleased to publish an article about you. The coverage of political trials was, however, a sore

Chapter 22

point, and I constantly received criticisms that we were not doing enough. Our reporting late in 1983 was strongly attacked by the *Mail's* political reporter, Anton Harber, in an article he wrote in the *Journalist* newspaper, in which he examined the *Mail's* heavy coverage of a treason trial of two young white people, Carl Niehaus and his girlfriend, Jansie Lourens. The sentencing of Niehaus to fifteen years' imprisonment was given thirty-one column inches. In contrast, only six column inches were given to the sentences of Alpheus Molotsi and Jacob Molefe, who were black, for eighteen and fifteen years, respectively. Harber also referred to other political trials, which had not been covered at all.

It was an easy criticism to make, and he was right to air it, but it ignored the news strength of a rare trial for treason of two young Afrikaners, which justified the story getting extra space. It also ignored the constant and impossible balancing act between reporting significant and readable news, maintaining a news mix—what other news to keep out so as to cover the plethora of political trials?—and trying to hold on to white readers when lack of advertising was drastically reducing the amount of space for news.

In my more somber moments, depressed by the compromises we were forced to make, I felt that it was time to hang a red light outside the front door to show what we had become. Younger reporters came into my office filled with anger because I had canned their stories or drastically edited them down. I found myself asking (and didn't like myself for it), "Where do you think you are? Do you think we have press freedom in South Africa and that we can publish what we like?" At the same time we kept stressing to reporters that they should not cut back on stories: their job was to report fully; the censorship came further up the line, in consultation with the lawyers if necessary. I also developed a precautionary drill. When a reporter came to me with what I could see was going to be a tricky story, I anticipated the likely outcome by saying, "You learned about this from an anonymous phone call, didn't you?" Sometimes I had to repeat the question several times in an ever-louder voice before the penny dropped.

It also bothered me that the government's information section, revamped after the Info scandal, was parading us abroad as proof of press freedom: look at all these editorials criticizing the government, they could say. The government's propaganda machine had become subtler, and where previously they had ignored us save for occasional attacks, they now habitually quoted the *Mail* and other English-language newspapers in their press summaries. Of course this also provided the opportunity to put across Nationalist views by quoting their own newspapers.

With all these reservations, at the end of most days I still believed that the *Mail* was doing enough as a newspaper to justify its existence and validate our reduced level of journalism. In our editorial comments we were hammering away at apartheid, declaring and upholding the notion of a decent society and the rule of law, and consistently arguing for a nonracial South Africa, all on a scale that no one else was doing.

The news desk, for all its problems, remained aggressive and energetic. Reporter Liz McGregor speaks of the "brutal, macho ethos" in the newsroom. Those of us on the executive side saw it as a commendable drive to obtain the news despite our inadequate resources. When McGregor went to check the effects of the drought in the Northern Transvaal, she had to face daunting obstacles. No photographer was available so she took her own pictures. The company car was in bad shape. Whenever she stopped, she had to assemble a crowd for a push start. She struggled to find her way to small mission stations in remote rural areas, but she nevertheless returned after a few days with a story and pictures about mass starvation, and it was strongly presented in the *Mail*. That's what counted.

Rich Mkhondo is one of those who has happier memories. He joined the *Mail* as a reporter at the start of 1984. Young as he was, he was pitched into political reporting and when his stories were cut, he did the normal thing—he complained. "The newsdesk was very open with me," he says. "They would tell me that a story could not be used because it had holes in it and we could not fill them and/or because of the law."

Mkhondo remembers the newspaper as becoming increasingly vocal against apartheid, especially in reaction to the government's plan for a tri-cameral parliament: one house for whites, another for coloreds, and another for Asians, with the white house holding the power. Blacks were excluded, as they were being herded into tribal "homelands." The scheme proved the catalyst for uniting the extraparliamentary opposition as never before. In August 1983 more than five hundred trade union, community, religious and sports organizations created the United Democratic Front, in effect the internal wing of the still-proscribed ANC. A year later the pent-up feelings erupted in violence on the East Rand near Johannesburg, another turning point in South African history. This time the resistance never halted for the next seven years until the breakthrough to freedom. Although no one could know the significance of the event, we recorded the start of the wave of violence with a large color photograph on the front page showing a surging crowd outside a burning building the previous day, September 4, 1984, in the township of Evaton. Events were moving fast. The first time the house of a black policeman living in a township ghetto was burned down was big news; within a year several hundred had been torched, and it became so commonplace that the latest episode rated only a brief paragraph. By then many black policemen had been moved with their families to safe areas.

By late 1984 white reporters could only safely enter the townships with police protection, riding inside an armored personnel carrier. A *Mail* reporter, Mauritz Moolman, who was Afrikaans, defied that because, as he explained, "credibility suffers because the press—traditionally in a sense the 'property' of the people—becomes identified with the oppressor." Under cover of darkness he walked into Sharpeville, which was ablaze as residents burned down schools, stores, and beer halls and killed local collaborators. Moolman succeeded in entering on his own and emerging alive three hours later because "I was able to say that I work for the *Rand Daily Mail*—the only 'white' newspaper with some credibility among blacks. Had I been working for any other paper, I would have had second thoughts. Secondly, the surprise of blacks over the unexpected appearance of an unarmed white in the township in the middle of the night—which implied my absolute trust in their hospitality. And thirdly, my preparedness to listen to their point of view."

At about the time that the United Democratic Front was founded, another organization also came into being: the National Front, a black-consciousness coalition. The *Mail* had been having problems with the Azanian Peoples' Organization (Azapo), the major black-consciousness group, because it often refused to allow white *Mail* reporters to cover its events. This caused us concern: Could we allow an organization to dictate to us who should report its activities? Would we be bowing to racism by agreeing to send only black reporters? The concern was, of course, late in the game, because we had traditionally gone along with the ruling mores by assigning only whites to cover white politics. With the entry of blacks into mainstream journalism, this had also been a practical policy. It would have been physically dangerous for a black reporter to attend a National Party congress because he or she could have faced violence. It had only recently begun to change with Ameen Akhalwaya, who was an Asian, reporting the white political scene in the Transvaal province.

On February 18, 1982, news of a "mystery blast" was carried on the *Mail*'s front page:

> An explosion ripped through the deserted building of an abandoned mine between Randfontein and Krugersdorp on Tuesday night, killing three black men.
>
> A fourth man was taken to hospital under police guard to be treated for shrapnel wounds after the explosion."

It seemed clear to us, based on what the police told us, that the men were insurgents and had been preparing a bomb, which blew up in their faces. It turned out we were hopelessly deceived. It took fourteen years before the truth behind that "mystery blast" became known. It had been a police set-up. The story emerged before the Truth and Reconciliation Commission, which sat from 1996 to 1998, hearing testimony from both victims and perpetrators of state-organized terror. Although no one could know it, by the start of the 1980s the government-created machinery for killing opponents had been well in place in what proved to be the last diehard attempts to hold on to white power.

The events of that fateful night in 1982 were described to the commission by the sole survivor, Zandile Musi. He and three friends, the youngest of whom was fourteen, had decided "to join the liberation movement," and were lured to the mine by the promise of training in guerrilla weapons. They were driven there by Joe "Scarface" Mamasela, a former freedom fighter who had become a police agent, unbeknownst to them. They were left alone in a room with two hand grenades and a "suspicious-looking" box. Musi said he was on his way to the box when there was a powerful explosion. Three of the youths died, and Musi was injured. The police arrived half an hour later. Musi was arrested, tortured, and charged with illegal possession of explosives. He was acquitted but was again arrested three years later, prosecuted, and served three years on Robben Island Prison. Musi told the Commission that his friends died for their country. "I want people to know these people did not die because they were just naughty, but because they were concerned about millions of South Africans," he said.

Mozambique, on South Africa's eastern border, was underreported with few contacts between the two countries. While ruled by Portugal, its capital, Lourenco Marques, had been an exotic holiday place for white South Africans. That ended when the Marxist Frelimo movement took over in 1975 after a war in the bush that had the additional effect of precipitating revolution and the overthrow of dictatorship in Portugal itself.

Under the new government, to go there for the *Mail* and the *Boston Globe* required drawn-out negotiations by telex for a visa. And as I discovered when I arrived at the airport in renamed Maputo in 1980, a journalist could only go there with government approval and cooperation. There were no buses from the airport to the city, and no cabs. Only senior government officials, diplomats, and aid agencies owned cars. Travel around the country was impossible without the government's assistance.

In reading up for the visit, I had come to realize how poorly the press had served South Africans in preparing them for the change in their neighbor, whose capital was a mere hour's flight from Johannesburg. Reporting during the bush war had been chiefly gung-ho stuff, based on Portuguese army briefings and going out on arranged sorties with troops; we had given little warning of the worm of discontent eating away inside the armed forces, little information about Portugal's dismal five-hundred-year colonial record—in addition to the tyranny, illiteracy was about 95 percent—and even less information about Frelimo's guerrilla struggle. Instead we had reinforced the deepest fears of South Africa's whites that the red peril was at the gates.

On this visit I found people fighting to survive. Basic foods were rationed, and supermarket shelves were bare except for tins of what were said to be Bulgarian sausage, which even hungry people considered too awful to eat, and rat poison. The tins of sausage and poison were neatly spaced out along the shelves, a gap of several yards between each of them. But the water flowed in the city's pipes and the electricity usually worked, once you allowed for the occasional breakdown.

The more I saw, the more impressed I was by the grit and the good humor of people in overcoming the awesome problems left by colonial neglect and the overnight loss of nearly all skilled workers with the departure of tens of thousands of settlers. Traditionally, small peasant farmers throughout the countryside had sold their cotton, corn, and cashew nuts to thousands of Portuguese storekeepers in exchange for salt and clothing, but with the flight of the storekeepers the internal economy collapsed. Peasants reverted to subsistence agriculture, and food production dropped catastrophically.

I was critical of the Marxist thinking and the baggage of totalitarianism, like the "re-education camps" for political dissidents, criminals, and prostitutes, and struggled within myself for fair and balanced conclusions. I ended up wary but sympathetic to Frelimo's efforts and my reports reflected that. It was unusual to have a good word said for the "enemy," and many in South Africa did not like it. That included our sister publication, the *Financial Mail*, no longer the intelligent and liberal paper it had once been. It now ran an editorial headlined "Through Rose-Tinted Glasses," which abused me and blamed all of Mozambique's troubles on Frelimo. Support for me came from Jonathan Kapstein, the Africa Bureau Chief of New York's *Business Week* magazine, who wrote to the *Financial Mail* to complain about its "pompous and strangely intemperate attack" on me. He said his own reporting of Mozambique confirmed my findings.

The narrow South African attitude towards Mozambique changed and suddenly the two governments were talking to each other. The Nkomati Accord was signed in March 1984, with each government promising not to harm the other's security. South Africa got what it wanted: a promise by Mozambique not to give sanctuary to the ANC. Overnight several dozen ANC members were ordered to leave the country. Until then South Africa had mounted raids across the border to attack what it claimed were ANC bases from which terrorism was planned or launched.

Mozambique, for its part, needed South African goodwill because Pretoria was helping to fund and arm Renamo, the rebel movement laying the country to waste. Renamo had a penchant for cutting off the ears of villagers. It was their trademark, apart from the wholesale destruction of rural clinics and schools. A Swedish-made television program once interviewed a victim, an elderly peasant woman: "If they go on like this, they will inherit a nation of people without ears," she said.

The Nkomati honeymoon did not last. The Mozambicans, I believe, kept their side of the bargain and cracked down on the ANC, but South Africa did not, as I learned during my next trip two months after the accord was signed. By that time Renamo had penetrated so far south that it was dangerous for anyone to go beyond the "green belt" surrounding Maputo. It was even perilous to drive the one and a half hours from or to the South African border because of the danger of land mines and ambushes.

On the plane to Maputo I met a reporter from a London newspaper and we agreed to cooperate. We set to work as soon as we reached the Polana Hotel, drawing up a set of questions and taking them to the Information Ministry, then sat at the hotel poolside in the sun and waited. A couple of times a day we walked to the ministry, always to encounter what by now I knew were the two most well-used words in Mozambique, "Patience. Wait." The government was thin on experience and talent, and you could rely on getting sense out of the top two or three officials in a ministry and very little thereafter. On one of our visits to the ministry we sat in the waiting room for over thirty minutes. No one came near us and we could hear no trace of activity, so we diffidently tiptoed down the passage and found the ministry's director sitting behind his bare desk, hands clasped, and staring into nothing. He was not the least bit embarrassed, and gave us the usual "Patience. Wait." We had arrived on Monday morning and the days drifted by; on Thursday the

London journalist ran out of patience and time, and a government car collected him at lunchtime to take him to the airport. At 1:45 P.M. I received a phone call and a voice said a car would fetch me in fifteen minutes. By 2:15 P.M. I was sitting in the office of a cabinet minister, followed by a string of other meetings with ministers, one after the other, until the final one in the evening with the Minister of Defense. This was the big one, because he told me that Mozambique was certain that South Africa was not observing the Nkomati Accord and was secretly still giving help to Renamo. I never discovered why I was given such preferential treatment; it was one of the mysteries in dealing with a secretive government. My report about Renamo appeared in the *Mail* and was predictably condemned by the South African Army. The poor Mozambicans were to suffer still more years of South African-fueled destruction.

In South Africa the Nationalists were preoccupied with trying to halt the flow of black people into Cape Town because it ran counter to their decree that only coloreds were allowed to work and live there. But that policy never worked, and, driven by poverty in the Ciskei and Transkei "homelands" on the east coast, blacks flocked to Cape Town in search of work, laying themselves open to arrest and prosecution under the pass laws. In the winter of 1984 the struggle between the government and black squatters reached a new peak. I went to Cape Town to report for both the *Mail* and the *Boston Globe*. Thousands of men, women, and children were living in shelters constructed with plastic sheeting draped over thin branches, pushed into the damp ground of the Cape Flats outside the city where the water table was high. The police came in each day to tear down the shelters, and built bonfires out of the plastic sheeting and the branches, leaving the squatters to sit in the open during the day with their few possessions. The plastic sheeting was provided by priests and paid for by the South African Council of Churches. Eventually the priests won a court order that the police could not burn the plastic sheeting but instead had to return it to the owner, the Council of Churches. So each daybreak the police tore down the shelters and handed the plastic sheeting to the priests. The priests would wait until dark to drive trucks along back roads in order to return the sheeting to the squatters.

One gray winter morning I received a phone call at my hotel telling me a big police raid against the squatters was under way. I hurried out there, but the police had cordoned off the area. I spent the day writing an article. Late that night I drove to the squatter camp for a last check, thinking that if I was turned back by the police again, I would have my last sentence for the article. The police, however, had withdrawn and I was able to get all the way to the squatters. Hundreds, perhaps thousands, of people were lying on the damp ground trying to find little hollows where they might find shelter from the cold. A large crowd of men was standing together and I made my way to the center. They were all blacks except for a few white Roman Catholic and Anglican priests. It was a prayer meeting and I would hear a voice coming out of the dark and asking God for help and then everyone would sing a hymn, and so it went on for some time. Then a voice next to me asked, "Will you pray with us?" Without stopping to think, the words came out of me, "I am a Jew, but we have the same God." A sigh went through the crowd, and I went on to pray aloud for God to touch the hearts of the police and government to be merciful and compassionate. A hymn was quietly sung and I stood there, stunned that I had broken the habit of a lifetime as a journalist and taken part in a public statement, and filled with emotion about the suffering of these people and the simple hope they put in God.

I wish I could say that the prayers were answered that day. But with the dawn the cycle began all over again. Eventually, through the weight of their numbers and refusal to yield, the squatters won, and the government legalized their existence and created a new ghetto for them.

Mamphela Ramphele was in the Black Consciousness Movement and after qualifying as a medical doctor worked with Steve Biko in Kingwilliamstown in the Eastern Cape. The Security Police served a banishment order on her and dumped her in a remote place many hundreds of kilometers away: they drove her there through the night, not even allowing her to take a change of clothes. But her lawyer, Raymond Tucker from Johannesburg, told her the banishment order was invalid because it misspelled her name and he advised her she could return home. She was back in town ten days after being carted away. The police went through the banishment again but this time gave her time to settle her affairs. Then she was dumped in Lenyenye village in the Lebowa tribal "homeland" in the far north, a few kilometers from the small town of Tzaneen, and in enervating tropical heat. Ramphele was pregnant with Biko's son; she was on her own in banishment when a few months later in 1977 Biko was killed by the Security Police. She named their son Hlumelo which means "a new seed growing from one that is dead."

Although she was the only doctor for a long distance in a rural slum of

60,000 people, the residents stayed away because the police warned them that they faced instant arrest if they were seen with her and also spread the story that she would steal their children and send them out of the country where they would become terrorists. But sick people started coming under cover of darkness and knocking at her window; she told them to come during the day and they would say that they were frightened of being arrested and she would give them the tart reply: "Then you're not sick enough." But mothers whose children fell ill insisted on defying the police and bringing them to Ramphele, and the barrier went down.

Anne and I went to visit her a few times and through her I began to learn about existence in the "homelands"—the tribal mini-states, supposedly independent but in fact vassals of the South African government, which were meant as a cornerstone of apartheid. She pointed out the local fat cat who had begun with a butcher shop, then expanded to a grocery store and then the ultimate moneyspinner, a liquor store, and who was profiteering at the expense of the local people who had nowhere else to go. "He is making as much money as he can because he knows it is not going to last," she said. As we drove around she spoke of the mass hunger, of families whose men had gone off to seek work, and people whose diet consisted of dry corn porridge supplemented by some wild spinach, with a treat to look forward to at the end of a month of a few chicken necks and feet. Deprivation on that scale looked all the worse amid such lush greenness; but people had neither time or energy to cultivate their own crops. If the husbands had deserted the family or died the women kept themselves and their children alive by seasonal work on white-owned farms: they were collected by truck as early as four A.M. and got home again as late as seven P.M., six days a week, and were paid a pittance. Driving along a main road, Ramphele warned me not to believe that other cars approaching stop signs would actually halt: the corruption was so general that drivers' licenses were easily bought and many drivers had no idea what a stop sign meant.

She had nearly seven years of banishment there and she transformed the lives of people, getting literacy classes going, gardening and brick-making, starting a clinic and then the building of a community center. After the banishment orders were finally not renewed she remained for a time to shepherd along her projects and told me how her stay had changed her: "It's hardened me a helluva lot, in the sense that I have had to learn to live with anger. I have to conserve my energy for other things. If I were to allow myself to get angry at every turn then I wouldn't have any energy left to do anything else. At the same time it's necessary some-times to really get angry in order to feel that you are alive because it can kill you inside to be seeing all this misery every single day."

Having said that she was also able to say, in what was an early expla-nation of the "South African miracle" that was to occur later, in 1994, with the largely peaceful transition to democracy: "Somehow there is something about blacks which probably is responsible for us allowing a lot of things to happen to us. We are very forgiving people. We are not given to hatred. There is a lot of laughter in the black community. There is something that is miraculous about us: we are able to laugh at ourselves, laugh at the world, and keep going under the most difficult of conditions."

Ramphele finally left Lenyenye and landed up teaching and studying at the University of Cape Town. She co-authored a study of poverty in South Africa and in 1995 was appointed principal of the university. Under her leadership the university became a shining example of how transformation to the new South Africa could be achieved. In 2000 she moved on to the international stage, joining the World Bank in Washing-ton DC as managing director for education, health and social services.

What Ramphele showed and told me in Lenyenye put flesh on what I had been hearing elsewhere for a long time, and especially from Sheena Duncan and her colleagues in the Black Sash who were going into the black rural areas: that standards of living in the "homelands," which had begun low, were declining still further. There was a severe drought at this time but it seemed it was not the fundamental reason for the mass poverty and hunger but was exacerbating what already existed. The situ-ation was hidden because it was so diffuse, much of it was away from the main roads and people were scared to say anything.

Rex Gibson and I agreed that this was an investigation which should be done but that it was beyond the *Mail*'s resources to do it properly; I sent a note to our morning newspaper partners proposing a joint nation-wide probe, pooling reporters and resources. What we needed was a Ramphele in every "homeland" who would have her guts, knowledge, and political savvy. That wasn't going to be remotely possible because people were too beaten down, but we had to find a whole range of peo-ple to work with us. Schoolteachers seemed the sort of people we should be searching out but they were also among the most controlled and scared of all. The *Cape Times* and *Eastern Province Herald* agreed to the project but the *Natal Mercury* and *Daily Dispatch* said no. This was late in 1984 and the pressures building up on the *Rand Daily Mail* did not allow us to allocate the needed staff and money so the investigation died. I rank this among our greatest failures: a hard-hitting newspaper series, adding to and pulling together all the bits and pieces of information that were known, would have exposed the wretchedness of the "homelands" as the end-result of apartheid on the scale that it deserved.

The war against Swapo, on the border between South West Africa (Namibia) and Angola—it went on for 25 years—was yet another creator of ambivalence inside the *Mail*. Not only were members of our staff required to do compulsory military duty but young South Africans, the sons of our readers, were dying on the border. The doings of the army, whether the annual call-up of white conscripts or public appeals for money to send comforts to the troops in the bush, were part of the news scene and were well-covered. We had a military correspondent and he relied on the army for facilities and information—which meant that like all the press in South Africa we were manipulated by the military to tell only what officialdom wanted told. The pressure to stay in line on the war was considerable because anyone who questioned too much was savaged by the government and its media as a traitor and friend of the Marxists in Angola, the Cubans and the Soviet Union. On the other hand, we opposed South Africa's presence in South-West Africa and even more the incursions into Angola and we went on saying so. We applauded "our boys" but objected to the politics of what they were being told to do.

One sphere in which we did try to keep cool was in language, both for the border war and the slowly escalating violence inside the country by the African National Congress. To the government, and most whites, the insurgents were terrorists. From the mid 1970s onward we tried to reduce the emotional temperature and to avoid demonizing Swapo and the ANC by using the word "terrorist" for those who attacked civilians; those who attacked the armed forces of the State, whether police or army, were "guerrillas." Only in direct speech did we publish whichever word a speaker had used. The emotive phrase, "freedom fighter," was barred unless in direct speech. The policy could lead to absurdities so that a group of insurgents who ambushed an army patrol in the morning were guerrillas but became terrorists when they attacked a white-owned farmhouse in the afternoon. Nor was it a universally popular policy—we affronted both right and left through it—and it wasn't always successful because "terrorist" tended to creep in as the word for all political violence. It's hard to stand back from the anguish and emotions when bombs are exploding and people are dying yet I think we were right to try to maintain a distinction and perhaps it contributed a tiny bit to ensuring that minds were not completely shut so that the government was finally able to sit down to reach peace with the ANC in South Africa and Swapo in Namibia.

Discussion of the ethics and practicality of violence was a no-go area, but I wrote a long editorial about it and got away unscathed. That was because I wrote about South Africa but did not mention South Africa; instead, the editorial was about the Somoza regime in Nicaragua which was in the international spotlight. "What must people do when democratic change is impossible?" was the theme of the leader. "At what stage, if ever, is violent attack on authority legitimate? What must the world's response be?" Nicaragua was "the personification of the authoritarian state, with parallels ready to hand elsewhere too: the majority of the people suffer intense poverty as land and wealth are concentrated in a few hands… There is a veneer of democracy with the existence of a parliament and an opposition… The rulers have traditionally enjoyed American support because, distasteful as is their rule, they have been viewed as providing a bulwark against Communism…"

During the next few days I heard there was muttering in Nationalist circles about the leader as they knew exactly what we had done but they could not do anything about it. We should probably have written more leaders like this, if only for the fun of getting away with otherwise unpublishable thoughts.

Someone one day is going to write an opera about Winnie and Nelson Mandela. The story line covers just about every aspect of human behavior and misbehavior, from love, steadfastness, and courage to greed, dishonor, and murder, ending with tragedy. Everyone forgets that Nelson Mandela, or Madiba as he is known by his tribal clan name, probably the world's most admired man, received little public attention both in South Africa and abroad during the late 1960s and well into the 1970s. But Winnie never gave up, and went on fighting to keep her husband's name alive. She did so with a personal passion, standing up to the Security Police to show her contempt for them and the system they enforced. In return she earned their total enmity. For several decades she was probably, for them, the single most hated person in South Africa.

For some thirty years the Security Police flung everything at Winnie they could. The least of it was the usual banning orders, the first one issued in 1962. She was also banished to Brandfort far from her home, was raided often, was repeatedly detained, and was kept in solitary confinement without trial. She was frequently charged in court on minor charges and even under the Terrorism Act. One prosecution was for assaulting a policeman; she knocked him down, inflicting serious injury , when he went into her bedroom. Only once were the police able to secure a conviction on a minor charge about a banning order. Employers were warned by the Security Police not to let her work. Several of her friends who visited her in banishment were jailed for refusing to disclose what they had talked about.

After Winnie was banished to Brandfort, Anne and I were among the friends who occasionally made the four-hour drive from Johannesburg to visit her. She was in a black township less than a mile from a "white" village, in a two-room house, even smaller than the usual Soweto house. Not much more than a bed could fit into her bedroom, but tucked away in the only available corner stood a small, four-shelf bookcase. Winnie said that it was the "library" she had started for township people. I came close to tears when I first saw it because of its message of determination: pieces of paper, each with a letter of the alphabet, were pinned to the shelves to separate the authors. The house was semidetached, with the other half occupied by a municipal policeman. A Security policeman lived in the house next door. She was watched every moment and she knew it.

The township ghetto was a desolate, dusty place. Winnie planted a lawn, flowers, and shrubs on her small piece of ground. Gradually her example spread, and within months green could be seen all around the township. She had to seek permission to visit Madiba in prison in Cape Town, and was not allowed to travel by road or rail, but only by air, which was a lot more expensive. She had to report to the police when she departed and when she returned. Winnie did not have a telephone, but each weekday she went to the "white" village and used the two public phone boxes outside the post office. This, she said, was her "office," and at eleven A.M. and again at four P.M., she made and received calls.

The pressures and isolation began to affect Winnie. It was upsetting to see it happening, and to hear her say, "What am I going to do with this old man when he comes out of jail? I'm the leader, not him."

Meanwhile I was writing occasional letters to Mandela, and regularly having my requests to see him turned down. In April 1984 I was on my annual visit to parliament and asked the minister of justice, Kobie Coetzee, about it.

"We are not allowing any journalists to visit him," he replied.

"I don't want to see him as a journalist but as a friend. I don't want to write about it," I said.

Later that day, the commissioner of prisons asked me to see him and we had a repeat of my morning conversation: I wanted a visit as a friend. That's as far as it went, until four months later, when Winnie returned from a visit and sent a message that I was being granted a visit and should grab it before they changed their minds. The next week I flew to Cape Town.

As I prepared for my visit with Madiba, I made up my mind not to be intimidated. I would say whatever I wanted, and it would be up to the prison authorities to censor me. My resolve lasted for less than a dozen steps into the cold concrete and brick of the prison because I realized that this was a guinea-pig visit. The authorities were waiting to see how it went, and as I later learned, it was the first visit allowed to a nonfamily person for many years. The warder explained to me that Mr. Mandela knew what he could not talk about; politics was not allowed.

I sat in a large interview room. On the other side of a thick pane of glass Madiba walked in and raised his arms high as he called out "hello," his voice disembodied through the amplifier. There stood the tall, erect man with wiry gray-white hair whose face had not been seen in public for two decades. It was one of those moments in life when you know that you are having an extraordinary and unforgettable experience and yet cannot quite believe that it is actually happening. Dressed in a neat green tunic and a white T-shirt, Madiba was sixty-six, and he was thinner and more athletic-looking than I remembered. He had a written list of what he wanted to discuss. Madiba wanted arrangements made for his daughter, Zinzi, to study in Cape Town, and for Makaziwe, the daughter from his first marriage, to obtain a scholarship for study in the United States. He asked about his friends from university days.

Madiba said he was studying again. He shared a cell with five other political leaders, and got up at three A.M. each day to run around the cell for an hour. (I wondered how his cellmates felt about this. Years later, one of them told me that they could not stand it, and Madiba had yielded to their pleas to stop running around the cell in the middle of the night). He then did an hour of push-ups, aerobics, and weightlifting. The food was good, but he took care with his diet: he had kept the chicken from the previous night's dinner and made it into a sandwich for breakfast that morning. They were getting a variety of newspapers, both local and foreign, and kept up to date with what was happening in the world. But they could not freely get books. These had to be sent via the prison authorities, who decided about them.

The forty minutes passed quickly and we stood up, said goodbye, and waved to each other. I gave the ANC's "thumb-up" salute and he did the same.

Mandela was by this point receiving world attention, and it was frustrating not to be able to write about my visit. Even a description of what he looked like and a report about his mental alertness and knowledge of the world would have been sensational. To add to my misery, a few months later a British reporter and European Parliament member, Lord Bethnell, was granted access to Madiba. His report was offered to the *Rand Daily Mail* for publication for the hefty fee, as I recall it, of £12,000. It was too expensive for us. Other newspaper interviews with Mandela followed swiftly.

I knew, chiefly from Winnie, that several approaches had been made to Madiba for his release, notably by his nephew, Paramount Chief Kaiser Matanzima, the head of the Transkei tribal "homeland." If he agreed to live in Transkei, he would be freed immediately. Madiba had turned it down. Johan Coetzee, then the commissioner of police, also visited him, and my information revealed that another offer of release had been made. But Coetzee denied it when I sent him a telex. "I visited Mr. Mandela after he had written me a personal letter in which he raised certain matters," he said.

In February 1985, State President P. W. Botha made a public offer to release Madiba if he would renounce violence. Madiba rejected it. Only free men could negotiate, he said, and prisoners could not enter into contracts. His youngest daughter, Zinzi, read his reply to a mass rally in Soweto. Our reaction at the *Mail* was that, as Madiba was banned, nothing he said could be quoted, and that Zinzi had broken the law. Out of curiosity I checked the date of his banning orders in our card index file. His name was not there. We checked and checked again, only to realize that his last bannings had expired some time in the 1960s, and had not been reimposed. It is of course likely that had we quoted Madiba in those later years, the government would have immediately "listed" him as a member of a banned organization, thus barring any further publication. We would also have had to avoid being charged with spreading the views of the banned ANC. But none of this relieved the great sense of embarrassment at the *Mail* that evening when we realized that, all these years we had been obeying a banning that did not exist.

The next time I saw Madiba in prison was in January 1986. This time the government required me to give a written promise that the meeting would not be for publication, which was even more frustrating, as a fever of interest was building up about him because of the deepening crisis in the country. Black resistance was reaching new heights, the government was constricting the press even more, and the previous August had seen a plunge in the economy when U.S. banks refused to roll over South Africa's loans.

Anne was with me this time, and we had a contact visit so we were able to shake hands when we met and sat in comfortable chairs in a small office with a prison colonel behind the desk taking notes. Madiba had arranged for a double visit—nearly an hour and a half—and after a while he asked the colonel how much time had elapsed. The colonel blushed and said he did not know because he did not have a watch. So, using my wristwatch, we agreed on the time, and I snatched an extra ten minutes in the process. My watch was digital and had a built-in miniature calculator, neither of which Madiba had ever seen, and they filled him with wonder. (I tried later to send him a watch and calculator, but prison headquarters would not allow it: "Why does he need a calculator in jail?" said an official, and was not impressed by my reply that it would help to prepare him for his release.) Madiba said that he had recently been taken on a drive around the prison grounds and had walked on grass for the first time since being taken to Robben Island in 1964. When he got into the car, he did not know how to open the door because the handles were recessed, which wasn't the way car door handles were the last time he had used them. He had had a prostate operation a few months earlier and was now on his own, seeing the other politicals when he wanted to. He told us about being under guard in a hospital room after the operation when Winnie came to see him: "The sun came into the room," he said.

He raised the issue of his release from prison. Madiba believed that it could be negotiated. He understood the government's problems in regard to him, but he believed his release would work to defuse the crisis in the country. He stressed his belief in nonviolence and reminded me that I knew that he was not a man of violence. He also indicated, if I understood him correctly, that he was not insistent about the simultaneous release of all political prisoners and that even this could be part of a negotiated package.

This was dynamite. When the interview ended, we had a minute or two standing close together in the reception area with no one else in earshot, and I softly asked him if he wanted me to convey these views to the government. Yes, he said.

Back in Johannesburg I phoned F. W. de Klerk, who was among the cabinet ministers I had gotten to know in my visits to parliament. He was minister of national education, so he was not involved with Mandela. But he was the head of the National Party in the Transvaal, and although his reputation at that stage was as a conservative, I felt he would be a reliable channel to the appropriate minister. I conveyed Madiba's message and he thanked me. Ten minutes later the phone rang. It was Justice Minister Coetzee and he said de Klerk had phoned him. "Why did you phone F. W.?" he complained. "You should have phoned me. I'm the minister of justice and I'm the one who deals with Mandela." With a laugh he went on, "You don't know that I have been having secret meetings with him for the last year." (In fact they began in November 1994.) The message from Mandela was important, he said, and he would pursue it. That's how I first learned about the discussions behind the scenes; it took another four years before Mandela was actually released.

While those events unfolded, Winnie's life grew messier. The imperiousness and self-confidence that had been part of her strength had by now become a weakness. She defied the government by leaving Brandfort and returning to the tiny Mandela house in Soweto, where she set off scandal by launching construction of a palatial house that local people dubbed "Winnie's Palace." She was right to fear for her safety—she had enough experience of official animosity—and she countered it by surrounding herself with young men in the Mandela United Football Club. But the bodyguards preyed on local residents and were soon hated. The description "Mother of the Nation" that the press had bestowed on her became, in graffiti on Soweto walls, "Mugger of the Nation." Then came the killing of Seipei "Stompie" Moeketsi, a teenage member of the club, and Winnie's ultimate trial and conviction. She is a South African tragedy, a victim of apartheid who brought herself down, doing to herself what the government had never been able to do.

I never thought that Madiba would totally break with her. I did not think that he would be able to bring himself to do it. She had been his emotional lifeline for all his twenty-seven years in jail, sustaining him and fighting for him. I always had in my mind his poignant statement of love: "The sun came into the room." Even while in jail he must have had an idea about the sleazy side of her life, but he turned away anyone who tried to bring stories about her, and never once during her visits did he raise his voice in anger against her. But after his release Winnie's financial extravagances grew so extreme, her love affairs so indiscreet and provocative, and her moves to set herself up as a populist leader so dangerous, that he finally did separate from her and insisted on divorce in 1996.

The *Mail* was suffering profoundly. We were being starved of resources. Saan's management was either openly against us or neglecting us outright.

The managerial neglect was pervasive, as Pat Sidley found out when she carried out a phone survey in 1984 for the SASJ of a dozen large advertising agencies in Johannesburg. "We asked them how the *Mail* was being sold and if they believed the *Mail* was being adequately sold: eleven out of twelve believed the *Mail* was being inadequately sold and that it was being tagged on to the back of the sale of *Sunday Times* advertising space. The twelfth agency, Lindsay Smithers, just believed the *Mail* was unsalable, left-wing, and nothing could ever be done about it. The overwhelming opinion was that the marketing people of Saan were shafting the *Mail*, not necessarily deliberately but that they were embarrassed about it."

Clive Kinsley and Nigel Twidale of Saan management

Chapter 23

did little to sell advertising for the *Rand Daily Mail*. Circulation was also a mess. A copy editor on the *Sunday Times* was appointed circulation manager for the company, but he was not particularly knowledgeable about the market, and his personal life happened to be in ruins. He reported to Twidale, who did not seem to recognize that the circulation department was falling apart.

Kinsley made it worse with two business decisions emanating from his personal resentment of the Argus Company, and his counterpart there, Hal Miller. First, he removed Saan's rural circulation from the Argus-controlled Allied Distribution Company, and set up Saan's own organization, claiming it would save money. Though Allied's service was poor, the breakaway proved a disaster, damaging sales and losing some fifteen million rand in the first year, and was subsequently abandoned. His second action came about from a panicky reaction to the Argus muscling into the Saturday-morning market. Kinsley dropped the *Mail*'s cover price from twenty-five cents to ten cents on Saturdays, which might not have been a bad strategy except that it was so poorly prepared for that it created mass confusion. Along the way, too, were sundry failed and money-chewing ventures into trade journals and book publishing.

As it was, the *Mail* had to contend with the government-funded *Citizen*. Perskor still owned the newspaper. It carried little advertising, with sales half of the *Mail*'s, yet it ran up to 70 percent more news space than we did. While on holiday at a resort south of Durban I was disturbed to find that only the *Citizen* was on sale. I phoned one of our circulation people in Johannesburg and he said that the *Citizen* chartered a plane that hopped its way down the Natal south coast each day dropping off newspapers at each resort. The paper was selling for twenty-five cents, but the cost of getting it there was at least four times that per copy. The *Mail* could do the same if we had the money, but of course, we didn't.

Perskor was not doing too well as a business, and it seemed that we could look forward to the day when the *Citizen* would be too heavy a burden, but that day never came. My guess was that the government was still pumping in money, but in a more roundabout way.

As the *Mail*'s business situation crumbled, Kinsley became a remote figure in the company in the early 1980s. Whether Kinsley was disintegrating as a person or was particularly driven by wanting to get rid of the *Mail* or both was never clear. Nearly a decade later, in an interview, he assured me that he had not been "agin the *Mail*." However, I had learned by then that he had been at the heart of secret maneuverings intended to kill off the *Mail*.

The key to this was that Kinsley commissioned the *Financial Times* in London "to advise on the future direction of the *Rand Daily Mail*." Gibson knew about it on a confidential basis, and believed Saan was looking at possible options. Kinsley encouraged him to make a quick trip to London to discuss it with the *Financial Times*. The commissioning of the *Financial Times* leaked out, and Gibson tried to use this to pressurize Kinsley to accept that the *Mail* should survive in lieu of being replaced by a financial daily. Kinsley addressed a meeting of anxious and angry editorial staff in March 1983, telling them that the newspaper's increasing losses were causing such concern that Saan's board had hired research teams to spend three months exploring ways of changing the

Mail in order to reduce the losses. He assured the staff that the board was not considering closing the *Mail* and that Saan would continue to publish a morning daily English-language opposition-supporting newspaper. Despite his emphatic words, a Saan journalists' union meeting the following day started working on a redundancy agreement.

Without knowing it at the time, journalists were right to fear the worst, because the trail dated back several months. Both Kinsley and the Saan board had proposed to transform the *Mail* into a financial daily, with staff reduced to less than half and a circulation target of one-third what it was. The board also agreed to hire the *Financial Times* to carry out a study. Darryl Phillips, the majority shareholder in a leading advertising agency in Johannesburg, was consulted.

"Kinsley and Twidale came in and swore me to secrecy and told me that a decision had been made by the [Saan] board to close the *Rand Daily Mail* and that they wanted to convert it into a financial newspaper," says Phillips. "Could I help them position it, how it should be done, and all this." He told them that this was beyond his competence but that he would make inquiries in London. Through his contacts he set up a meeting with a team of senior management and editorial staff at the *Financial Times*, "and I explained my background and the purpose of my mission and I asked them if they would be prepared to undertake a consultancy to help launch a financial daily in South Africa. They made it very, very clear that on the condition that the decision had been taken formally and firmly to close the *Rand Daily Mail*, they had no problem with it, but that they couldn't be party to any decision to close the *Rand Daily Mail*. I told them I had been assured that this was the case." Phillips returned to South Africa and reported to Kinsley, who was "very excited." Phillips arranged for the two of them to meet *Financial Times* executives, who agreed to draft a research proposal.

When the *Financial Times*' involvement eventually leaked out, "that put me, I felt, in a terrible position," says Phillips. "I wrote a stinking letter to Clive and I wrote a letter of apology to the *Financial Times* saying that I had been misled by Clive and that I therefore wished to dissociate myself from any of this, and I dropped out of the picture." But not for long, because when the *Financial Times* sent a research team to Johannesburg, Phillips helped it with arrangements. With soured relations with Kinsley, Phillips said it took about four months to recover from

Saan the cost of his first-class air ticket, and he was paid only after threatening to go public with what had been going on.

Twidale, Kinsely, and Phillips were the people determining the *Mail's* fate. Editorial had no idea that Kinsley was in cahoots with Phillips in trying to close the *Mail*.

Dennis Kiley, the managing editor of syndication at the *Financial Times*, (he was from Johannesburg, and had worked at the *Golden City Post* in the early 1960s), met Kinsley and Phillips, who conveyed that "they felt the *Rand Daily Mail* was in dire straits and they wanted us to come and study it and they wanted us to confirm their view that it could not continue in its present form because its demographics were out of kilter—advertisers were white and readers were black. They thought the *Mail* should be closed down to be replaced immediately by a business daily. What they wanted from us was firstly to confirm that this was the right strategy, and secondly to show them how to do it—to send a whole team from the *Financial Times* to show them how to set up a successful daily business newspaper."

Kiley said he and his colleagues quickly agreed among themselves about potential damage to the *Financial Times* because "the public upshot was likely to be headlines to the general effect: '*FT* Advises Closure of *RDM*,' and the longer subhead would read: 'Capitalist Organ Shuts Down Last Surviving Bastion of Liberalism in South Africa.' That would have been disastrous publicity for the *FT*. We also saw through what we believed was their real agenda, which was to make use of the hefty reputation of the *Financial Times* to do their dirty work for them, to sanitize their intentions by enabling them to say we've had the great *Financial Times* in here and they agree that we have to close the *Rand Daily Mail*. So the *FT* would have taken worldwide political flak. The *Rand Daily Mail* had a big reputation in the world."

What that could mean became apparent when the widely read British satirical magazine *Private Eye* heard what was afoot from Pat Sidley, commenting: "The *Financial Times* looks set to combine with the South African government to abolish the last vestiges of the free press in that country. . . As well as being the only paper that raises a whimper of dissent, the *RDM* also happens to have a very large readership (sixty to seventy percent) among educated blacks. If the paper were suddenly to devote its space to the discussion of stocks and shares, most of this readership would desert it."

Kiley and his colleagues decided to proceed with caution, and "try and get rid of them by setting a high fee, which we hoped would frighten them off." Kiley roughly estimated how many staff members would be needed, added an "extremely generous" markup, and told Kinsley and Phillips it would not cost less than £250,000, a colossal amount to money. "They looked me straight in the eye and said okay, that sounds reasonable, go ahead." (The Saan board seemingly endorsed this).

Kiley decided to send a small team—the night editor and a business representative—for a preliminary investigation, excluding the South Africans at the *Financial Times* to avoid their being embroiled in local politics. They went for a week, returning with a damning report. Apart from the political publicity dangers, they said, there was no possibility whatsoever of proceeding with a project of this nature with Saan because the company's management, in their professional view, could "not be trusted with running a small whelk store." According to Kiley, Jones was scathing about Phillips, who had revealed his deeper purpose: Phillips "had no hesitation in telling Jones, after only a few days' acquaintance, that as soon as he could get control of the group, his first move would be to fire Kinsley."

Some overlapping and contrasting assessments were made by other *Financial Times* executives who dealt with Phillips and Kinsley. The deputy manager of the *Financial Times*' syndication department, Raymond Whitaker, was at the initial lunch with them in London and thought Kinsley was "irresolute." Whitaker explained, "he seemed very confused and pulled this way and that. On the one hand he was tired of all the political trouble—pressure from the government—and on the other hand he was much more aware of the political fallout there would be from closing down the *Mail*. I think he was torn between fear of the consequences of either course." Phillips, however, "kept urging him to close it down. He was very blunt in his language. The gist of Phillips's attitude was that the *Mail* was a money-loser and a political embarrassment to Saan: all it did was upset the government."

Jones did not witness Kinsley's indecisiveness in his home in Johannesburg. Instead he said, "he was a bully, he was very tough and a smart operator inside organizations. It was very much his determination to close the *Rand Daily Mail*. He had written it off." Within two days Jones concluded that there was a hidden agenda. "I began to realize that we were being used," and halfway through the week, Jones phoned Joe Rogaly at the *Financial Times* to reveal his concern. Rogaly, once a *Mail* reporter in the 1950s, was a chief executive of the *Financial Times*' Business Enterprises Division. He wanted to end the contract forthwith but agreed that it should be completed, with a report written in return for their fee. The thirty six-page report began emphatically:

1. The poor performance of the *RDM* is largely a consequence of the group's inappropriate management structure and inconsistent departmental objectives.

2. There is little prospect of finding a solution to the *RDM's* problems without extensive management changes.

3. The constraints on the quality, availability, and recruitment of editorial talent are so severe that it will prove impractical to relaunch the *RDM* on the basis of radically changed editorial quality.

4. The newspaper has considerable strengths, which appear not to have been properly researched or exploited.

5. A feasibility study of business daily option should not be undertaken until other work has been completed.

Understandably these words cheered us in editorial. As I later learned, Kinsley had initially told the *Financial Times* executives that the report should be handed only to him, but suspicious that it might go no farther, they insisted on sending a copy to every Saan board member. A copy also ended up with editorial, and several of us made copies to distribute them far and wide in Johannesburg. A summary appeared in the *Journalist*.

The report, however, contained worrying facts about the *Mail's* viability. In 1982 surveys showed that while estimated total readership dropped to 739,000 from the high point of 933,000 in 1977, white readership was down to 28 percent, while black readership was up to 72 percent. The financial loss in 1982 was 7 million rand and was budgeted to rise to 8.2 million rand in the current year. Although the post-tax losses were smaller, the figures were disconcerting for Saan's long-term development. As the report stressed, first get the shop fixed up before exercising possible options.

We waited for swift action to clean up management and to get to grips intelligently and purposefully with the *Mail's* problems. To our astonishment nothing happened. The report sank without a trace. Kinsley told the members of the board that the *Financial Times* had not understood the complexities of the newspaper market in South Africa, and the board left everyone intact. Years later I learned that Leycester Walton rejected the report. He thought that it was poor and offered no new insights. Walton believed that the *Financial Times* team had been got at by the *Mail's* editorial staff.

We had always considered Walton our champion on the board, a liberal voice, on whose support we could count. Unknown to us he had reached the conclusion that the *Mail* could not survive. He did not want to see the *Rand Daily Mail* die, but he did want it to become something different.

Gibson was firing off memos to Kinsley, urging resolution of the *Mail* situation. He warned that staff were feeling dejected, senior journalists were drifting away, the staffing level had dropped, and it was months since he had received any job applications of caliber. He also warned of the corrosive effects of the constant rumor mongering among the newspapers that opposed the *Mail*. They were floating every possible angle, from the *Mail*'s closing down to its becoming a financial newspaper to its becoming a newspaper for blacks. The *Financial Mail* also published "speculation" about the imminent demise of the *Mail*, and this was damaging, coming from a Saan magazine, and obviously fed by sources high up in the building.

Ostensibly the *Financial Mail*'s negative statements derived from the belief that the *Mail*'s losses threatened to kill the company as a whole. Its editor, Stephen Mulholland, openly said this, and it was echoed by his deputy, Nigel Bruce. Yet there was more to it because both were abrasively right-wing and fiercely criticized the *Mail*'s liberalism and condemnation of white rule. I suspected that the *Mail*'s standing, both at home and abroad, drove them into a frenzy.

Amidst the muddle and trauma a proposal emerged from Gibson for a separate business section in the *Rand Daily Mail*, and a second section for the townships, leaving the main body of the newspaper for all readers. Kinsley embraced the idea. For Gibson it was a genuine development to meet the needs of the moment, but it was soon revealed as the means of putting Saan's hidden agenda into effect. An upbeat announcement named Howard Preece, the *Mail*'s financial editor, or editor of the business tabloid. Saan's reputation for bungling was confirmed when the first that Preece learned of it was when he was called in to the boardroom and shown the public statement, which described his enthusiasm for the project. It was to begin after a quick six-week start-up time. Financial journalists were in short supply, and Preece had difficulty hiring extra staff.

Preece overcame the problems, *Business Day* emerged on time, and it looked good. Crucially, management assigned specific representatives to sell advertising space, and the tabloid inserted in the *Mail* was an immediate success, striking proof of the value of dedicated advertising representatives. Even then, though, the lesson was not carried over for the newspaper as a whole.

A few voices in editorial worriedly asked, "Why don't management want to call it *Business Mail* in line with the style of the rest of the paper, like *Sports Mail* and *Inside Mail*? Why are they naming it *Business Day*? Is it because they intend the child to take over from the father and the father to be killed?" These voices were outweighed by the hope that if the child was successful, there would be no call to kill the parent.

Preece believed in the *Rand Daily Mail* and was devoted to it. He thought that *Business Day* had been created to save the *Mail* and he worked hard for it. Looking back, he said it was a "total lie" and "we never had a chance from the beginning."

Gordon Waddell was the growing force behind the scenes. Anglo American Corporation's control of Argus was exercised through Johannesburg Consolidated Investments, and once Waddell was appointed chairman of JCI in 1981, he became Anglo's point man for the press, directly with Argus and indirectly with Saan (through Argus's nearly 40 percent holding in Saan, as well as the Advowson Trust holding of some 20 percent). In 1983 three former *Rand Daily Mail* editors, Gandar, Louw, and Sparks, went to see Waddell to warn him that the newspaper was being starved of money and resources. Waddell said he knew of the problems and that something would be done before the end of the end of the year. By 1984 nothing had been done, and Gandar and Louw went to see him, but were politely brushed off.

Chapter 24

In September 1984, JCI bought the Bailey Trust shares in Saan, the last remnants of Sir Abe Bailey's holdings from early in the century, and was in direct control. For the first time Anglo American was the visible hand in some 90 percent of South Africa's English-language press. And where previously the Oppenheimer family had shrunk from being viewed as the power behind the press, Waddell was open about his hands-on approach. The Anglo American ethos had changed since the retirement of Harry Oppenheimer at the start of 1983 and his replacement as chairman by Gavin Relly.

A statement by Kinsley was put on notice boards in the Saan building. It read that the company was now in "friendly hands," a well-received piece of news. But that feeling was tempered by apprehension. It was believed that Waddell intended to reduce costs by closing down newspapers, ending the competition between Saan and Argus not only in Johannesburg but in Cape Town and Durban. Pat Sidley went to see him and was alarmed by his repeated declaration, "In this office, ma'am, we're concerned about the bottom line." She returned to tell us that she was convinced the *Mail* was going to be closed.

The *Mail*'s claimed losses mounted, reaching fifteen to sixteen million rands in 1984. Crisis became part of everyday existence, as did rumors. Each Saan board meeting was anxiously awaited. The board held emergency meetings, and there was talk about looking at alternative ways to go forward, but which way?

None of it mattered, as it turned out, because the real decision was being made by Waddell in consultation with Anglo American's board. By early 1985, the decision to shut down the *Mail* had already been made, but only a small number of insiders knew of it. Kinsley learned about it in mid January. Waddell was adamant about it, and in retrospect from then on everything was a charade. The Saan board and the journalists continued holding their meetings, and the lobbying went on, but Anglo American had made their decision.

Word of the sixteen-million-rand loss seemed to freeze everyone. Many of our influential friends turned their backs. Max Borkum, who had been a prime mover in staving off Louis Luyt in 1975, and was close to both Anglo American and Oppenheimer, said he could not understand why anyone should think he or his Progfed friends could do anything. Even Helen Suzman turned away from us. The losses were too great, was the refrain. We learned that the Progressive Federal Party leader, Frederik van Zyl Slabbert, had tried to persuade Waddell not to destroy the *Mail*, but was soothed with the promise that whatever replaced it would back the Progfeds.

Kinsley had promised Gibson that he would be consulted before any final decision was made. On March 15th, Gibson was called to a board meeting. He addressed the board for fifteen minutes, stressing that destroying the *Mail* would destroy Saan. Gibson was surprised by the response of the Advowson Trust representative, Charl Celliers, who said, "Some of us, some of the members of the board, argue the opposite, that not to close the *Mail* will destroy the company." It seemed strange to Gibson that the Advowson representative should be more caring about the company than about the *Mail*, but at that point he realized the battle was lost and that he was there as a rubber stamp. He angrily returned to his office. Twenty minutes later, Kinsley asked Gibson to read a statement prepared by the board announcing the closing of the

Mail. It had obviously been written in advance of Gibson's speaking to the board. A daily financial newspaper, *Business Day*, was to replace the *Mail*; the child was to become the father.

When a fuming Gibson told me about the formal decision, I felt relief. It surged through me like a physical thing. At last we knew where we stood. We had been living with uncertainty and strain for so long. But the relief ended quickly as the consequences came flooding back into my mind. Editorial people gathered in the newsroom. "When one has bad news to tell, it is best to tell it quickly," Gibson told them. "The *Mail* will close on April 30, 1985."

A different tone was heard that night from State President P. W. Botha, who offered his happy reaction: "I would say a new South African-ism is taking control over South Africa and the media will have to take notice of this… I am glad to see things developing in this direction." His choice of words was significant: since 1979 Botha had been holding a series of large conferences designed to bring the business community to his side. Many hundreds of English-speaking businessmen were reacting favorably to him, and there was reason for Botha to be pleased with what he saw as "a new South Africanism." From his point of view and that of the businessmen eager to cooperate with him, the *Mail* was totally out of step. A message emanating from the Saan board that reached us was that the *Mail*'s unending criticisms of Botha were impeding cooperation; another message was that Botha had advanced the cause of change in South Africa so far that there was no longer any need for us.

Gibson wanted the *Mail* "to die with dignity" and not get into "sniping arguments." Some of the *Mail* staff, including me, would have preferred more kicking out as we went down, but he would not hear of it. Perhaps he was right; the quality of the newspaper was sustained until the last moment. Instead of an immediate closure, the *Mail* had to keep going for another six weeks so that its replacement could be put into place. It became a matter of pride for the *Mail*'s reporters and copy editors to produce the best possible newspaper day after day.

Letters and messages poured in from the public. Some welcomed our disappearance, but overwhelmingly they were horrified that the *Mail* was closing. The *Mail*'s final issue appeared, as planned, on April 15, 1985. When the newspaper had been put away for the last time, editorial staff brought their spouses to the newsroom for a last drink together. I made an impromptu speech about the great things the newspaper had done for South Africa, and praised Gibson for "giving the

Mail its soul again." Then I went to my office and cleared out my computer files.

An epitaph appeared that morning in the *Sowetan* newspaper written by its news editor, Thami Mazwai:

> From one's high school days the *Mail* had a special place in the hearts of the black community. It was the first paper to regard them as human beings.
>
> It fought for them.
>
> Its blend of inspirational and aggressive writing was talk of the times.
>
> For one to be seen tucking it under his arm was a sign of intellectualism. Whether one could read or not did not matter.
>
> Even reporters from the *Mail* were at some stage regarded as a cut above other reporters. If you announced yourself as from the *World* [newspaper] people would look at your feet.
>
> When from the *Mail* you stood a good chance of getting a free drink and unbounded hospitality. The *Mail* as a flagship of black aspiration had made its mark.

In contrast to the *Mail*, our sister paper, the *Sunday Express*, closed immediately. The chief purpose of the *Express* had been to protect the *Sunday Times* against interlopers, but its fate had been sealed the previous year when the Argus Company destroyed its hold on property advertising by giving discounts of 75 percent, guaranteed for four years. Advertisers grabbed it and ran. When Saan protested about its long history of cooperation with them, a can of worms opened: property salespeople expressed outrage about the poor service Saan had given them for so many years.

The formal rites over the *Mail* came a few months later when the Society of Journalists presented its Pringle Medal for Press Freedom to "the journalists of the *Rand Daily Mail*," and I gave the annual Fairbairn Memorial Address. The medal and address were named after two early nineteenth century defenders of the press in Cape Town. I raised the following issue, which resounds today as much as it did then: "Many questions remain to puzzle us," I said. "Instead of terminating the *Mail*, and instead of allowing the claimed loss to mount up, why wasn't remedial action taken?"

With the *Mail* off the scene, the government announced that a planned new commercial television channel would be given to the newspaper industry. On the morning that this report appeared, three friends phoned me—Nadine Gordimer, Sydney Kentridge, and John Dugard, a professor of law at the University of the Witwatersrand. Each said, "Now we know why the *Mail* was closed. This was the deal." There has never been any direct proof that the *Mail* was closed in collusion with the government, but it's an intriguing story. At that time the country's newspapers were deeply worried about the effects of television advertising on their income, and Afrikaans and English companies submitted a joint application for a stake in the promised new service. I represented the *Mail* at several meetings of editorial executives to discuss the issue. We were told that the most we could hope for was 25 percent, and could count ourselves fortunate if we even got that. The strong contender likely to get the majority share, if not the whole lot, was Satbel, an entertainment group recently bought by a flamboyant hotelier, Sol Kerzner, hoping to use it to get into the new channel. Now the newspaper industry was given 100 percent. The explanation given was that Nasionale Pers, the chief Afrikaner newspaper company, had persuaded P. W. Botha to do it as the means to keep the Afrikaans press groups alive. Botha is said to have agreed and the goodies were shared out, with Nasionale in charge and taking a larger proportion than the other newspaper groups. A company, M-Net, was created to run the new service.

So, was a deal struck between the government and Anglo American? Close the *Mail* and we will give the industry a television channel to safeguard your newspapers? Was this the clinching factor in killing the *Mail?* Waddell says that he has no evidence of it and that in fact he had to persuade the Saan board to keep the investment in M-Net. "The board lost their nerve. I told them we must keep it," he says.

Waddell's denial should silence any conspiracy theory—except for nagging suspicion about the remarkable coincidence in the timing of the *Mail's* closure and the M-Net license decision, and the lingering thought that a deal could have been agreed to at a higher level, without him knowing about it. That could have happened because Waddell was openly derisory about the developing links between business and the government, and this would have excluded him from the wink and a nod that would have been how any deal would have been struck with P. W. Botha.

We were discarded like dirty old socks. The right-wingers were riding high.

My more than twenty-six years of work on the *Mail* counted against me. The only person with a longer history was Ian Reid, a columnist who sported a monocle and who had joined a year before me. He was also tossed out without a parting thank-you. Jill and Ernie Wentzel were so affronted by Saan's behavior that they presented me with a silver picture frame, the sort of gift given to someone upon retirement. My name and the date were engraved on the front. Another, private message was engraved out of sight: "Not even 'Goodbye' from *der Grobbes*" (Yiddish for "the uncouth").

On the other side of the fence, McPherson was fired, but tried to hold on to his post and was allowed to stay on until midyear. Kinsley was fired, too, but his pay was first increased 40 percent so that he could retire in comfort. The new managing director, John King, was a former telephone engineer whom I thought harmless, but he proved me wrong and showed it by denying me use of the Saan library. I was told that it was not open to members of the public. I thought of the uncountable number of words in that library that had been written, edited, and inspired by me. Ernie Wentzel had previously acted, at my request, for both Raymond Louw and for Allister Sparks when they were fired and had improved their financial packages. I asked him to do the same for me, but he said there was nothing to be done and that I should accept whatever they gave me, which was the minimum. Only later did I understand that he had been unable to do much because he was too ill; although then unknown, the cancer from which he died a year later was already deep inside him.

The Advowson Trust was noticeably silent in the closing of the *Mail*. It had been set up in 1975 with Anglo American Corporation money to beat off the attempted Saan takeover by Louis Luyt. The *Mail* was the government's target, so it was only natural to believe that the trust would continue maintaining its protection. The five trustees were "not subject to the direction of anybody or any person." Their role in ensuring that the *Rand Daily Mail* survived was clear enough to me in my meetings from time to time with its chairman, Issy Maisels, an eminent barrister and leader in the Jewish community.

But when the crunch came, the trust played no role at all, because it was not consulted. The trustees were simply told that the *Mail* was being closed, and this was conveyed to them only the night before the board's formal decision. They had last met in November the previous year and did not meet again until more than five weeks after the closure decision had been announced.

Interestingly enough, what had started as a political rescue operation proved to be an investment of surpassing profit. Buying into Saan in the name of the Advowson Trust in 1975 had cost 1,616,924 rand. By 1982 the market value of the shareholding had risen to more than 5 million rand, the next year it was more than 6.5 million rand and it reached 9.7 million rand in 1984. The dividends were also healthy: 735,000 rand in 1982, more than 1.1 million rand in 1983, and 755,000 rand in 1984. Only during the year the Mail closed did the shares' market value drop to 5.5 million rand, with dividends down to 99,000 rand.

An even more glittering bonanza was eventually reaped. The later recovery of the company, the dazzling effect of the M-Net holding on its share price, the splitting of the company's shares, and a series of share swaps resulted in the original 1,616,924 rand reaching a market value of 129,290,860 rand by 1991. At that stage, Anglo American received shares valued at 112,288,368 rand. The original investment had increased nearly eighty times in the space of sixteen years.

Those responsible for closing the paper sought to put a spin on it. A month after the closure, Relly kept up the story about the *Mail*'s losses when he spoke at a banquet for the Businessman of the Year event, which ironically, had been started by the *Mail* and taken over by its replacement newspaper. "I think we have to go along with the judgment of the market in its broadest sense," he said. "The demise of the *Mail* was a market judgment, however regrettable, and had nothing to do with the quality of its journalism or the values for which the paper stood."

Four years later Oppenheimer offered another public explanation:

Personally I admired the *Rand Daily Mail* and felt close sympathy for the views it expressed. Nevertheless, it now seems to me that by addressing itself to too distant a goal and by attacking apartheid almost exclusively on moral grounds, while laying little emphasis on the damaging effects of apartheid on the economy, it not only gave offense to conservative whites but tended to open up a gap between leaders of black opinion and the businessmen who, partly on moral grounds but also for strong reasons of self-interest, should have been their natural allies. This was and unfortunately still remains a grave misfortune for South Africa.

I was able to ask Oppenheimer about this during an interview on October 28, 1996, coincidentally the day that he was celebrating his eighty-eighth birthday. His speech had puzzled those on the *Mail* who had given so much attention on the news pages, the business pages, and in leaders to the effects of apartheid on the economy, I told him. Could he explain what he had meant? Oppenheimer replied, "I must say to you that when you read that [his statement] now I am inclined to agree with you. I don't know quite why I said that at the time." As far as he knew, the *Mail* was closed "because it was making very big losses"; it was a "business decision" taken by JCI, and Anglo American's role "took the form more of concurring with what had been decided at JCI".

Speaking of Anglo American Corporation's involvement with the press, Oppenheimer said, "We knew nothing about newspapers and didn't want to. That was the trouble. I think, looking back, we were foolish because we either at all costs should have got out, or we should have accepted our responsibility. We did neither of these things."

Waddell, meanwhile, has had second thoughts. Two years after the closing, he left South Africa to return to Britain. *Leadership* magazine interviewed him, saying to him, "There will always be a black mark on your career. You will be seen, in the nature of history, as one of those who participated in the decision to close the *Rand Daily Mail*."

He replied, "It is a matter of the greatest possible regret. I say with conviction that it was unnecessary... I think that the problem with Saan was always seen as the style of the editors. I don't think the problem lay there at all. The problem lay with the management of the business as opposed to the editorial side. To the extent that I failed to carry that point of view, then I must have been guilty."

Waddell took that even farther in a later interview with me. He had never had problems with the *Mail*'s editorial stand, and had supported it, but "I was speaking for a very small minority," he said. The newspaper was not popular inside the top echelons of Anglo American: "They took great offense to the editorial line of the *Rand Daily Mail*... 'We can't stand it,' they said. 'Why should we support sixteen million rand of losses with something with which we don't agree.'"

Saan's management had been "appalling," said Waddell, but he could not do anything about it until he had control of the company, nor could he do anything about the *Financial Times*' recommendations for management changes. He argued within Anglo American for action. The Oppenheimer attitude had reigned—not to be seen to be in control of the English-language press. Only when JCI acquired the Bailey Trust shares in September 1984 did he gain control and move in on Saan. Everyone on the Anglo American board was consulted about closing the *Mail*. No decision like that could be taken without consulting them, including the retired Oppenheimer.

Why, when Waddell finally had the power to act, did he close the *Mail*? It was "dead," he said, and its losses were "putting the whole of the English-language press in jeopardy."

He wasn't convincing, if only because during the same month of the *Mail* closing, Anglo American was engaged in a fierce battle with the National Union of Mineworkers. The several hundred thousand black workers on the gold mines had always been an exploited group but were now joining this union, which was led by Cyril Ramaphosa (who later became the ANC's secretary-general and co-chairman of the assembly that wrote South Africa's democratic constitution). Anglo American had welcomed the emergence of the union, but later seemed to have grown nervous about its power. Labor trouble at the company's Vaal Reefs mine went on for some seven weeks in 1985 and culminated in exceptionally tough action in a showdown with the union: fourteen thousand workers were summarily sacked. An Anglo American spokesman said that the cost of the dispute had been about 25 million rand, far exceeding the *Mail*'s reputed loss.

There was another factor. It is never unusual for a flagship newspaper to lose money and still receive support from other divisions in a corporation. The year before the *Mail* was closed, the *Guardian* in London lost money but was kept alive through its parent company's evening newspaper, a motor magazine, and free newspapers published in Manchester. Since then the *Guardian* has in some years lost money and been subsidized. The *Times* in London lost colossal amounts of money in the 1960s, but its owner, Lord Thomson, believed in its existence and drew on his private funds to support it. Since then its losses under the ownership of Rupert Murdoch have run into tens of millions of pounds. At the end of December 1996 the *Independent* in London estimated that the *Times*, engaged in a circulation war, had lost £80 million that year. Murdoch has used profits from his tabloid newspaper, the *Sun*, to carry other parts of his media empire.

In the same way there was no reason why, in South Africa, Saan's *Sunday Times* should not have carried the *Mail* until the political and economic tide turned.

Gordon Waddell's "bottom line" machismo provided the kick-start. Ultimately, however, support for the *Rand Daily Mail* ceased because the will did not exist. Anglo American Corporation board members, the Saan board, management, and its right-wing editors were affronted by the fuss created by the *Mail* in its aggressive attacks on racial discrimination. They rejected its belief in a nonracial South Africa, they were seduced by P. W. Botha's call for whites to stand together, and they were uncaring about the hope the newspaper represented for the majority of South Africans, who were black.

A final insight comes from two men, Terry Moolman and Noel Coburn, who pioneered the freesheet market in South Africa and went on to build a newspaper empire. In 1983, they met Waddell and offered to buy Saan. Waddell was not yet directly linked with Saan and had no authority from Anglo American's headquarters to deal with the press but they went on meeting. He turned down their offer but they watched as the company went on the skids.

"The *Mail* was a victim of several factors," they say. "You had a profitable company in Saan and then you had this crazy management which changed it through the distribution system and by going into an advertising rate war with the Argus Company. Straightaway the profitability went overboard. Television was also in full swing and was hurting every newspaper; it was a difficult market. The losses for the company were mounting and a decision had to be taken for the entire company and you really had to exercise some damage control. The management was deeply hostile to the *Mail* so the *Mail* was fingered as the culprit."

Looking at it from outside, they say that Saan's costs were unfairly loaded on the *Mail*. They blame "a complete absence of high-quality accountants in the business." They estimate that the *Mail* was losing only 4 million to 5 million rand, nowhere near the claimed double digits which persuaded so many that it was a basket-case.

The aftermath of closing the *Rand Daily Mail* was every bit as catastrophic as Waddell and the Saan board had been warned it would be. Saan's bank overdraft zoomed to 44 million rand within less than two months. JCI bought the Saan building, the presses were sold and shipped abroad, and agreement was reached with Argus for joint printing and distribution. Blows rained down on editorial departments in

Port Elizabeth, Durban, and Cape Town, with drastic cuts to numbers and resources. In Cape Town and Durban the Saan morning newspapers were made subservient to the Argus afternoons. Van Zyl Slabbert was sold short because *Business Day* did not help the Progfeds. It could not have done so even if it wanted to because for the next few years it was a miserable product. The Saan name was so discredited that the company was renamed Times Media Limited. In this guise it went into profit, and that was hailed as a great thing. It even went on to publish a local version of *Playboy* magazine, unsuccessfully. The few voices that complained about the dire effects on the quality of journalism and the disservice done to South Africa were ignored. Editors and columnists in Saan's major publications who now held sway were mostly ignorant about black thinking, and stoked up white fears and resistance. The *Citizen*, with its newly rising circulation, gave vent to the same sort of outlook, albeit in cruder form. The cumulative effects in influencing the outlook of whites were incalculable in delaying the coming of political change.

Getting news to Saan's newspapers in the coastal cities largely collapsed, leaving readers there ignorant about what was happening in the heart of the country. The end of the pacesetting *Mail* led to a drastic falloff in the pursuit of news. South Africans knew less and less. Yet more information than ever before was needed because the Nationalists entered what was to be the final phase of their defense of white rule, and their enforcement of emergency decrees to suppress information grew deadlier.

In the first year following the closing, an official of the Society of Journalists estimated that 120 of the organization's 750 members emigrated. Among many of those whom I knew, a prime reason for leaving was sheer disgust with what Anglo American and Saan/Times Media had done to the press. The mass departure was a staggering loss for the country and severely affected the standard of journalism. It was all the more serious because it went together with the government's repression. Others simply quit newspapers altogether.

The *Mail* as an interracial bridge was gone, as was its assault on apartheid and its challenge to the Afrikaner Nationalists. So was its upholding of basic values of decency and the rule of law and hope for the future. No other newspaper could match what it had been and how it was viewed by most South Africans. Had the *Mail* still existed, might the next few years have been less bloody and painful for South Africa? Might the road to eventual democracy have been less difficult? Might the *Mail* have played a unique role, too, in postapartheid South Africa, as a supportive but critical voice in the transition? It might have been none of this, or all of it.

In July 1999, I learned about a hoard of secret files preserved from the apartheid era. My file, No. 2/3/2/1457, was among them, classified under "Internal Security: Control of Persons" in the "Directorate of Security Legislation."

The file exists because of a mistake. Early in the 1990s, as the end of apartheid rule loomed, the three government security agencies—the Security Police, National Intelligence Service, and Military Intelligence—systematically destroyed their thousands of dossiers. But they forgot that there was another set of files, kept by the Minister of Justice and containing material referred to him by the security agencies. In 1995, about a year after the beginning of democratic government, someone woke up to the existence of these files and an attempt was made to get them. But the then Minister of Justice, Dullah Omar, ordered that the files be kept

Epilogue

and in due course they landed up in the National Archives in Pretoria.

Reading my file, I discovered that I had twice been a candidate for banning orders, in 1965 and 1978. Had they been imposed, my life would have been fundamentally different: I would have been barred from writing and working as a journalist, attending meetings with more than one person, or going outside Johannesburg without permission.

Both times I had been the subject of a secret investigation, a secret assessment, and a secret judgment. But I was not banned. The first time, I was facing trial after my Prisons reports and the Minister of Justice made a handwritten note that the file should be referred to him when the trial was over; the trial ended only four years later and it seems that the note was forgotten. The second time, the then Minister of Justice, Jimmy Kruger, wanted banning orders imposed but the police recommended against it because of the "propaganda material it will give our enemies."

According to the police, I was "one of the strongest and most effective critics of the South African government," adding, however, that there was no information that I was engaged in "unlawful or subversive activities." The file also contained a list of "leftwing" meetings and social parties which I was said to have attended—and which provides a chilling insight into the incompetence of authoritarian rule and reliance on informers. For I was not at those social parties, and my attendance at the meetings was in my capacity as a newspaper reporter.

The file is marked "Part 1" and ends on April 26, 1978. I could not find later records.

White minority rule ended after 342 years when the first nonracial and democratic elections were held in April 1994. The African National Congress won with 62.6 percent of the national vote. Nelson Mandela was chosen as president, confirming the worldwide view of him as an icon, who more than anyone else in the twentieth century represented the struggle for freedom and reconciliation with enemies.

A mere nine years earlier, when the *Rand Daily Mail* was closed, it had all seemed an impossible dream. At that time, Afrikaner Nationalists were so securely in power, and so determined to remain there, that their collapse within the foreseeable future was simply not conceivable.

No single pressure brought about the end. Taken together, it was the ruinous price of apartheid. A combination of factors, not necessarily in order of significance, ground down the economy and eroded morale because whites were treated as international pariahs: boycotts of South African goods and disinvestment by multinational corporations; expulsion from world sports, from the Olympic Games to the rugby and cricket which were the passions of whites; the country's exclusion from a wide range of international organizations; the costly war in Angola on the northern border of South-West Africa; unceasing and spreading resistance by blacks, both in internal mass action and guerrilla warfare directed from outside; and domestic problems because blacks were consigned to inferior education and there weren't enough whites to provide the skills the country needed. The collapse of the Soviet Union was pivotal: the ANC lost military support and Western nations, especially the

United States and Britain, felt encouraged to turn away from supporting the status quo of white rule.

But the Afrikaner Nationalists did not go easily. Their last years were marked by increasing savagery. The police grew more violent in using gunfire against protesters, and government secret death squads were also let loose. In July 1985, the government imposed a State of Emergency, giving the police and army virtually unlimited power in the major urban centers. During the next eight months, more than 8,000 people were detained without trial, including half the United Democratic Front's national and local leaders. Mass meetings were banned; so were advertisements and T-shirts deemed to be stoking resistance.

The harshness did not stem the resistance. If anything, it had a boomerang effect, fueling popular anger. On June 12, 1986, the State of Emergency was extended to the entire country. Within the next year, 26,000 people were imprisoned without trial; 40 percent were below the age of 18.

Amid the detentions and shootings, the government did its utmost to curtail information. On December 11, 1986, a government decree took restrictions to new levels, prohibiting journalists—print, sound, and television—from being "on the scene, or at a place within sight, of any unrest, restricted gathering, or security action." So the moment any unrest occurred, all journalists, and their helpers such as anyone carrying their camera or sound equipment, had to remove themselves unless they had police permission to be present.

Even more, it became an offense to publish without permission any information about any security actions. Most newspapers were already weak and feeble and radio and television were strictly controlled. South Africans were now denied even elementary information about what was happening in their country, unless sanctioned by the government. But as other governments have discovered at other times, that did not end the resistance because it did not deal with the motivating causes.

Violence also went beyond the government. The mid 1980s saw a power struggle between the UDF and the heirs of Black Consciousness in the Azapo movement, with indications also of murky police involvement: an estimated 260 people died before the UDF triumphed. It was the horrifying period, too, of "necklacing," killing by putting a gas-filled tire around a victim's neck and setting it alight. Aimed at government "collaborators," it also became the means to settle scores and to get rid of personal enemies. Township vigilantes are estimated to have "necklaced" 350 to 625 people during 18 months from early 1985.

President P. W. Botha wavered between tough talk and action and recognizing that an era had ended. Many black areas became ungovernable: rents on government housing went unpaid for years on end, and policemen could enter townships only in groups and heavily armed.

Contacts with Mandela became more frequent: cabinet ministers visited him in prison and he was secretly taken to a meeting with Botha. Mandela's jail conditions changed dramatically. First, he and five other ANC leaders were transferred from Robben Island to Pollsmoor prison on the mainland (which is where I visited him), and later he was installed in his own set of cells, with a warder to care for his needs; then he was transferred to live in style in a prison officer's house at Victor Verster prison in the countryside outside Cape Town, and a stream of leaders of the resistance visited him.

The government see-sawed about Mandela's release. It was frightened that letting him loose on the streets would trigger an uncontrollable mass uprising, and was even more frightened that he might die in prison, setting off an even bigger mass upheaval and leaving a legacy of martyrdom for evermore.

Botha, old and tired, was forced into retirement in 1989 by the National Party. He was succeeded as party leader and president by F. W. de Klerk, leader of the Transvaal, the biggest and most conservative of the provinces. Once in power, de Klerk was anything but conservative: in February 1990, he made the momentous announcement that the bans on the African National Congress, the Pan-Africanist Congress, and the Communist Party were to end and that Mandela was to be freed from jail.

The tumultuous scenes of Mandela's release from 27 years of imprisonment, strolling out of the prison's front gates hand in hand with Winnie, were relayed to the world on television screens and in newspaper photographs and words. Preparations began to write a new constitution to represent all South Africans. The future looked good.

But the suffering was not yet over. As events showed, Afrikaner Nationalist leaders were not ready to abdicate or even share power. It appears that they decided that the African National Congress, now in full view as a legal body, was not as fearsome as they had thought and that there was scope for continuing white control. Destabilization and division swiftly became the aims and were pursued by unleashing violence on a scale previously unknown. At the heart of it was the State Security Council, set up in the early 1980s with members drawn from the cabinet and the security agencies, and a countrywide network of committees on the ground.

In cities, mass murders became commonplace. There were repeated attacks on trains, with commuters axed, bludgeoned, and shot to death. There were attacks on people at bus, train, and cab stations. In August 1990, some 1,000 "political" deaths were recorded; during the next year, 572 people died in violence on the trains. A mysterious "Third Force," of men from the army and police, was said to be behind the carnage.

The tribal "homeland" of KwaZulu became a particular area of battle as Zulus loyal to Chief Gatsha Buthelezi fought for control against Zulus who backed the African National Congress. The violence began less than six months after Mandela's release with an average of 101 deaths a month; within the next three years, the deaths totaled more than 3,600.

Judge Richard Goldstone did extraordinary work during 1992 in digging into the killings and exposing government involvement. Press investigations exposed secret government funding and training of Buthelezi's Inkatha party. The events of this time were later chronicled by the Truth and Reconciliation Commission, headed by Archbishop Desmond Tutu, when it reported in 1998 after a two-year investigation. It heard evidence about the Civil Co-operation Bureau, the innocent-sounding title of the killing and violence-fomenting agency set up inside the army. It also heard details about Vlakplaas farm, the headquarters of the police unit which carried out assassinations.

Even amid the bloodshed, discussions went on about the future. ANC and Communist leaders returned from exile to meet with government leaders. Joe Slovo, the Communist Party general secretary and head of Umkhonto weSizwe, was hated and feared by most whites (his wife, Ruth, was assassinated in Mozambique in 1983 by a South African letter bomb), but he was in the discussions from the start. He later told me of his bemusement at being greeted by a police general at the first ANC-government meeting in 1990: "Mr. Slovo, I have been put in charge of security and I want to assure you that I will, if necessary, lay down my life to protect you."

In December 1991, the Convention for a Democratic South Africa (Codesa) opened with 228 representatives of 19 political parties taking part; Buthelezi, however, stayed away as did extreme right-wing Afrikaners. Nearly two years later, despite agreement on many details, the talks were deadlocked; Slovo broke through by getting the ANC to agree to "sunset clauses" to meet white fears—a guarantee of a coalition to run the country initially, and job security for existing government officials. De Klerk made a monumental contribution by persuading most whites, and especially Afrikaners, to accept a nonracial society. In November 1993, South Africa went ahead to its first democratic elections. Mandela and de Klerk shared that year's Nobel Peace Prize.

I watched the changes from a distance. The closing of the *Rand Daily Mail* left me drained of energy and spirit, filled with disgust about the deceit and blindness of the newspaper's management and owners, and in despair about South Africa. I felt I was unemployable in the climate of the time; the one possibility was to find a job as a correspondent for a foreign newspaper but I did not want to do that if I could not also write for South Africans.

I was also worried about our youngest son, Gideon: he was 12 and within about five years would face conscription into the army. I had nightmare visions of him being sent to Soweto with a gun to face the children of friends. I hoped that Gideon would refuse to serve if he was drafted; but that would mean imprisonment for up to six years and I thought that was an unfair burden to put on a teenager.

When the *Weekly Mail* was started by young journalists made redundant by the closing of the *Rand Daily Mail* and the *Sunday Express* I felt honored that they asked me to propose the toast at their launch party; but I knew that this was a new generation who were picking up the baton and I was required to give only limited help. So, with my family, I went to Britain in January 1986, to become foreign editor in launching *Today*, which was meant to be a new type of newspaper, a serious soul in tabloid dress. It did not succeed and I was relieved to be laid off.

Searching for a cause took me to Panos, a London-based organization devoted to Third World issues. As editorial director I edited books and features about development, the environment, and AIDS, and initiated a book about the effects of apartheid on the environment. Then it was back to newspapers, at the *Independent* in London as chief foreign copy editor and then as a copy editor handling world news; then to Boston, as editor of *The WorldPaper*, an odd and interesting venture in reporting global issues through the eyes of local writers.

I tried to shake off South Africa. But it was not possible, especially when the news from there was so grim. Among my return visits, *Today* sent me there on assignment and old and trusted friends gave me startling information about the scale of government-directed killings. In the hands of my tabloid editors my staid reports were transformed into powerful, colorful presentations. The series drew a Peace Prize from the United Nations Association of Great Britain.

The big, big questions through the end of the 1980s were: when will Nelson Mandela be freed? What role will he play? And how to assess the flow of information alleging that Winnie Mandela was involved in kidnapping and killing? A handful of us, South Africans living in exile in London, became the commentators and interpreters for BBC television and radio, Sky television, and other international agencies. When events in South Africa were really hot, I did six or seven broadcasts a day.

I also returned to South Africa in 1992 for the *Independent* to interview General Hendrik van den Bergh, the former head of BOSS. I went to his farm at Bronkhorstspruit, an hour's drive from Johannesburg, he proudly walked me through his sheds with 100,000 cheeping baby chickens, and agreed to be interviewed. He spoke nonstop for five hours. He would not allow me to use a tape recorder or write a single word. I listened and turned my brain into a filing cabinet, trying to remember as much as I could but finally called a halt when I could absorb no more.

Talking about the huge enmity between him and P. W. Botha, he gave me a glimpse into the struggles behind the scenes among the Nationalist rulers. Military Intelligence had broken into his BOSS offices, he said, and had burgled the safe: they removed documents which Botha believed showed that BOSS was trying to destroy him.

I asked van den Bergh about the political murders which had begun after he was put in charge of security. He knew nothing about them, he insisted. Impossible, I said, you were the most powerful man in the country, the power behind the prime minister—political assassinations could not have happened without your knowledge. His answer was revealing: "It depends how far up the line the reports came," he said. "No reports reached me. I did not know about killings." I did not see van den Bergh again and he died in 1997.

A separate discussion with John Horak, the former journalist/police spy, put van den Bergh's answer into context. After becoming a full-time policeman, Horak sat on a security committee and saw the system at work: the Nationalists created a structure for carrying out killings and arranged for its funding. Decisions about murders or instigating violence were phrased in euphemisms such as "transfer" or "remove from society" (which a Nationalist leader has since claimed merely meant removal to other towns). A cut-off point was built in for reporting back. Thus a killing would be ordered, would be carried out and the report about it would go back up the chain of command, stopping at a predetermined point; that enabled the people at the top to put their hands on their hearts and declare that they had nothing to do with the killing, and knew nothing about it.

Horak quit the police in 1992 and came to see me in London in search of a job and with the suggestion that we write a book about his experiences. He joined the ANC and Patrick Lekota, then in charge of ANC security (and now Minister of Defense), told me he had been invaluable in explaining how the government was running its murder squads. Horak was able to show how the bits and pieces fitted into an overall strategy. The *Independent* published an interview with him.

In the new South Africa, Horak was hired by the National Intelligence Service. He retired in 1996 and went to work for an apostolic church.

In July 1998, Ferial Haffajee of the *Mail&Guardian* (the renamed *Weekly Mail*) phoned me from Johannesburg to say that one of the government witnesses who had testified against Laurence Gandar and me 30 years earlier wanted to come clean. Did I remember Willem Boshoff, she asked. Indeed I did. He was an Afrikaans journalist jailed for fraud who was among those who gave lying evidence against us, claiming that prisoners enjoyed excellent conditions. Boshoff had been so reprehensible a person that his previous employer, the Afrikaans newspaper, *Vaderland*, took the amazing step of giving our lawyers overnight access to its personnel files so that we could search for information to attack him.

Now, all these years later, Boshoff, 58 and destitute, "has apologized for his role in a trial which chalked up a dark age for media freedom," reported Haffajee. She said that Boshoff wanted a new set of dentures and a few hundred rand—but his decision to apologize was apparently spurred by a higher calling because he said: "As my life is coming to an end, I want at least to leave a clean copy behind. I want to tell them I'm very, very sorry… I twisted the truth."

Boshoff said that he had previously been a member of the Afrikaner Nationalist Youth Movement, the Jeugbond. In prison, a friend brought him a personal message from John Vorster who "wanted me to assist the state. He said it was my National Party and Afrikaner duty to testify against the English press." Boshoff said that, after testifying, his five-year sentence was reduced by three years; when released, he was given generous credit facilities after Vorster's aides spoke to his bank manager.

Some months before Boshoff's apology, I had given evidence to the Truth and Reconciliation Commission about the apartheid restrictions on press freedom and the crookery in the Prisons trials; I asked that the convictions of Gandar and me be expunged. Walking off the witness stand, I felt a deep relief: the opportunity to speak publicly from an official platform about the wrongs of the past was a cathartic experience.

I listened as others testified, people who had suffered immeasurably more than I had, from torture, unjust imprisonment, or the murder of family members. There was relief among them, too, but some who testified at the commission's hearings up and down the country were left profoundly dissatisfied because the retribution they wanted was not forthcoming. The Truth Commission worked on the basis that perpetrators could apply for amnesty and this could be granted, freeing them from criminal and civil penalties, if it was believed they had told the full truth. Amnesty could be denied if their crimes were so serious as to demand criminal prosecution. Many victims thought it wrong that most perpetrators of apartheid crimes were able to get away unscathed.

I sympathized with their hurt but thought that the Commission had gone as far as it should; to have pursued perpetrators further would have been to enter into Nuremberg-style punishment, which could have destroyed the reconciliation between blacks and whites for which the ANC strove, and which Mandela exemplified so nobly.

The Truth Commission was also criticized from the right, for allegedly favoring the ANC and furthering divisions instead of fostering reconciliation. This attitude was based on the notion that the ANC had on its side committed atrocities during its freedom struggle, by killing and maiming civilians in bomb attacks and killing ANC members thought to be informers.

The ANC had certainly perpetrated some human rights offenses and leaders and members applied for, and were granted, amnesty. What the right-wing was trying to do was to create a level playing field of morality between the ANC and the apartheid government. That, I thought, was obscene. It was as though the French Resistance in the Second World War was to be condemned for killing Germans.

The Truth Commission did well to reveal and record the terrible past and to enable many people to learn what had happened to their loved ones. It has been healthier to do this than to seek to hide everything under the carpet.

A major failure of the Truth Commission was the refusal of former president P. W. Botha to testify. Living in retirement, but as aggressive as ever, he said he had nothing to answer for. F. W. de Klerk did testify, and then obtained a court interdict to block the Commission from publishing its findings about him. A question mark hangs over de Klerk: he insists that he did not know about the mass murders and the instigation of violence by the police and army, and that he learned of these only at a late stage. Is it really possible that he could have been so ignorant or so incompetent?

The Commission did deliver a searing judgment on Nelson Mandela's former wife, now known as Winnie Madikizela-Mandela. Recalling the nightmare days of the 1980s, it said she was accountable for crimes committed by members of her Mandela United Football Club—"killing, torture, assaults and arson in the community." She "had knowledge and/or participated in the activities of club members" and those who had opposed her and the club were "branded as informers and killed." Despite this, Madikizela-Mandela is a survivor: she remains a heroine to many people who still await the benefits of the post-apartheid era; they feel that she speaks for them. She is a member of parliament, elected to the ANC slate by popular acclaim.

Laurence Gandar was left bereft by the death of his wife, Isobel, in 1989 after 45 years of marriage. A while later he told me that he had contemplated suicide. But he was excited by the birth of his grandson, Owen, and by the collapsing Soviet Union, and decided he wanted to stay alive for at least another two years to see what happened. In fact he went on until November 1998, when he died at the age of 83.

Raymond Louw, his energy seemingly undiminished, has continued all these years to publish the weekly *Southern African Report* newsletter from Johannesburg. He has also been as forceful in arguing for press freedom under the ANC government as he was under the previous regime. Allister Sparks reported the last years of apartheid for major newspapers abroad and wrote highly praised books about that period. After the *Rand Daily Mail* closed, Rex Gibson went to the *Star* as deputy editor and after retirement turned to public relations and writing books.

My two closest friends and soul-mates both died in their prime, when they had so much to give to South Africa. Robert Sobukwe died of cancer in February 1978, aged 53, while under banishment, house arrest, and banning orders in Kimberley. Government harassment grew worse after the cancer had been diagnosed and a lung removed: the Security Police cruelly controlled where he could convalesce and monitored his movements. When he died, he had last been free 18 years before, when he set out on his early-morning walk to offer himself for arrest at Orlando police station on March 21, 1960. He and I had drawn closer over the years and his death devastated me; South Africa lost a towering figure who could have been one of the inspiring leaders on the road to nonracism.

Ernest Wentzel also died of cancer, in Johannesburg in April 1986, aged 52. We had grown up in the same suburb in Cape Town and had known each other since we were knee-high. We went to different schools and became friends as students at the University of Cape Town. In the liberal student tradition of keeping the line of leadership going, I took him on as a protégé and fostered his entry into student politics. He took to it with gusto and his rise was meteoric, gaining election as president of the National Union of South African Students and then going into the Liberal Party. His principles and beliefs kept him there, leavening the dangers with an outrageous sense of humor and a booming laugh. He was, too, a brilliant lawyer who gave unstintingly to those in need.

A story he told about his detention during the State of Emergency in 1960 was to do with the few dozen white political men kept at the Fort. The prison commandant told them that Helen Suzman was being allowed to visit them but warned: "You are not allowed to tell her about your conditions in jail. If you say anything to her I will end the interview immediately." The prisoners lined up and Suzman came into the courtyard. The first prisoner, looking at the commandant, said in a loud voice: "Colonel, can I tell Mrs. Suzman that we are on a hunger strike?" "No, you may not tell her that." The next man in the line said: "Colonel, can I tell Mrs. Suzman that we don't have enough blankets and that we are cold?" "No, you may not tell her that." The next in the line said: "Colonel, can we tell Mrs. Suzman that there are worms in the soup?" "No, you may not tell her that." "Colonel, can we tell Mrs. Suzman that we are not allowed to get newspapers?" "No, you may not tell her that." So it went on down the line, each detainee, straightfaced, conveying details of their conditions to Helen Suzman, who struggled to contain her laughter.

During turbulent periods of my life Ernie was my friend and private adviser. When I was most under attack by the government he and his wife, Jill, were the ones I first consulted about what best to do. When I married for the second time I asked him to be the best man. But my father did not like it because Ernie was not Jewish. It was true that the custom of having a best man was a recent innovation, said my father; he was not part of the Jewish religious ceremonial and did not really stand under the "chupah," the wedding canopy. But it would not look good to have a non-Jew and he asked me not to do it. For the first time I told my father about the role that Ernie had played behind the scenes. His face lit up: "Then he is one of the Righteous Gentiles—Christians who have risked themselves to save Jews. We will be honored to have him in the wedding ceremony."

Ernie proved his value at the wedding reception: I heard that one of the elderly white women working for the caterers was refusing to serve our black friends among the guests and I begged Ernie to sort it out. He returned a few minutes later, giggling. He had charmed the woman by putting his arm around her and whispering: "I don't like it either, but what can we do?"

Kelsey Stuart also died young, of a heart attack in 1981 when he was only 52. That was a heavy loss for the press, but his legal firm, Bell, Dewar and Hall, carried forward his media expertise. It was significant in helping local journalists and foreign correspondents to deal with the tightening coils of government restrictions in the 1980s and early 1990s. Sydney Kentridge emigrated to Britain and became as distinguished a barrister there as in South Africa; he was later knighted by the Queen. Arthur Chaskalson, who had defended Theron, was appointed President of the Constitutional Court when democracy came to South Africa. Judge Cillie died but Percy Yutar has survived, to be forgiven by Mandela for his zealous prosecution of him in the Rivonia trial; many others, however, continue to despise him as a Security Police lickspittle.

Harold Strachan still lives in Durban, and after many years of working on art restoration, has also become a fiction writer. Norma Kitson, in Britain, became involved with a London branch of the anti-apartheid movement and organized a 24-hour, seven-days-a-week vigil outside the South African embassy in Trafalgar Square to protest Mandela's imprisonment. The ANC feared it would be counter-productive and ordered her to stop. But she refused to back off and the vigil remained, and took on the status of a tourist site, until Mandela's release. David Kitson, whom she had divorced, was meanwhile freed after serving the full 20 years to which he had been sentenced and they came together again and eventually settled in Harare, Zimbabwe.

Nearly six years after the coming of democracy, there is no black and white about South Africa. There are no easy descriptions to offer about where the country is and where it might be going. Instead, there is a lot of gray. The gray existed even during the heavy years of white rule: despite apartheid, nothing was straightforward and there was more warmth and acceptance between blacks and whites than seemed likely or possible. But at least the moral lines were clear: apartheid was evil, opposition was good.

Now it is not so simple. The gray has deeper shades and the texture is more complex as the ANC, now led by President Thabo Mbeki, is into its second five-year period of office after winning the elections in May 1999.

On the dark side is the crime. It is every bit as scary and pervasive as countless news reports and visitors to South Africa say it is. In Johannesburg, you must always be on your guard against criminals, watching out for possible carjackers as you pull up at traffic lights, and looking around nervously as you drive in and out through the electronic gates of houses (many of which are like fortresses, protected by high walls, razor wire and alarms). The fear goes beyond mere robbery because the great unknown is whether your attacker is a psychopath who might shoot to kill just for the hell of it.

Much of what is happening can be explained in terms of the past. Crime was widespread under apartheid: no white person in his right mind would have thought of walking at night in any of Johannesburg's wealthy "white" suburbs; at the same time, people in the black townships were at the mercy of gangsters and the police did little to protect them. Now, some say, rampant crime has simply crossed over into the "white" areas.

But that is only a partial explanation because the black criminals do not strike only at whites but with equal mercilessness also at people of their own color. In Cape Town, crime in the mixed-race colored areas has reached new depths of brutality, especially in attacks on young women, exceeding even the past. Gang rapes, with or without murder, are common.

The government has repeatedly threatened fierce action against criminals. But little has been achieved and the crime has gone on.

To say that is easy (and it's a refrain among many whites). The real question, however, is what the government can actually do, at least in the short-term. Many in the national police are a carryover from apartheid when they were an oppressive force. Morale is low, racism flourishes, pay is poor, and corruption is rife.

So what can be done? Lock up suspected criminals? Smash them up? Chop off their heads, legs, and arms, as the leader of the PAC has urged? The human rights culture of the new South Africa does not allow rough arbitrary action, or at least it hasn't thus far. Mass jailing also will not work if only because the prisons are already overflowing—and corruption opens the doors to escapes.

The obvious, if long-term, answer to the crime is employment and social welfare. But there is no money for the latter and unemployment is estimated at anything from 30 to 60 percent. Like crime, no one yet knows what to do about it. After the end of apartheid, the great hope was that the world would rush in with huge amounts of job-generating money. But so far it hasn't happened and foreign money comes in but is mainly for stock market investment.

Beggars, both black and white, stand at traffic lights in Johannesburg with hands outstretched. One enterprising man holds a piece of cardboard, with scrawled letters: "I don't want to do crime—help me."

Many whites rate corruption as a big problem, but they forget that the previous Afrikaner Nationalist government was deeply corrupt. Perhaps it is worse now because of the attitude of "entitlement" found among blacks—that they deserve as much as they can get, by fair means or foul, after the years of racial degradation. But whether as bad or worse than before, much of the present corruption is known because it is publicized in a way that was impossible under Afrikaner rule. Transparency is now the norm.

While that is to the credit of the country, the government has also sometimes condoned or been slow to confront misuse of public money in highly publicized episodes involving its own supporters.

Health has its dark/light shades too. Private medical care is life-saving for the relatively few with money, but public hospitals in cities are in crisis, with repeated warnings of outright collapse because of dire shortages of doctors, nurses, medicines, and everything else. Doctors are in despair about the plummeting state of some university training hospitals, which in the past produced doctors of international standard. Almost the least of it are stories of patients having to use their own sheets and towels because the hospital issue has been stolen.

An obvious problem in health is under-funding—but it is not as simple as that. A reason for the lack of money is the government's determination to make health care available for everyone, to get away from the apartheid-era situation whereby some 6 million whites enjoyed the best possible medical attention and the bulk of the 40 million people were deprived. Heart transplants were carried out for tiny numbers while most children were not given basic inoculations. The government has been tackling this by concentrating on primary health care, creating and upgrading thousands of clinics, especially in rural areas where about half the black population live.

Spectacular progress has been achieved: more than six in ten South Africans now live within 6 km of a health care facility, and three out of four children aged between 23 months and 12 years are fully immunized. Money for the clinics was switched from the teaching hospitals; hence their crisis. At the same time, many rural clinics are not functioning well because of staff and equipment shortages—so people continue to flock to the cities to the major hospitals, which are even less able to cope than before.

AIDS is jeopardizing progress. An estimated 3.6 million people are infected with HIV, with an estmated 1,500 new cases every day, giving South Africa the unhappy distinction of being a world leader in the growth of HIV infection.

On the positive side…

The government's target for the first five years was an ambitious, probably over-ambitious, one million houses. About 800,000 were completed or were being built, no mean feat. Some say that the quality of many houses is poor, but at least roofs are being given to people. And rudimentary services are increasingly being provided for the millions who move to the cities from impoverished rural areas, and who live in squatter camps.

Getting clean water to people who have never had it is another success story. So is providing electricity and telephones. And education—it's ensnarled in problems to do with shortages of everything, but the apartheid system has been dismantled and thousands of schools made nonracial with only occasional trouble; now the backlog of apartheid neglect in previously blacks-only schools—from classrooms, desks, books and blackboards to water, toilets and phones—is being tackled.

As any visitor can see, the country runs efficiently. There are holdups and hiccups because skills are short and people are learning on the job. But from post office counters and banks, to water and electricity and traffic lights and clean city streets, to the quality of the food, this is a well-functioning society, certainly in the cities.

It is also a troubled society. The people brutalized by apartheid—black victims as well as white perpetrators—are still around. Scarred souls and societies do not heal quickly.

The world is right to believe in the "miracle" of South Africa's peaceful change: that is exactly what has happened and in general there is an easy traffic between blacks and whites in everyday life. But it is not a place of perfect interracial harmony. Scratch the surface and racial antagonisms do reveal themselves: among whites there is resentment at having lost political power, and sneering about black competence.

White arrogance remains, especially in rural areas. Hence a revealing report in mid 1999 by Chris McGreal in the *Mail&Guardian* that "the many abuses of white rule continue on the South African farms that provide a precarious existence for five million blacks. Deplorable working conditions and paltry wages in return for long hours remain the norm. Some laborers still sleep in the sties and stalls of the animals they tend.

"But, for many workers, the worst thing is the continuing impunity with which white farmers abuse, beat, and even kill their laborers and other blacks, and then walk free because of indifferent or incompetent police and friendly judges."

Among Afrikaners there seems to be astonishment—and a growing rage among some—that they yielded power so rapidly. They are frustrated at their declining role, seen for example in Afrikaans-language universities, once citadels of power, which are giving lectures in English to accommodate increasing numbers of black students. Among young, professional blacks there is simmering resentment: whites are holding back and not giving of themselves to the new South Africa, they say.

But the barriers can be surmounted: a black woman of 24 with a Bachelor of Science degree who works as a medical representative for a drug company told me that there are many white Afrikaner doctors in the territory she handles outside Johannesburg. When she first started working two years previously it was usual for a doctor to tell her bluntly: "I am sorry but I do not deal with black reps." To which she replied: "I'm not a black rep, I'm a medical rep and I know my job." Those doctors are now her customers and friends, she said.

Democracy is strong. The composition of Mbeki's cabinet reflects the "rainbow nation," the phrase popularized by Archbishop Tutu. Democracy was given a huge boost in June when Nelson Mandela, having completed his five-year term, stepped down as President—an action which will, hopefully, be an exemplar for rulers in Africa who, more often than not, have tyrannically clung to power.

The press is largely free of restriction. But simultaneously, newspapers, radio, and television are unable to put their freedom to good purpose because standards of journalism, especially in investigation and analysis, remain depressingly poor, apart from a few shining exceptions.

After spending nearly a month in the new South Africa in mid 1999 the single strongest impression left on my mind was the caliber of the black elite whom I met. They are men and women in their twenties and thirties, usually well educated at home or abroad, self-confident, articulate, believing in themselves and in what they can do for their country. If there are enough of them around then the future is secure.

I asked one of them for an assessment: Justice Malala, a political writer on a Sunday newspaper, said: "It has been a tough five years and many issues like our nationhood and race remain unresolved. But I understand as well that the first five years were essentially about turning around a system designed for a minority towards one created to serve a majority, while the more psychological aspects of liberation have been on the backburner.

"Things will be worse in this country before they get better. Joblessness will rise, poverty will touch more people. However, this is an inevitable curve that most if not all transitions go through. But in ten years we will have emerged from the worst of it, and we will be a prosperous, great and beautiful country and people."

And while there is no shortage of sour voices among whites, the view which excited me came from Peter Hawthorne, British-born, who has been the *Time* magazine correspondent in the region for more than 15 years. Hawthorne has covered war, famine and destruction up and down the African continent; he is as crisis-hardened as any journalist can be. Yet he lights up when he speaks about South Africa's future, and says he believes Mandela ensured racial reconciliation; now Mbeki will energetically take the country forward.

"Somehow, notwithstanding the crime and unemployment, the gap between the haves and have-nots, the racism that will take another generation, maybe to finally burn out, there's something special about being a South African. This country has been in the troughs of crisis and despair. Most people, blacks for sure, whites in a slow process of realization, know that it will never be like that again."

I also sought the views of Nadine Gordimer, Nobel Literature prize-winner and always a friend of the *Rand Daily Mail* in the past: "Each period in a country's progress towards fulfilling democracy requires a certain quality of leadership," she told me. "The right leader is the one who is equipped to meet the demands of that certain period. We were greatly blessed in having exactly the right, perhaps the only, man equal to the demands of the first five years of South Africa's transition.

"The demands of the present period are different and call for someone equal to those—political, economic, social—of this stage in our evolution from the burdens of the apartheid past. We have great problems to solve. I believe Thabo Mbeki is the man to meet these demands.

"There is still so much that we have not achieved," she said. "But the rest of the world judges us strangely. They expect us, in five years, to achieve a democracy that has taken them several hundred years, and not achieved properly. Give us time."

That tallies with my own optimism about South Africa.

While living in London I became friends with Rabbi Michael Rosen, the founder of Yakar (Hebrew for "precious"), a Jewish learning center. I was drawn by his warm, embracing Judaism, and the fact that as an Orthodox rabbi, he stressed ethical behavior and tolerance for "the other." He emigrated to Israel and launched another Yakar in Jerusalem.

In due course he asked me to come and start a Center for Social Concern—to stimulate Israelis into thinking afresh about problems, and to encourage Israeli-Palestinian cooperation. Anne and I came in September 1997. There is ample scope for applying lessons learned in South Africa, in working for peace by making contact across lines of division and creating trust between people.

Jerusalem, January 2000

INTERVIEWS CONDUCTED WITH:

Akhalwaya, Ameen
Behrman, Neil
Bisseker, Trevor
Cockburn, Noel
Duval, Syd
Fleischer, Anthony
Gandar, Laurence
Gibson, Rex
Goodwin, June
Gregory, James
Hall, Laurie
Holiday, Anthony
Holroyd, Paul
Horak, John

Mervis, Joel
McGregor, Liz
Mkondo, Rich
Moolman, Terry
Nackan, Bernard
Omar, Dullah
Oppenheimer, Harry
Palestrant, Vita
Palmer, George
Paulson, Roy
Phillips, Darryl
Preece, Howard
Rees, John
Rees, Mervyn

Sources

Ivey, John
Jaroschek, Emielia
Jones, David
Kiley, Dennis
Kinsley, Clive
Kleinot, Pam
Krut, Riva
Lee, Kate
Lee, Marshall
Legum, Colin
Louw, Raymond
Magubane, Peter
Maisels, Issy

Sidley, Pat
Sisulu, Walter
Stein, Sylvester
Stiles, Sean
Swanepoel, Gerry
Tucker, Raymond
Waddell, Gordon
Walton, Leycester
Wellman, Peter
Wessels, Bernardi
Whitaker, Raymond
Woods, Donald

BOOKS AND OTHER MATERIAL CONSULTED

A Coat of Many Colors: The Memoirs of Clive Corder (Published by the author for private circulation, Cape Town, 1977)

A Dictionary of South African History by Christopher Saunders and Nicholas Southey (David Philip, Cape Town, 1998)

A Shanty Town in South Africa by Andrew Silk (Ravan Press, Johannesburg, 1981)

Censorship and Press Control in South Africa by Alex Hepple (Published by the author, Johannesburg, 1960)

Changing Faces: A History of the Guardian, *1956-88* by Geoffrey Taylor (Fourth Estate, London, 1993)

Edgar Wallace: The Biography of a Phenomenon by Margaret Lane (The Book Club, London, 1939)

Flashpoint South Africa by Bob Hitchcock (Don Nelson, Cape Town, 1977)

Heart of Whiteness: Afrikaners Face Black Rule in the New South Africa by June Goodwin and Ben Schiff (Scribner, New York, 1996)

How Can Man Die Better: Sobukwe and Apartheid by Benjamin Pogrund (Peter Halban, London, 1990)

In No Uncertain Terms by Helen Suzman (Sinclair-Stevenson, London, 1993)

Jan Smuts: An Illustrated Biography by Trewhella Cameron (Human & Rousseau, Cape Town, 1974)

Lessons of Struggle: South African Internal Opposition, 1960-1990 by Anthony W. Marx (Oxford University Press, New York, 1992)

Let My People Go by Albert Luthuli (Fount, London, 1982)

Long Walk to Freedom by Nelson Mandela (Little, Brown, New York, 1994)

Major Political Events in South Africa 1948-90 by Eileen Riley (Facts on File, Oxford, 1991)

Mandela: The Authorized Biography by Anthony Sampson (Harper-Collins, London, 1999)

Muldergate by Mervyn Rees and Chris Day (Macmillan, Johannesburg, 1980)

Nelson Mandela by Benjamin Pogrund (Exley Publications, Watford, 1991)

No Neutral Ground by Joel Carlson (Crowell, New York, 1973)

Operation Q-018 by Gerard Ludi (Nasionale Boekhandel, Cape Town, 1969)

Rand Daily Mail, 1902-86

Rebel Pity: The Life of Eddie Roux by Eddie and Win Roux (Rex Collings, London, 1970)

Revolution in My Life by Baruch Hirson (Witwatersrand University Press, Johannesburg, 1975)

Rivonia's Children by Glenn Frankel (Farrar, Straus and Giroux, New York, 1999)

South Africa: A Different Kind of War by Julie Frederikse (Ravan Press, Johannesburg, 1986)

South African Dispatches: Letters to my Countrymen by Donald Woods (Henry Holt, New York, 1986)

Survey of Race Relations in South Africa (SA Institute of Race Relations, Johannesburg): annual reports 1946-85

The Black Sash of South Africa by Cherry Michelman (Oxford University Press, London, 1975)

The Development of the Rand Daily Mail *as an Intercultural Newspaper* by Gavin Stewart (BA Hons thesis, University of South Africa, Pretoria, 1980)

The Fourth Estate by Joel Mervis (Jonathan Ball, Johannesburg, 1989)

The Last Trek, A New Beginning by F.W. de Klerk (Macmillan, London, 1998)

The Long Way Home by Annmarie Wolpe (Virago Press, London, 1994)

The Newspaperman's Guide to the Law, 3rd edition, by Kelsey Stuart (Butterworth, Durban, 1982)

The Press as Opposition by Elaine Potter (Chatto & Windus, London, 1975)

The Red Trap: Communism and Violence in South Africa by Chris Vermaak (APB, Johannesburg, 1966)

The Rise of African Nationalism in South Africa: The African National Congress 1912-1952 by Peter Walshe (C. Hurst, London, 1970)

The Rivonia Story by Joel Joffe (Mayibuye Books, Bellville, 1996)

The World That Was Ours by Hilda Bernstein (S. A. Writers, London, 1989)

Total Onslaught: The South African Press Under Attack by W.A. Hachten and C.A. Giffard (The University of Wisconsin Press, 1984)

Unofficial Dispatches of the Anglo-Boer War by Edgar Wallace (Struik: Africana Collectanea, Cape Town, 1975)

Index

Abe Bailey Trust, 228
Abendroth, Keith, 134
Abolition of Passes and Coordination
    of Documents Act, 61
Abramson, David, 303
Abyssinia, 30
Adamson, George, 26
Adonis, Lizzie, 33
Advowson Trust, 333, 334, 338, 339
African Explosives and Chemical
    Industries, 48, 51
African National Congress, 42, 68,
    251, 317, 318, 341, 357
African Nationalist group in, 49, 50,
    51, 52, 76–77
All-in African National Action
    Council, 95, 96, 97
banning of, 19, 87, 95, 127, 235
boycotts by, 78
church support for, 114
congress meetings, 74

cultural differences in, 77
farm labor and, 77
Federation of South African
    Women, 64
financing for, 76
Freedom Charter, 50–51
in government, 346
legality of, 44
lifting of bans on, 348
in Mozambique, 312
policy on nonviolence, 98, 99, 100
Program of Action, 50
protests by, 83, 93, 95
strikes by, 67, 93, 95, 98, 99
support for, 75
violence by, 21, 101
Women's League, 82
Youth League, 10, 49
African Nationalist group, 49, 50,
    51, 52, 76–77

African Opinion, 28
African Resistance Movement, 150
Africa South, 44
Africa Today, 166
Afrikaner Nationalist Party, 30, 32, 38
  change to white rule and, 346
  coming to power, 41
  control of information by, 89, 238, 39
  corruption in, 237
  last years in power, 346–348
  moral rules, 126
  opposition to, 73
  press control and, 89, 90, 91, 92
  protection of police by, 87
  religion and, 102–108
  separate development policy, 67, 75,
    81, 137
  States of Emergency by, 83, 84, 85,
    89, 92, 93, 95, 127, 234, 346–347
  universities and, 39
  war on opponents, 128
AIDS, 359
Akhalwaya, Ameen, 309
Alcock, Neil, 136
Alexandra, 78, 260
Allied Distribution Company, 325
All-in African National Action Council,
  95, 96, 97
American Newspaper Publishers Association, 210
American Women's club, 259
ANC. *See* African National Congress
Andrews, Bill, 156
Anglo American Corporation, 57, 64,
  286, 333, 334, 338, 339, 340, 341,
  342
Anglo-Boer War, 22, 27, 102
Angola, 238, 317–318
Anti-Semitism, 109, 110, 304
Apartheid
  beginnings, 30–31
  churches and, 102–108
  enforcement of, 9, 34, 46
  Grand, 254
  opposition to, 53, 76
  petty, 255
  relaxation of, 247, 255, 267, 268, 269
  repression, 83
  research on, 129–130
  university, 36, 37, 38, 39, 40, 41, 70
  world opinion on, 215
Appeal Court, 108, 208, 217
Argus Company, 57, 71, 133, 151, 196,
  276, 295, 325, 326, 333, 334, 336,
  342, 343
Arnett, Patricia, 37
Arnold, Rosemary, 256
Ashe, Arthur, 254
Asians, 28, 29, 81, 115, 235
Asingeni Fund, 113, 115
Athlone, 39
Atomic Energy Act, 237
Aucamp, Pieter, 223
Authoritarianism, 13
Azanian Peoples' Organization,
  309, 346–347

Bagley, Desmond, 87
Bailey, Abe, 26, 27, 28, 49, 333
Bailey, Jim, 58, 228
Bailey Trust, 333, 341
Ballinger, Margaret, 42, 61
Ballinger, William, 42
Banda, Hastings Kamuzu, 246
Bans, 298, 345
  African National Congress, 19,
    127
  antiapartheid organizations, 283
  Communist Party, 41–42
  demonstration, 40
  lifting, 348
  on Luthuli, 75
  on Mandela, 60
  newspaper, 235, 283
  Pan-Africanist Congress, 127, 244
  Ramphele, 314, 315, 316
  reporters, 267
Bantu Authorities, 75
Bantu Commissioners Courts, 65
Bantu Resettlement Board, 71
Bantustans, 137, 138
Bantu World, 71
Baragwanath Hospital, 130–131, 134
Barrie, F.G., 287

Basutoland, 59, 84, 118–120, 120–122, 122
Bechuanaland, 117, 118
Beeld, 252, 272, 283
Bell, Dewar and Hall law firm, 107, 191, 356
Benoni, 144
Benson, Ivor, 53, 58, 59, 68, 151
Berman, Myrtle, 251
Bernhard, Norman, 110
Berrange, Vernon, 197
Bethal, 297, 298
Beyers, C.F., 276
Beyers, General, 47
"Big Jingo," 47
Biko, Steve, 114, 130, 283–285, 293, 314
Bishop's Committee of Thirteen Anti-Apartheid Organizations, 84
Bizos, George, 298
Black Consciousness Movement, 283, 309, 314, 346–347
"Black Pimpernel," 19
Black(s)
    education, 257, 269, 276, 346, 359
    in exile, 84, 120
    freehold tenure for, 48
    journalism, 117, 294, 295
    labor, 27, 48, 79–81, 255, 257
    living conditions, 34, 134, 136
    militancy, 42, 291
    nationalism, 51
    as "native problem," 29
    on Newspaper Press Union, 28
    politics, 59
    population size, 136
    prisoners, 94
    resistance, 297, 308, 346–347
    students, 36
    voting rights, 29, 43, 106
    in World War II, 30
Black Sash, 64, 66, 77, 130, 171, 227, 244, 316
    Advice Offices, 64, 65
Blakplaas, 120
Blasphemy, 237, 238
Bleomfontein, 281

Bloomberg, Charles, 96
Boers, 21, 22, 26
Boksburg, 168
Bonhoeffer, Dietrich, 105
Booth, Charles, 37, 136
Bophelong, 83
Borkum, Max, 286, 302, 334
Boshoff, Willem, 352
"Boss boys," 77
Boston Globe, 271, 313
Botha, P.W., 263, 288, 289, 290, 291, 293, 294, 335, 337, 342, 346–347, 348, 351, 353
Botha, Robert, 107, 108
Botha, T.J., 242
Botswana, 119
Botting, Alex, 48
Brandfort, 319
Bridgett, Geoff, 175
British Colonial Service, 59
British Institute of Journalists, 210
British Union of Fascists, 58
Brooks, Allan, 204, 205
Brooks, John, 222
Brown, Andrew, 185
Bruce, Nigel, 331
Bureau for State Security, 248, 250, 251, 351
Burger, 30, 166, 177
Business Day, 331, 332, 335
Buthelezi, Chief Gatsha, 246, 349
Butler, Lord, 227

Calvinism, 102
Cape Argus, 300
Cape Flats, 36
Cape Herald, 295
Cape Provincial Committee, 42, 43
Cape Times, 32, 40, 51, 73, 180, 256, 300, 316
Cape Town, 34, 41, 59, 61, 81, 120, 166, 229, 263, 300, 313, 334, 342, 343, 348
Carlson, Joel, 77
Carnegie Corporation, 112
Carruthers, Hugh, 46
Cartwright, A.P., 48

Casper, Bernard, 110, 111
Celliers, Barend, 182, 183, 184, 186, 189
Celliers, Charl, 334
Censorship, 23, 237, 238, 281, 307
  political, 91
  of press, 91, 92
Center for Social Concern, 362
Central Mining Investment Company, 27
Chamber of Mines, 21, 27, 29
Chaskalson, Arthur, 216, 356
Children's rebellion, 260, 268, 271, 272, 298
Chisholm, Jill, 123, 199
Christie, Ernie, 124
Christmas Comfort Fund, 26, 259
The Church and the Race Problem, 105
Churches
  Anglican, 105, 106
  Dutch Reformed Church, 30, 103, 105, 270
  Nederduitsch Hervormde Kerk, 102, 104
  Nederduitse Gereformeerde Kerk, 103, 105
  views on apartheid, 102–113
  views on violence, 106
Cillie, Piet, 221, 222, 224, 225, 226, 227, 276, 277, 278, 356
Cinderella prison, 167–170, 186, 215
Ciskei, 137, 313
Citizen, 113, 286, 287, 288, 290, 326, 343
Civil Cooperation Bureau, 349
Clarkson, Terence, 131–132
Clay, George, 40
Coaker, John, 220, 222
Coalbrook mine, 79–81
Coburn, Noel, 342
Codesa, 349
Coetzee, Johan, 112, 228, 250, 251, 303
Communist Party, 38, 41–42, 50, 99, 107, 108, 132, 133, 156, 172, 177, 183, 197, 203, 249, 255, 256, 349
Congress Alliance, 42, 43, 99

Congress of Democrats, 42, 100, 127, 133
Constitutional Court, 216, 356
Contact, 42, 59, 147
Convention for a Democratic South Africa, 349
Cook, Claud, 46
Cooper, David, 38
Corder, Clive, 72, 229
Corner House, 27
Corruption, 61, 138, 157–158, 237, 285, 287, 358
Craighead, David, 42
Crime, 48, 348, 349, 357
Criminal Investigation Department, 146
Criminal Law Amendment Act, 146–147, 234
  Section 83, 147
Criminal Procedure Act, 92
  Section 205, 235
Cyanimid Corporation, 260

Dagbreek, 165, 166, 178
Daily Dispatch, 196, 283, 316
Daily Mail, 165
Daily Tribune, 58
Day, Chris, 287
Dean, Geoffrey, 182, 183
De Beers Company, 48
Defense Act, 238, 289
Defense and Aid Fund, 94, 95
de Klerk, F.W., 348, 349, 350, 353
de Kock, Wessel, 132
Delayed Action (Geyser), 103
Demonstrations. *See* Protests
Department of Colored Affairs, 40
Department of Indian Affairs, 40
Department of Information, 285, 287, 303
Department of National Education, 40
Department of Native Affairs, 40
Deportations, 106
Detention without trial, 83–84, 92, 94, 122, 154, 194, 235–236, 266, 298, 346–347
de Villiers, Les, 289

de Villiers Graaff, Sir, 72
Devlin, Lord, 227
de Wet Nel, Daan, 135, 137
Dhlamini, Dumisa, 122, 123, 124
Dirker, Carel, 85, 86
Divestiture, 255
d'Oliviera, Basil, 255
Drum (magazine), 49, 141
Dugard, John, 336
Duncan, Patrick, 42, 59, 147
Duncan, Sheena, 65, 316
Durban, 39, 57, 74, 77, 160, 164, 300, 334, 342, 343
Durr, C.J.M., 146, 149
Dutch Reformed Church, 30, 103, 270
Duval, Syd, 257

East Africa, 30
Eastern Province Herald, 73–74, 316
Edmunds, G.R. "Bob," 72, 73
Education, 13, 359
    Bantu, 260, 270
    black, 257, 260, 269, 276, 346, 359
    English speaking, 269, 270
    funding for, 259, 269
    Rand Bursary Fund, 259, 260, 266
    university, 36, 37, 38, 39, 40
    white, 259, 269
Elections, 32, 127, 172, 254, 255, 256, 286
Ellis, G. Rayner, 45, 47
Emdon, Clive, 272
"English Mails," 25
Erasmus, Frans, 126, 146
Ethiopia, 30
Evans, David, 204
Evans, Harold, 156, 262
Evening Post, 51, 52, 73
Extension of University Education Act, 40, 235

Factories Act, 296
Fairbairn Memorial Address, 336
Farrell, David, 241, 242
Federal Hotel, 241
Federation of South African Women, 64

ffrench-Beytagh, Gonville Aubrey, 106
Financial Mail, 331
Financial Times, 327, 328, 329, 330, 340
Fischer, Bram, 193
Fleischer, Anthony, 214
Fordsburg, 96
Foreign Correspondents Association, 89, 90
Fort Hare University College, 119
Freedom Charter, 50–51
Freeman Cohen, Harry, 23, 24, 26
Frelimo movement, 310, 311
Fridjohn, Harold, 69
Friedman, Bernard, 89

Galgut, Oscar, 284
Gandar, Isobel Ballance, 70, 177, 354
Gandar, Laurence, 21, 51, 52, 57, 58, 62, 63, 69, 70, 71, 72, 91, 93, 97, 127, 128, 135, 136, 151, 156, 157, 158, 159, 164, 165, 167, 169, 170, 172, 176, 179, 192, 193, 210, 211, 212, 213, 214, 215, 218, 221, 227, 228, 229, 249, 333, 352, 354
Gangs, 48, 56, 357
Garment Workers Union, 156, 244
Geldenhuys, F.E. O'Brien, 105
General Law Amendment Act, 237, 292
Germany, 30, 113, 158, 296
Geyser, Albert, 102, 103, 104
Gibson, James, 43
Gibson, Rex, 162, 243, 262, 276, 304, 305, 306, 316, 326, 331, 334, 335, 354
Gluckman, Jonathan, 284
Goldberg, Dennis, 202, 204, 205, 206
Goldberg, Marcelle, 86
Goldberg, Victor, 86
Golden City Post, 49, 53, 71, 144, 171
Golding, George, 41
Goldstone, Richard, 115, 116, 349
Goodhead, M.E., 197, 200, 203, 206, 207, 208
Goodman, Isaac, 47
Gordimer, Nadine, 336, 361
Gottlieb, Solly, 257
Grahamstown, 39

Grand Apartheid, 254
Great Britain, 30, 122, 158, 166, 346
  colonial rule, 21, 25
  links with, 25
Greyshirts, 30
Group Areas Act, 81, 115
Groutville, 75
Guardian, 107, 166
Gxogyia, Absalom, 46

Habonim, 38
Hadebe, James, 75, 76
Haffajee, Ferial, 352
Hall, Elsie, 45
Hall, Laurie, 295
Harber, Anton, 306
Harris, John, 248
Hawthorne, Peter, 361
Hazelhurst, David, 266, 289
Hazelhurst, Peter, 215, 216
Health care, 130–131, 358–359
Heard, George, 92, 147
Heath's Hotel, 23
Herstigte Nasionale Party, 245, 246
Hertzog, Albert, 90, 245, 248, 290
Hertzog, J.B.M., 29, 30, 89
Heunis, Chris, 299
Hillbrow, 115, 143
Hirson, Baruch, 44
Hjul, Peter, 43
Hoek, Jan, 83
Holiday, Anthony, 254, 255, 256
Homelands, 78, 121, 137, 138, 313,
  314, 315, 316, 349, 359
Hope, Sydney, 265
Horak, John, 249, 250, 303, 351, 352
Horrell, Muriel, 42
Hospitals, 130–131, 134, 182
Houghton, 73, 127
Howick, 99
Huddleston, Trevor, 106
Hughes, A.B. "Barno," 69, 86, 212
Hurley, Denis, 105

Immorality Act, 108, 126
Imperial Chemical Industries, 48
Imvo Zabantsundu (newspaper), 28

"Infogate," 291, 307
Ingram, Derek, 165
Ingwenyama, the Lion, 122
Inkatha party, 273, 349
Inquests Amendment Act, 293
Inside BOSS (Winter), 252
Institute for Democracy in Africa, 120
Internal Security Act, 273
International Union of Students, 38
Israel, 108, 110, 256
Italy, 30
IUS. *See* International Union of Students
Ivory Coast, 245
Iyer, Letchmee, 96

Jabavu, Tango, 28
Jackson, Ralph Ward, 27
James, Neville, 279–280
Jeugbond, 352
Joffe, "Bully," 47
Johannesburg, 21, 22, 34, 46, 61, 64, 73,
  77, 84, 87, 96, 110, 113, 117, 121,
  124, 211, 255, 259, 300, 308, 334
Johannesburg Consolidated Investment
  Company, 286, 333, 340, 341, 342
Johannesburg Sunday Times, 96
Johnson, M.A. "Johnny," 133–134, 195,
  212, 286
Johnson Foundation, 112
Joseph, Adelaide and Paul, 96
Journalism
  accuracy in, 71
  advocacy, 71
  bias in, 71
  black, 117
  British standards, 47, 48
  codes of conduct in, 282
  confidentiality in, 146
  independent, 10
  investigative, 134
  objectivity in, 58–59
  political control of, 89, 90, 91, 92
  training courses, 295–296
Judaism, 108–111

Kahn, Sam, 41
Kambule, Wilkie, 260

Kantor, Jimmy, 54
Kapstein, Jonathan, 311
Katzen, Kitt, 287
Kennedy, Brian, 168, 169
Kentridge, Sydney, 220, 222, 224, 227, 277, 285, 336, 356
Kenya, 166
Kerzner, Sol, 337
Kiley, Dennis, 144–145, 328, 329
Killarney, 193
Kimberley, 284, 354
King, John, 338
Kingswell, George, 28
Kingswilliamstown, 284, 314
Kinsley, Clive, 276, 300, 301, 302, 303, 304, 325, 326, 327, 329, 330, 331, 333, 334, 338
Kitson, David, 154, 204, 206, 356
Kitson, Norma, 154, 155, 158, 214, 218, 356
Kleinot, Pam, 297
Koornhof, Piet, 112, 262, 282
Kroonstad prison, 157, 193
Kruger, Jimmy, 278, 280, 283, 284, 291, 346
Kruger, Paul, 156
Krugersdorp, 223
Kuiper, Henri, 57, 58, 72, 73, 210, 212, 213
Kupugani, 134, 135, 136, 137
Kwashiorkor, 134–135
KwaZulu, 349

Labor
  black, 27, 48, 79–81, 156, 255, 257
  farm, 77, 78
  guest, 138
  seasonal, 315
  shortages, 27
  skilled, 81, 156, 275, 311
  white, 27, 81, 156
Labor Party, 41
Lady Selborne township, 82
Lane, Margaret, 23, 24
Langham Hotel, 246
Laurence, Patrick, 145
Lazar, Robin, 216, 217

Leabua Jonathan, Chief, 119
Leballo, Potlako, 51, 120–122, 122
Lebowa, 314
Lee, Kate, 242, 243
Lee-Warden, Len, 43
Legum, Colin, 45
Lekota, Patrick, 352
Lelyveld, Joseph, 202
Lenasia, 71
Lenyenye, 314, 316
Lesotho, 59, 118–120
Lesotho Liberation Army, 119
Levitan, Esther, 130
Libel, seditious, 237
Liberal Party, 10, 42, 48, 49, 51, 58, 103, 127, 132, 146, 355
Lindsay, G.K., 228
Loginov, Yuri, 249
London Daily Mail, 23
Long, Athol, 125, 126
Lourens, Jansie, 306
Louw, Eric, 70, 90
Louw, Raymond, 47, 69, 80, 134, 148, 151, 207, 212, 213, 214, 215, 228, 239, 240, 241, 249, 257, 265, 266, 274, 275, 276, 286, 300, 301, 333, 338, 354
Ludi, Gerard, 133, 249
Luthuli, Chief Albert, 74, 75, 86, 99–100
Luyt, Louis, 285, 286, 287, 288, 334, 338

McGoff, John, 288
McGreal, Chris, 359
McGregor, Liz, 307–308
McLeod, Lewis Rose, 29, 30
Macmillan, Harold, 81
McPherson, Ian, 275, 276, 304, 305, 338
Madiba. *See* Mandela, Nelson
Magistrates Court, 55, 56, 60, 61, 62, 67, 70, 191
Magubane, Peter, 266, 267, 272, 273
Mail&Guardian, 352, 359
Main Reef, 21
Maisels, Issy, 338

Maize Board, 258
Malan, D.F., 30
Malan, Giliam, 186
Malanazis, 31
Malawi, 145, 245, 246
Malnutrition, 134, 135
Mamasela, Joe "Scarface," 310
Mandela, Nelson, 9, 19, 59, 62, 95, 96,
    226, 227, 318–324
    banning, 60
    jailing, 99
    law practice, 59, 60
    Nobel prize for, 350
    as president, 346
    in prison, 120, 225
    release from jail, 348
    Rivonia Trial, 173, 202
    sabotage trial, 153
    underground activity, 19–20, 96, 97,
    98
Mandela, Winnie, 251, 318–324, 351,
    354
Marais, Dave, 40, 199
Margolies, Hank, 53
Marxism, 310, 311
Maseko, Macdonald, 123
Matthews, Joe, 77
Mayekiso, Lawrence, 265
Mazwai, Thami, 336
Mbeki, Govan, 202–203
Mbeki, Thabo, 203, 357, 360, 361, 362
Mdluli, Joseph, 278–279, 280, 284
Meadowlands Tswana School Board,
    269–270
Media Workers' Association of South
    Africa, 294, 295
Mendelssohn, Emmanuel, 23
Menell, Monica, 39
Mervis, Joel, 181, 215, 217, 218
Meyer, Johannes Petrus, 22
Meyers, Lou, 54, 55
Mhlambiso, Thami, 157
Militancy, 75
Miller, Hal, 325
Milner, Lord, 26, 27
Mindolo Ecumenical Foundation, 105,
    106

Mining, 21, 22, 27, 79–81, 341
Minority Rights Group, 229
Missionaries, 136–137
Mkhondo, Rich, 308
M-Net, 337, 339
Modderbee prison, 144, 158
Mofolo, 49, 82, 111
Mokhehle, Ntsu, 119, 120
Molefe, Jacob, 306
Molema, S.M., 118
Molotsi, Alpheus, 306
Moolman, Mauritz, 308
Moolman, Terry, 342
Mosala, Leonard, 271
Moseley, Oswald, 58
Moshoeshoe, 118–120
Mothopeng, Zephaniah, 297
Motlana, Sally, 292
Motsuenyane, Sam, 295
Mozambique, 84, 184, 215, 216,
    310–313, 349
Mulder, Connie, 260, 262, 264, 282,
    285, 287, 288, 289, 290
Muldergate (Rees and Day), 287
Mulholland, Stephen, 331
Munsieville, 46
Murder squads, 249
Murdoch, Rupert, 341
Murray, A.H., 50, 51
Murray, Bill, 86, 87
Musi, Obed, 144, 158
Musi, Zandile, 310
Mutambikwa, Jairus, 39
Mwasa. *See* Media Workers' Association
    of South Africa
Myburgh, Tertius, 302, 303, 304, 305

Namibia, 317–318
Nasionale Pers, 337
Nataller, 150, 151
Natal Mercury, 74, 207, 316
Natal province, 28, 34, 37, 77, 258
National Front, 309
National Socialism, 30, 31
National Supplies Procurement
    Amendment Act, 293
National Union of Mineworkers, 341

National Union of South African Students, 37, 38, 39, 244, 355
Native Administration Act, 234, 235
Native Advisory Board, 46
Natives Act, 61
Naught for Your Comfort (Huddleston), 106
Nazism, 30, 31, 47, 89, 105, 108, 183
Necklacing, 346–347
Nederduitsch Gereformeerde Kerk, 103, 105
Nederduitsch Hervormde Kerk, 102, 104
Netherlands, 166
NEUM. *See* Non-European Unity Movement
New Age, 71
Newclare, 86
Newlands, 34
Newspaper Bill, 282
Newspaperman's Guide to the Law (Stuart), 152
Newspaper Press Union, 28, 91, 238, 239, 282, 284, 293
Newspapers, Afrikaner, 93, 113, 132, 143, 166, 171, 172, 196, 246, 266, 283, 290, 293
Newspapers, English-language, 47, 52, 57, 63, 73, 89, 90, 128, 171, 239, 263, 291, 293, 327, 333, 341
New Unity Movement, 37
New York Times, 166, 181, 202, 248
Nicholas, H.C., 185, 196, 197, 198, 204, 206, 207
Niehaus, Carl, 306
Nkamela, K., 270
Nkomati Accord, 312, 313
Nkosi, Willie, 274
Nobel prizes, 100, 350
Noffke, Ferdie, 132
Nokwe, Duma, 251
Non-European Affairs Department, 66, 98, 111, 131, 259
Non-European Unity Movement, 37, 92, 244
New Era Fellowship, 39
Nonviolence, 20–21, 98, 99, 100, 112

Norton, Victor, 73
NPU. *See* Newspaper Press Union
Nquku, J.J., 122
Nusas. *See* National Union of South African Students
Nutrition Corporation, 134
Nyanga, 61
Nyasaland, 145

O'Connor, Harry, 32, 33, 53–54, 55, 69, 80, 133, 213, 219
Odendaal, M.J., 201
Official Secrets Act, 233, 288
Oliver, George, 47
Omar, Dullah, 34–35, 345
Oosthuizen, A.J.G., 104
Oosthuizen, J.J., 132
Operation Damp Squib, 146, 150, 247
Operation Q-018 (Ludi), 133
Operation Snowball, 259, 266
Oppenheimer, Harry, 58, 286, 333, 334, 339, 340, 341
Orange Free State, 28, 235, 291
Orlando Community Hall, 67
Orlando High School, 260, 261
Ossewa Brandwag, 30
Oudtshoorn, 34
Owen, Ken, 302, 303, 304, 305

PAC. *See* Pan-Africanist Congress
Pan-Africanist Congress, 68, 82, 83, 119, 120–122, 251, 297, 298
banning of, 87, 95, 127, 235, 244
lifting of bans on, 348
Panos, 350
Pappert, Errol, 259
Pass laws, 60–62, 64, 65, 66, 67, 77, 82, 234–235, 298
Passport withdrawals, 70, 84–85, 129, 178, 211, 214, 262
Paton, Alan, 42, 103
Payne, Cecil, 213, 214, 220, 228, 274, 275
Petersen, Hector, 271
Pfeffer, Yitzik, 38
Phillips, Darryl, 327, 328, 329
Phillips, Sir Lionel, 27

Pide, 84
Pietermaritzburg, 37, 39, 74, 95
Pines, Nome, 108
Pitje, Godfrey, 107
Player, Gary, 286
Pogrund, Benjamin
  as African Affairs reporter, 117–126
  assistant editor, 258
  at *Boston Globe*, 271, 272
  deputy editorship, 276
  joins *Rand Daily Mail*, 53–55
  journalistic views, 58, 59
  loss of passport, 178
  night editor, 233, 240, 241, 250, 257, 258
  political views, 58
  in prison, 146–152
  prison reports, 142–149, 157–170, 184–209
  resignation from political parties, 10
  on trial, 220–228
  as *Umhlabeni*, 59
Polaroid Corporation, 255
Police
  attacks by, 61, 62, 76, 83
  brutality, 9, 87
  at children's rebellion, 271
  Criminal Investigation Department, 146
  detention without trial, 83–84, 92, 94, 96, 122, 154, 194, 235–236, 266, 298, 346–347
  evidence planting, 106
  informers, 204
  interrogations, 155
  Murder and Robbery Squad, 87
  protection for, 87, 142, 173, 174, 249, 279, 284, 285, 292
  raids on activists, 63–64
  raids on squatters, 313–314
  searches without warrant, 92
  security, 10
  spies, 10
  surveillance, 189, 208, 218, 265
  toleration of, 142
  wiretapping by, 76
Pollock, Mac, 73–74

Pollsmoor prison, 348
Poqo, 120–122
Port Elizabeth North End prison, 159, 160, 182, 201
Portugal, 310, 311
Poverty, 138, 257, 313, 316
Pratt, David, 88
Preece, Howard, 331, 332
Press Code, 282, 283
Press Council, 283, 284, 293, 298
Press Identity Cards, 297
Press-Police Agreement, 238
Pretoria, 60, 61, 64, 82, 94, 110, 130
Pretoria Central prison, 161, 163, 190, 192, 198, 199, 206
Pretoria Local prison, 154, 163, 203, 204
Pretoria University, 37, 177
Pringle Medal for Press Freedom, 336
Prins, Gideon, 169
Prins, Marthinus, 285
Prinsloo, Sampie, 86
Prisoners
  black, 144, 163, 164, 182, 225
  information on, 141
  political, 143, 202, 225
  treatment of, 94, 145, 148, 149, 150, 160–162, 163, 168, 182, 201, 202, 216, 284
  white, 143, 144, 157, 190, 225
Prisons
  Cinderella, 167–170, 186, 215
  conditions in, 94, 143, 144, 148, 160–162, 168, 179, 200, 201, 202
  corruption in, 157–158
  electric shock in, 168, 169, 174, 179, 184, 186, 187, 188, 216, 298
  executions in, 161
  Fort, 141, 142, 143, 149
  information from, 144
  Kroonstad, 157, 193
  Modderbee, 144, 158
  Pollsmoor, 348
  Port Elizabeth North End, 159, 160, 182, 201
  Pretoria Central, 161, 163, 190, 192, 198, 199, 206

Pretoria Local, 154, 163, 203, 204
Robben Island Prison, 106, 120, 200, 225, 226, 227, 310, 348
Victor Verster, 348
Zonderwater, 157
Prisons Act, 141, 145, 160, 196, 215, 228, 233, 235
  Sections 44(e) and (f), 141, 142, 143, 153, 158, 183, 185
Prisons Department, 217, 218, 223, 224, 225
Prisons Trial, 220–228, 276
Prisons Trials, 352
Private Eye, 328
Program of Action (ANC), 50
Progressive Federal Party, 286, 334
Progressive Party, 73, 127, 128, 210, 286
Protests, 40, 130
  banning, 40, 130
  by children, 113
  pass law, 82, 83
  by Poqo, 120–122
  university, 129
Protter, David, 256, 257
Publication and Entertainment Act, 237–238
Public Safety Act, 234
Putter, Paul, 190, 191, 192, 194

Q agents, 222

Race Classification laws, 265
Racial laws, 52
Racism
  antiwhite, 51, 68, 120, 121
  Bantustans and, 138
  church views on, 102–108
  defining, 27–28
  early, 27–28
Rafferty, Pat, 223, 224
Ramaphosa, Cyril, 341
Ramphele, Mamphela, 314, 315, 316
Rand Bursary Fund, 259, 260, 266
Rand Club, 21, 45
"Rand Daily Liar," 47

Rand Daily Mail
  Adamson editorship, 26
  advertising, 25, 211, 240, 300, 301, 307, 325, 331–332
  African Affairs desk, 117
  apartheid views, 53, 71, 114, 115, 129
  Asians and, 28
  board of directors, 72, 212, 213, 228, 229, 274, 326, 327
  Cartwright editorship, 48
  centralization at, 301
  changing demographics at, 299–302
  character of, 27, 93, 97
  circulation, 93, 211, 240, 257, 274, 299, 301, 304, 325
  in collusion with government, 337
  computers at, 275
  creation of, 21, 24
  crime reporting, 63, 132
  debt at, 299
  demise of, 302–305, 330, 331, 333–344
  editorial views, 69, 93, 127, 135, 136, 167, 169, 179, 180, 266, 302, 318
  education projects, 259, 260
  Ellis editorship, 45, 47
  Extra editions, 265, 266, 267
  Gandar editorship, 21, 51, 52, 57, 58, 62, 63, 69, 70, 71, 72, 91, 93, 97, 127, 128, 135, 136, 156, 169, 179, 180
  Gibson editorship, 306, 331, 334, 335
  government repression of, 164, 165, 167, 172, 173, 174, 178, 179, 181, 220–228, 282, 284, 291, 292–294, 298, 299, 329
  investigative reporting, 134, 156
  Jackson editorship, 27
  "Just In Passing" column, 69
  Louw editorship, 207, 213, 214, 239, 240, 241, 265, 266, 276
  McLeod editorship, 29, 30
  McPherson editorship, 275, 276
  management hostility to, 300–301
  managerial neglect at, 325
  military reporting, 317–318

morale at, 80, 211, 304, 306, 331
Morning Final edition, 268
on Nelson Mandela, 19, 20
nonwhite reporters at, 265
opposition from other papers, 74
opposition to Afrikaner Nationalist
    Party, 47, 129
paternalism on, 46
political reporting, 63, 69, 70, 114,
    115, 172–173
"Political Viewpoint" column, 52, 69
prejudice on, 71, 72
prison reports, 142–149, 157–170,
    184–209
racial tensions at, 266
radicals on, 132, 133
raids on, 169–170, 176, 177
readership, 93, 265, 266, 299, 300,
    302, 307, 330
reputation of, 27
respect from blacks for, 20
segregation at, 296
slip editions, 266
Sparks editorship, 276, 284, 288, 293,
    302, 303
special editions, 20, 80, 98, 266, 267,
    302
spies at, 132–133, 162, 249, 250, 251,
    252, 303
support for Progressive Party, 73
Township Mail, 266
transformation to financial daily,
    327–331
at trial, 196–209, 220–228
use of sources for stories, 131
Wallace editorship, 24–26
World Press Achievement Award to,
    210, 211
Randpark Golf Club, 267
Rand Show, 87
Rapport, 266, 283
"Red danger," 38
The Red Trap (Vermaak), 132
Rees, Cecil, 197, 205
Rees, John, 111, 112, 113, 114, 115, 116
Rees, Mervyn, 114, 272, 285, 287, 288

Rees-Mogg, William, 227
Reeves, Ambrose, 84, 85, 106
Reid, Ian, 337–338
Relly, Gavin, 333, 339
Renamo, 312, 313
Renewed National Party, 245, 246
Republic Day, 19, 146, 208
Revolt, 256
Rezelman, Dirk, 258
Rhodesia, 55, 105, 151, 212, 215, 216,
    256
Rhoodie, Eschel, 285, 287, 289, 303
Richard, Dirk, 178
Rights
    personal, 233
    of press, 233
    restrictions on, 74
    voting, 28, 64, 93, 106
Riotous Assemblies Act, 234
Robben Island Prison, 106, 120, 200,
    225, 226, 227, 310, 348
Robinson, John, 74
Roelofse, Eugene, 114, 115
Rogaly, Joe, 329
Rosen, Michael, 362
Rozwadowski, Vincent, 125
Rustenburg, 81
Rwanda, 111

Saan. *See* South African Associated
    Newspapers
Sabotage, 159, 202
Sabotage Act, 235
Sachs, Solly, 156
Sacks, Andrew, 223, 224, 225
Sacks, Harold, 62, 63, 64, 82–83
Salt River, 34
Satbel, 337
Schlebusch, Alwyn, 263, 264, 293
Scholes, Johnny, 225, 226
Schonfrucht, Arnold, 55
Scott-Smith, Robin, 146, 147, 150
"Search for Alternatives," 112–113
Security Branch, 84
Segal, Ronald, 44
Segale, Steve, 10, 49, 85, 86

Segregation
  academic, 36
  beach, 35, 40
  hotels, 117
  at *Rand Daily Mail,* 296
  residential, 34, 37, 115, 313
  social, 36
Sekukuniland, 132
Sentinels of the Ox-Wagon, 30
Serache, Nat, 273, 274, 276
Setshedi, Isaac, 169, 184, 186, 187, 188
Shadrack, Matthew, 56
Sharpeville, 10, 19, 83, 86, 93, 127, 239, 309
Sidley, Pat, 325, 328, 334
Silk, Leonard, 248
Sinclair, Jean, 65
Sisulu, Albertina, 76
Sisulu, Walter, 76, 77, 251, 294
Sisulu, Zwelakhe, 294, 295
699 Down, 26
Slovo, Joe, 109, 349
Slovo, Ruth, 349
Smith, Ian, 212, 215
Smuts, Granny, 33
Smuts, Jan Christian, 30, 32, 86, 89
Snoyman, Hymie, 241
Sobhuza, King, 122, 123–124, 124, 125
Sobukwe, Robert, 9, 49, 51, 59, 68, 82, 106, 120, 145, 200, 201, 251, 283, 294, 297, 354
Somerset, Charles, 92
Sondagstem, 196
Sophiatown, 45, 48, 49, 71, 85, 106
South Africa
  anti-Semitism in, 109, 110, 304
  British colonial rule in, 21, 25
  current problems in, 13
  economy, 21
  international attention on, 111, 183, 255, 285, 287
  Judaism in, 108–111
  mining in, 21, 22
  new constitution, 348
  partitioning of, 137, 138
  relations with Great Britain, 122
  relations with Lesotho, 119
  as republic, 93, 95
  sanctions on, 299, 346
  ties with Great Britain, 93
South African Associated Newspapers, 57, 72, 73, 151, 176, 185, 217, 220, 221, 228, 250, 267, 274, 275, 276, 286, 288, 291, 295, 296, 300, 325, 327, 330, 331, 333, 335, 338, 339, 342, 343
South African Board of Jewish Deputies, 109
South African Broadcasting Corporation, 171, 172, 173, 246, 294
South African Colored Peoples Organization, 43
South African Council of Churches, 111, 113, 114, 115, 313
South African Institute of Race Relations, 29, 42, 243
South African Medical Journal, 182
South African Morning Group, 73, 250, 275
South African Press Association, 128, 164, 235, 297
South African Railway, 34
South African Society of Journalists, 89, 90, 343
South-West Africa, 238, 256, 317–318, 346
Sowden, Lewis, 69–70, 142
Sowetan, 283, 336
Soweto, 9, 50, 67, 71, 82, 111, 116, 130, 244, 259, 260, 271, 272
Sparks, Allister, 194, 276, 284, 288, 293, 301, 302, 303, 333, 338, 354
Spear of the Nation. *See* Umkhonto weSizwe
Spengler, Att, 84, 86, 87, 97, 150
Spengler's List, 84
Sports, 36, 37, 254, 255, 262, 268
Standard and Diggers News, 22
Star, 27, 131, 142, 145, 173, 180, 181, 196, 240, 246, 259, 299, 354
Starvation, 134, 135, 308, 315, 316
State Security Council, 348

States of Emergency, 83, 84, 85, 89, 92, 93, 95, 127, 234, 343, 346–347, 355
Stegeman, Sadie and George, 189
Stein, Archie, 131
Stein, Sylvester, 45, 46, 47, 49
Stellenbosch Farmers' Winery Journalism Awards, 274
Stellenbosch University, 132
Steyn, J.C., 142, 144, 160, 172, 192, 193, 223, 224
Steyn, Louis, 162
Stirling, Tony, 221
Strachan, Harold "Jock," 157, 158, 160, 164, 165, 166, 170, 184, 196, 198, 200, 201, 202, 203, 207, 208, 209, 222, 225, 251, 298, 356
Strijdom, J.G., 90
Strikes, 19, 20, 67, 93, 95, 98, 99, 122, 123, 124, 295
Stuart, Kelsey, 146, 148, 150, 151, 158, 159, 160, 166, 167, 168, 169, 174, 176, 184, 197, 206, 215, 217, 218, 277–278, 289, 305, 356
Suicides, 64, 88, 124, 132, 194, 204, 207, 254, 278, 289
Sunday Chronicle, 171, 196
Sunday Express, 107, 194, 195, 212, 276, 287, 304, 336
Sunday Times, 9, 27, 31, 126, 168, 169, 181, 182, 195, 217, 266, 301, 303, 336
Suppression of Communism Act, 41, 107, 108, 142, 235, 273
Supreme Court, 115, 206, 207, 220
Sutherland, John, 51, 73
Suzman, Helen, 73, 109, 127, 128, 165, 166, 190, 192, 193, 203, 210, 223, 227, 255, 280, 334, 355
Swanepeol, Bosman, 246
Swanepoel, Gerry, 300, 301
Swapo, 317–318
Swart, C.R., 141, 142
Swaziland, 84, 122–126, 150, 197
Swaziland Progressive Party, 122
Syfrets, 72, 210, 211, 213, 214, 228, 229, 274

Taimo, Filisberto, 168, 169, 184, 185, 186
Tambo, Oliver, 44, 59, 60, 67, 68, 84
Tamsen, Oscar, 84, 85, 251
Tanzania, 122
Television, 90, 336, 337, 342, 351
Temba, Can, 49
Terrorism Act, 106, 235, 273, 276, 297, 298, 319
Theron, Johannes, 167–170, 174, 184, 216, 217, 356
"Third Force," 349
Thoms, Raymond, 203, 204, 205, 206, 207
Thomson, Lord, 255, 341
Thwane, S.G., 270
Times Media Limited, 343
Today, 350
Torch, 92
Township Mail, 266
Townships, black, 9
Trade Union Council of South Africa, 156, 244
Transkei, 78, 121, 137, 313
Transvaal Indian Congress, 96
Transvaal province, 19, 21, 28, 34, 36, 49, 50, 59, 67, 81, 132, 134, 135, 291, 309
Transvaal Provincial Committee, 48
Transvaler, 93, 135, 165, 172, 228
Treason Trial, 50, 51, 60, 96
Treurnicht, Andries, 270, 271
Trewhela, Paul, 133
Tribalism, 76, 77, 124
Trouw, 166
Truth and Reconciliation Commission, 310, 349, 352, 353
Tsafendas, Dimitri, 245
Tucker, Raymond, 314
Tucsa. See Trade Union Council of South Africa
Tugwana, Jan Gabu, 273, 274, 283
Turok, Ben, 100, 101
Tutu, Desmond, 111, 115, 349
Twidale, Nigel, 325, 327
Typographers Union, 275
Tzaneen, 314

Umboti Mission Reserve, 75
Umhlabeni, 59
Umkhonto weSizwe, 99, 101, 154, 159, 349
Union of South Africa, 28, 52
Unions, trade, 89, 90, 156, 244, 341
United Democratic Front, 308, 309, 346–347
United Nations, 70, 110, 157, 171–172
UNESCO, 262
United Nations Association of Great Britain, 350
United Party, 29, 33, 36, 41, 47, 52, 72, 73, 89, 127, 128, 162, 165, 210, 214, 254, 286
United States, 112, 113, 288, 289, 346
University of Cape Town, 36, 39, 40, 50, 316, 355
University of the Witwatersrand, 36, 37, 39, 49, 70, 87, 104, 107, 244, 296, 337
Unlawful Organizations Act, 235
Unna, Yitzhak, 257

Vaal Reefs mine, 341
Vaderland, 132, 166, 352
van der Bergh, Hendrik, 147, 247, 248, 249, 251, 252, 253, 257, 285, 288, 289, 351
van Gass, Hendrik, 118
van Rensburg, Nooientjies, 168
van Schalkwyk, Gysbert Johan, 168, 169, 173, 174, 175, 176, 179, 180
van Vuuren, "Fires," 200
van Zyl Slabbert, Frederik, 334, 343
Vereeniging camp, 23
Vermaak, Chris, 132
Verwoerd, Hendrik, 67, 75, 81, 86, 87, 88, 95, 128, 197, 245
Victor Verster prison, 348
Vine, Owen, 52, 69
Vlakplaas farm, 349
Vorster, John, 128, 136, 154, 165, 167, 169, 171, 172, 173, 179, 183, 185, 195, 211–212, 219, 242, 243, 245, 246, 247, 254, 255, 256, 258, 268, 270, 281, 282, 283, 285, 287, 289, 352
Voting, 28, 41, 64
  qualifications, 42–43
  rights, 93, 106
Waddell, Gordon, 286, 302, 333, 334, 337, 341, 342
Waldeck, Thomas, 195
Wallace, Edgar, 23, 24, 25, 26, 102, 259
Walters, Tom, 150
Walton, Leycester, 72, 73, 210, 211, 212, 215, 240, 274, 275, 276, 330, 331
Waring, Frank, 177
Washington Star, 288
Wayburne, Sam, 134, 135
Weech, Paddy, 256
Weekly Mail, 294, 350
Wentzel, Ernest, 84, 85, 100, 108, 109, 154, 213, 215, 338, 355, 356
Wentzel, Jill, 130, 148, 338, 355
Wessels, Bernardi, 243, 260, 262, 263, 281, 282
Western Native Township, 48
West Rand Administration Board, 273
Whitaker, Raymond, 329
White, Jill, 213
White, Vic, 213
White(s)
  education, 269
  labor policy, 27
  political divisions among, 29, 30
  protection of power of, 77
  working class, 34
Wilson, Andrew, 196, 206
Wilson, Harold, 215
Winter, Gordon, 195, 252
Wolpe, Harold, 37, 54
Women's League (ANC), 82
Woods, Donald, 283, 284
Woodstock, 34
World, 274, 283, 336
World Council of Churches, 103, 105
World War II, 30, 57, 89, 158
Xuma, Mrs. A.B., 243

Yad Vashem Holocaust memorial,
    108
Youth League (ANC), 10, 49
Yutar, Percy, 54, 173, 174, 175, 177,
    179, 180, 182, 186, 187, 216, 217,
    276, 277, 356

Zambia, 105, 119, 154, 245
Zimbabwe, 216, 356
Zionist Hall, 34
Zonderwater prison, 157
Zululand, 136
Zulu tribe, 77, 138, 273, 349